"Eight outstanding scholars make a compelling case biblically, theologically, and historically for the deity of Jesus. If he is God incarnate, then Christianity is true. If he is not, then the Christian faith is false. Powerful arguments are marshaled, and convincing evidence is set forth in this volume that demonstrates that Jesus is indeed the God-man. Read this book for your mind as well as for your soul. Both will be blessed."

Daniel L. Akin, President, Southeastern Baptist Theological Seminary

"As you read this volume your spirit will breathe a heartfelt 'thank you' to the editors and writers. They write of the deity of Christ—the north star of Christian doctrines—with fresh perspective and historical foundation, theological depth and personal challenge. The strength of biblical evidence for the deity of Jesus expressed in these pages is wonderfully overwhelming!"

Tom Holladay, Teaching Pastor, Saddleback Church, Lake Forest, California; Purpose Driven Connection; P.E.A.C.E. Plan

"This is a well-crafted, faithfully biblical, meticulously worked-out study of the deity of Christ that brings us from the Old Testament through the New Testament and into the modern world. This is a superb study."

David F. Wells, Distinguished Senior Research Professor, Gordon-Conwell Theological Seminary

"Nothing should be more important and more interesting to a Christian than Jesus. And nothing is more important or more interesting about Jesus than the fact that he is God. His deity is at the heart of the gospel's wonder for the believer, and it is the blunt force of the traumatic offense of the gospel to those who disbelieve. I cannot imagine a more important truth to unpack. Morgan and Peterson have organized an indispensable resource for this fundamental doctrine. *The Deity of Christ* achieves the rare balance between scholarly credibility and accessible practicality. Reading its pages generated waves of worship from each chapter. This volume will inform your mind and feed your soul with the undeniable, undiminished deity of Jesus."

Rick Holland, Executive Pastor, Grace Community Church, Sun Valley, California

"Morgan and Peterson are to be commended for putting together another outstanding volume for Crossway's Theology in Community series. The editors have assembled a first-rate group of authors to produce this highly commendable work. The subject of the deity of Christ is carefully explored and clearly expounded from the perspectives of biblical, historical, and systematic theology. Important and timely applications for apologetics and missiology are also appropriately included. The deity of Christ is an essential doctrine of the Christian faith, and *The Deity of Christ* should be essential reading for faithful followers of Jesus Christ."

David S. Dockery, President, Union University

"More than a collection of academic essays, this book pulsates with the life of Jesus—evident in the passion of the writers and the life change he has produced in each of them. Affirming the deity of Jesus is not, ultimately, about winning arguments with detractors or proving points to the academy; it is about encountering Jesus! Reading these essays will challenge you intellectually and enrich you spiritually, deepening both your understanding of Jesus and submission to him as Lord."

Jeff Iorg, President, Golden Gate Baptist Theological Seminary

The Deity
of Christ

THEOLOGY IN COMMUNITY
A series edited by Christopher W. Morgan and Robert A. Peterson

Other titles in the Theology in Community Series:
Suffering and the Goodness of God (2008)
The Glory of God (2010)

The Deity
of Christ

Christopher W. Morgan
and Robert A. Peterson

EDITORS

CROSSWAY

WHEATON, ILLINOIS

The Deity of Christ
Copyright © 2011 by Christopher W. Morgan and Robert A. Peterson
Published by Crossway
   1300 Crescent Street
   Wheaton, Illinois 60187

Cover design: Jon McGrath, Simplicated Studio
Interior design and typesetting: Lakeside Design Plus
First printing 2011
Printed in the United States of America

Unless otherwise indicated, Scripture quotations are from the ESV® Bible (*The Holy Bible, English Standard Version*®), copyright © 2001 by Crossway. Used by permission. All rights reserved.

Scripture quotations marked KJV are from the *King James Version* of the Bible.

Scripture quotations marked NASB are from *The New American Standard Bible*®. Copyright © The Lockman Foundation 1960, 1962, 1963, 1968, 1971, 1972, 1973, 1975, 1977, 1995. Used by permission.

Scripture references marked NEB are from *The New English Bible* © The Delegates of the Oxford University Press and The Syndics of the Cambridge University Press, 1961, 1970.

Scripture references marked NIV are taken from the Holy Bible, New International Version® . Copyright ©1973, 1978, 1984 Biblica. Used by permission of Zondervan. All rights reserved. The "NIV" and "New International Version" trademarks are registered in the United States Patent and Trademark Office by Biblica. Use of either trademark requires the permission of Biblica.

Scripture references marked NRSV are from *The New Revised Standard Version*. Copyright © 1989 by the Division of Christian Education of the National Council of the Churches of Christ in the U.S.A. Published by Thomas Nelson, Inc. Used by permission of the National Council of the Churches of Christ in the U.S.A.

Scripture references marked REB are from The Revised English Bible. Copyright ©1989, 2002 by Oxford University Press and Cambridge University Press. Published by Oxford University Press.

Scripture references marked RSV are from *The Revised Standard Version*. Copyright © 1946, 1952, 1971, 1973 by the Division of Christian Education of the National Council of the Churches of Christ in the U.S.A.

All emphases in Scripture quotations have been added by the authors.

Hardcover ISBN:	978-1-58134-979-5
PDF ISBN:	978-1-4335-3116-3
Mobipocket ISBN:	978-1-4335-3117-0
ePub ISBN:	978-1-4335-3118-7

Library of Congress Cataloging-in-Publication Data
 The deity of Christ / Christopher W. Morgan and Robert A. Peterson, editors.
   p. cm.—(The community in theology)
  Includes bibliographical references and index.
  ISBN 978-1-58134-979-5 (hc)
   1. Jesus Christ—Divinity. I. Morgan, Christopher W., 1971– II. Peterson, Robert A., 1948– III. Title.
 IV. Series.
 BT216.3.D45 2011
 232'.8—dc22

                            2010051421

To our presidents,
Bryan Chapell of Covenant Theological Seminary
and Ron Ellis of California Baptist University,
for their vision, leadership, and commitment to the Great Commission

Contents

List of Abbreviations

ABD	*Anchor Bible Dictionary*
AUSS	*Andrews University Seminary Studies*
BECNT	Baker Exegetical Commentary on the New Testament
Bib	*Biblica*
BNTC	Black's New Testament Commentaries
BBR	*Bulletin for Biblical Research*
CBET	Contributions to Biblical Exegesis and Theology
ChrCent	*Christian Century*
CTR	*Criswell Theological Review*
EBC	Expositor's Bible Commentary
EvQ	*Evangelical Quarterly*
HTR	*Harvard Theological Review*
HTS	Harvard Theological Studies
JETS	*Journal of the Evangelical Theological Society*
JSNTSup	Journal for the Study of the New Testament: Supplement Series
LCC	Library of Christian Classics
NIB	*The New Interpreter's Bible*
NICNT	New International Commentary on the New Testament
NIGTC	New International Greek Testament Commentary
NIVAC	NIV Application Commentary
NSBT	New Studies in Biblical Theology
NTAbh	Neutestamentliche Abhandlungen
NTS	*New Testament Studies*
PNTC	Pillar New Testament Commentary
Prax.	*Against Praxeas*
R&T	*Religion and Theology*
SBLDS	Society of Biblical Literature Dissertation Series

SNTSMS   Society for New Testament Studies Monograph Series
TNTC   Tyndale New Testament Commentaries
TUGAL   Texte und Untersuchungen zur Geschichte der altchristlichen
           Literatur
WBC   Word Biblical Commentary
WUNT   Wissenschaftliche Untersuchungen zum Neuen Testament

Series Preface

As the series name, *Theology in Community,* indicates, *theology* in community aims to promote clear thinking on and godly responses to historic and contemporary theological issues. The series examines issues central to the Christian faith, including traditional topics such as sin, the atonement, the church, and heaven, but also some which are more focused or contemporary, such as suffering and the goodness of God, the glory of God, the deity of Christ, and the kingdom of God. The series strives not only to follow a sound theological method but also to display it.

Chapters addressing the Old and New Testaments on the book's subject form the heart of each volume. Subsequent chapters synthesize the biblical teaching and link it to historical, philosophical, systematic, and pastoral concerns. Far from being mere collections of essays, the volumes are carefully crafted so that the voices of the various experts combine to proclaim a unified message.

Again, as the name suggests, theology *in community* also seeks to demonstrate that theology should be done in teams. The teachings of the Bible were forged in real-life situations by leaders in God's covenant communities. The biblical teachings addressed concerns of real people who needed the truth to guide their lives. Theology was formulated by the church and for the church. This series seeks to recapture that biblical reality. The volumes are written by scholars, from a variety of denominational backgrounds and life experiences with academic credentials and significant expertise across the spectrum of theological disciplines, who collaborate with each other. They write from a high view of Scripture with robust evangelical conviction and in a gracious manner. They are not detached academics but are personally involved in ministry, serving as teachers, pastors, and missionaries. The contributors to these volumes stand in continuity with the historic church, care about the global church, share life together with other believers in local churches, and aim to write for the good of the church to strengthen its leaders, particularly pastors, teachers, missionaries, lay leaders, students, and professors.

For the glory of God and the good of the church,
Christopher W. Morgan and Robert A. Peterson

Acknowledgments

We have many people to thank for their help on this project.

Allan Fisher, senior vice president for book publishing; Jill Carter, editorial administrator; and Lydia Brownback, editor extraordinaire, of Crossway, for their faithfulness, diligence, and kindness.

Covenant Theological Seminary's librarians James Pakala and Steve Jamieson, for timely, gracious, and expert assistance.

Beth Ann Brown, for expertly editing the entire manuscript. Rick Matt, for proofreading the indexes and bibliography.

Robert's teaching assistants for their help: Kyle Dillon and K. J. Drake, for reading parts of the manuscript; Jeremy Ruch, for working on the indices and bibliography.

Tony Chute, our friend and Chris's colleague at California Baptist University, for reading parts of the manuscript and offering suggestions for improvement.

Contributors

Gerald Bray (DLitt, University of Paris-Sorbonne), Research Professor of Divinity, Beeson Divinity School

Alan W. Gomes (PhD, Fuller Theological Seminary), Professor of Historical Theology, Talbot School of Theology

J. Nelson Jennings (PhD, University of Edinburgh), Professor of World Mission, Covenant Theological Seminary

Andreas J. Köstenberger (PhD, Trinity Evangelical Divinity School), Professor of New Testament and Greek, Southeastern Baptist Theological Seminary

Christopher W. Morgan (PhD, Mid-America Baptist Theological Seminary), Professor of Theology, California Baptist University

Stephen J. Nichols (PhD, Westminster Theological Seminary), Research Professor of Christianity and Culture, Lancaster Bible College and Graduate School

Raymond C. Ortlund Jr. (PhD, University of Aberdeen), Pastor, Immanuel Church, Nashville, Tennessee

Robert A. Peterson (PhD, Drew University), Professor of Systematic Theology, Covenant Theological Seminary

Stephen J. Wellum (PhD, Trinity Evangelical Divinity School), Professor of Christian Theology, Southern Baptist Theological Seminary

Introduction

CHRISTOPHER W. MORGAN
AND ROBERT A. PETERSON

Peter Kreeft and Ronald K. Tacelli, in their *Handbook of Christian Apologetics: Hundreds of Answers to Crucial Questions*, correctly state that the deity of Christ is "crucially important for at least six reasons." We list their reasons because they are cogent:

1) The divinity of Christ is the most distinctively Christian doctrine of all.
2) The essential difference between orthodox, traditional, biblical, apostolic, historic, creedal Christianity and revisionist, modernist, liberal Christianity is right here.
3) The doctrine works like a skeleton key, unlocking all other doctrinal doors of Christianity.
4) If Christ is divine, then the incarnation, or "enfleshing" of God, is the most important event in history.
5) There is an unparalleled existential bite to this doctrine. For if Christ is God, then, since he is omnipotent and present right now, he can transform you and your life right now as nothing and no one else possibly can.
6) If Christ is divine, he has a right to our entire lives, including our inner life and our thoughts.[1]

---

[1] Peter Kreeft and Ronald K. Tacelli, *Handbook of Christian Apologetics: Hundreds of Answers to Crucial Questions* (Downers Grove, IL: InterVarsity, 1994), 151–52.

Kreeft and Tacelli make a lot of sense. The deity of Christ is vital to Christian faith and practice. In fact, nothing is more important than whether or not Jesus Christ is God. If Jesus is not God incarnate, then Christianity is not true; if he is, then it is true. The critical importance of Christ's deity is sufficient reason for this book. But there are other reasons too.

Contemporary Challenges to Christ's Deity

We will make a case for Christ's deity for at least four additional reasons—all contemporary challenges to his deity:

1) Lost Gospels

A recent challenge to the deity of Christ has emerged in the popularization of noncanonical and Gnostic gospels, such as the so-called gospels of Thomas, Peter, Judas, etc. Dan Brown's 2003 bestselling book, *The Da Vinci Code*, and its subsequent movie catapulted such works into pop culture.[2] Through the fictional character Sir Leigh Teabing, a conspiracy theory is alleged: just about all that church history has taught about Jesus is wrong—including his deity. Jesus' deity was merely one view among many and became the politically dominant view after the Council of Nicaea in AD 325, so the character Teabing claims.[3]

Questioning the validity of the Christ of historic Christianity grew more and more widespread. On December 22, 2003, *Time* focused on such supposed "lost gospels" and related theories as its cover story.[4] *National Geographic* partnered with various organizations in the 2006 translation of the *Gospel of Judas* and continues to promote it, even devoting a website to it.[5] Competent evangelical responses to these views have appeared.[6]

Some critics of historic Christianity use such recent interest in the *Gospel of Judas* and the *Gospel of Thomas* to promote their view that the Christ of Christianity is contrived and to put forward their variant portrait of Christ—one that is human but not divine.

---

[2]Dan Brown, *The Da Vinci Code* (New York: Doubleday, 2003).
[3]Larry Hurtado, "Ungodly Errors: Scholarly Gripes about *The Da Vinci Code*'s Jesus," *Slate*, May 22, 2006 (http://www.slate.com/id/2142157/?nav=tap3).
[4]David Van Biema, "The Lost Gospels," *Time*, December 22, 2003.
[5]http://www.nationalgeographic.com/lostgospel.
[6]For three such responses, see Darrell L. Bock, *The Missing Gospels: Unearthing the Truth Behind Alternative Christianities* (Nashville: Nelson, 2006); Darrell L. Bock, *Breaking the Da Vinci Code* (Nashville: Nelson, 2006); Darrell L. Bock and Daniel B. Wallace, *Dethroning Jesus: Exposing Popular Culture's Quest to Unseat the Biblical Christ* (Nashville: Nelson, 2007).

2) The Worldwide Expansion of Islam

Although the majority of Muslims live in Asia and Africa, with its primary center of influence still in the Middle East, today Islam has spread around the world. "A comprehensive 2009 demographic study of 232 countries and territories reported that 23 percent of the global population, or 1.57 billion people, are Muslims."[7] Islam and Christianity make common cause of some beliefs and issues, including affirming monotheism and opposing abortion. The two faiths even agree on some things about Jesus, who is mentioned in the Qur'an twenty-five times: he was a prophet of God, miraculously conceived via the virginal conception, born of Mary, and he performed miracles, ascended to heaven, and will come again.[8] Yet Islam and Christianity do not agree on everything about Jesus. Islam rejects the Christian doctrine of the incarnation, that Jesus was the Son of God, and that he died, holding instead that he was taken alive to heaven. Most importantly for our present purposes, Islam rejects the deity of Christ, his substitutionary atonement, and resurrection. Because of Islam's worldwide reach and faulty doctrine of Christ, a defense of Christ's deity is important.

3) Religious Pluralism

Pluralists hold that all religions and forms of spirituality are complex histori-cally and culturally conditioned human perceptions, conceptions of, and responses to the one divine reality. Each of those responses can be effective, bringing forth the desired outcome, whether it is salvation, enlightenment, liberation, or some sort of ultimate fulfillment. Thus, according to pluralism, Christians can view Jesus as unique and normative for them, but they can-not maintain that this is objective or universal.[9] This view obviously leads the vast majority of pluralists to view Jesus as less than fully divine. Instead, they tend to see him as enabled by the Spirit to embody moral qualities that reflect the divine.[10] This view of Jesus is natural for pluralism because if Jesus were indeed unique and divine, then he would be the universal Lord and the only Savior, whom all must worship. Many pluralists maintain that those who believe that Jesus is divine and therefore the only way to God are intolerant and narrow-minded.

---

[7]"Islam," Wikipedia.

[8] Norman L. Geisler and Abdul Saleeb, *Answering Islam: The Crescent in Light of the Cross*, 2nd ed. (Grand Rapids, MI: Baker, 2002), 233–77.

[9]Harold Netland, *Encountering Religious Pluralism: The Challenge to Christian Faith and Mission* (Downers Grove, IL: InterVarsity, 2001), 52–54.

[10]An influential example of this is John Hick, *The Myth of God Incarnate* (Philadelphia: West-minster, 1976).

4) The Proliferation of Cults

An outstanding resource defines a cult as follows: "A cult of Christianity is a group of people, which claiming to be Christian, embraces a particular doctrinal system taught by an individual leader . . . or organization, which (system) denies . . . one or more of the central doctrines of the Christian faith as taught in the sixty-six books of the Bible."[11] As this resource unpacks this definition, it includes the deity of Christ among the "central doctrines of the Christian faith."[12] One of the most prolific cults in the world is the so-called Jehovah's Witnesses. According to the 2009 Report of Jehovah's Witnesses Worldwide listed on their official website, "276,233 people were baptized in 2009 helping to comprise a total number of 7,313,173 Witnesses."[13]

The same website is forthright in its rejection of the deity of Christ:

> Jesus is the only one directly created by God. Jesus is also the only one whom God used when He created all other things (Colossians 1:16). . . . Is the firstborn Son equal to God, as some believe? That is not what the Bible teaches. As we noted in the preceding paragraph, the Son was created. Obviously, then, he had a beginning, whereas Jehovah God has no beginning or end (Psalm 90:2). The only-begotten Son never even considered trying to be equal to his Father. The Bible clearly teaches that the Father is greater than the Son (John 14:28; 1 Corinthians 11:3). Jehovah alone is "God Almighty" (Genesis 17:1). Therefore, he has no equal.[14]

With great zeal the Witnesses continue to spread their message. And a key part of that message is a denial of Christ's deity. This is a significant pattern in most cults, which continue to proliferate today.

A Road Map

A road map of the book's contents will guide readers. We have mentioned a few reasons why Christ's deity is important. Stephen J. Nichols, research professor of Christianity and culture at Lancaster Bible College and Graduate School in Lancaster, Pennsylvania, winsomely explores these reasons and more in our first chapter, "The Deity of Christ Today."

Of utmost weight is the testimony of Scripture. For that reason, the heart of this volume is comprised of the work of noted biblical scholars. Raymond C. Ortlund Jr., formerly a seminary professor and currently pastor

---

[11]Alan W. Gomes, *Unmasking the Cults*, Zondervan Guide to Cults and Religious Movements (Grand Rapids, MI: Zondervan, 1995), 7.
[12]Ibid., 10.
[13]http://www.watchtower.org/.
[14]Ibid.

of Immanuel Church in Nashville, Tennessee, pens "The Deity of Christ and the Old Testament." Noteworthy is the caution that Ortlund exercises as he does not overreach the evidence for Christ's deity in the Old Testament.

Key chapters on Christ's deity in the New Testament follow. Stephen J. Wellum, professor of Christian theology at The Southern Baptist Theological Seminary in Louisville, Kentucky, contributes "The Deity of Christ in the Synoptic Gospels" and "The Deity of Christ in the Apostolic Witness." Wellum's careful attention to both the big picture and individual texts shines.

Andreas J. Köstenberger, professor of New Testament and Greek at Southeastern Baptist Theological Seminary in Wake Forest, North Carolina, also writes two important chapters, "The Deity of Christ in John's Gospel" and "The Deity of Christ in John's Letters and the Book of Revelation." Köstenberger's ability as one of the foremost evangelical Johannine scholars is evident in his treatment of Jesus' deity in John's Gospel, letters, and the Apocalypse.

Essays by biblical scholars make up the core of this volume, but not all of it. It is imperative to build a good historical and theological superstructure upon the solid biblical foundation. Gerald Bray, research professor of divinity at Beeson Divinity School in Birmingham, Alabama, writes "The Deity of Christ in Church History." Bray traces the history of the doctrine of Christ's deity from its beginnings until recent times, insightfully focusing on current implications of truth and error concerning the person of Christ. Robert A. Peterson, professor of systematic theology at Covenant Theological Seminary in St. Louis, Missouri, authors "Toward a Systematic Theology of the Deity of Christ." Peterson attempts to bring together in a fresh manner some of the most important theological arguments for Christ's deity.

Alan Gomes, professor of historical theology at Talbot School of Theology in La Mirada, California, contributes "The Deity of Christ and the Cults." Gomes, a recognized authority on the cults and editor of the fifteen-volume Zondervan Guide to Cults and Religious Movements, shows that there is little new under the sun, comparing contemporary cults to ancient heresies. J. Nelson Jennings, associate professor of world mission at Covenant Theological Seminary, writes "The Deity of Christ for Missions, World Religions, and Pluralism." Jennings takes readers in some surprising directions as he shows the indispensability of the church's confession of its Lord's deity for its worldwide mission.

We invite readers to join us on this contemporary, biblical, historical, theological, practical, and missional journey investigating a grand theme—the deity of our Lord and Savior Jesus Christ.

1

The Deity of Christ Today

STEPHEN J. NICHOLS

D an Kimball cleverly titles his engaging, prophetic, and at times disturb-ing book, *They Like Jesus but Not the Church: Insights from Emerging Generations.*[1] Kimball discusses with quite revealing results the views of Christianity by the unchurched. Let me suggest a sequel, this time with discussions about Christianity by the churched. It could be titled *They Like Jesus but Not Christology.* Such a judgment may seem harsh, perhaps even wide of the mark. But, as I will try to make the case here (as I have attempted to make it elsewhere), such a judgment may actually be right on target.[2]

The deity of Christ is a cardinal doctrine in the life of the church. As the early church fathers came to understand, not to mention fight and for some even die for, this doctrine is of the utmost importance. The doctrine of the deity of Christ has everything to do with the doctrine of the work of Christ. The gospel is, to put it frankly, at stake. As the following essays of

---

[1]Dan Kimball, *They Like Jesus but Not the Church: Insights from Emerging Generations* (Grand Rapids, MI: Zondervan, 2007).
[2]I am thankful to my friend William Evans and his colleagues and students at Erskine College in Due West, SC, for inviting me to deliver the Staley Lectures in February 2010, which afforded me the pleasure of working out some of these ideas before an incarnate audience.

25

this book unfold, the centrality and urgency of the doctrine of the deity of Christ will be all the more apparent.

That being the case, some self-awareness and potential self-criticism regarding how we think about Christ and how we express those thoughts may be in order. We would be wise to explore the current horizons of thought on the deity of Christ. From my limited vantage point, a few places along the horizon do not bode well for the church and her proclamation of a biblically faithful and compelling gospel. There is, in other words, some unhealthy thinking on the person of Christ in many places of American evangelicalism. Of course, it would be wrong to limit the discussion to merely the American corner of the horizon. Further examination beyond the fifty states can also be instructive. The majority of our discussion here, however, will focus on the American corner. We will proceed along two lines—first, the making of contemporary christology, and second, the unmaking of contemporary christology.

"My Own Personal Jesus": The Making of Contemporary Christology[3]

Depeche Mode's 1989 song "Personal Jesus," with its recurring line "Your own personal Jesus," well captures three elements of contemporary thinking about Christ, namely that such thinking of him is intensely personal, intensely—if not exclusively—experiential, and decidedly counter-confessional and counter-creedal. Such thinking received cinematic expression in a deeply satirical scene from the spoof, *Talladega Nights: The Ballad of Ricky Bobby*. This particular scene starts off with a prayer, uttered by Will Ferrell's character, to "Baby Jesus." The scene quickly spirals downward and inward, with each person around the table offering his or her personal take on what Jesus looks like and how he would act. The Jesus of American culture is not only multiplex but sadly and strangely far removed from the original, biblical depiction.

The same is true of the Jesus of contemporary religious thought. Here, the overriding factor seems to be a cultural predilection to tolerance and inclusivity in light of pluralism. The work of John Hick stands out on this score. Hick reduces Christ to metaphor, zapping Christ of both his historical particularity and his divine identity. The incarnation acts as a metaphor, too, a metaphor for making the presence of the Real (Hick's preferred designation for God) known. Hick chalks up the language of the New Testament

---

[3]The pages to follow draw upon Stephen J. Nichols, *Jesus Made in America: A Cultural History from the Puritans to the Passion of Christ* (Downers Grove, IL: IVP Academic, 2008).

Gospels' claims to deity as inauthentic and instead regards those claims as creations of the later Christian community, efforts to trump up the figure at the center of their religious devotion. As he summarizes the thesis of much of his own work, Hick notes, "Jesus himself did not teach that he was God and that this momentous idea is a creation of the church."[4] Hick proceeds to deconstruct literalist Christologies, such as those put forth at Nicaea and Chalcedon.[5] Those who take Jesus and his claims to deity literally, Hick argues, miss the point altogether. Jesus is nothing more than a metaphor.

Veli-Matti Karkkainen shows the connection between Hick's metaphorical (and mythological) Christology and Hick's pluralism, as he notes, "Christ is depicted as the embodiment of divine love, complementary to the intense experience of the release from suffering in Buddhism or the source of life and purpose in Hinduism."[6] Hence, the essence of the Christ event may be found in all religions. What matters most for Hick is what Christ represents, not some quest to uncover and put forth, as the creeds do, who Christ is.

The pluralist Christ may be found in many places beyond the work of John Hick. In the new globalism, as Christianity continues to interface with world religions, the pluralist option continues to gain popularity. Marcus Borg, of the Jesus Seminar, published a book simply placing the sayings of Jesus side by side with the sayings of Buddha.[7] This pluralistic Christ has become so ideologically distorted that he can no longer be recognized.

The Transformation of the American Jesus

In the hands of American pop culture or in the hands of scholars of world religions, Christ does not fare well. At this point we may very well ask, how did this happen? How did we get here? Stephen Prothero makes the case that the American Jesus went through a three-stage transformation, moving from a creedal Jesus with an emphasis on dogma, to a biblical Jesus with an emphasis on his humanity and closeness, to a Jesus liberated from Christianity and the Bible. This Jesus of contemporary American culture wears many faces, reflecting the tastes of postmodern and pluralist times.[8]

From impersonal to personal. According to Prothero, the American Jesus was first shaped by the strict, dogmatic ideals of the Puritans. The transition

---

[4]See John Hick, *The Metaphor of God Incarnate: Christology in a Pluralistic Age*, 2nd ed. (Louisville: Westminster, 2006), 2.

[5]Ibid., 100–104.

[6]Veli-Matti Karkkainen, *Christology: A Global Introduction* (Grand Rapids, MI: Baker Academic, 2003), 183.

[7]Marcus Borg, *Jesus and Buddha* (Berkeley, CA: Ulysses Press, 2002).

[8]Stephen Prothero, *American Jesus: How the Son of God Became a National Icon* (New York: Farrar, Straus & Giroux, 2003). See also Richard Wightman Fox, *Jesus in America: Personal Savior, Cultural Hero, National Obsession* (San Francisco: HarperSanFrancisco, 2004).

from the first to the second stage, then, involved the dramatic shift away from the Christ of the Puritans. As Prothero notes, "In the early nineteenth century, evangelicals liberated Jesus first from Calvinism and then from the creeds." He explains that while evangelicals were not rejecting Christ's deity, they were much more comfortable discussing and fixating on his humanity, transforming Jesus from "a distant god in a complex theological system into a near-and-dear person, fully embodied with virtues they could imitate, a mind they could understand, and qualities they could love."[9]

This "near-and-dear" Jesus tended to be more reassuring, more affirming, and hence to be preferred even more than God, who remained distant, shrouded in mystery, and ready to judge. Simultaneously, the New Testament gained an upper hand on the Old Testament. In the Old Testament, God is a God of wrath, a judge and warrior, whereas in the New Testament, Jesus is love, a friend of sinners. This Jesus of "biblicism" as opposed to the Christ of the creeds offered a kindlier and gentler savior. As such, this transformation from the first stage to the second purportedly took Jesus away from man-made creeds to a focus on the Bible alone.

Some would argue that this move was a positive one. But we should pause before we condone that conclusion. First, it's a faulty dichotomy to pit the Christ of the creeds against the Christ of the Bible. The early creeds, such as the Apostles' Creed and the Christologically charged Nicene and Chalcedonian Creeds, are extremely biblical, reflecting biblical language and, in my view, quite helpful summaries of wide swaths of biblical teaching on the person of Jesus Christ.[10] It may very well be unwise and presumptuous to assume that the Bible and the three aforementioned creeds are at odds.

Second, the Jesus of biblicism can be potentially harmful given the way biblicism tends to play out. The creeds force us to consider the "whole counsel of God," whereas we tend to have our favorite places and preferred texts in the biblical canon. To put the point directly, the Jesus of the Bible tends not to be the Jesus of the whole Bible. Rather, he tends to be the Jesus of the parts of the Bible one happens to like. We can see this especially in nineteenth-century American culture. To Victorians, Jesus espoused Victorian virtues of tenderness and gentleness. He was a meek and mild savior, who always had time for children. One of the favorite episodes from the Gospels, and an oft-reproduced image on cards and lithographs, was Jesus welcoming the children.[11] We can also see a personalized Jesus, if

---

[9]Prothero, *American Jesus*, 13.
[10]See the essay by Gerald Bray, "The Deity of Christ in Church History," in this volume.
[11]See Nichols, *Jesus Made in America*, 74–97.

we move ahead a bit, into the counterculture movement of the 1960s and 1970s. Here the popular image is of Jesus as a countercultural rebel, with the favorite episode being Jesus' throwing the money-changers from the temple. The Jesus of biblicism is rarely the complex and mysterious Jesus of the *whole* Bible.

Third, the Jesus of biblicism proved problematic in American culture due to the demise of biblical authority in American culture. Mark Noll argues that this decline, which was generally in the wake of the Civil War, was due to the use of biblical arguments for slavery. Noll explains, "The country had a problem because its most trusted religious authority, the Bible, was sounding an uncertain note."[12] Couple that with the encroachment of biblical higher criticism in the surrounding decades, and you end up with a doubly damning cocktail for biblical authority.[13] The upshot of it all is that the Bible no longer held the place of the most trusted religious authority it had once held. And this leads to the next step in the making of contemporary christology.

From personal to liberated. As the first stage of the American Jesus, the creedal Jesus of the Puritans, gave way to the second, the biblical Jesus of the nineteenth century, so the second stage would give way to the third. Back to Prothero's thesis: as Scripture waned in American culture, and in other places as well, Jesus was liberated from the Bible and from Christianity itself.[14] At the turn of the twentieth century this dynamic played itself out in the fundamentalist and modernist controversy. The liberal side, championed by such figures as Harry Emerson Fosdick, called for a radically different Jesus from the Jesus of orthodoxy. Fosdick made the case that from the beginning, Christ had been "interpreted." The disciples themselves interpreted him, using the cultural models of their place and time to express how Christ speaks to the "deep and abiding" or perennial needs of humanity. This Fosdick takes as the license to embark on his own interpretation of Jesus in light of the cultural models of his own day. The Jesus that emerges in Fosdick's reinterpretation, not surprisingly, is strongly, if not heroically, human—not the Jesus Christ of the creeds, the God-man.[15] J. Gresham Machen captures the difference between Fosdick and liberalism's christology and that of an orthodox, biblical christology. He declares

---

[12]Mark A. Noll, *The Civil War as a Theological Crisis* (Chapel Hill, NC: University of North Carolina Press, 2006), 50.

[13]See Stephen J. Nichols and Eric T. Brandt, *Ancient Word, Changing Worlds: The Doctrine of Scripture in a Modern Age* (Wheaton, IL: Crossway, 2009).

[14]Prothero, *American Jesus*, 13–14.

[15]Harry Emerson Fosdick, *The Man from Nazareth* (New York: Harper, 1949), 246–48.

with a bit of rhetorical flourish, "Liberalism regards Jesus as the fairest flower of humanity; Christianity regards him as a supernatural person."[16]

The American Jesus Today

As the twentieth century rolled on, the Jesus of the creeds and the Bible continued on its downward trajectory toward the intensely personal Jesus of one's own making. In the closing decades of the twentieth century at least three factors have come into play, which have exacerbated this anti-biblical and pluralistic trend. These include the many portrayals of Jesus in film, the all-consuming consumerism and commodification of culture, and the invoking and enlistment of Jesus in politics. For the unchurched of our culture, movies, trinkets, and the buzz of political ideologies inform them far more about Christ than do the pages of the sacred text.

Film. First, consider movies. Two of the most controversial movies of recent decades have been cinematic portrayals of Jesus, Martin Scorsese's *The Last Temptation of Christ* (1988) and Mel Gibson's *The Passion of the Christ* (2004). Also making the list is Ron Howard's *The Da Vinci Code* (2006). There has been much debate over these movies, but I do not wish to enter that debate here. I wish to make only a single point: when you add up all the box office receipts and DVD rentals, you realize the power of these films in communicating Christ to culture. For many, the only Jesus they will ever know is the Jesus of these and other films.

One of the difficulties film faces in depicting Christ concerns the subject at hand, his deity. How do you portray the deity of Christ on screen? His humanity comes through rather easily, and in the case of Scorsese's film, all too easily. Even Gibson's *The Passion*, despite all the praises heaped upon it by evangelical leaders, faces limitations in presenting Christ as the God-man and in presenting a theological interpretation of all that suffering depicted on the screen.

Consumerism. Film isn't the only place Jesus shows up in culture. He also appears seemingly ubiquitously on bracelets, necklaces, stickers, backpacks, T-shirts, and even (*sic*!) rubber duckies. Contemporary American culture clearly stands out as the most consumer-driven culture of all time. And even Jesus has been sucked up in its wake. Religious kitsch or "holy hardware" has another name: Jesus junk—two words that clearly don't belong together. The upshot of this commodification of Jesus, spurred on for the most part by well-intentioned evangelicals, is twofold: the trivialization of Christ and a detrimental witness before a watching world. To put the

---

[16]J. Gresham Machen, *Christianity and Liberalism,* new ed. (Grand Rapids, MI: Eerdmans, 2009). For more on Machen and Fosdick, see Nichols, *Jesus Made in America,* 98–121.

matter directly, when we reduce Jesus to a vinyl rubber ducky or to copped advertising slogans on T-shirts and golf balls ("Got Jesus?"), we are not speaking persuasively and compellingly for the gospel. We simply look silly.

Politics. And then there's politics. Here Jesus has been caught in an ideological tug-of-war between the left and the right, both sides claiming to be the true bearers of his mantel. This also has resulted in a twofold problem. The first problem concerns us directly. In zeal to appropriate Christ, some go too far, making Christ captive to their political agenda. The second problem concerns a watching world. When unbelievers look for Christ, they see one dressed as either a Republican or a Democrat, but they can't see past that to get to the real thing. The truth is that Christ's agenda is far too capacious to be restricted to a political party, not to mention the problems incumbent when every issue of social ethics is reduced to the confines of the American two-party system.

So much of contemporary culture is left with a panoply of personal Jesuses—personal Jesuses who look far more like their makers than like the Jesus of sacred Scripture and the historic creeds. Given this context, it's helpful to ask how this Jesus of contemporary culture, broadly speaking, has influenced the Jesus of contemporary evangelicalism. Such questions are healthy as they lead to self-awareness. Such questions can also be painful as they lead to self-criticism. Even a casual observer of contemporary evangelicalism can see the influence of this personal Jesus. Evangelicals stress that Jesus is our friend. They stress the humanness of Jesus, they stress experiencing Jesus, and they show an aversion to dogmatizing about him. As the popular expression testifies, I don't want to know *about* God, I want to know God. So we could paraphrase, I don't want to know *about* Jesus, I want to know Jesus. That, of course, is a faulty approach, not to mention nonsensical.

Here's what the author of Hebrews has to say about Jesus, serving well as a foil against all that has been written here so far:

> Long ago, at many times and in many ways, God spoke to our fathers by the prophets, but in these last days he has spoken to us by his Son, whom he appointed the heir of all things, through whom also he created the world. He is the radiance of the glory of God and the exact imprint of his nature, and he upholds the universe by the word of his power. (Heb. 1:1–3a)

The author of Hebrews offers a corrective to this trajectory that led away from Scripture and the creeds toward a "personal" Jesus. Hebrews invites us back to Scripture and to dogma, to robust theological reflection on the person of Christ. Having traced the making of contemporary christology, we now turn to its unmaking.

"When the Man Comes Around": The Unmaking of Contemporary Christology

Perhaps amidst all this critique of American culture and American evangelicalism, one thing should be noted in its favor. Perhaps we should applaud the sincerity of the movement, especially the sincerity of well-intentioned evangelicals. The Depeche Mode song referenced at the beginning of this essay comes into play again here. Johnny Cash covered "Personal Jesus" on his Rick Rubin-produced *American IV*. Cash takes a song that mocks, in the hands of Depeche Mode, and turns it into a song that pleads. Cash's desperate reach for an answer, for someone to be on the other side of the line, is met with a person. For Cash, Jesus is real, as real and as flesh-and-blood as his own existence. His aging voice sincerely and desperately needs Jesus.

But even Cash recognizes that sincerity only goes so far. He recognizes that something more is necessary when it comes to understanding who Christ is. He recognizes that the something more is submission: not submission to the Jesus that culture wants, the made-to-order, personal Jesus, but submission to Jesus as he stands before us and presents himself to us in Scripture. This is submission to the full, undiluted, and unmitigated person of Jesus—and submission to his claims—as he comes to us in the pages of God's authoritative and inerrant word.

Johnny Cash titled *American IV* after an original song he wrote for the album *When the Man Comes Around*. "Listen to the words long written down," Cash declares, "when the man comes around." In this song, Christ speaks with the voice of the whirlwind, the voice of weighty judgment. He is the one who comes in terrible display of splendor that sends all to their knees:

> The hairs on your arm will stand up
>   at the terror in each sip and each sup.
>   Will you partake of that last offered cup?
>   Or disappear into the potter's ground?
> When the man comes around.

Cash reminds us that sincerity only goes so far. If we are to move beyond the Jesuses of contemporary culture, we take the first step by submitting to Christ as he presents himself to us in his Word.

This type of submission requires submitting ourselves to two things: the biblical text and tradition, in that order. By submitting to the text—all of it and not just the preferred parts—we are challenging the assumed ascendancy of the subjective and experiential. The Jesus of subjective experience will never rise to the level of the full complexity of the Jesus of Scripture. By submitting to tradition, we are challenging the widely held assumption of the ultimacy of our time. Americans in general and American evangelicals in particular tend to suffer from a sort of ahistoricism in their display of disdain and ignorance toward the past. "Newer is better," as the saying goes, is a reflection of the hubris of our age that tends to disregard the experiences of those who have gone before us.

Submission to tradition and the text helps break us of addictions to the idols of our time, such as consumerism and politics, which have exacerbated the problem of faulty contemporary christologies. For now, we will briefly sketch how a posture of submission to tradition can help us forge an orthodox christology, and then briefly explore submission to the biblical text.

Submission to Tradition

In terms of tradition, two stops suffice. The first concerns the christological creeds of the early church, the Nicene and Chalcedonian creeds. Before we even step out of the pages of the New Testament, controversy arises over the person of Christ. Given the philosophical currents of the first century, tilting as they did toward Platonism, the early controversy over Christ surrounded his humanity. This is true of the New Testament epistles and true of much of the first two centuries of the church's life. "It is his flesh," church father Tertullian would say, "that is in question."[17] But by the beginning of the AD 300s the tables had turned and the issue centered on Christ's divinity. Largely through the teachings of Arius, the idea circulated that Christ was less than and different from God. So strongly raged the controversy over this issue that a council was convened at Nicaea in 325. Nicaea, along the shores of Lake Iznik just south of Istanbul in Turkey, served as a summer retreat for Constantine.

On the other side of Arius and his teachings stood Athanasius, a young but insightful and courageous bishop. Athanasius argued for the word *homoousian*, meaning "of one or of the same substance," to describe the relationship of Jesus to God. While an extrabiblical word, *homoousian* summarizes biblical teaching. That which God is, Jesus is. They are identical in being. Athanasius's other significant contribution at Nicaea comes in the

---

[17]Tertullian, "On the Flesh of Christ," in *The Ante-Nicene Fathers*, vol. 3: *Latin Christianity*, ed. A. Cleveland Coxe (Grand Rapids, MI: Eerdmans, 1957), 521.

phrase "for us and for our salvation," a reminder that the person of Christ has everything to do with the work of Christ.

While the bishops who gathered at Nicaea affirmed the creed in 325, the ensuing decades saw an unraveling of that decision and the encroachment of Arian views in the church. Arian bishops won the favor of Constantius, and on no less than five occasions Athanasius himself faced exile. Athanasius used his time in exile, which added up to nearly more years than that of his time as a seated bishop, to write such works as *On the Incarnation of the Word* and many tracts refuting Arianism. Those writings served to answer many of the Arian party's objections. Just after Athanasius's death in 373, Theodotius I convened a council at Constantinople in 381. Athanasius's decades of championing the cause for orthodoxy came to fruition as the Nicene Creed from 325 was reaffirmed and firmly planted in the church.[18]

The work of Athanasius firmly established both the full and unmitigated humanity and deity of Christ. However, it left undone the work of expressing how those two natures, the human and divine, came together in the person of Christ. In the decades after Constantinople I, various views were put forth to explain how the two natures conjoin—and not always with the best of results. Thus, the tables were set for another conference, this time at the city of Chalcedon in 451. Here Leo I, though not in attendance himself, helpfully guided the church. His famous work, dubbed *Leo's Tome*, expresses the matter succinctly, that Christ is fully God and fully human, two natures, conjoined in one person. The Greek term used for person was *hypostasis*, from which we derive the doctrine of the hypostatic union.[19]

These two creeds, the Nicene Creed (325, 381) and the Chalcedonian Creed (451), form the basis of orthodox christology, informing us that Christ is fully God and fully human, and that those two natures conjoin perfectly and fully in one person. These councils and their creeds did not put an end to christological controversies, however. Such controversies continue to this day. But they do represent the boundaries for the church in her expression of the person of Christ, and they do confront the potential challenges to a biblically faithful christology. Views of Christ err when they deny or limit the humanity of Christ, deny or limit the deity of Christ, or confuse how the two natures come together. Since all christological heresies trace back to one (or more) of these three errors, Nicaea and Chalcedon provide the boundaries to keep us from such errors.

---

[18]*Nicene and Post-Nicene Fathers*, Second Series, vol. 4: *Athanasius* (Grand Rapids, MI: Eerdmans, 1957).

[19]For the full text of *Leo's Tome*, which is his letter to Flavian, see Stephen J. Nichols, *For Us and for Our Salvation: The Doctrine of Christ in the Early Church* (Wheaton, IL: Crossway, 2007), 123–33.

Current evangelicals may be ignorant of these creeds and the issues they deal with, but they are so to their own peril. There is even a move by some to consciously downplay the value of such creeds for the church today. Tony Jones, former National Coordinator of Emergent Village, delivered a paper at the 2007 Wheaton Theology Conference. In the abstract to the paper he asks, "Does Chalcedon Trump Minneapolis?" Here's how he answers his own question in the paper, titled "Whence Hermeneutical Authority?":

> [The Council of Chalcedon] was a messy, messy meeting. That's another way to say that it was a *human meeting*. That's why I can only imagine what Michel Foucault would have said, had he been in attendance in 451. It's not too hard to imagine: he would have found an event laced with the politics of power. . . . And what came out of this messy meeting? Oh, only the standard, orthodox articulation of Christology. The Chalcedonian creed of the two natures—one person of Jesus Christ, as well as every other theological construction from every other council, has human fingerprints all over it. These were messy meetings, rife with power and politics.

This leads Jones to advance his thesis: "Orthodoxy happens. (And here, I could just as easily say, 'Truth Happens,' 'Gospel Happens,' or 'Christianity Happens.') Orthodoxy is a *happening*, an occurrence, not a state of being or a state of mind or a state-ment."[20]

Jones understands Chalcedon to be messy because of a controversy over Dioscorus. Jones claims that the controversy centered around Pope Leo's attempt to excommunicate Dioscorus. In efforts to calm this upheaval, the council forced Dioscorus to sit in the lobby. But Jones fails to tell the whole story. Leo's attempt to excommunicate Dioscorus did not spring from an ambitious power play. In 449 Dioscorus convened a synod at Ephesus, dubbed the "Robber Council." In his desire for power, he oversaw this council that sought to creedalize the views of Eutyches, who taught that the union of the two natures in Christ resulted in a new being altogether: Christ was neither human nor divine but a third thing (*tertium quid*). Flavian, bishop of Constantinople, refused to sign this synod's statement. Dioscorus, having the blessing of the emperor, Theodosius II, dispatched an armed guard to pressure Flavian to sign this errant statement of the synod. Flavian refused. He was then beaten so badly he died a few days later.

Consequently, Leo sought to excommunicate Dioscorus. Only after Theodosius II died in 450 could another council be convened—the Coun-

---

[20]Tony Jones, "Whence Hermeneutical Authority?" a paper delivered at the 2007 Wheaton Theology Conference.

cil of Chalcedon in 451, the council that produced its eponymous creed. Indeed, Jones is correct when he claims that power politics were present at Chalcedon. Fortunately for the church, they remained situated in the lobby.

The crucial issue here is not so much that Tony Jones didn't quite relay the whole story. The issue is the way he so casually dismisses Chalcedon. In his view Chalcedon does not trump the views of Minneapolis and his church, Solomon's Porch. Chalcedon warrants more credence, however, than Solomon's Porch. But before the argument can be made in favor of Chalcedon, a caveat is in order. The Chalcedonian Creed is not Scripture, not inerrant, and not authoritative. For that matter, the Chalcedonian Council was an historically situated event with flawed human participants who were not biblically, theologically, or epistemologically perfect, neutral, objective automatons.

Nevertheless, Chalcedon trumps current theological ideologies. First, its creed is a faithful retelling of Scripture, always the criterion for orthodox theology. To be sure, it employs extrabiblical language, but by the time of Chalcedon the heresies had grown rather complicated. Complex heresies require a complex response. In that complex response, the Chalcedonian Creed echoes Scripture. Second, can the church of today, in any city, improve on declaring, as did Chalcedon with its gathering of 520 bishops, that Christ is fully God and fully human, with two natures united perfectly in one person?

Again, our ahistoricism leads us to disdain and neglect the past, but only to our peril. These early creeds offer us a sure place to stand when we think of the person of Christ. They call on us for an attitude of submission, submission to the whole Christ of the whole Scripture. Without these "statements" we easily get lost in the tall grass of our subjective experience and our cultural predilections. If this generation decides to throw off Nicaea and Chalcedon in favor of a Christ that reflects our own cultural moment, then we may very well be living on borrowed theological time. When it comes to the doctrine of Christ and a two-nature christology, the church cannot afford to be fluid. The church must be static—teaching, affirming, and abiding by the true statements of Scripture and of those who have paved the way before us.

Our first stop on the road of tradition was the Nicene and Chalcedonian Creeds. We can learn something else from the early centuries of the church's life that could be helpful, this time from the side of Eastern Orthodoxy. Our second stop in terms of tradition is one of the depictions of Christ in Eastern traditions—that of Pancreator or Pantocrator, meaning "Almighty" or "Ruler of All."[21] In most Eastern Orthodox churches this understanding of Christ is rather visibly felt, as the image of Christ as Pantocrator covers the ceiling, towering above and over the worshipers beneath. This is the perfect antidote to Jesus as a vinyl rubber ducky or even an "I Love Jesus" sticker.

What I am not suggesting is that we employ icons (my Presbyterian sensibilities are intact). But I am suggesting that seeing Christ as Pantocrator, towering over and above us, could go a long way in correcting our tendency to trivialize and over-familiarize Jesus. If we suffer from an overemphasis on the humanity of Jesus, then we need some correction. We need sustained reflection and teaching on the deity of Christ. Jesus Christ as sovereign Lord of the universe should be taught just as quickly and as passionately as we evangelicals teach of Jesus as friend. Going one step further, evangelical popular writers should put a moratorium on gushing, reflections over Jesus' precious little baby feet and speculations on Jesus' living next door and instead give honor to the almighty Son of God, Christ Pantocrator.

Submission to the Text

Tradition can save us from ourselves, from the cultural static and distortion of our age. But it too has its limitations. Ultimately, if we are going to unmake our cultural christology and make a biblically faithful christology, we must submit to Scripture. As we turn to Scripture, we need to be reminded that we are required to submit to the whole counsel of God. Of course, we would prefer to pick and choose. We would prefer the loving Jesus, the merciful Jesus, the compassionate Jesus, not the Jesus of judgment, not the Jesus who curses a fig tree for not having figs when it's not even the season (Mark 11:12–14). All one has to do is read through the Gospel accounts to see that Jesus continually surprises his followers by challenging their most basic assumptions. We might prefer a Christ who understood the value of social hierarchies and maintained safe distances from the social undesirables—one who kept the marginalized on the margins. Instead, we find a Jesus who rebuked power and cast his lot with the poor, with those of questionable character; we find a Jesus who sat with the blind, with the lame.

Moreover, we would prefer the human Jesus, the man from Nazareth, the one we can relate to, the one who is near and dear. The God-man of dogma stretches our mind beyond that which we can conceive. But it was Paul who declared that in Christ "the whole fullness of deity dwells bodily"

---

[21] The Greek word *Pantocrator* is used by Paul in 2 Cor. 6:18 and frequently by John in Revelation. Though the New Testament references are to God the Father, by the fourth century Eastern theologians applied the term specifically to Christ.

(Col. 2:9). As Spurgeon once put it, Christ is at once infant and infinite. Such are the marvels of the mystery of our faith. And it is because of the work of him—the infinite-infant, the God-man—on the cross that our trespasses are forgiven and we are raised in newness of life (Col. 2:13). Christ is the God-man, in the ancient words of the creed, "for us and for our salvation."

The Gospels and the Epistles do not shrink back from presenting a complex Christ who makes substantial demands on those who would follow him. The deity of Christ legitimizes the claims he makes about his own identity and the demands he makes about what he would have us do. John 6 portrays this vividly. At the beginning of the chapter, great crowds engulf Jesus. And Jesus does not disappoint. But then his teaching takes a turn. Christ sets himself forth as the "bread of life," one of the string of "I am" statements in this Gospel, adding that only by eating of him, only through him, may one come to the Father. This teaching did not sit well with the crowd, and they grumbled. They grumbled because they thought Christ overplayed his hand. They grumbled because they could not get past the humanity of Christ—"Is not this Jesus, the son of Joseph, whose father and mother we know?" (John 6:42). They grumbled at his claim and at his demands, and eventually they left.

John leads us to believe that by the time Jesus had finished teaching, the crowds of thousands had given way to just the Twelve by the end of chapter 6. Jesus turns to the Twelve and asks if they are going to leave, too. Peter speaks up for the group, asking rhetorically, "Lord, to whom shall we go? You have the words of eternal life, and we have believed, and have come to know, that you are the Holy One of God" (John 6:68–69).

Peter here offers a confession, a creed. The English word *creed* comes from the Latin word *credo*, meaning "I believe." Whether or not he realizes it, Peter is confessing the fundamental beliefs, the cardinal doctrines, of Christianity, centering on the person and work of Christ. In light of his confession, we see how profoundly rhetorical Peter's question is: "Lord, to whom shall we go?" Why would we go to the Jesus of culture, American or otherwise? Why would we go to the Jesus of our subjective experience? We should only go to the Jesus of sacred Scripture, God incarnate, who lived and died and rose again and is now seated in power at the Father's right hand.

. . . .

2

The Deity of Christ
and the Old Testament

RAYMOND C. ORTLUND JR.

. . . .

The Nicene Creed defines the Christian's faith in "one Lord Jesus Christ, the only-begotten Son of God, begotten of the Father before all worlds; God of God, Light of Light, very God of very God; begotten, not made, being of one substance with the Father, by whom all things were made." This is the belief of the instructed Christian. This is not only the conscious thought but also the intuitive awareness of the believer that one both human in sympathy and suffering and divine in power and perfection, and only such a one, can save us. To what extent does the Old Testament declare this faith?

The following three categories will structure our consideration of the eight primary passages relevant to the question: (1) Old Testament passages inaccurately construed to reveal the deity of the Christ; (2) Old Testament passages accurately construed to reveal his deity; and (3) Old Testament passages not clear enough for the reader to be certain one way or the other.

Old Testament Passages Inaccurately Construed to Reveal the Deity of the Christ

Psalm 2

The figure central to Psalm 2 is called the Lord's Anointed (v. 2), his King (v. 6), and his Son (vv. 7, 12). The capitalization of these titles in the ESV could imply the deity of this royal figure, predictive of the Lord Jesus Christ, while the lowercase titles in the NRSV—anointed, king, son—locate the psalm more historically in ancient Israel without further necessary reference.[1] The very translation of the psalm into English reveals one interpretative orientation or the other. The crux is verse 7:

> I will tell of the decree:
> The LORD said to me, "You are my Son;
>   today I have begotten you."

Two questions arise. One, to what does the word "today" refer? Two, what is the nature of this begetting?

First, to what does the word "today" refer? Augustine interprets "today" as an eternally unending reality:

> The word *today* signifies the present, and in eternity there is nothing which is past, as though it had ceased to be, nor future, as though not yet in existence; there is present only, because whatever is eternal always is. By this phrase, *today have I begotten you*, the most true and Catholic faith proclaims the eternal generation of the Power and Wisdom of God, who is the only-begotten Son.[2]

By "the eternal generation" of the Son, Augustine does not mean that the Father adds the Son to himself, for God cannot grow, but that in a wonderful sense beyond our knowing the Father is forever Father to the Son and the Son is forever Son to the Father, not in essence but in loving relationship.[3] The word "today," therefore, whispers to us something of the endless intensity between God the Father as Father and God the Son as Son.

The eternal generation of the Son, while a human doctrinal construct, is evoked by biblical evidences. "He was in the beginning with God" (John 1:2). "The only God, who is at the Father's side . . ." (John 1:18). "As the Father

---

[1] The word *son* does not appear in v. 12 of the NRSV for technical reasons, which need not detain us here.

[2] Maria Boulding, trans., *The Works of Saint Augustine: Expositions of the Psalms, 1–32* (Hyde Park, NY: New City Press, 2000), 73.

[3] See Donald Macleod, *The Person of Christ* (Downers Grove, IL: InterVarsity, 1998), 131–35.

has life in himself, so he has granted the Son also to have life in himself" (John 5:26). Though faithful interpreters have articulated this reality at various levels of precision, they have agreed that the Son is "begotten of the Father before all ages."

But is the eternal generation of the Son the category of thought intended in Psalm 2:7? That leads to our second question: What is the nature of this begetting? God taught Israel to see him as their Father and themselves as his corporate son (Ex. 4:22–23; Deut. 1:31; 8:5). His intimate identification with his people came to a representative focal point in their Davidic king. God covenanted with David regarding his son, "I will be to him a father, and he shall be to me a son" (2 Sam. 7:14), revealing the unique divine care pledged to the line of David. Israel and the nations must not regard the house of David (2 Sam. 7:11) as a merely human dynasty; they are the royalty of God on earth, the more solemnly to be reckoned with.[4] This assertion of divine authority is consistent with the emphasis of the Hebrew text, which falls on the word "I": "I myself beget you today."[5]

Within the context of this historic covenant with David, the begetting of Psalm 2:7 is to be explained not in terms of Trinitarian relationships but in terms of political empowerment. This metaphorical begetting, prompted by the father/son language, is the Davidic king's installation into office. Psalm 2 should then be read as a coronation hymn, perhaps appropriate to an occasion such as is alluded to in 2 Kings 11:12, and the *today* marks the moment of the king's crowning. In his sacred position of unique access to God, the royal son was authorized to pray into existence a new world of peace and justice (Pss. 2:8; 89:26–27).

But the Old Testament line of David failed to live up to its high calling. "Israel draped the magnificent royal psalms as robes on each successive king, but generation after generation the shoulders of the reigning monarch proved too narrow and the robe slipped off, to be draped on his successor."[6] The New Testament confirms, however, that God's decree, rehearsed in Psalm 2:7, was not wasted breath. Jesus is the ultimate Son of the Most High, ruling from the throne of his father David with endless success (Luke

---

[4] The cultural location of—and possible polemic embedded in—the biblical covenant is suggested by an Egyptian pyramid text that reads, "Recitation by Nût, the greatly beneficent: The King is my eldest son who split open my womb; he is my beloved, with whom I am well pleased." Cf. R. O. Faulkner, *The Ancient Egyptian Pyramid Texts* (Oxford: Oxford University Press, 1969), 1.
[5] John Goldingay, *Psalms*, vol. 1: *Psalms 1–41* (Grand Rapids, MI: Baker, 2006), 93.
[6] Bruce K. Waltke, *An Old Testament Theology* (Grand Rapids, MI: Zondervan, 2007), 889. Cf. Bruce K. Waltke, "A Canonical Process Approach to the Psalms," in *Tradition and Testament: Essays in Honor of Charles Lee Feinberg*, ed. John S. Feinberg and Paul D. Feinberg (Chicago: Moody, 1981), 3–18.

1:32–33). He is God's beloved Son, with whom he is well pleased (Matt. 3:17) and to whom we must listen (Matt. 17:5). He fulfilled Psalm 2:7 through his resurrection from the dead (Acts 13:32–33). By his resurrection Jesus "was declared to be the Son of God in power" (Rom. 1:4) after so many centuries of Davidic weakness and failure. Jesus is superior even to angels (Heb. 1:5).[7] Angels are merely ministering spirits (Heb. 1:14), but the Son alone, crowned with glory and honor, is bringing many sons to glory (Heb. 2:9–10). Nor did Jesus exalt himself to this role; he was appointed by none less than God (Heb. 5:5).

Psalm 2 says much about the Christ—his unique role in God's plan for history, his inevitable judgment of the nations, all fulfilled in Jesus as the final son of David. But Psalm 2 does not reveal his deity.

Proverbs 8
The book of Proverbs urges upon the reader reverence for wisdom as present with God prior to the creation (Prov. 8:22–31). "When he established the heavens, I was there," wisdom says (Prov. 8:27). And the point? "And now, O sons, listen to me: blessed are those who keep my ways" (Prov. 8:32). Wisdom is more than plausible concepts and handy tips; wisdom is the reality in which we live, to which we must adjust.

Christian theologians have read Proverbs 8 as the voice of the divine Christ, the Wisdom of God, preexistent to and instrumental in the creation of all things. The New Testament reveals, "All things were made through him" (John 1:3; cf. 1 Cor. 8:6; Col. 1:15–16; Heb. 1:2). It is not surprising that Christians have seen in Proverbs 8 an Old Testament witness to the deity of Christ. The crux is verse 22:

> The LORD possessed me at the beginning of his work,
>   the first of his acts of old.

That the passage should be interpreted as of Christ was not at issue in the early Christian centuries. There was broad agreement in that respect. The debate raged over which christology it taught. The Septuagint translated the key words as "The Lord created me," a possible rendering of the Hebrew and one certainly useful to the Arians. But the Hexaplaric revisers—Aquila, Symmachus, Theodotion—construed it as "The Lord possessed me," bring-

---

[7]The "begetting" in Heb. 1:5 is "the begetting of the *incarnate* Son," according to Philip Edgcumbe Hughes, *A Commentary on the Epistle to the Hebrews* (Grand Rapids, MI: Eerdmans, 1977), 55; emphasis original.

ing the Greek tradition back into line with what they perceived to be the more likely sense of the Hebrew.[8]

Gregory of Nazianzus contended for the orthodox view of an uncreated Christ by explaining Proverbs 8 this way:

> Since then we find here clearly both the "created" and the "begetteth me,"[9] the argument is simple. Whatever we find joined with a cause we are to refer to the manhood, but all that is absolute and unoriginate we are to reckon to the account of his Godhead.[10]

Gregory finds in the two natures of Christ a ready way to explain the two kinds of assertions in the LXX text of Proverbs 8:22–31: Christ in his manhood was created (v. 22); Christ in his deity was begotten (v. 25). The theological pre-understanding he brings to the text finds corresponding evidences in the text. If we hesitate to agree with him that "the argument is simple," we can at least sympathize with him that it is textually observable and therefore worthy of a thoughtful, rather than a dismissive, reply.

It is at this point that modern interpreters would press upon Gregory the question, but is this passage even about Christ? One historian considers the antagonists in the Arian controversy, as far as their biblical exegesis is concerned, "two blindfolded men trying to hit each other."[11]

What is Proverbs 8 meant to accomplish? The passage personifies wisdom as an ideal woman ("her voice" in v. 1), in contrast with the seductive woman of chapter 7 ("her smooth talk" in v. 21). Proverbs 8:22–31 commends wisdom to the reader because of wisdom's primordial antiquity and joyful outlook on life. Waltke proposes that the passage is meant to accomplish three things:[12] (1) It lifts Solomon's wisdom to a height of nobility and authority superior to all rival wisdoms. (2) It commends his wisdom to us as better qualified to counsel, since preexistent wisdom knows the whole story. (3) The transcendent wisdom pervading the creation can come down to help human society. Established by God's decree ($\sqrt{hqq}$, v. 29), cosmic wisdom can be replicated on a small scale by the decrees

---

[8]That there remains uncertainty regarding this Hebrew verb is reflected in the English versions. KJV, NASB, NIV margin, ESV: "possessed." RSV, NRSV, NEB, REB, JPS *Tanakh*: "created." NIV: "brought forth."

[9]That is, "created me" in v. 22 and "begetteth me" in v. 25 of the LXX.

[10]Edward Rochie Hardy, ed., *Christology of the Later Fathers*, LCC, vol. 3 (Philadelphia: Westminster, 1954), 178.

[11]R. P. C. Hanson, *The Cambridge History of the Bible*, ed. P. R. Ackroyd and C. F. Evans (Cambridge: Cambridge University Press, 1970), 1:440.

[12]Bruce K. Waltke, *The Book of Proverbs: Chapters 1–15* (Grand Rapids, MI: Eerdmans, 2004), 407–8.

of wise human leaders ($\sqrt{hqq}$, v. 15). By these three strategies Proverbs 8 directs the reader away from the degrading pleasures of reckless living (chap. 7)—Pascal called it "licking the earth"—toward the dignifying joys of wise living (chap. 8).

It is true that all the treasures of wisdom and knowledge are hidden for us in Christ alone (Col. 2:2–3). But taking Proverbs 8 on its own terms, arguments here for the deity of the Christ are misplaced efforts.

Old Testament Passages Accurately Construed to Reveal the Deity of the Christ

Psalm 45

> Your throne, O God, is forever and ever.
> The scepter of your kingdom is a scepter of uprightness;
> you have loved righteousness and hated wickedness.
> Therefore God, your God, has anointed you
> with the oil of gladness beyond your companions. (Ps. 45:6–7)

If Psalm 2 and Proverbs 8 were wrongly interpreted in earlier times because the exegesis did not take sufficiently into account the historical context of the literature, Psalm 45 has been wrongly interpreted in later times because the exegesis has been overly historical and insufficiently canonical. Even the grammar of Psalm 45:6, the crucial verse, has been forced. The RSV of 1952 famously mistranslates the verse as "Your divine throne endures for ever and ever,"[13] which seems tautological since a divine throne must endure forever. Other problematic English versions include the NEB of 1970 ("Your throne is like God's throne, eternal") and the REB of 1989 ("God has enthroned you for all eternity"). But the plain sense of the Hebrew is clear in most English translations: the KJV of 1611 ("Thy throne, O God, is for ever and ever"), the NASB of 1971 ("Thy throne, O God, is forever and ever"), the NIV of 1978 ("Your throne, O God, will last for ever and ever"), the NRSV of 1989 ("Your throne, O God, endures forever and ever") and the ESV of 2001 ("Your throne, O God, is forever and ever"). This understanding of the Hebrew is corroborated by the ancient versions: the Septuagint in Greek ("Your throne, O God, is forever and ever"), Targum in Aramaic ("Your throne, O God, is in the heavens[14] forever and ever"), and Jerome's Hebrew-based Psalter in Latin ("Your throne, O God, is ongoing

---

[13]The RSV margin offers as alternatives "your throne is a throne of God" or "your throne, O God."
[14]The theologically motivated insertion "in the heavens" is typical of targumic method and has no bearing on the question before us here.

and eternal"). Not least, the New Testament quotes, "Your throne, O God, is forever and ever" (Heb. 1:8).

The interpretation of the Hebrew syntax standing behind the RSV is not impossible,[15] but neither is it likely.[16] If we allow the Hebrew to speak in its most natural way, what meaning does the psalm willingly yield?

Psalm 45 presents itself as "a love song," according to the superscription, specifically intended for a royal wedding. In the context of the Old Testament, a Davidic son is taking a bride. But the description of this king is so extravagant that Psalm 45 cannot be predicated of the sons of David prior to Jesus Christ. The king envisioned here is handsome above all others (v. 2), a formidable fighter for truth, meekness, and righteousness (vv. 3–5), reigning eternally, never doing anything wrong, always happy and successful (vv. 6–9), ruling the world through his dynasty, and praised by the nations forever and ever (vv. 16–17).

Still, some interpreters reduce the psalm to categories of meaning small enough to fit down inside a historic situation in ancient Israel. Commenting on verse 6, *The New Interpreter's Bible* argues this view as reasonably as it can be argued:

> [The word *God*] occasionally designates human beings who exercise God-given authority over others (see Exod 4:16, where Moses is "God" for Aaron, and Exod 7:1, where Moses is "God" to Pharaoh).... This seems to be the case here. While other ancient Near Eastern cultures viewed the king as divine, and while Israel certainly accorded the king special relatedness to God (see Ps 2:7), it is not likely that Israelite or Judean kings were viewed as divine.[17]

Appealing to Exodus 4:16 is a less compelling argument, because the expression there is qualified: "You shall be *as* God *to him.*" The Exodus 7:1 reference is more forceful: "See, I have made you God to Pharaoh."[18] This way of explaining Psalm 45:6 goes back at least to Rashi.[19] But Exodus 7:1 is not a fitting parallel with Psalm 45:6. In the Exodus passage God exalts Moses as prophet to Pharaoh during that particular conflict, with

---

[15]Cf. Num. 25:12, in W. Gesenius, E. Kautzsch, and A. E. Cowley, *Gesenius' Hebrew Grammar*, 2nd English ed. (Oxford: Clarendon Press, 1910), § 128 d, "thy divine throne" is allowed for.
[16]Peter C. Craigie, *Psalms 1–50*, WBC, vol. 19 (Nashville: Nelson, 1983), 337, refers to "the obvious syntax of MT (viz. that ["God"] is vocative)." Analogies to the grammar appear in Pss. 44:4; 48:10.
[17]*NIB* (Nashville: Abingdon, 1996), 4:862.
[18]The ESV reads, "See, I have made you like God to Pharaoh," softening the text, as do most English versions. Of the English Bibles I am able to consult, only the Geneva Bible of 1560 translates the Hebrew text literally, with this appropriate marginal gloss: "I have given thee power and authority to speak in my name and to execute my judgments upon him."
[19]See Mayer I. Gruber, *Rashi's Commentary on Psalms* (Leiden: Brill, 2004), 350.

the ironic twist that Aaron will do his talking for him (Ex. 4:10–16). In Psalm 45:6 the king is celebrated as enthroned forever. The eternality of his sovereign reign is the point of the verse, consistent with the grandeur of the psalm as a whole, and the historic sons of David were not deified. The uniqueness of Israel's God was too clear to allow confusion on the matter, and the weaknesses of Israel's kings were too obvious for ancient Near Eastern ideological bluff. What we are left with is this staggering assertion in the context of a royal psalm of Israel: "Your throne, O God, is forever and ever."

Psalm 45 illustrates the value of interpreting the Old Testament not only in its historical setting, which can be too confining, but also in its biblical setting, which cannot, as a matter of principle, lead our understanding astray. The writer to the Hebrews illuminates the meaning of verse 6 and its theological implications. His citation even includes verse 7 to good effect:

> But of the Son he says,
> "Your throne, O God, is forever and ever,
>> the scepter of uprightness is the scepter of your kingdom.
> You have loved righteousness and hated wickedness;
> therefore God, your God, has anointed you
>> with the oil of gladness beyond your companions." (Heb. 1:8–9)

The author's purpose is to validate from the Old Testament the conviction that Jesus, as the Son of God, is superior to angels. And to what other being in heaven or on earth has God said such a thing as Psalm 45:6–7? The writer to the Hebrews wants us to think about that.

We have already noted his use of Psalm 2:7. Now he uses Psalm 45:6–7 to make a bolder claim, because Psalm 45 is itself bolder. Psalm 45:1 begins, "I address my verses to the king," and in the unfolding coherence of the psalm the vocative "O God" of verse 6 addresses that king. But verses 6 and 7 foresee a divine-human king—divine because of "O God" in verse 6, human because of "God, your God" in verse 7.

We saw how Gregory interpreted the language of Proverbs 8 in terms of the two natures of Christ, as Christian interpreters often do in the Bible, because the biblical evidences require it (e.g., John 1:1, 14; 20:17). There is no question about the principial validity of this line of reasoning but only of its appropriate application on a passage-by-passage basis. We know, moreover, that the Davidic covenant did not emerge by merely historical development. It came down as a matter of divine revelation, which Nathan the prophet, acting in his official capacity as a prophet, received by night (2 Sam. 7:1–4, 17). "Of old you spoke in a vision to your godly one" (Ps. 89:19). It should not offend us that the Davidic covenant, as expounded in Scripture, contains surprises from a historical point of view. Psalm 45 celebrates that covenant with its vision of a divine-human Savior King. Indeed, its paradoxical assertions are "consistent with the incarnation, but mystifying in any other context."[20]

Psalm 45, therefore, acknowledged by even Jewish interpreters as messianic,[21] could hardly be overlooked by the author to the Hebrews in advancing his purpose. He saw, as all can see, that the historic Davidic line failed to establish a throne "forever and ever." The disaster of 586 BC, when Jerusalem fell to Babylon, made that painfully obvious. But it is equally clear that there is a son of David, one only, whose glory fills out the prophetic vision foreseen by the psalmist. The beautiful bride and stately wedding, anticipated in verses 10–15, add the promise that the whore shamefully exposed elsewhere in the Old Testament will be presented to her King "without spot or wrinkle or any such thing."[22]

Psalm 45, if allowed to speak for itself, demands recognition as a prophecy of a divine-human Messiah and the joy of his ultimate glories with his people.

Psalm 110

> The LORD says to my Lord:
> "Sit at my right hand,
> until I make your enemies your footstool." (Ps. 110:1)

The interpretation of Psalm 110 is clarified by its superscription: "A psalm of David." This is the evidence our Lord points to in his own argumentation from the psalm:

> And as Jesus taught in the temple, he said, "How can the scribes say that the Christ is the son of David? David himself, in the Holy Spirit, declared,
>
> > 'The Lord said to my Lord,
> > Sit at my right hand,
> > until I put your enemies under your feet.'

---

[20]Derek Kidner, *Psalms 1–72* (Downers Grove, IL: InterVarsity, 1973), 172.
[21]See Targum, Radak.
[22]Eph. 5:27; cf. Raymond C. Ortlund Jr., *God's Unfaithful Wife: A Biblical Theology of Spiritual Adultery* (Downers Grove, IL: InterVarsity, 2003), 171–76.

> David himself calls him Lord. So how is he his son?" And the great
> throng heard him gladly. (Mark 12:35–37)

It was assumed on all sides that Psalm 110 was Davidic in authorship and messianic in vision and that "the Christ is the son of David." Jesus wants his hearers to press into the implications of the messianic son of David also, according to David himself, being the lord of David.

Psalm 110 is exegetically difficult at some points. But the aspects of the psalm critical to our interest here are clear enough, in verses 1 and 4.

First, verse 1 begins with "The LORD says," which is "an almost completely fixed technical expression introducing prophetic oracles."[23] David is speaking with prophetic revelation—"in the Holy Spirit," as Jesus puts it. The message concerns, from David's standpoint, "my Lord." This language is suitable for a master/servant relationship (Gen. 24:12), a king/subject relationship (1 Sam. 22:12), or just as a courteous admission of superior rank (Gen. 24:18). "The LORD says to my Lord," then, assumes levels of authority. Taking into account a wider Old Testament outlook, there are the surrounding nations, to be ruled by Israel as God's kingdom of priests (Ex. 19:4–6). Then central to Israel is the king, the son of David, ruling over God's people (1 Sam. 10:1; 2 Sam. 7:12–16). Then there is this "my Lord" here in Psalm 110:1, to whom David looks as ruling over the Davidic throne. Finally, there is Yahweh, "the LORD," putting honor upon David's Lord.

What then did Jesus expect the attentive reader of Psalm 110 to surmise from the vision evoked by verse 1? The Messiah certainly is the son of David, as other passages affirm. But the Messiah is greater than David, by David's own admission.[24] He is greater even than angels (Heb. 1:13). He is established at God's right hand—"From the Old Testament point of view it was wholly unthinkable, even in metaphor, to describe a mortal as seated on Yahweh's right hand"[25]—and ruling his enemies from there with triumphant finality, as David and his historic sons never did. Psalm 110

---

[23]Ludwig Koehler and Walter Baumgartner, *The Hebrew and Aramaic Lexicon of the Old Testament* (Leiden: E. J. Brill, 1995), s.v. *ne'um*.

[24]"Twice Jesus emphasizes it was "David himself" who confessed the lordship of the one above him at Yahweh's right hand (Mark 12:36–37). Peter too, in his sermon at Pentecost, noted that it was "David himself" who foresaw the exaltedness of the Messiah (Acts 2:34).

[25]A. B. Ehrlich, quoted in Waltke, *Old Testament Theology*, 895. Cf. Richard Bauckham, *Jesus and the God of Israel* (Grand Rapids, MI: Eerdmans, 2008), 176: "The concern of early Christology was not to conform Jesus to some pre-existing model of an intermediary figure subordinate to God. The concern of early Christology, from its root in the exegesis of Psalm 110:1 and related texts, was to understand the identification of Jesus with God."

demands a divine Christ, which made Jesus' argument unanswerable and the great throng's response delighted.

Some modern scholars follow a different line of reasoning. Beginning with a less boldly prophetic view of the royal psalms, some see the messianic vision of these psalms emerging under the hammer blows of affliction in the course of Israel's history. For example, "So far as the main essential of the 'messianic' hope was concerned, this derived from the expectation of the restoration of the Davidic family to the kingship of a renewed Israel after the Babylonian exile." In this view, the royal psalms, originally written to celebrate the sons of David as historic figures, "must have appeared obsolete at a time when Judah had no king." So these psalms were reinterpreted "out of a genuine hope that Israel would again need them."[26] The New Testament's christological reading of these psalms is therefore not original.

But if "David himself" wrote Psalm 110, this psalm precludes such an understanding of itself. Within the thought world of Psalm 110, David is not an idealized figure from the past for other kings to live up to; David is the humble servant of his coming Lord. There is no reason not to receive the psalm's own witness to this effect, once the reader allows its prophetic claim ("The Lord says") to carry its full force. Beginning not with mere historical processes but with divinely inspired Scripture—that is, miracle—we have no principial reason for which David could not see at Yahweh's right hand a better future for his kingdom and the whole world in his Son, who is also his Lord. The result, as far as this study is concerned, is a revelation of the Messiah as both human and divine. David declared it, Jesus affirmed it, and he expected us to acknowledge it.

The second aspect of Psalm 110 important here is verse 4, which supplements the vision of divine glory foreseen by David in verse 1. Another oracle sounds forth, this one a divine oath:

> The Lord has sworn
>   and will not change his mind,
> "You are a priest forever
>   after the order of Melchizedek."

Unlike the ancient kings of Israel, the Messiah is a king-priest—and forever, after the analogy of Melchizedek. The priestly King Melchizedek of Genesis 14:18–20 appears suddenly in the biblical narrative "without father or mother or genealogy, having neither beginning of days nor end of life,

---

[26]Ronald C. Clements, *Old Testament Theology: A Fresh Approach* (Atlanta: John Knox Press, 1978), 150–51.

but *resembling the Son of God*" (Heb. 7:3). As one prior to and independent of the Aaronic priests, who could not give rest to human consciences, the "priest forever" who is also the king at God's right hand triumphs for us over our greatest enemy, our sin. The victory is complete, achieved by no historic son of David or of Aaron.

Isaiah 9
The mainstream tradition of the English translation of Isaiah 9:6 is represented by the ESV:

> For to us a child is born,
>   to us a son is given;
> and the government shall be upon his shoulder,
>   and his name shall be called
> Wonderful Counselor, Mighty God,
>   Everlasting Father, Prince of Peace. (Isa. 9:6)[27]

The prophet rejoices in the glories of the Messiah, who is a human child born to us but also the Mighty God and Everlasting Father exalted above us. No explanation of this paradox is offered; it is simply asserted. But the titles of the Messiah are presented in terms of such grandeur that some English translations soften the language. The REB, for example, reads:

> . . . and his title will be:
> Wonderful Counsellor, Mighty Hero,
> Eternal Father, Prince of Peace.

The most debated of the titles is, in Hebrew, *'el gibbôr*. Is the proper sense "Mighty God" or "Mighty Hero"? Is the Messiah being celebrated for his divine might or for his human prowess? Or is some other leader in view? The ancient versions do not establish a single interpretative vector for our guidance. The LXX seems downright confused: "His name will be called Messenger of great counsel, for I will keep peace upon the rulers, peace and health for him." Targum evades the import of the Hebrew: "And his name will be called before the Wonderful Counselor, the Mighty God existing forever, 'The messiah in whose days peace will increase upon us.'" The Vulgate fails to discern the structure of the Hebrew: "And his name will be called Wonderful, Counselor, God, Strong, Father of an age to come, Prince of peace."

---

[27] This line of translation is followed by the KJV of 1611, the RSV of 1952, the JB of 1966, the NASB of 1971, the NIV of 1978, and the NRSV of 1989.

The interpretation "Mighty Hero" is possible but not plausible. It is possible because of Ezekiel 32:21, where the plural 'elê gibborîm means "the mighty chiefs." The application of this meaning to 'el gibbôr in Isaiah 9:6 is traceable back to Ibn Ezra, who saw King Hezekiah as the figure described here: "I think that all these words are names of the child; . . . he is called 'Mighty Chief,' for Hezekiah was powerful."[28] The implausibility of this interpretation, however, is tacitly recognized even by other Jewish exegetes—Rashi, for example—who acknowledge the force of this language as "Mighty God" but remove the theological difficulty by realigning the syntax of the verse to say, "And the Wonderful Counselor, the Mighty God, the Everlasting Father, will call his name 'prince of peace.'" That is, God, with his several titles, will call Hezekiah "prince of peace," since there was peace during his reign (Isa. 39:8). This understanding of the syntax is forced. The emphasis of the verse falls on the royal child born to us, on his authority and majesty. The list of titles belongs to *him*, as most commentators recognize. And Hezekiah cannot be the king Isaiah is referring to, because the endless triumph of verse 7 goes far beyond the accomplishment of any historic son of David:

> Of the increase of his government and of peace
>   there will be no end,
> on the throne of David and over his kingdom,
>   to establish it and to uphold it
> with justice and with righteousness
>   from this time forth and forevermore. (Isa. 9:7)

The more plausible interpretation of 'el gibbôr in Isaiah 9:6 is suggested by this same title reappearing in the very next chapter, where its meaning is unmistakable: "A remnant will return, the remnant of Jacob, to the mighty God" (Isa. 10:21). Even the REB of that verse reads, "A remnant will return, the remnant of Jacob, to the mighty God"—materially the same sense. In the usage of Isaiah, the word 'el always refers to deity, most often to the God of Israel.[29] Moreover, this divine title had been created long before, in Deuteronomy 10:17: "For the LORD your God is God of gods and Lord of lords, the great, the mighty, and the awesome God [ha'el haggadol haggibbor wᵉhannôra(')]."[30] The whole point of the passage in Isaiah 9 is to set the Messiah apart from historic saviors. Gideon the hero (gibbôr, Judg.

---

[28]M. Friedländer, ed., *The Commentary of Ibn Ezra on Isaiah* (New York: Philipp Fledheim, n.d.), 52.
[29]In Isa. 44:17 (twice) and 45:20, the word refers to a false, idolatrous god.
[30]Neh. 9:32 alludes to Deut. 10:17, as does Jer. 32:18, with the same sense.

6:12) is suggested by verse 4, where "as on the day of Midian" alludes to Judges 6 and 7. But Isaiah is saying that the Messiah is an *'el gibbôr*, a God of a hero, that is, a heroic, victorious, mighty God.[31] The Messiah will not simply conquer; he will bring an end to all conquest (Isa. 9:5, 7). In other words, he will overcome the world (John 16:33).

The other messianic title relevant to our study is "Everlasting Father." The English versions are in broad agreement on the correct translation. The question is theological. What expectation does this title—literally, "Father of eternity"—communicate about the Christ?

At this point in the unfolding of biblical revelation, the title "Father" is not yet to be understood in a Trinitarian sense. The Old Testament uses the word *father* figuratively for a provider (Job 29:16), a guardian (Isa. 22:21), and a guide (2 Kings 2:21), as is naturally understandable. God himself, not surprisingly, is called the Father of his people (Ps. 68:5; Isa. 63:16; 64:8). Isaiah's use of the Hebrew noun *ʿad* is also clear:

> But Israel is saved by the LORD
>   with everlasting salvation;
> you shall not be put to shame or confounded
>   to all eternity [*ʿad*]. (Isa. 45:17)

> For thus says the One who is high and lifted up,
> who inhabits eternity [*ʿad*], whose name is Holy. (Isa. 57:15)

The hope embedded in the compound messianic title "Everlasting Father" is that, with fatherly benevolence toward his own, he shall reign forever and ever. The dynastic succession that began with David will never again stumble in failure or be degraded by selfishness or even be interrupted through death. Among all the sons of David, the divine Messiah alone will be able to say to his people, "I will not leave you as orphans" (John 14:18).

Daniel 7
Paralleling the dream of Nebuchadnezzar in chapter 2, Daniel records his own dream-vision of the final triumph of the kingdom of God. He sees the humane character of that kingdom, as opposed to the beastly nature of man-made cultures of power. "Like a lion," "like a bear," and "like a leopard" are answered by "one like a son of man" (Dan. 7:4, 5, 6, 13). The victory of humanness is a gift of heaven:

---

[31]Cf. Gen. 21:33, where *'el 'ôlam*, God of eternity = eternal God, and Ps. 31:5, where *'el 'emet*, God of faithfulness = faithful God.

> I saw in the night visions,
>> and behold, with the clouds of heaven
>>> there came one like a son of man,
>> And he came to the Ancient of Days
>>> and was presented before him.
>> And to him was given dominion
>>> and glory and a kingdom,
>> that all peoples, nations, and languages
>>> should serve him;
>> his dominion is an everlasting dominion,
>>> which shall not pass away,
>> and his kingdom one
>>> that shall not be destroyed. (Dan. 7:13–14)

Who is this "one like a son of man"? The sense of the Aramaic *bar ʾenash* is not difficult. The ESV's "a son of man" is faithful as a literal translation, and the JPS *Tanakh*'s "a human being" is faithful as a paraphrase.[32] What is debated is the referent. Some interpreters identify this figure as a human collectivity, viz., the people of God "personalized and Messianized."[33] This proposal can be validated from the interpretation of the vision recorded by Daniel himself:

> But the saints of the Most High shall receive the kingdom and possess the kingdom forever, forever and ever. (Dan. 7:18)

> And the kingdom and the dominion
>> and the greatness of the kingdoms under the whole heaven
>> shall be given to the people of the saints of the Most High;
> their kingdom shall be an everlasting kingdom,
>> and all dominions shall serve and obey them. (Dan. 7:27)

If the kingdom is given to "one like a son of man," and if the text identifies the saints as the heirs of the kingdom, then the collective interpretation is not unreasonable. But a more nuanced understanding is both required and illuminating.

It is true that Daniel does not make a sharp king/kingdom distinction. The four beasts rising from the sea signify four *kings*, according to

---

[32] In Dan. 2:25, 5:13, and 6:13, "the sons of the exile" = the exiles. Ernestus Vogt, *Lexicon Linguae Aramaicae Veteris Testamenti* (Rome: Pontifical Biblical Institute, 1971), s.v. *bar*, glosses *bar ʾenash* as *aliquis similis homini*, "someone like a man."

[33] James A. Montgomery, *A Critical and Exegetical Commentary on the Book of Daniel* (Edinburgh: T&T Clark, 1927), 317–24.

verse 17,[34] and four *kingdoms*, according to verse 23. But Daniel does make a clear heaven/earth distinction, so much so that some consider his thought dualistic. In his vision, the "one like a son of man" is invested with power on high, while the people of God are oppressed on earth. The human-like figure presented at the heavenly court comes "with the clouds of heaven," at a level fit for deity (Pss. 97:2; 104:3; Isa. 19:1). Daniel is communicating to his persecuted people a hope that depends for its cogency on its divine transcendence, above all historic and earthly processes of causation:

> You, O king, the king of kings, to whom the God of heaven has given the kingdom, the power, and the might, and the glory. (Dan. 2:37)

> The Most High rules the kingdom of men and gives it to whom he will. (Dan. 4:17, 25, 32)

> I, Nebuchadnezzar, lifted my eyes to heaven, and my reason returned to me. (Dan. 4:34)

> The Most High God rules the kingdom of mankind and sets over it whom he will. (Dan. 5:21)

Daniel 7 reveals that this sovereign God has formally given to a human-like person "coming out of obscurity into manifestation,"[35] a someone with status above the angelic millions in the heavenly court, a king who can occupy a throne where "a river of fire was pouring out, flowing from [the Ancient of Days'] presence" (Dan. 7:10, NLT)—God has given to this one an eternal kingdom of divine authority (cf. Dan. 4:3, 34; 6:26). The people of God are not being encouraged to see their hope for the future emerging from any earthly domain, but they are encouraged to see a magnificent future for themselves in this mysterious royal person above. Such a vision would have strengthened this generation of God's people after all earthly hopes, including the sons of David, had failed them. God alone remained, and God alone sufficed—in this "one like a son of man."

There would come a time "when the saints possessed the kingdom" (Dan. 7:22). But *how* the dominion given to the man-like one, who is exalted in heaven, would also be "given to the people of the saints of the

---

[34]The Aramaic text is apparently emended to "kingdoms" by the translators of the NEB, NIV, and REB. This change is unnecessary.

[35]B. B. Warfield, "The Divine Messiah in the Old Testament," in *Biblical and Theological Studies* (Philadelphia: Presbyterian and Reformed, 1968), 118.

Most High" (Dan. 7:27), who are suffering on earth—that connection is not revealed here. The king and his people are bound together in destiny. But to *equate* the heavenly man with the earthly saints defeats the hope of the text.

This vision has long been construed as individual and messianic even within the Jewish interpretative tradition.[36] But the exegete who explains this "one like a son of man" most unequivocally is Jesus, who applied it to himself.[37] The force of his thinking will sway the reader depending on the reader's entire view of Jesus. If Jesus' exegesis needs validation from beyond himself, then Jesus is, in the view of the reader, another thinker in the course of history, perhaps to be admired, but still limited. If however his exegesis, while requiring explication, needs no validation beyond his own authority, then Jesus occupies, in that reader's mind, the position Jesus himself demanded. The most striking thing about his use of the Danielic vision is how implicitly he saw his own identity there. He did not argue the matter as much as he assumed it. Indeed, he asserted it by adding the definite article: "*the* son of man," as if to say, "Yes, the one in Daniel 7."

> Again the high priest asked him, "Are you the Christ, the Son of the Blessed?" And Jesus said, "I am, and you will see the Son of Man seated at the right hand of Power, and coming with the clouds of heaven." And the high priest tore his garments and said, "What further witnesses do we need? You have heard his blasphemy." (Mark 14:61–64)

Jesus answered their suspicions about his messianic self-understanding, and he took it further. Yes, he is the human messianic son authorized to rule the nations in Psalm 2. But he is also the divine Son of Man empowered by the Ancient of Days in Daniel 7, and he is also the human son and divine Lord of David, empowered at the right hand of Yahweh, in Psalm 110. Still more, the high priest and his allies[38] will see all this fulfilled—implying that they are, in opposing Jesus, joined with the beastly powers of earth doomed to destruction at his hand, perhaps even implying that the high priest himself is acting in the role of the little horn with "a mouth speaking great things" (Dan. 7:8).

---

[36] See *1 En.* 46–48; *Babylonian Talmud*, Sanhedrin 38b, 98a; Rashi; Saadia Gaon.

[37] See Johann Albert Bengel, *New Testament Commentary* (Grand Rapids, MI: Kregel, 1981), 1:208: "This title, Son of Man, is frequent in the Evangelists, and is to be carefully observed; no one was so called but Christ himself, and he by no one, while he walked on earth, save by himself."

[38] The "you" in v. 62 is plural.

Daniel saw his vision as a dream at night (Dan. 7:1–2, 13a). It perplexed him, and he kept it to himself (Dan. 7:28). But the high priest and the others on his side will see the reality played out in history. It will not be perplexing or private. "Behold, he is coming with the clouds, and every eye will see him, even those who pierced him, and all tribes of the earth will wail on account of him. Even so. Amen" (Rev. 1:7).

Old Testament Passages Not Clear Enough to Be Certain One Way or the Other

Isaiah 7

Matthew 1:18–25 makes clear that Isaiah's prophecy of Immanuel is fulfilled in Jesus Christ. It is less clear, however, by what hermeneutical line of reasoning Matthew drew the connection. If he quoted Isaiah 7:14 as a direct prediction of Jesus, then the name Immanuel ("*God* with us") could be construed as revealing a divine Messiah. But if Matthew saw in Isaiah 7:14 an indirect foreshadowing of Jesus, then the divine element in the name Immanuel does not necessarily identify the nature of the child.

> Therefore the Lord himself will give you a sign. Behold, the virgin shall conceive and bear a son, and shall call his name Immanuel. (Isa. 7:14)

According to the one interpretation, Isaiah is predicting the birth of Jesus by his virgin mother, Mary. But then it is difficult to make sense of the immediately following context, verses 15 and 16, where the prophet connects the birth of this child with the crisis in Isaiah's own day. Neither was Jesus himself actually named Immanuel: "And he called his name Jesus" (Matt. 1:25).

According to the other interpretation, also arguable from the biblical text itself, Isaiah is predicting the birth of Maher-shalal-hash-baz (Isa. 8:1–4). Understood in this way, the effectiveness of the birth as a sign to Ahaz and his generation is more apparent. Matthew certainly allows for typological uses of the Old Testament (Matt. 2:13–15). But then one must explain the use of "virgin" in the prophecy: "And I went to the prophetess" (Isa. 8:3). It also seems odd that Isaiah's son would be addressed in royal terms: "Your land, O Immanuel" (Isa. 8:8).

Neither understanding is free of difficulties, as the ongoing discussion of the verse among interpreters makes plain. But the message conveyed by this birth is certain. Matthew makes it explicit by his parenthetically added explanation: "And they shall call his name Immanuel' *(which means, God with us)*." In quoting Isaiah 7:14, Matthew affirms the virginity of the mother, obvious from the facts and already established in his own narrative; but his purpose in the quotation is to emphasize the God-with-us significance of the Son. Jesus embodied the true meaning of "Immanuel," his deity intensifying the relevance of that name as never before. But God's saving presence with his people was clearly true in Isaiah's time, it was truly communicated through the birth of that sign-child, and it was the principal burden of the prophecy.

To sum up: the Messiah's deity is consistent with Isaiah 7:14 but not necessarily revealed there.

Micah 5

> But you, O Bethlehem Ephrathah,
>   who are too little to be among the clans of Judah,
> from you shall come forth for me
>   one who is to be ruler in Israel,
> whose coming forth is from of old,
>   from ancient days. (Mic. 5:2)

The scholars of Jesus' day saw this text as a prophecy of the birth of the Christ (Matt. 2:1–6). Even as David was a surprising choice as king, so the birthplace of the son of David would also surprise. Out of little Bethlehem, of all places, would come the glorious kingdom of God to save the world. The irony is clear. But the final assertion of the prophecy is problematic: "Whose coming forth is from of old, from ancient days." What is Micah accomplishing by this time reference?

One possibility is suggested by the AV of 1611: "Whose goings forth have been from of old, from everlasting." Similarly, the NASB of 1971 reads, "His goings forth are from long ago, from the days of eternity." If this is the intended sense, then Micah's point is the preexistence, and thus the deity, of the Messiah:

> The third line [of the verse] refers to the 'goings forth' of the Messiah (in the person of the preexistent Son or Logos) in eternity past to create the world (see John 1:1–3; Col. 1:16–17; Heb. 1:2), to his numerous subsequent 'goings forth' as the 'Angel of the Lord' from Patriarchal to Davidic times, and to his constant 'goings forth' providentially to sustain and to uphold all things by the word of his power (Col. 1:17; Heb. 1:3).[39]

The case can be made that the Hebrew time-words are capable of eternal reference.[40]

---

[39]Robert L. Reymond, *Jesus, Divine Messiah* (Fearn: Mentor, 2003), 133.
[40]See *miqqedem* in Ps. 74:12 and Hab. 1:12; *'ōlam* in Gen. 21:33; Deut. 33:27; Isa. 40:28; and Jer. 10:10.

The other possibility is suggested by, among others, the ESV: "Whose coming forth is from of old, from ancient days." If this is the intended sense, then the point is the antiquity of the Messiah's Davidic roots. Deity is not the message. Authenticity is. God will bypass the many generations of corrupt failures on the throne of David, go all the way back, and restore the kingdom with another man after God's own heart. "Messiah is no upstart or afterthought in God's program. His origins began when God chose David in the first place."[41] The Hebrew is congenial with this sense also, the time-words useful with reference to the historic past.[42]

On balance, the latter interpretation seems to function more meaningfully within the David-focused vision of the verse. But the former is not impossible.

Conclusion

"And the Scripture, foreseeing . . ." (Gal. 3:8). There is a forward tilt built into the Bible. It is not imposed by the dogmatist. It is embedded within. As the story moves forward from the "unfinished symphony" of the Old Testament to the denouement of the New, its truths intensify in clarity. There is no reason why that progress of thought should not include the deity of the Christ. Not all Christian exegesis of the relevant texts is convincing in all respects, and doubtless some of my proposals here have failed to satisfy some readers. Still, "the Scripture, foreseeing" requires the faithful interpreter to allow for the clearer light of the New Testament to dawn in the Old. I believe that is warranted in the case of the divine Christ.

Disciplined by cautious exegesis—indeed, compelled because of that caution—I must conclude that the deity of the Christ is unmistakably, if mysteriously, revealed in Old Testament texts. The key passages raise questions more than they answer questions. But that is a valid function of the Old Testament, for incomplete revelation is still revelation and a fitting preparation for the full Christ of the New Testament. Psalm 45 rejoices in one who is both royal groom and eternal Ruler. Psalm 110 esteems the son of David who also towers over David as God's final answer to worldwide human rebellion. Isaiah 9 celebrates the birth of a child who, as our divine warrior and endless benefactor, will advance David's kingdom successfully and infinitely. Daniel 7 reveals heaven's decree of worldwide, eternal author-

---

[41]Bruce K. Waltke, in *The Minor Prophets: An Exegetical and Expository Commentary*, ed. Thomas Edward McComiskey (Grand Rapids, MI: Baker, 1993), 2:705.

[42]See *miqqedem* in Neh. 12:46; Pss. 77:5, 11; 143:5; *yᵉmê ʿôlam* in Isa. 63:9, 11; Amos 9:11; Mic. 7:14; and Mal. 3:4. Micah's inclusion of *yᵉmê* should be carefully noted as suggestive of historic time.

ity conferred on a celestial being who stands forth also as a man. These passages cannot convincingly be made to say less, and their assertions are consistent with the later faith of the Christian church.

To quote Canon Liddon, "Do we not already seem to catch the accents of those weighty formulae by which Apostles will presently define the pre-existent glory of their Majestic Lord?"[43] But divorce the text of the Old Testament from the hope of a divine Messiah—"how full of difficulties does such language forthwith become, how overstrained and exaggerated, how insipid and disappointing!"[44]

---

[43]H. P. Liddon, *The Divinity of Our Lord and Saviour Jesus Christ* (London: Longman, 1890), 63.
[44]Ibid., 91.

3

The Deity of Christ in the Synoptic Gospels

STEPHEN J. WELLUM

Jesus Christ has been and still is an enigma to many people. Jaroslav Pelikan has rightly observed, "Regardless of what anyone may person-ally think or believe about him, Jesus of Nazareth has been the dominant figure in the history of western culture for almost twenty centuries,"[1] and yet a majority of people are still confused as to his identity. This should not surprise us since the confusion regarding his identity is nothing new. Even in Jesus' time there were diverse viewpoints about him. On one occasion, at Caesarea Philippi, Jesus asks his disciples the all-important question, "Who do people say that the Son of Man is?" (Matt. 16:13). The responses they recited, as in our own day, were diverse and confused— some people identified him superstitiously with a resuscitated John the Baptist, while others thought of him as one of the great Old Testament prophets. But when Jesus asks his own disciples the same pointed ques-tion, Peter, speaking for them, rightly responds: "You are the Christ, the Son of the living God" (Matt. 16:16).

---

[1]Jaroslav Pelikan, *Jesus through the Centuries: His Place in the History of Culture* (New Haven, CT: Yale University Press, 1999), 1.

It is Peter's statement that Scripture and the church continue to con-fess in regard to the identity of Jesus. In fact, the church, on the basis of Scripture, has affirmed this confession that Jesus' identity is nothing less than the Lord Christ, the Lord of glory who existed as God the Son from all eternity, coequal with the Father and the Spirit, who at a specific point in time took to himself our human nature for the purpose of saving us from our sin by his glorious life, death, resurrection, and ascension. Or, as summarized by the Chalcedonian Creed: "Jesus is fully God and fully man, one person existing in two natures now and forevermore."

Throughout church history, especially since the Enlightenment, some have questioned for a number of reasons whether the church has gone too far in her claim that Jesus is God the Son incarnate.[2] Some have questioned the truthfulness of the entire Christian position. Others who broadly iden-tify with Christianity have questioned whether Scripture actually makes such a uniform claim, given its varied portrayal of Jesus.[3] The purpose of this chapter is to affirm that such skepticism is unjustified. This will be done by laying out some of the biblical evidence from the Synoptic Gospels which demonstrates that Scripture teaches that Jesus is God the Son incarnate, and what's more, how it does so precisely because this is Jesus' self-identity.

Before we proceed, it is necessary to make two important distinctions. First, we must distinguish between Jesus' self-consciousness and his self-identity.[4] The former term is psychological in orientation and has to do with one's inner awareness, which includes a whole host of factors such as moral and religious desires, fears, joys, anxieties, and so on. Most acknowledge that access to a person's self-consciousness is nigh impossible, especially historical individuals who can no longer be interviewed, talked with, and questioned. If we are trying to determine Jesus' self-consciousness, this is not available to us.[5] Instead, we should think in terms of Jesus' self-identity, which interprets his sayings, actions, and gestures within an overall con-

---

[2]For a helpful discussion of this time period see Colin Brown, *Jesus in European Protestant Thought: 1778–1860* (Grand Rapids, MI: Baker, 1988) and Alister E. McGrath, *The Making of Modern Ger-man Christology: 1750–1990*, 2nd ed. (repr. Eugene, OR: Wipf & Stock, 2005).

[3]For a current example, see J. D. G. Dunn, *Christology in the Making*, 2nd ed. (Grand Rapids, MI: Eerdmans, 1996).

[4]For this distinction see David F. Wells, *The Person of Christ: A Biblical and Historical Analysis of the Incarnation* (Wheaton, IL: Crossway, 1984), 36–37. Cf. Dunn, *Christology in the Making*, 22–33.

[5]Contra Dunn, *Christology*, 22–33, who seems to think that a person can have access to another person's self-consciousness. In seeking to answer the question, "Did Jesus speak or think of himself as God's Son?" Dunn constantly frames the discussion in terms of "Jesus' consciousness of divin-ity" or "Jesus' messianic consciousness" (23) and hence seems to equate "self-consciousness" and "self-understanding" (25). This is a mistake.

text and interpretive framework, which for us is Scripture and which is discoverable.

Second, we must distinguish between the "implicit and explicit" sayings, actions, and gestures of Jesus as a way of interpreting his self-identity.[6] On the one hand, "implicit" refers to those gestures and actions that Jesus performs in which his identity is revealed. For example, Jesus explains his life in terms of the inauguration of God's kingdom. But given the nature of God's kingdom in Scripture, i.e., it is *God's* saving reign breaking into the world, Jesus' identification of himself with the coming of the kingdom reveals who he thinks he is. On the other hand, "explicit" refers to what Jesus says about himself by way of assertion. For example, Jesus applies various titles to himself, such as the "Son" or his favorite self-designation, the "Son of Man." These titles, placed within the storyline of Scripture, communicate who Jesus thinks he is.

With these distinctions in place, let us now turn to the Synoptic Gospels to demonstrate that they (and Jesus) teach us that he is God the Son incarnate. We will do so in two steps. First, we will discuss succinctly some foundational and biblical framework matters. It is important to remember that Jesus does not come to us in a vacuum—we cannot grasp Jesus' identity apart from placing him within the storyline of the Bible, which provides the categories, content, and interpretive grid to do so. Second, with these structures in place, we will then turn to the implicit/explicit christology of the Synoptics, which teach that Jesus is *God the Son* incarnate.

Biblical Foundations for Understanding the Identity of Jesus

The Nature of Scripture

How we think of Scripture is crucial for understanding the identity of Jesus. Here we will assume the full authority and reliability of Scripture as God's Word, not merely because it is the church's book but also due to its self-testimony.[7] Minimally, this view entails that the Jesus presented in the text, though interpreted by the biblical authors, is the Jesus of history, and that their interpretation of him is God-given and thus accurate and true.[8] Even though Scripture does not exhaustively say everything about

---

[6]See, e.g., Wells, *Person of Christ*, 37; Dunn, *Christology in the Making*, 22–25.

[7]On the Bible's claim for itself see Sinclair B. Ferguson, "How Does the Bible Look at Itself?" in *Inerrancy and Hermeneutic*, ed. Harvie M. Conn (Grand Rapids, MI: Baker, 1988), 47–66, and Wayne Grudem, "Scripture's Self-Attestation and the Problem of Formulating a Doctrine of Scripture," in *Scripture and Truth*, ed. D. A. Carson and John D. Woodbridge (Grand Rapids, MI: Zondervan, 1983), 19–59.

[8]This view of Scripture rejects the infamous Enlightenment dichotomy between the "Jesus of history" and the "Christ of faith" because this distinction assumes from the outset that Scripture is not

the identity of Jesus (see, e.g., John 21:25), whatever it does say, it does so infallibly and correctly.

In drawing christological conclusions, then, we must read the Bible intra-textually, i.e., approaching the biblical text as being in its final form precisely because it is divine revelation. In this way, Scripture not only provides the raw data for understanding who the historical Jesus is, but it also provides the God-given interpretive framework, structure, and categories by which we grasp his identity and thus construct an objectively grounded and warranted christology. In this way, Scripture serves as our epistemological norm for understanding who Jesus is apart from all historical-critical reconstructions of the text. In fact, all attempts to understand Jesus' identity apart from the overall framework and storyline of Scripture and/or pick and choose aspects of that framework while rejecting others will lead only to imaginative, subjective, and arbitrary interpretations of Jesus—something, unfortunately, which has been done for centuries.[9] Now, given the fact that we must understand who Jesus is within the framework of the Bible, it is important briefly to discuss two categorical/structural issues central to grasping Jesus' identity.

The Promise-Fulfillment Motif

The promise-fulfillment theme is a major scriptural motif that is central to understanding Jesus' identity. What is the promise? It is simply this: the eternal, sovereign, personal God who created the universe, who entered into personal relations with his creatures, and who, in light of sin's entrance into this world due to Adam's disobedience, has *promised* to redeem us. This promise, given immediately after the fall, albeit in embryonic form, is to reverse the disastrous effects of sin upon the world through a coming deliverer (Gen. 3:15). Sometimes known as the "first good news" (*protoeuangelion*), this promise anticipates the coming of a Redeemer, the "seed of the woman," who though wounded himself in conflict, will destroy the works of Satan and restore goodness to the created order. As God's plan unfolds in history, this initial promise is given more definition as God enters into covenant relationship with Noah, Abraham, Israel, and David. Step by step, God, by his mighty acts and words, prepares his people to anticipate

---

reliable either in terms of its recounting of events or in its interpretation of them and thus requires extrabiblical criteria to determine what to believe in regard to the Scripture's presentation of Jesus.
[9] I discuss this point in more detail in Steve Wellum and John Feinberg, *Christology* (Wheaton, IL: Crossway, forthcoming). For a discussion of intratextual and other methodological issues, see my "Postconservatism, Biblical Authority, and Recent Proposals for Re-Doing Evangelical Theology: A Critical Analysis" in *Reclaiming the Center*, ed. Paul K. Helseth et al. (Wheaton, IL: Crossway, 2004), 161–97.

the coming of a Messiah—a Messiah who, when he comes, will *fulfill* all God's promises by ushering in God's saving rule and reign of this world.[10]

What is important for our discussion here is the identity of this Messiah. On the one hand, Scripture teaches that the fulfillment of God's promises will be accomplished through a man, and this idea is revealed through various typological persons such as Adam, Moses, Israel, and David. On the other hand, it is also clear that this Messiah is more than a mere man, for he is identified with God. How so? In fulfilling God's promises he literally inaugurates *God's* saving rule and shares the very throne of God—something no mere human can do—which reveals that his identity is intimately tied to the one true and living God.[11] This observation is further underscored in the next foundational truth important for understanding the identity of Jesus.

The Kingdom of God and Inaugurated Eschatology
When one reads the Gospels, particularly the Synoptics, one is struck by the fact that the kingdom of God is central to Jesus' life and teaching; he cannot be understood apart from it.[12] Now to grasp fully the significance of Jesus' inaugurating God's kingdom for understanding his identity, we must first set the "kingdom" within its Old Testament context. Even though the expression "the kingdom of God" is not found in Scripture until much later, the idea of it is found as early as creation.[13] God, as the Creator and Lord,

---

[10]For a development of these points see Graeme Goldsworthy, *According to Plan: The Unfolding Revelation of God in the Bible* (Downers Grove, IL: InterVarsity, 1991); Stephen G. Dempster, *Dominion and Dynasty: A Theology of the Hebrew Bible*, NSBT 15 (Downers Grove, IL: InterVarsity, 2003).

[11]See Wells, *Person of Christ*, 21–81; Richard Bauckham, *Jesus and the God of Israel: God Crucified and Other Studies on the New Testament's Christology of Divine Identity* (Grand Rapids, MI: Eerdmans, 2008). Some specific texts I have in mind are Psalms 2; 45; 110; Isa. 7:14; 9:6–7; Ezekiel 34; Daniel 7.

[12]In the Gospels, the kingdom is mentioned directly thirteen times in Mark, nine times in sayings common to Matthew and Luke, twenty-seven additional instances in Matthew, twelve additional instances in Luke, and twice in John (Mark 1:15; 4:11, 26, 30; 9:1, 47; 10:14, 15, 23, 24, 25; 12:34; 14:25; Matt. 5:3 [Luke 6:20]; 6:10 [Luke 11:2]; 6:33 [Luke 12:31]; 8:11 [Luke 13:29]; 10:7 [Luke 10:9]; 11:11 [Luke 7:28]; 11:12 [Luke 16:16]; 12:28 [Luke 11:20]; 13:33 [Luke 13:20]; 5:10, 19, 20; 7:21; 8:12; 13:19, 24, 38, 43, 44, 45, 47, 52; 16:19; 18:1, 3, 4, 23; 19:12; 20:1; 21:31, 43; 22:2; 23:13; 24:14; 25:1; Luke 4:43; 9:60, 62; 10:11; 12:32; 13:28; 17:20, 21; 18:29; 21:31; 22:16, 18; John 3:3). Even though John's Gospel does not use kingdom terminology as often, John refers to these same realities in the language of "eternal life" (see I. Howard Marshall, *New Testament Theology* [Downers Grove, IL: InterVarsity, 2004], 498; D. A. Carson, *The Gospel According to John* [Grand Rapids, MI: Eerdmans, 1991], 187–90). For John, eternal life belongs to the "age to come," which is, importantly, identified with Jesus (John 1:4; 5:26; 1 John 5:11–12) since Jesus himself is the "life" (John 11:25; 14:6). In this way, John ties eternal life to Jesus, just as the Synoptics link the kingdom with Jesus in his coming and cross work. We are not to view the Synoptic Gospels' emphasis on the fulfillment of God's promises by speaking of God's kingdom and John's focus on the fulfillment of God's promises by speaking of eternal life as if they are opposed to each other. See Andreas J. Köstenberger, *John*, BECNT (Grand Rapids, MI: Baker, 2004), 123, who argues this point.

[13]See Goldsworthy, *According to Plan*, 94–95, who makes this precise point.

rules over his creation and creatures regardless of whether they acknowledge him. After the fall, even though God is not obligated to save us, he chooses, by his own sovereign grace, to bring his saving kingdom to this world through his Messiah (see Gen. 3:15). As one unpacks the biblical storyline, God's saving kingdom comes to this world, at least in anticipatory form, through the biblical covenants and covenant mediators—Adam, Noah, Abraham and his seed centered in the nation of Israel, and most significantly through David and his sons. Ultimately, the arrival of God's kingdom is tied to the dawning of the new covenant.[14]

Jeremiah 31 is probably the most famous new-covenant text in the Old Testament, although teaching on the new covenant is not limited to this passage. New-covenant teaching is also found in the language of "everlasting covenant" and the prophetic anticipation of the coming of the new creation, the Spirit, and God's saving work among the nations. In fact, among the post-exilic prophets there is an expectation that the new covenant will have a purpose similar to the Mosaic covenant, i.e., to bring the blessing of the Abrahamic covenant back into the present experience of Israel and the nations.[15] Yet there is also an expectation of some integral differences from the old covenant, all of which are outlined in Jeremiah 31. Probably what is most "new" about the new covenant is the promise of complete forgiveness of sin.

In the Old Testament, forgiveness of sin was normally granted through the sacrificial system; however, the Old Testament believer, if spiritually perceptive, knew that this could never be enough, as evidenced by the repetitive nature of the system. But here in Jeremiah 31:34 we are told that sin will be "remembered no more," which certainly implies that sin will be finally dealt with in full.[16] Ultimately, when other texts are considered,

---

[14]For a discussion of this point see my "Baptism and the Relationship between the Covenants," in *Believer's Baptism: Sign of the New Covenant in Christ*, ed. Thomas R. Schreiner and Shawn D. Wright (Nashville: B&H Academic, 2007), 97–161.

[15]The "new covenant" will bring about the Abrahamic blessing in that it will benefit both Israel and the nations. Within the Old Testament, the new covenant is viewed as both national (Jer. 31:36–40; 33:6–16; Ezek. 36:24–38; 37:11–28) and international (Jer. 33:9; Ezek. 36:36; 37:28). In fact, its scope is viewed as universal, especially in Isaiah (42:6; 49:6; 55:3–5; 56:4–8; 66:18–24). These Isaiah texts project the ultimate fulfillment of the divine promises in the new covenant onto an "ideal Israel," i.e., a community tied to the Servant of the Lord located in a rejuvenated new creation (Isa. 65:17; 66:22). This "ideal Israel" picks up the promises to Abraham and is presented as the climactic and ultimate fulfillment of the covenants that God established with the patriarchs, the nation of Israel, and David's son (Isa. 9:6–7; 11:1–10; Jer. 23:5–6; 33:14–26; Ezek. 34:23–24; 37:24–28). As the new-covenant texts are picked up in the New Testament, they are viewed as fulfilled in Christ and then by extension to the church.

[16]The concept of "remembering" in the Old Testament is not simple recall (cf. Gen. 8:1; 1 Sam. 1:19). That is why in the context of Jer. 31:34 for God "not to remember" means that no action

the Old Testament anticipates a perfect, unfettered fellowship of God's people with the Lord, a harmony restored between creation and God—a new creation and a new Jerusalem—where the dwelling of God is with men (see Ezek. 37:1–23; cf. Isa. 25:6–9; Dan. 12:2; Rev. 21:3–4). That is why, with the arrival of the new-covenant age, we also have God's saving kingdom brought to this world, which is precisely the fulfillment of the *protoeuangelion.*

A crucial question to ask in thinking about the fulfillment of God's promises and the entire new-covenant age is this: who is able to inaugurate these great promises and realities? In biblical thought, the answer is clear: God alone can do this, and no one else.[17] Is this not the message of the Old Testament? As the centuries trace the history of Israel, the need for the Lord alone to act to accomplish his promises becomes evident. Who can achieve the forgiveness of sin? Who can usher in the new creation, final judgment, and salvation? Certainly none of these great realities will ever come through previous covenant mediators; they have all failed. Nor will these things come through Israel as a nation, for their sin has brought about their exile and judgment. God *himself* must come and usher in salvation and execute judgment; the arm of the Lord must be revealed (Isa. 51:9; 52:10; 53:1; 59:16–17; cf. Ezekiel 34). Just as he once led Israel through the desert, so he must come again, bringing about a new exodus in order to accomplish salvation for his people (Isa. 40:3–5).[18]

However, alongside this emphasis that God *himself* must come and accomplish these great realities, the Old Testament also stresses that the Lord will do so through another David, a human figure, but a human figure who is closely identified with the Lord himself. Isaiah pictures this well. This king to come will sit on David's throne (Isa. 9:7) but he will also bear

---

will need to be taken in the new age against sin. In the end, to be under the terms of *this* covenant entails that one experiences a full and complete forgiveness of sin. See W. J. Dumbrell, *Covenant and Creation* (Carlisle, UK: Paternoster, 1984), 181–85.

[17] See Bauckham, *Jesus and the God of Israel,* 184, who argues this point. Bauckham labels this teaching of the Old Testament "eschatological monotheism." By this expression he stresses not only God's unique lordship, but also, as sole creator and Lord, there is the expectation that "in the future when YHWH fulfills his promises to his people Israel, YHWH will also demonstrate his deity to the nations, establishing his universal kingdom, making his name known universally, becoming known to all as the God Israel has known." On this same point see N. T. Wright, "Jesus" in *New Dictionary of Theology,* ed. Sinclair B. Ferguson et al. (Downers Grove, IL: InterVarsity, 1988), 349, who describes three features of first-century Judaism as: "a. belief in the one creator God who had entered into covenant with Israel; b. hope that this God would step into history to establish his covenant by vindicating Israel against her enemies . . . ; c. the determination to hasten this day by remaining loyal to the covenantal obligations enshrined in the law (Torah)."

[18] See R. E. Watts, "Exodus," in *New Dictionary of Biblical Theology,* ed. T. D. Alexander et al. (Downers Grove, IL: InterVarsity, 2000), 478–87.

the very titles and names of God (Isa. 9:6). This king, though another David (Isa. 11:1), is also David's Lord, who shares in the divine rule (Ps. 110:1; cf. Matt. 22:41–46). He will be the mediator of a new covenant; he will perfectly obey and act like the Lord (Isa. 11:1–5), yet he will suffer for our sin in order to justify many (Isa. 53:11). It is through him that forgiveness will come, for "the LORD is our righteousness" (Jer. 23:5–6). In this way, Old Testament hope and expectation, which is grounded in the coming of the Lord to save, is joined together with the coming of the Messiah—one who is fully human yet also bears the divine name (Isa. 9:6–7; Ezekiel 34).

These foundational structures serve as background to the New Testament's staggering assertion that Jesus is the one who inaugurates God's kingdom, and, if properly understood, this assertion presents Jesus as God the Son incarnate. Given the fact that the kingdom he inaugurates is *God's* kingdom, Jesus identifies himself with God—the Son in relation to his Father (see Matt. 11:1–15; 12:41–42; 13:16–17; Luke 7:18–22; 10:23–24; cf. John 1:1–3; 17:3). David Wells states it this way:

> This "age," we have seen was supernatural, could only be established by God himself, would bring blessings and benefits which only God could give, would achieve the overthrow of sin, death, and the devil (which only God could accomplish), and was identified so closely with God himself that no human effort could bring it about and no human resistance turn it back. If Jesus saw himself as the one in whom this kind of Kingdom was being inaugurated, then such a perception is a Christological claim which would be fraudulent and deceptive if Jesus was ignorant of his Godness.[19]

In other words, to say, as Jesus himself says, that he has *fulfilled* all God's promises, that he has inaugurated *God's* saving rule and has ushered in the "age to come," has to be understood as a claim to deity. This is why the New Testament presents Jesus in an entirely different category from any mere creature. In fact, Scripture so identifies Jesus with Yahweh in all his actions, character, and work that he is viewed, as Wells reminds us, as "the agent, the instrument, and the personifier of God's sovereign, eternal, saving rule."[20]

---

[19]Wells, *Person of Christ*, 38. For a similar view see Robert L. Reymond, *Jesus, Divine Messiah: The New and Old Testament Witness* (Ross-shire, Scotland: Mentor, 2003), 239–41, and G. E. Ladd, "Kingdom of Christ, God, Heaven," in *Evangelical Dictionary of Theology*, ed. W. A. Elwell (Grand Rapids, MI: Baker, 1984), 609.

[20]Wells, *Person of Christ*, 172. Gerald Bray, "Christology," in *New Dictionary of Theology*, ed. Sinclair B. Ferguson et al. (Downers Grove, IL: InterVarsity, 1988), 137, makes the same point when he writes: "The New Testament claims that Jesus, the son of David and inheritor of the kingly tradition of Israel, became the high priest and victim of the atoning sacrifice, made once for all upon the cross in order to save men from their sins. Only God had the authority to overturn the

Understanding Jesus' identity, then, within the foundational categories of Scripture—specifically themes of promise-fulfillment and the kingdom of God—is basic to grasping who he is. Everything Jesus says and does, implicitly or explicitly, must be interpreted within this overall biblical framework; otherwise we will fundamentally misunderstand who he is. Now, with these biblical structures in place, let us turn to the Synoptics and briefly unpack their implicit and explicit christology.

Implicit Christological Claims to Deity in the Synoptic Gospels

We want to focus on four examples of Jesus' actions and gestures that *implicitly* present him as God the Son incarnate. As we do so, it is important to place these examples within the biblical structures developed above, since Jesus' words and actions come to us embedded within them and his identity, meaning, and significance cannot be understood apart from these structures.

Jesus as the Fulfillment of the Old Testament

The fulfillment theme is found everywhere in the Synoptics. It is part of the larger promise-fulfillment motif built off the storyline of the Old Testament. When located within the biblical framework, this theme implicitly asserts that Jesus is more than a mere man since he alone fulfills all of God's redemptive promises. In this way, he is closely identified with God himself precisely because he does works that only God can do. Two broad areas underscore this point.

First, Jesus is presented as the fulfillment of all God's saving promises in his person and work. For example, Matthew (1:1–17) and Luke (1–3) immediately tie Jesus genealogically to the Abrahamic promises and the Davidic line. In these passages, Jesus is clearly linked to Abraham and thus the entire Abrahamic covenant thereby emphasizing "that Jesus is the one through whom God's promises of universal blessing—a promise that will include all nations—is fulfilled."[21] In fact, it is not by accident that Matthew ends his Gospel with the Great Commission to make disciples of all nations (Matt. 28:18–20), thus having the Abrahamic promises frame the entire book.[22] As Thomas Schreiner comments, "We note that this command is

---

established order of Israelite society in this way, and establish a 'new way.' That this took place is consistent with the first Christians' claim that Jesus was God in human flesh, and this is in fact implicit in the frequent discussions of his authority which occur in the gospels."

[21] Thomas R. Schreiner, *New Testament Theology: Magnifying God in Christ* (Grand Rapids, MI: Baker, 2008), 171.

[22] See D. A. Carson, *Matthew*, EBC 8 (Grand Rapids, MI: Zondervan, 1984), 596, who makes this precise point.

given because 'all authority in heaven and on earth has been given' to Jesus (Matt. 28:18). Clearly, God himself has delegated such authority to Jesus, and it is his intention that all peoples be blessed through him as the son of David and Abraham."[23]

However, as important as it is to stress that Jesus is the true seed of Abraham and David's long-awaited son, the Gospels also announce that Jesus is greater than any Abrahamic or Davidic son since he is also God's Son (Matt. 11:25–30; cf. John 5:18–29). This is especially seen in the opening verses of John's Gospel where the Word is identified with God from eternity past and viewed as the agent of creation (John 1:1–3), an affirmation consistent with the rest of the New Testament (e.g., Col. 1:15–17; Heb. 1:1–3). But it is also stressed in the birth narratives (Matthew 1–2; Luke 1–2) where Jesus is presented as the fulfillment of the Old Testament and utterly unique. Jesus is unique in his virginal conception by the Spirit (Matt. 1:18, 20; Luke 1:34–35)—teaching which not only picks up Old Testament predictive prophecy (Isa. 7:14) tied to the coming of the Lord but also Old Testament expectation of the relation of the Spirit to the Messiah in the "age to come" (Isa. 11:1–5; 42:1–4; 61:1–3). Jesus is also the one who "will save his people from their sins" (Matt. 1:21). With this assertion, Jesus is viewed as the Mediator of the new covenant—a covenant which, in the Old Testament, is intimately tied to the eschatological coming of God himself.

Second, Jesus is presented as the fulfillment of all the Old Testament types and patterns. For example, Jesus is presented as the true Israel who, like the Israel of old, was called out of Egypt (Matt. 2:13–15; Hosea 11:1), was tested in the wilderness but did not fail, and triumphed over the Evil One through obedience to God and his Word (Matt. 4:1–11).[24] Related to Jesus as the true Israel is also the emphasis that in him a "new exodus" is coming to pass (Matt. 2:16–18; Jer. 31:15). He is the one who will act as God's servant, and he will do so obediently (Matt. 3:15). In these ways, Matthew "indicates that Jesus is the true Israel who fulfills what God always intended when he chose Israel to be his people. He is the obedient Servant of the Lord who always does the will of the Father."[25]

In addition, Jesus is presented as the antitype of a whole host of Old Testament persons, events, and institutions. John, for example, argues that

---

[23]Schreiner, *New Testament Theology*, 171.

[24]Donald A. Hagner, *Matthew 1–13*, WBC 33a (Dallas: Word, 1993), 62, nicely makes this point: "Thus Jesus, the embodiment of Israel and the fulfiller of all her hopes, repeats in his own experience the experience of Israel—with, of course, one major difference, that whereas Israel failed its test in the wilderness, Jesus succeeds, demonstrating the perfection of his sonship." Cf. Schreiner, *New Testament Theology*, 170–79.

[25]Schreiner, *New Testament Theology*, 173.

the Old Testament pattern of the tabernacle (John 1:14–18) and temple (John 2:13–22) is ultimately fulfilled in him. Jesus is viewed as the antitype of Moses in a variety of ways: the Old Testament law given under Moses now finds its fulfillment in him (Matt. 5:17–20); he is the giver of a greater food than manna (John 6); he inaugurates a new covenant which replaces the old (Hebrews 8–10); and he not only is the prophet Moses predicted (Acts 3:17–26) but is far greater because he is God's last and final Word (Heb. 1:1–2; 3:1–6). Jesus is also the antitype to the priests and kings of the Old Testament: he fulfills the role of the great High Priest in his person and work (Heb. 1:3; 2:17–18; 5:1–10) yet eclipses the Levitical priests by coming from an entirely different order (Hebrews 7). He is David's son (Matt. 1:1; Rom. 1:3–4; cf. Psalm 2; Isa. 7:14; 9:6–7; 11:1; Ezek. 34:23–24), yet far greater (Matt. 22:41–46; Heb. 1:4–5; Ps. 110:1). In contrast to Adam, Jesus comes as the last Adam who undoes the work of the first one through his obedience to his Father (Rom. 5:12–21; 1 Cor. 15:20–28; Heb. 2:5–18).

Some may think this data stresses only Jesus' humanity, but this is a misunderstanding. Placed within the storyline of Scripture, it is impossible merely to view Jesus as a human being. No doubt he is that, but he is also the one who fulfills all God's promises, the one who outstrips the figures of old, and the one to whom the Old Testament pointed. Even more, it is in him that the very rule of God comes to this world. In this way, the Gospels and the entire New Testament present Jesus as God the Son incarnate, thus fulfilling Old Testament expectation of the simultaneous coming of the Lord and of "another David" (see Isa. 9:6–7; Ezekiel 34). That is why repeatedly in the New Testament we have Old Testament references of Yahweh unambiguously applied to Jesus (see, e.g., Ex. 3:14 with John 8:58; Isa. 44:6 with Rev. 1:17; Ps. 102:26–27 [LXX] with Heb. 1:11–12; Isa. 45:23 with Phil. 2:10–11), as well as the title *theos* explicitly applied to him (see John 1:1, 18; 20:28; Rom. 9:5; Titus 2:13; Heb. 1:8–9; 2 Pet. 1:1).[26] The Synoptics *implicitly* teach and announce this very same christological point as does the entire New Testament. In Jesus the Christ, we have the coming of the eternal Son, now become incarnate, in order to fulfill God's plans and purposes.

The Baptism of Jesus

What does Jesus' baptism, the event which marks the beginning of his ministry (Matt. 3:3–17, par.), implicitly signify about him? Understood in light of the biblical framework, it identifies him with the Lord and thus reveals that he is God the Son incarnate. Let us turn to this point.

---

[26]On this last point see Murray J. Harris, *Jesus as God: The New Testament Use of* Theos *in Reference to Jesus* (Grand Rapids, MI: Baker, 1992).

Each of the Gospel accounts has distinctive features in terms of Jesus' baptism, but they unite in a twofold emphasis. First, in all accounts the Spirit falls on Jesus, which in the context of the Old Testament signifies that he is the Messiah and that the messianic age has dawned (Matt. 3:13–4:11, par.; cf. John 1:32–34).[27] To have the Spirit in this way not only fulfills the types and shadows of the great anointed leaders found in the Old Testament and signifies that he is the Messiah, but it also signifies that he is identified with Yahweh in the closest of relationships. In Old Testament expectation the coming of the Spirit, tied to the "age to come," is so identified with God's sovereign rule that the question regarding the nature of *this* man who inaugurates God's reign has to be raised. The only answer that can be given is that he is God the Son incarnate.

Second, in all the baptismal accounts Jesus hears the words of affirmation from the Father, which underscore the first point—"This is my beloved Son, with whom I am well pleased" (Matt. 3:17). These words are probably a combination of Psalm 2:7 and Isaiah 42:1.[28] Anyone familiar with the Old Testament would hear these words as messianic. Here is David's greater son, who is also linked with the suffering servant who, in the words of Jesus himself, has come to "fulfill all righteousness" (Matt. 3:15). Jesus, then, in this context understands himself to be the obedient Son who not only identifies with his people but in so doing has come to inaugurate God's saving reign in this world.[29] Moreover, the title "Son" underscores this. As will be developed below, the title "Son" takes on typological connotations—Jesus in all of his humanness is the fulfillment of Israel and supremely of David—but it is more than this. Given the emphasis on the virginal conception in Matthew and Luke (Matt. 1:18–25; cf. Luke 1:26–38), the emphasis on the "beloved" (*agapētos*) Son, and the entire context of Jesus as the one who inaugurates God's reign, it is certainly legitimate to regard Jesus' sonship in more than merely functional terms. This title also carries a hint of ontological sonship (which is made explicit in such places as Matthew 11:25–27 and John's Gospel).[30]

---

[27]See R. T. France, *The Gospel of Matthew*, NICNT (Grand Rapids, MI: Eerdmans, 2007), 121–22; Carson, *Matthew*, 106–10; Schreiner, *New Testament Theology*, 172–73; Max Turner, *The Holy Spirit and Spiritual Gifts* (Peabody, MA: Hendrickson, 1996), 19–30; Sinclair B. Ferguson, *The Holy Spirit* (Downers Grove, IL: InterVarsity, 1996), 45–52; Graham A. Cole, *He Who Gives Life: The Doctrine of the Holy Spirit* (Wheaton, IL: Crossway, 2007), 149–77.

[28]See France, *Matthew*, 123–24; Carson, *Matthew*, 106–10; Schreiner, *New Testament Theology*, 172–73.

[29]See France, *Matthew*, 119–21; Carson, *Matthew*, 107–8.

[30]See Carson, *Matthew*, 109–10.

Thus, in the act of baptism and the affirmation of the Father, we have Jesus presented as the Davidic king who inaugurates God's kingdom, the suffering servant and representative of his people, and the "Son" of God both functionally and ontologically. That Jesus realized he was fulfilling God's promises and bringing with him the messianic age, at least from the time of his baptism, should not be disputed. As Wells comments: "It was visibly signaled and audibly declared. And the Synoptic authors plainly wanted their readers to understand this."[31] Who, then, did Jesus understand himself to be? At least in this event, one has to say that he understood himself to be the Son, uniquely related to his Father, and the one who was charged to do only what God can do.[32]

The Life and Ministry of Jesus

As in his baptism, so in his life and ministry, Jesus understands himself to be the Son, uniquely related to his Father, and the one who inaugurates God's kingdom in this world. Where is this seen? It is specifically evident in his teaching and miracles. For example, twice Matthew tells us that Jesus "went throughout all Galilee, teaching in their synagogues and proclaiming the gospel of the kingdom and healing every disease and every affliction among the people" (Matt. 4:23; cf. 9:35). As Murray Harris notes, these two verses are carefully placed in the narrative as an *inclusio*, which encases Jesus' teaching (5–7) and healing ministry (8–9).[33]

It is imperative, as noted above, that we set Jesus' teaching and healing ministry within the larger context of the inauguration of the kingdom. When we do so, Jesus' teaching and miracles are presented qualitatively different than anything that has preceded him, thus signifying his unique identity vis-à-vis his Father and all those who preceded him. In other words, in his teaching and healing ministry, Jesus is not presented as a mere man— even a sinless man—who is specially endowed by the Spirit with incredible wisdom and power. After all, in the Old Testament, there were numerous

---

[31]Wells, *Person of Christ*, 39.

[32]What is stressed at Jesus' baptism is also reaffirmed at the transfiguration (Matt. 17:1–8; Mark 9:2–8; Luke 9:28–36). Many have questioned the authenticity of this account, but there is no reason to do so (see Carson, *Matthew*, 383–84 and Reymond, *Jesus, Divine Messiah*, 316–25). The transfiguration fits literarily and logically in the narrative, and the only reason one would reject it is by assuming that Jesus had no consciousness of his deity or preexistence, but that is what is central to the debate. Within the plotline of Scripture and the Gospels themselves there is no reason to doubt this. Given this event, one has to say that Jesus understands himself as the Messiah, the suffering servant, God's Son, both functionally and ontologically, and one who is superior to all the Old Testament forerunners as represented by Moses and Elijah. Jesus understands himself to be uniquely different and in another category altogether. For a discussion of the transfiguration see Wells, *Person of Christ*, 39–40; Reymond, *Jesus, Divine Messiah*, 316–25.

[33]See Murray J. Harris, *3 Crucial Questions about Jesus* (Grand Rapids, MI: Baker, 1994), 82–83.

Spirit-empowered individuals who performed mighty works of God (e.g., Moses, Elijah), and even in the New Testament, the twelve disciples are commanded "to heal every disease and every affliction" (Matt. 10:1) and to teach and preach (Matt. 28:20). The crucial difference, however, is that none of these people's teaching and actions were understood as inaugurating God's long-awaited and promised kingdom, which is why Jesus is viewed in an entirely different category than any previous prophet, priest, or king. In fact, everything that the disciples would do later was solely based on the fact that they received their authorization and power from Jesus himself, though it was never reciprocal (see Acts 3:6; 4:10; 9:34; Matt. 28:18–20). Additionally, it is crucial to note that the contemporaries of Jesus were astonished at his teaching and his healing (Mark 1:22; cf. Matt. 7:28). Whereas the duly licensed teachers of the day expounded the Old Testament and the traditions, Jesus gave his own teaching on his own authority— "I say unto you"—and he viewed his miracles as evidence that in him, God's supernatural reign had now arrived.

A good example of this is how Jesus understands himself in relation to the Old Testament law. One of the most important texts in this regard is Matthew 5:17–20. Debate has surrounded how best to interpret Jesus' words.[34] In my view, the best interpretation stresses the antithesis between "abolish" and "fulfill" so that Jesus is claiming that he "fulfills" the Law and the Prophets in that they point forward to him.[35] This interpretation understands "fulfill" to have the exact same meaning as its use in Matthew 1 and 2 and elsewhere in Matthew, where great emphasis is placed on the prophetic nature of the Old Testament and how the Old Testament anticipates and points forward to Jesus, particularly through typological persons, events, and institutions, but is not limited to them. What Jesus, then, is claiming, as D. A. Carson notes, is not that he is abolishing the Old Testament as canon but that "the Old Testament's real and abiding authority must be understood through the person and teaching of him to whom it points and who so richly fulfills it."[36]

In this sense, the nature of the Law and the Prophets' valid continuity is established only with reference to Jesus himself. The antitheses which follow in verses 21–48 are not given by Jesus primarily to correct or intensify the Old Testament law but to show "the direction in which it points, on the basis of his own authority (to which, again, the Old Testament points)."[37]

---

[34]For a discussion of the various options, see Carson, *Matthew*, 140–47; France, *Matthew*, 177–91.
[35]For a defense of this view, see Carson, *Matthew*, 143–45; cf. France, *Matthew*, 182–84.
[36]Carson, *Matthew*, 144.
[37]Ibid.

The christological claim is simply staggering. Jesus understands himself to be the eschatological goal of the Old Testament, the one that the Old Testament has always been pointing forward to, ultimately the one in whom all God's plans and promises are realized, and thus he is the Old Testament's sole authoritative interpreter. In other words, Jesus understands himself as having the authority of God and is thus identified with him; indeed he claims to be the one in whom God's entire plan finds its culmination and *telos*.

But it is also in his miracles that Jesus displays a unique sense of deity. We must not view the miracles of Jesus as merely evidence of a Spirit-empowered individual who acts on behalf of God. Rather, all Jesus' miracles are set within the larger context of the inauguration of the "age to come"— something which only God can do. The healing miracles are evidence of the arrival of the messianic age (Luke 7:22–23; cf. Isa. 29:18–19; 35:5–6; 61:1). They are visible manifestations of the presence of the supernatural rule of God coming in and through Jesus. For example, the nature miracles are displays of the work of God. In Matthew 8:23–27 we are told that Jesus exercises his authority over nature. He speaks a word, and the storm instantly calms. But what would this bring to mind for the Old Testament reader? It would remind them of the Lord himself, who triumphs over the stormy sea (see Ps. 107:23–32; cf. Job 9:8; Pss. 65:7; 77:19; Isa. 43:16; 51:9–10; Hab. 3:15).

In a similar nature miracle when Jesus walks on the water (Matt. 14:25; Mark 6:48; cf. John 6:19), Old Testament readers would be reminded of the Lord who walks upon the sea (Job 9:8 lxx; cf. Ps. 77:19; Isa. 51:9–10).[38] In fact, as the Gospels present this account each one of them recounts how the disciples were filled with terror. But, as Schreiner points out, "Jesus replies with the exact same words: *egō eimi, mē phobeisthe* ("I am; do not fear")."[39] As Schreiner rightly argues, in John's Gospel *egō eimi* is full of christological import and hearkens back to "Exodus 3:14 and to texts in Isaiah that refer to the one and only God (e.g., Isa. 41:10; 43:10; 45:18). Given John's Christology, it is clear that Jesus is considered to be God—*theos* (John 1:1)."[40] That is why in the Gospels the proclamation of the gospel of the kingdom is accompanied by many miracles, healings, and exorcisms of demons (Matt. 4:23; 9:35; 10:7–8; Luke 9:11; 10:9, 17; 11:20). In fact,

---

[38]See Simon J. Gathercole, *The Pre-existent Son: Recovering the Christologies of Matthew, Mark, and Luke* (Grand Rapids, MI: Eerdmans, 2006), 64. Gathercole states: "The reference to walking on the sea is a 'theophany' motif which is taken over from Yahweh to Jesus.... For the moment, however, the combination of the two passages showing Jesus' mastery of the sea (Matt. 14:22–33; Mark 6:45–52) points very strongly to a close identification of him with Yahweh in the Old Testament."
[39]Schreiner, *New Testament Theology*, 181–82.
[40]Ibid., 182. Cf. Gathercole, *The Pre-existent Son*, 64.

Matthew 12:28 makes clear that Jesus' exorcisms of demons by the power of the Spirit is proof-positive that God's saving reign has now come to this world. Jesus' miracles, then, as Schreiner correctly notes, "are signs of the kingdom, manifestations of the new creation."[41] In light of this, what is Jesus' self-understanding? It is this: he is not only the Messiah but also the unique Son vis-à-vis his Father and thus closely identified in authority and power with him.[42]

In addition to Jesus' mighty acts, we should also note how Jesus says that he can do works that only God can do—works all associated with the arrival of the "age to come." For example, Jesus understands himself to be the person appointed by his Father to exercise divine judgment (Matt. 7:22–23; 16:27; 25:31–33, 41; cf. John 5:22–23). But Scripture is clear: judgment is the work of God alone (Deut. 1:17; Jer. 25:31; Rom. 2:3, 5–6; 14:10; 1 Pet. 1:17). Yet, Jesus understands himself to be the one the Father has appointed to judge all humanity. In fact, Jesus' verdict and sentence determines each individual's destiny as either eternal punishment or eternal life (Matt. 25:46; cf. John 5:29; 2 Cor. 5:10). Exercising divine judgment is *implicit* evidence of Jesus' self-understanding that he is in unique relation to his Father and has divine authority to do the very works of God.

Jesus' Understanding of His Death and Resurrection

As Jesus approached his death, he did not view it as martyrdom but as central to his divinely planned messianic mission. This is evident at Caesarea Philippi (Matt. 16:21–23 par.). After he blesses Peter for identifying him as the Christ, he then goes on to explain to his disciples that he *must (dei)*

---

[41] Schreiner, *New Testament Theology*, 66. For this same emphasis see Reymond, *Jesus, Divine Messiah*, 259–69; Wells, *Person of Christ*, 40.

[42] This understanding of the significance of Jesus' miracles is different from others who affirm a functional kenotic Spirit-christology. For a discussion of this view see Oliver D. Crisp, *Divinity and Humanity* (Cambridge: Cambridge University Press, 2007), 118–53. For a good example of this view see Gerald F. Hawthorne, *The Power and the Presence* (repr. Eugene, OR: Wipf & Stock, 2003). Hawthorne argues that in becoming a human being, the eternal Son chose to renounce his divine powers and to "live fully within those limitations which inhere in being truly human" (208). In regard to his life and ministry, then, Jesus' divine attributes were only latent and not operative. Thus, when Jesus teaches with authority or acts supernaturally he is not doing so by the use of his divine attributes but by the power of the Spirit (211–19). Even though there is truth in this view, ultimately it does not do justice to the Bible's storyline. Jesus nowhere is presented merely as a Spirit-empowered man, similar yet greater to those who preceded him. Rather he is identified with Yahweh, the one who effects the sovereign reign of God, and whose miraculous works demonstrate that he is the Lord himself. Hawthorne's view has a difficult time accounting for how Jesus is presented within the larger biblical framework of Scripture. For others who promote this view see Garrett DeWeese, "One Person, Two Natures: Two Metaphysical Models of the Incarnation," 114–53, and Klaus Issler, "Jesus' Example: Prototype of the Dependent, Spirit-Filled Life," 189–225, in *Jesus in Trinitarian Perspective*, ed. Fred Sanders and Klaus Issler (Nashville: B&H Academic, 2007).

suffer and die and then in three days rise again. At this point, the disciples do not grasp what he is saying. They believed with Peter that Jesus was the Messiah, but they did not associate the Messiah with suffering. Their concept of the Messiah fell in line with Old Testament prophecy in regard to a coming Davidic king. They did not, however, think of the Messiah as both a priest *and* king, indeed a suffering king. Nonetheless, Jesus interprets his death as the fulfillment of the vocation of the servant of the Lord, who by his cross work will inaugurate God's sovereign rule and reign on earth. For this reason his death is viewed in terms of a divine necessity (see Matt. 16:21; Mark 8:31; Luke 9:22; cf. Luke 24:26) and that "everything that is written about the Son of Man by the prophets will be accomplished" (Luke 18:31). As John Stott comments, "the Synoptic evangelists bear a common witness to the fact that Jesus both clearly foresaw and repeatedly foretold his coming death."[43] In other words, Jesus views his death as a voluntary, obedient act together with his Father (Mark 10:45; cf. John 10:17–18), planned before the foundation of the world. This plan, in the context of the Old Testament, is ultimately tied to the inauguration of the entire new-covenant age—an age which only God can effect. As Wells comments, "His actions, in this regard, had an implied christological significance, for who can forgive sin but God alone? (Mark 2:7/Luke 5:21)."[44]

Explicit Christological Claims to Deity in the Synoptic Gospels

It is not only Jesus' gestures and actions that implicitly reveal his divine identity; it is also his *explicit* statements, specifically statements that speak of his unique Father-Son relationship. What, then, is Jesus' self-understanding? In the Synoptic Gospels, Jesus understands himself to be God the Son incarnate. Let us briefly look at some of the evidence for this assertion.

Jesus' Use of Abba

In each of the Synoptics, Jesus addresses God by the Aramaic term *Abba*, which reveals how he perceived his relationship vis-à-vis the Father (see Matt. 6:9; 11:25–26; 26:39, 42; Mark 14:36; Luke 10:21; 11:2; 22:42; 23:34, 46). As Joachim Jeremias has shown in his study of the contemporary Jewish literature, "there is *no analogy at all* in the whole of Jewish prayer for God being addressed as Abba."[45] The reason for this reticence was due to the fear that one needed to give proper deference to God's holiness and

---

[43]John Stott, *The Cross of Christ* (Downers Grove, IL: InterVarsity, 1986), 28.
[44]Wells, *Person of Christ*, 41.
[45]Joachim Jeremias, *The Prayers of Jesus* (Philadelphia: Fortress, 1989), 57.

majesty. Yet Jesus, as Wells notes, "with utmost regularity, addresses God by this term of intimacy and familiarity."[46]

Also important to note is how Jesus distinguishes his use of *Abba* from that of his disciples, and how Jesus does not associate with the disciples when he teaches them to pray, "Our Father" (Matt. 6:9; John 20:17). Later in Scripture, Paul says that Christians, as adopted sons of God, are free to call God *Abba* (see Rom. 8:15; Gal. 4:6), but it is only through Jesus that this is possible. In other words, it is only because we are united by faith to the Son that we have access to the Father by the Spirit (John 1:12; cf. 14:6; 17:26; Rom. 8:15). As such, our use of the term is only made possible because of the Son in relation to his Father, which is another way of underscoring Jesus' unique sonship.

Jesus, then, by the use of this term understands himself to be the unique Son in relation to the Father. What is the precise nature of this sonship? No doubt, it is not explained by the term alone; ultimately one requires the entire plotline of Scripture to unpack the meaning of sonship. But when one does so, it is clear that Jesus' sonship is not merely functional but also ontological. This point is demonstrated in Jesus' use, understanding, and application of the title "Son" to himself. Let us now turn to this important self-designation.

Jesus' Self-Identity as the "Son"

This title describes the unique relationship of Jesus to God. It is found throughout the Synoptic Gospels (Matt. 3:17; 11:25–27; 28:19; Mark 1:1, 11; 9:7; Luke 1:32; 3:32; 9:35) and occupies a central role in John's Gospel (3:16, 17, 35–36; 5:19–23; 6:40; 8:36; 14:13; 17:1).[47] The New Testament states that the title originated with Jesus himself and this certainly makes sense of the data (Matt. 11:27; cf. Mark 12:6; 13:32). The title was used of him at his baptism (Mark 1:11), temptation (Luke 4:9), and transfiguration (Mark 9:7; Matt. 17:5; Luke 9:35). It was used in address by the centurion (Mark 15:39), the high priest (Mark 14:61), and by the demons (Mark 3:11; 5:7). It also occurs frequently in John; indeed the entire purpose of the Gospel is to demonstrate that Jesus is the "Son of God" (John 20:31).[48]

It is certainly the case that this title can be used in a number of ways in Scripture, specifically carrying a strong functional/representational mean-

---

[46]Wells, *Person of Christ*, 43.
[47]For a fine treatment of the title in John's Gospel see Andreas J. Köstenberger and Scott R. Swain, *Father, Son and Spirit: The Trinity and John's Gospel*, NSBT (Downers Grove, IL: InterVarsity, 2008), 75–92. Also cf. Carson, *John*, 246–59.
[48]See ibid., 87–95.

ing.[49] For example, it can refer to finite, heavenly beings (Gen. 6:2; Job 1:6; 38:7; Pss. 29:1; 89:7). It can also be applied to Israel as a nation (Ex. 4:22–23; Jer. 31:9; Deut. 14:1; 32:5; Isa. 43:6; Hos. 11:1), as God's "firstborn son" (Ex. 4:22). As applied to Israel, the term stresses the unique functional/representational role Israel, as a nation, plays in God's redemptive plan. Israel is to carry on the work that Adam was to do, but failed. Just as Adam, as the "image" and "son" (Luke 3:38), was to represent God and be under his sovereign rule, as a creature, along with the entire human race, so Israel is to act and represent the Lord to the nations. They are to be an obedient "son" in relation to God as their father (Deut. 32:6; Jer. 3:4) since they are in covenant relationship with the Lord, but unfortunately they failed.

Probably the most significant use of the title is in relation to the Davidic king, who stands as the representative of Israel (he is called God's "firstborn," Ps. 89:26–27) and is in a unique relationship to the Lord—a Father-son relationship (2 Sam. 7:14; 1 Chron. 17:13). In this way, the Davidic kings are "sons" who function as representatives of the Lord to carry out his rule in this world, similar to Adam before them. In the prophetic literature there is a growing anticipation that a Davidic king will come and rule over the nations as God's vicegerent (Psalms 2, 72; Isa. 9:6), which fuels messianic expectation. In this sense the Davidic king functions as God's unique son, as a representative figure—the Messiah—for Israel as a nation and to the nations of the world.

When the title "Son" is applied to Jesus, and when Jesus applies it to himself, it minimally refers to these typological patterns rooted in the Old Testament. When Matthew 2:15 says that Jesus' return from Egypt fulfills Hosea 11:1, the stress is placed on Jesus as the true Son of God, i.e., the true Israel.[50] Even at Jesus' baptism and transfiguration the divine voice identifies him as God's "Son" (Matt. 3:17; 17:5 and par.), minimally underscoring that he is the long-awaited Messiah, David's greater son. Thomas Schreiner rightly argues that "the titles 'Christ' and 'Son of God' were synonyms, denoting that Jesus was the Messiah of Israel."[51]

This point is important to stress since Jesus as the "Son," in this first sense, strongly teaches his full humanity and necessarily so. Without his being the "Son" and fulfilling the role of Adam, Israel, and David, we would not have a covenant mediator who is able to represent us and reverse the effects of sin and death that are the results of the fall. That is why the New Testament does not hesitate to emphasize a strong functional aspect to

---

[49]See Schreiner, *New Testament Theology*, 234–48; Gathercole, *The Pre-existent Son*, 272–83.
[50]See Carson, *Matthew*, 90–93; Schreiner, *New Testament Theology*, 170–73.
[51]Ibid., 236.

christology in the sense that Jesus, by virtue of what he *does*, is appointed Son and Lord. In other words, the eternal Son by becoming incarnate (John 1:1, 14), obediently identifying with and acting on our behalf—by virtue of his entire work—is now appointed as Son and Lord (see Rom. 1:3–4; Phil. 2:6–11).[52] Yet, this is only half of the story. In typological relations, the antitype is always greater than the type, and such is the case here. It is not enough to say only that Jesus as the "Son" is a reference to him as the Messiah. Rather, when Jesus speaks of himself as the "Son," we must think of it ontologically, not merely functionally, i.e., he is the eternal, divine Son vis-à-vis his Father.

Think of how the ontological is emphasized throughout the New Testament. Jesus is the Son from all eternity who takes on flesh and who becomes Jesus of Nazareth (John 1:1, 14; cf. Heb. 1:1–2; Col. 1:14–17). He is described as always having been in the bosom of the Father (John 1:18; 17:5). As such, he is *the* Son of God (Luke 1:31–32; John 1:34; 1 John 5:20), God's *own* Son (Rom. 8:3, 32), whose sonship is prior to ours and the foundation for how we become "sons of God" (John 1:12; Rom. 8:15; Gal. 4:6), and so on. In all these ways, the New Testament stresses that Jesus' sonship is utterly unique. In the Gospels, this emphasis is particularly developed in John where Jesus clearly views himself in this way (see, e.g., John 5:16–30). But Jesus' use of this title is not limited to the fourth Gospel; it is also found in the Synoptics, specifically Matthew 11:25–27, sometimes labeled the "thunderbolt from the Johannine heaven."[53] Let us briefly look at how this text teaches the uniqueness of Jesus' sonship.

The entire chapter of Matthew 11 is one of incredible christological importance.[54] Already in Matthew's Gospel, Jesus is presented as the one who fulfills all God's plans and purposes. For example, this is made evident from the opening genealogy (1:1–17), to the stress on his virginal conception (1:18–25), to how he fulfills the typological structures of the Old Testament as the true Israel (2:15) and brings the exile to an end (2:16–18), and to how he alone ushers in God's sovereign rule to this world (3–4). As we noted above, Matthew recounts the dawning of the promised "age to come" in Jesus by describing his incredible teaching (5–7) and divine acts (8–9), which all demonstrate that the messianic age has arrived and that sin, death, and the Devil are now being put to flight.

---

[52]See Douglas Moo, *The Epistle to the Romans*, NICNT (Grand Rapids, MI: Eerdmans, 1996), 44–53; P. T. O'Brien, *Commentary on Philippians*, NIGTC (Grand Rapids, MI: Eerdmans, 1991), 205–53.

[53]Reymond, *Jesus, Divine Messiah*, 203. Reymond attributes this expression to K. A. von Hase.

[54]See Carson, *Matthew*, 259–79; France, *Matthew*, 416–51.

Building on this, chapter 11 begins a section (11–13) which recounts growing opposition to Jesus, thus raising questions about the kind of messiah he is. If the people expect a royal messiah who will win political victory, their disappointment is growing. Even John the Baptist has doubts (vv. 2–19) and as such sends his disciples to ask Jesus: "Are you the one who is to come, or shall we look for another?" (v. 3). Jesus responds by describing his own miracles and teaching in the language of Isaiah 35:5–6; 61:1, which is thoroughly messianic. He does indeed say that the long-awaited kingdom has dawned in him, but he purposely does not speak of divine judgment, which was expected as part of the coming of the messianic age.[55] In his response, Jesus challenges John and his disciples to rethink their concept of the Messiah, especially in terms of a suffering messiah. Now what is significant in this entire discussion, especially for our purposes, is how incredibly egocentric Jesus is as he speaks of who he is as compared to John (vv. 11–18) and then as compared to his Father (vv. 25–27). Let us look at those two relationships in turn.

First, as Jesus speaks of who he is in relation to John, he begins by focusing on John's greatness: "Truly, I say to you, among those born of women there has arisen no one greater than John the Baptist. Yet the one who is least in the kingdom of heaven is greater than he" (v. 11). Jesus is clearly defining John's greatness in terms of himself! John is great because he has the supreme privilege, as the last of the Old Testament prophets, to predict and anticipate the coming of the Messiah and the dawning of the messianic age. No prophet in redemptive history had this unique privilege. But, as Jesus elaborates, those least in the kingdom are greater than John precisely because they live after John. They, unlike John, will be able to bear witness to Jesus greater than he could ever have done. They will be able to speak of Jesus' cross, resurrection, ascension, and the dawning of the Spirit at Pentecost. They will know in a far greater way who Jesus is as the Lord and thus bear witness to him in a greater way than John. But note: this only makes sense if Jesus sees himself as the focal point of history, the one who brings to pass all God's plans and purposes in himself—quite a claim indeed, and quite an egocentric view to have of himself.

But Jesus says more. He now develops his sonship in terms of his relationship to his Father (vv. 25–27). After addressing God as "Father, Lord of heaven and earth," Jesus thanks God for concealing the significance of his miracles from some as an act of judgment upon their sin, and, by grace, revealing it to others. Why has the Father done so? Ultimately it is due to the

---

[55]See Carson, *Matthew*, 262.

Father's own good pleasure (v. 26). Incredibly, Jesus now adds that in this concealing/revealing activity of the Father, he is the exclusive agent of that revelation: "All things have been handed over to me by my Father, and no one knows the Son except the Father, and no one knows the Father except the Son and anyone to whom the Son chooses to reveal him" (v. 27). Here we discover how Jesus understands his relation to the Father—a relation that can only be understood as a claim of deity. It is presented in the most unique of ways and is unpacked in terms of two affirmations.[56]

First, the Father-Son relationship is spoken of in terms of an exclusive, mutual knowledge that each has of the other. Initially, it is not surprising that Jesus says, "No one knows the Son except the Father," for the Father is omniscient. But when he states, "No one knows the Father except the Son," this is a staggering claim. As Robert Reymond contends, this statement "lifts Jesus above the sphere of the ordinary mortal and places him in a position, not of equality merely, but of absolute reciprocity and interpenetration of knowledge with the Father."[57]

Furthermore, the only way one can make sense of this reciprocal/mutual knowledge of the Son is in categories that are antecedent to Jesus becoming Messiah. Why? Because it is nigh impossible to think of Jesus' knowledge as merely a consequence of his messianic mission; it has to be tied to pre-temporal, even eternal relations. That is why "sonship" cannot merely be reduced to functional categories. Rather, as George Ladd has argued, "sonship precedes messiahship and is in fact the ground for the messianic mission."[58] Second, the Father-Son relation is further developed in terms of a mutual sovereignty whereby both the Father and the Son must take the initiative to reveal each other in order for anyone to come to a saving knowledge.

When these two affirmations are united, it is fair to say that no higher expression of parity between the Father and the Son can be given. Jesus' self-identity as the Son has to be understood in divine terms. B. B. Warfield, many years ago, said it correctly:

> Not merely is the Son the exclusive revealer of God, but the mutual knowledge of the Father and Son is put on what seems very much a par. The Son can be known only by the Father in all that He is, as if His being were infinite and as such inscrutable to the finite intelligence; and His knowledge alone—again as if He were infinite in His attributes—is competent to compass the depths

---

[56]See Reymond, *Jesus, Divine Messiah*, 206–10.
[57]Ibid., 207.
[58]George E. Ladd, *New Testament Theology* (Grand Rapids, MI: Eerdmans, 1974), 167.

of the Father's infinite being. He who holds this relation to the Father cannot conceivably be a creature.[59]

Now it is within this context that we need to think carefully about Jesus' famous confessed ignorance, or lack of knowledge of the *parousia*, which many argue count against viewing him as *God* the Son. Jesus says: "But concerning that day and hour no one knows, not even the angels of heaven, nor the Son, but the Father only" (Matt. 24:36; cf. Mark 13:32). Throughout the history of the church, beginning with the Arian controversy, this text has been used to undercut the deity of Christ since surely if Jesus were God he would have known this information. Certainly, this text deserves a detailed discussion, more than is possible here, but it is crucial to point out that it does not provide grounds to undercut the deity of Christ. Rather, it is better understood in terms of the unique Father-Son relationship as discussed above,[60] as well as the nature of the incarnation during the state of humiliation as Jesus acts as the obedient Son in order to accomplish our salvation. But with that said, even Jesus' admission of ignorance instead of leading us to deny his deity actually underscores his unique self-identity as the Son. How so? As noted above, the very use of the title "Son" speaks of his unique filial relation to the Father. In addition, the context of this statement is centered in Jesus speaking of his coming in divine judgment, something which only God can do. Moreover, as Reymond rightly observes, the fact that the phrase "not even the Son" comes *after* the reference to angels, proves that Jesus views himself in a category all by himself—greater than any human or angel. In biblical thought, this carries with it an unmistakable divine claim.[61]

---

[59]B. B. Warfield, *The Lord of Glory* (repr. Grand Rapids, MI: Baker, 1974), 83. There is even more in this text which could be developed in terms of Jesus' divine self-identity. In vv. 28–30, Jesus invites the burdened to come to him. In itself this is an incredible christological statement, an echo of Jer. 31:25, which in its Old Testament context is an anticipation of the arrival of the new-covenant age—an age which only Yahweh can usher in. On this point, see Carson, *Matthew*, 277–79. All of this together, like John 5, leads us to conclude that Jesus' self-identity is that he is God the Son incarnate.

[60]France, *Matthew*, 940, makes a helpful observation. He notes that in the immediate context, Jesus is not embarrassed by this statement. That is why it is best understood in terms of "the relationship between Father and Son which is implied here and in 11:27, one which combines a uniquely close relationship with a recognition of priority and subordination, a paradox neatly summed up in the Johannine declarations 'I and the Father are one' (John 10:30) and 'The Father is greater than I' (John 14:28)." Also see Carson, *Matthew*, 508, for a similar point. Carson wisely admits that the text does not tell us how to combine the New Testament's insistence on Jesus' deity with its insistence on his ignorance and dependence, but "attempts to jettison one truth for the sake of preserving the other must be avoided."

[61]Reymond, *Jesus, Divine Messiah*, 216. Reymond writes: "[Jesus] classifies himself with the Father rather than with the angelic class, inasmuch as elsewhere he represents himself as the Lord of the angels whose commands the angels obey (Matt. 13:41, 49; 24:31; see Heb. 1:4–14)."

Thus, instead of undercutting Jesus' claim to deity, this text underscores it, albeit in ways that unpack the unique Father-Son relationship.

Jesus' Self-Identity as the "Son of Man"

This title is Jesus' most common self-designation, and if properly understood *explicitly* testifies to the fact that he is God the Son incarnate. It appears in all the Gospels (used some fifty times) and in every instance by Jesus himself which proves that the title originates with him.[62] In order to grasp what Jesus meant by "Son of Man," it is crucial to understand the title within the storyline of Scripture and its Old Testament background.[63]

In the Old Testament, the title is used both generally and specifically. First, generally, it is used as a synonym for humans within the context of our role in creation (see Ps. 8:4; cf. Num. 23:19; Job 25:6; Isa. 51:12; 56:2; Jer. 49:18, 33; 50:40; 51:43). In Psalm 80:17 there is a dispute as to its reference. This psalm recounts God's saving acts on behalf of Israel and its present devastation under foreign nations. Israel is compared to a vine that the Lord planted but has now been cut down. The Lord is petitioned to take regard for "the son whom you made strong for yourself" (v. 15), and in verse 17 a similar request is made: "Let your hand be on the man of your right hand, the son of man whom you have made strong for yourself." In this context, "man" and "son of man" could be a reference to Israel, due to the earlier reference to "son" (cf. Ex. 4:22) and "vine" (cf. Isa. 5:1–7), yet, in the context of the entire Psalter, it may also refer to the anointed king who represents Israel as a whole. If the latter, which is quite probable, then the reference takes on strong associations with the language of "son" in terms of an entire typological pattern from Adam to Israel, and finally to David, as a term that not only has messianic overtones but also speaks of a unique representative human.[64]

Second, specifically, in Daniel 7:13–14 this title takes on the significance of a superhuman figure who functions alongside the "Ancient of Days" (who is clearly God in judgment). In this vision, four kingdoms are depicted as four different beasts; they arise from the sea (7:3), belong to this world,

---

[62]Matthew uses the title thirty times, Mark fourteen, Luke twenty-five, and John thirteen. Outside the Gospels, the term is used with reference to Jesus only in Acts 7:56; Heb. 2:6; and Rev. 1:13; 14:14. The title is not used at all after Jesus' death except in Acts 7:56. Wells, *Person of Christ*, 78, argues that this "suggests that this was *his* term and not a formulation placed on his lips by the early church as Rudolf Bultmann and Norman Perrin propose. If this title was the creation of the church, we would also expect to encounter it in the epistles."

[63]See Schreiner, *New Testament Theology*, 213–31; cf. Gathercole, *The Pre-existent Son*, 253–71; C. F. D. Moule, *The Origin of Christology* (Cambridge: University Press, 1977), 11–22.

[64]See Schreiner, *New Testament Theology*, 213–16; cf. Dempster, *Dominion and Dynasty*, 194–202, 215–17.

and terrorize the peoples of the world. However, the kingdom of God will ultimately triumph and destroy all these kingdoms, and it is this eternal kingdom which God gives to the "son of man," who comes on the "clouds of heaven" (7:13, a reference to deity) and whose realm is supernatural and eternal (7:14). He will subjugate all other kingdoms to himself; the kingdoms of this world will disappear, but his will not. What is also important about this vision is that the four beasts (kingdoms) are represented by four kings who act as representative heads for each kingdom, while the Son of Man is presented as an individual who represents those who receive God's kingdom, namely God's saints, probably a reference to Israel and by extension to all God's people (Dan. 7:18, 22, 27). This implies, then, that the Son of Man, who has already been identified with God (7:13), also identifies with God's corporate people, yet he is also differentiated from them. Schreiner summarizes the overall significance of this vision when he writes: "Indeed, the son of man in Daniel does not grasp rule through military conquest by which he brutally rules over other human beings. He is given the kingdom of God himself, and thereby he fulfills the role for which human beings were created (Ps. 8)."[65]

In light of this background, the "Son of Man" title is applied to Jesus in three main areas: (1) Jesus' ministry (Mark 2:10, 28; Luke 7:34; 9:58; 19:10); (2) Jesus' suffering and resurrection (Mark 10:45; Luke 17:24–25; 22:48; 24:7; John 3:14; 6:53; 8:28; 12:23; 13:31); and (3) Jesus' future coming (Mark 8:38; 13:26; 14:62; Luke 12:8–10, 40; 17:22–30; 18:8; Matt. 10:23; 19:28; 24:30; 25:31).[66] The Son of Man sayings together lead to the conclusion that "Jesus employed a term which has specific content in the Old Testament, but in applying it to himself and his work it came to have a meaning both larger and more complex than it does in the Old Testament."[67] This is the case because Jesus' self-identity is that of *God the Son*; hence the reference to *the* "son of man" from Daniel 7:13–14, as well as God the Son *incarnate*; hence the true representative man, the Messiah, who triumphs and wins victory through suffering and death. In this way, this title fits wonderfully with the entire storyline of Scripture in which Jesus is affirming his solidarity with human beings and fulfilling all that Adam was intended to be but failed to become (see Ps. 8:4; cf. Gen. 1:26–27; Heb. 2:5–18).

But he also knows himself to be more than a mere man, for he speaks of himself in ways that are unashamedly divine and corporate. This, of course, fits with his self-identity as the Son who ushers in the "age to come" and

---

[65]Schreiner, *New Testament Theology*, 216.
[66]See Wells, *Person of Christ*, 80; Schreiner, *New Testament Theology*, 219–21.
[67]Wells, *Person of Christ*, 80.

all that is entailed by that age. But precisely because the inauguration of God's kingdom is ultimately tied to his cross work, Jesus explicitly speaks of himself as the "Son of Man" in relation to his death and resurrection. Thus the title is used by him both in his humiliation to save the lost (Matt. 8:20; Mark 10:45) and in his authority to forgive sins and powerful resurrection (Mark 2:10; Matt. 17:9)—all acts that are part of the promised age he inaugurates. The title is also included in his ascension and his return in glory (Matt. 19:28; 24:30), for without these events, what he started in his first advent would not be complete. In these ways, the title "Son of Man" explicitly speaks of his deity and humanity, which is consistent with his self-identity as God the Son incarnate.

Jesus' Self-Identity in Other Explicit Statements

Two other explicit kinds of statements further underscore Jesus' divine self-identity. First, there are statements related to Jesus' understanding of the purpose of his coming—"I have come to . . ."—which not only presuppose that Jesus is preexistent, but also identify him with God in a deliberate way. The recent work of Simon Gathercole, *The Pre-existent Son*, is probably the best treatment of such statements along with their christological implications. I can only summarize his main arguments here. Gathercole's study divides these statements into three categories.

First, on two occasions demons ask whether Jesus has come to destroy them (Mark 1:24 par.; Matt. 8:29). Jesus is portrayed in exalted terms on both occasions and his heavenly origin is evident when he is identified as the "Holy One of God" and the "Son of God." Jesus' coming in order to destroy the demons is presented as a visit from the heavenly realm, and, as such, it presupposes not only his preexistence but also that he transcends the human realm and is identified with God. Second, there are six sayings in which Jesus declares why he has come. He has come to preach the good news of the kingdom in Israel (Mark 1:38 par.); to call sinners to himself (Matt. 9:13 par.); to fulfill rather than to abolish the Old Testament (Matt. 5:17); to cast a fire onto the earth (Luke 12:49); to bring a sword and division rather than peace to earth (Matt. 10:34 par.); and to divide family members against one another (Matt. 10:35). In each of these statements, especially Luke 12:29, Jesus understands himself to have preexisted and that his work has a transcendent quality about it, identified with the work of God. Third, there are two "Son of Man" sayings where Jesus states the purpose of his coming. The Son of Man came to serve others and to offer his life as a ransom (Matt. 20:28 par.); and he came to seek and to save the lost (Luke 19:10). In the context of the Old Testament, this activity uniquely identifies Jesus with God himself who seeks his sheep and is the shepherd of the flock (Ezekiel 34), so that Jesus understands himself in the role of the Lord. All these statements, Gathercole argues, especially when viewed in light of how Jesus is presented in the Synoptic Gospels in heavenly terms, let alone the rest of the New Testament—e.g., Jesus' transfiguration (Matt. 17:1–8 par.), his role in sending the prophets (Matt. 23:34–36), his role in the heavenly council (Luke 10:20), etc.—explicitly reveal to us that Jesus' self-identity is that his origin transcends the sphere of humanity and is identified with God.

Second, there are statements in which Jesus explicitly states that he does the work which God alone does. For example, in Mark 2 Jesus announces that he has the authority to forgive sins. In light of the fall, humanity's greatest problem is sin against a holy and righteous God. Ultimately, God is the only one with the authority to forgive sin, because sin first and foremost is against him. In fact, at the heart of the "newness" of the new covenant is the promise of the full forgiveness of sin (Jer. 31:34). Under the old covenant, sin was forgiven, but only in a temporary, anticipatory, typological fashion. It is only with the arrival of the new covenant that God is said to remember our sin no more. That is why it is staggering to hear Jesus say to the paralytic: "Son, your sins are forgiven" (Mark 2:5). In one respect, the response of the religious leaders was theologically correct. They were right to think that only God can forgive sins (2:7), but they were wrong in charging Jesus with blasphemy, since they failed to recognize his identity as God the Son incarnate. Jesus with a fullness of knowledge and perception knew what they were thinking, so he challenged them in regard to his identity: "Why do you question these things in your hearts? Which is easier, to say to the paralytic, 'Your sins are forgiven,' or to say, 'Rise, take up your bed and walk'?" (2:8–9).

In explaining this rhetorical question, R. T. France argues that it implies "that if the 'harder' of the two options can be demonstrated, the 'easier' may be assumed also to be possible."[68] He then suggests that to forgive sins is the harder, since only God can do it, but Jesus' question "is not about which is easier to *do*, but which is easier to *say*, and a *claim* to forgive sins is undoubtedly easier to make, since it cannot be falsified by external events, whereas a claim to make a paralyzed man walk will be immediately proved true or false by a success or failure which everyone can see."[69] The logic of what follows then is: "Jesus' demonstrable authority to cure the disabled

---

[68]France, *Matthew*, 346.
[69]Ibid., 346.

man is evidence that he also has authority to forgive sins."[70] No doubt this is true, but there seems to be more here. Remember that in the Synoptics this healing is placed in the overall context of the inauguration of the king-dom. As noted above, Jesus' miracles are no mere display of power but a graphic demonstration that the promised "age to come" has now dawned in him. His healing of the paralytic, then, is a miracle which one ought to have expected if God's rule and reign has truly broken into this world (see Matt. 8:17; cf. Isa. 35:5–6; 53:4; 61:1). Yet, tied to the inauguration of the "age to come" is the complete forgiveness of sin (Jer. 31:34).

So Jesus lays out the options: which is easier, to heal this man as evidence that the kingdom has dawned, or to pronounce the forgiveness of sin, which is also evidence that the new-covenant age is now here? These options are both acts of the dawning of the new-covenant age—an age that only God can effect. This is why Jesus ties his authority to the title "Son of Man": "But that you may know that the Son of Man has authority on earth to forgive sins" (2:10). For, as argued above, this title speaks of Jesus' identity as God the Son incarnate, who has the authority to inaugurate the promised age and all that is entailed by that age—judgment, the granting of eternal life, including the authority to forgive sins. Ultimately, as Carson notes, "This is the authority of Emmanuel, 'God with us' (Matt. 1:23), sent to 'save his people from their sins' (Matt. 1:21)."[71] And note: all this takes place *outside* the temple so that Jesus is signifying that forgiveness of sin, now that he has come at this point in redemptive history, is found in him alone. After all, he is the one to which the entire old covenant pointed in its priesthood, sacrificial system, and entire temple structure. Jesus' claim then, set within the storyline of Scripture, is an explicit claim of deity.[72]

---

[70]Ibid.

[71]Carson, *Matthew*, 222.

[72]See N. T. Wright, *The Challenge of Jesus: Rediscovering Who Jesus Was and Is* (Downers Grove, IL: InterVarsity, 1999), 62–73, who argues a similar point. However, Wright rejects the conclusion that Jesus' self-identity was that of God the Son incarnate. Wright argues that Jesus believed himself called to act as the new temple, which, he admits, in a Jewish mind-set would be an implicit claim "to be the place where and the means by which Israel's God was at last personally present to and with his people" (114). He also argues that Jesus believed he was not merely a new Moses "but in some sense or other a new YHWH" (114) since in his teaching, the living God was somehow present. In addition, Jesus believed that he was acting to bring about the new exodus so that in his actions he was revealing the personality of Yahweh in action, embodied in human form (116). In all these ways, Jesus, in terms of his vocation, "believed he had to do and be, for Israel and the world, that which according to Scripture only YHWH himself could do and be" (122). But Wright argues that Jesus' awareness of his vocation is not the same as him knowing that he is God the Son. However, Wright's conclusion is not correct. Within the storyline of Scripture, all the actions Wright says Jesus knew he was doing are only actions that God can do and as such, Jesus' identity is a divine identity. In addition, Jesus' identity in relation to the Father is more than a messianic

Conclusion

Who do the Synoptic Gospels say Jesus is? Who does Jesus say he is? We have argued that both teach, implicitly and explicitly, that he is God the Son incarnate. The Synoptic presentation of Jesus, when placed within the storyline, framework, and theology of Scripture, announces that in Christ alone the promised "age to come" has dawned—an age that only God can truly effect. In *this* specific man, we find the Messiah who is also the Lord (Luke 1:31–35; 2:11). In this way, the Synoptics are a perfect example of what Bauckham labels a "divine identity Christology," i.e., Jesus is identified directly with the one God of Israel in all his actions, character, and work.[73] In him all God's sovereign plans and purposes are fulfilled, for he is not merely a man, but he is also Immanuel, God with us. In Jesus the Christ, we see the perfectly obedient son who is also God the Son from all eternity. In him, we see the two strands of Old Testament eschatological expectation unite: he is the sovereign Lord who comes to rescue and save his people and who simultaneously is the great Davidic king. In this way, Jesus fulfills all the types of the Old Testament: he is the last Adam, the true seed of Abraham, the true Israel and Davidic son, the great prophet, priest, and king, yet he is also identified with Yahweh and thus God the Son incarnate, forever to be praised, trusted, loved, and adored—King of kings and Lord of lords.

---

relation; it is one which must be understood in terms of eternity. He knows that he is the eternal Son who has come in obedience to his Father's will, who has taken upon our humanity in order to do what only God could do, namely to forgive his people of their sins (Matt. 1:21). Ultimately, Wright's explanation does not do justice to Jesus' own statements placed within the entire biblical-theological framework of Scripture.

[73]See Bauckham, *Jesus and the God of Israel*, 1–59.

4

The Deity of Christ in John's Gospel

ANDREAS J. KÖSTENBERGER

John's Gospel is rooted in the soil of first-century Jewish monotheism. It was composed by an eyewitness of the events surrounding Jesus' earthly ministry and has as its major purpose the demonstration that Jesus is the Christ and Son of God in order to instill faith in its readers resulting in eternal life (20:30–31).[1] While the other canonical (Synoptic) Gospels are less overt in presenting Jesus as divine, John unapologetically and from the very outset claims that Jesus was God who existed prior to, and was God's agent in, creation (1:1–3).[2] In what follows, I will first explore the monotheistic environment of first-century Judaism to understand John's presentation of Jesus as divine in its proper historical setting. This will be followed by an exploration of John's multifaceted teaching on Christ's divinity and by probing its important theological implications.

---

[1]For a thorough discussion of the relevant introductory issues for John's Gospel, see Andreas J. Köstenberger, L. Scott Kellum, and Charles L. Quarles, *The Cradle, the Cross, and the Crown: An Introduction to the New Testament* (Nashville: Broadman, 2009), chap. 7. On the Gospels as eyewitness testimony, see Richard Bauckham, *Jesus and the Eyewitnesses: The Gospels as Eyewitness Testimony* (Grand Rapids, MI: Eerdmans, 2006).

[2]On Jesus' preexistence in the Synoptics, see Simon Gathercole, *The Pre-existent Son: Recovering the Christologies of Matthew, Mark, and Luke* (Grand Rapids, MI: Eerdmans, 2006).

Historical Setting

John's Teaching on Jesus as God and First-Century Jewish Monotheism
The Jewish belief in one God finds early and significant expression in two
major passages in the Hebrew Scriptures: (1) the first two commandments
in the Decalogue, which forbid the Israelites from having or worshiping any
gods other than Yahweh (Ex. 20:2–6; Deut. 5:6–10); and (2) the injunction
commonly referred to as the Shema (from the Hebrew "to hear"), "Hear,
O Israel: The LORD our God, the LORD is one" (Deut. 6:4). Throughout
Israel's history, as attested in the Hebrew Scriptures, it is this God who
acts both in terms of revelation and redemption, who delivers his people
from bondage, enters into covenant with them, gives them the law, and
communicates with them through the prophets. This God, with whom
Israel enters into various covenants, they acknowledge as both the creator
and the sovereign ruler over all things.[3]

From this set of beliefs it also follows that God alone is to be worshiped.
This constituted a major distinctive of Jewish religion in the ancient world:
"Judaism was unique among the religions of the Roman world in demanding
the exclusive worship of its God."[4] In fact, "the worship of one and only one
God set Israel apart from the polytheistic beliefs and practices of its pagan
neighbours, including the Greco-Roman pantheon, which was made up of
dozens of gods."[5] Greco-Roman historians regularly recognized monotheism
as a hallmark of Jewish faith.[6] As Christopher Wright observes, the "theo-
centric, monotheistic worldview of first-century Jews," in turn, constituted
"the assumptive bedrock of Jesus and all his first followers."[7] Not only was
this God the God of Israel; the Jews believed that Yahweh was also the God
to whom all nations owed submission and worship.

In light of this firmly entrenched set of Jewish monotheistic beliefs, it
is manifest that any claim to deity by a person such as Jesus would meet
with vehement opposition by first-century Jews. As John's Gospel attests,
this is what in fact ensued when Jesus' Jewish contemporaries repeatedly
set out to stone Jesus on account of blasphemy (see, e.g., John 5:18; 8:59;
10:31–33; cf. 11:8). What is more, while other reasons were initially given

---

[3]On the deity of Christ in the Old Testament, see the chapter by Ray Ortlund Jr. in this volume.
See also Günter Reim, "Jesus as God in the Fourth Gospel: The Old Testament Background," *NTS*
30 (1984): 158–60.
[4]Richard Bauckham, "Jesus, Worship of," *ABD* 3.816.
[5]Andreas J. Köstenberger and Scott R. Swain, *Father, Son and Spirit: The Trinity and John's Gospel*,
NSBT 24 (Downers Grove, IL: InterVarsity, 2008), 34.
[6]Thus Tacitus wrote, "The Jews conceive of one God only" (*Hist.* 5.5).
[7]Christopher J. H. Wright, *The Mission of God: Unlocking the Bible's Grand Narrative* (Grand
Rapids, MI: IVP Academic, 2006), 105.

by the Jews in John's Gospel why Jesus must die—such as the claims that he was a criminal and lawbreaker and that he constituted a threat to Roman imperial power (18:30; 19:12)—in the end the real reason emerged: Jesus "must die, because he claimed to be the Son of God" (19:7 NIV). In keeping with the Synoptic testimony, therefore, John states unequivocally that the primary reason Jesus was condemned to die was that he claimed to be God (cf. Matt. 26:65).[8]

Some scholars argue that Second Temple Judaism adhered to a strict form of monotheism that would have made it unlikely for people of that culture to attribute divinity to anyone other than God. These scholars argue that only a radical break with first-century Judaism would have allowed Jesus' followers to claim he was divine. Maurice Casey, for example, maintains that "the deity of Jesus is . . . *inherently* unJewish. The witness of Jewish texts is unvarying belief that a second being is God involves departure from the Jewish community."[9] Other scholars, however, contend that Second Temple Judaism was considerably more flexible and point to a variety of intermediary figures including angels, exalted human beings, or personified divine attributes, maintaining that these features constitute Jewish precedents for the Christian practice of attributing deity to Jesus.[10]

In this context, it is helpful to note that in several places in the Old Testament and in Second Temple literature, beings other than Yahweh are called "god." The Alexandrian Jewish philosopher Philo refers to Moses as "god" (*Mos.* 1.155–158; *Prob.* 42–44; cf. Ex. 7:1); as Jesus himself points out, human judges are called "gods" (Ex. 22:27 LXX; cf. John 10:34–38), as are angels (Pss. 8:6; 82:1, 6; 97:6; 138:1) and the enigmatic figure of Melchizedek in the Dead Sea Scrolls (11QMelch 2.24–25). Nevertheless, the fact must be given full weight that these kinds of intermediary figures were clearly understood as creatures, and firm boundaries were in place between God the creator and the beings he had made (e.g., Ezek. 28:2; Hos. 11:9). Rather than diluting the distinction between deity and humanity, beings listed in the examples above are professedly not divine, and their correlating texts portray them only as exercising prerogatives usually reserved for deity.

---

[8]See Darrell L. Bock, *Blasphemy and Exaltation in Judaism: The Charge against Jesus in Mark 14:53–65* (Grand Rapids, MI: Baker, 2000).

[9]Maurice Casey, *From Jewish Prophet to Gentile God: The Origins and Development of New Testament Christology* (Louisville: Westminster, 1991), 176; emphasis original. But see the critique of Casey by Larry W. Hurtado, *Lord Jesus Christ: Devotion to Jesus in Earliest Christianity* (Grand Rapids, MI: Eerdmans, 2003), 43–44; and James D. G. Dunn, "The Making of Christology—Evolution or Unfolding?" in *Jesus of Nazareth: Lord and Christ. Essays on the Historical Jesus and New Testament Christology*, ed. Joel B. Green and Max Turner (Grand Rapids, MI: Eerdmans, 1994), 437–52.

[10]See esp. Hurtado, *Lord Jesus Christ*.

Thus any such reference to Jewish intermediary figures as precedents for John's presentation of Jesus as God remains precarious.

More likely, the early Christians, including John, identified "Jesus directly with the one God of Israel" and included him "in the unique identity of this one God."[11] It is sometimes alleged that John stands only at the climax of an evolution of Christian consciousness, culminating with the idea that Jesus was God, which it took decades, in fact over a half-century, to develop. However, as Bauckham contends, to the contrary:

> The highest possible Christology, the inclusion of Jesus in the unique divine identity, was central to the faith of the early church even before any of the New Testament writings were written. . . . Although there was development in understanding this inclusion of Jesus in the identity of God, the decisive step of so including him was made at the beginning.[12]

Even more importantly, contra scholars such as Maurice Casey, John's high christology is completely reconcilable with strict first-century Jewish monotheism. This would explain why neither John nor the other canonical Gospels evince even the least bit of discomfort with the notion that Jesus was divine, a fact that is remarkable especially since all of Jesus' first followers were Jews. While Jesus' inclusion in the unique deity was a new development, it did not therefore necessarily conflict with, or compromise, first-century Jewish monotheism. As Bauckham observes, "Nothing in the second temple Jewish understanding of divine identity contradicts the possibility of interpersonal relationship within the divine identity."[13]

A case in point is provided by repeated instances in John's Gospel where Jesus is shown to appropriate the divine name *'anî hû'* (*egō eimi* in the Septuagint).[14] As Scott Swain and I have written:

> In keeping with Isaiah's vision of a new exodus for God's people, the Gospels provide a new narrative of God's acts. Just as Israel knew God as the one who

---

[11]Richard Bauckham, *God Crucified: Monotheism and Christology in the New Testament* (Grand Rapids, MI: Eerdmans, 1998), 4.

[12]Ibid., 27. Contra James D. G. Dunn, *Christology in the Making: A New Testament Inquiry into the Origins of the Doctrine of the Incarnation*, 2nd ed. (Grand Rapids, MI: Eerdmans, 1996).

[13]Bauckham, *God Crucified*, 75.

[14]See esp. 4:26; 6:20; 8:24, 28; 13:19; 18:5, 6, 8. See Philip B. Harner, *The "I Am" of the Fourth Gospel* (Philadelphia: Fortress, 1970); David M. Ball, *"I Am" in John's Gospel: Literary Function, Background and Theological Implications*, JSNTSup 124 (Sheffield: Sheffield Academic Press, 1996); Catrin H. Williams, *I Am He: The Interpretation of 'ani hu' in Jewish and Early Christian Literature* (Tübingen: Mohr-Siebeck, 2000); and Richard Bauckham, "Monotheism and Christology in the Gospel of John," in *Contours of Christology in the New Testament*, ed. Richard N. Longenecker (Grand Rapids, MI: Eerdmans, 2005), 153–63.

delivered the nation out of Egypt and told the story of that God, the New Testament writers identify God as the God of Jesus Christ and tell the story of Jesus as the account of the deliverance of God's people from sin.[15]

This new story, for its part, organically flows from the Old Testament representation of God and his redemptive acts on behalf of his people Israel, yet is new in the way in which God has now revealed himself and provided salvation in a definitive and universal manner (1:18; cf. Heb. 1:1–3). In Jesus, the creator and sovereign ruler of the world has become its universal savior (John 4:42; cf. Luke 2:1).

Before moving on to an investigation of John's presentation of Jesus as God, it will be important to clarify the most likely background for John's portrayal of Jesus' preexistence. As mentioned, it is often argued that Jewish belief in divine intermediaries provides the connecting link between Old Testament monotheism and the Christian worship of Jesus as God. However, it is considerably more likely that, on a historical level, the portrayal of Jesus as divine in all four canonical Gospels is predicated upon the early Christian interpretation of Psalms 110:1 and 2:7 in light of Jesus' self-understanding as the Son of God.[16] In Psalm 110:1, the early church found biblical warrant for interpreting Jesus' resurrection as his exaltation to God's right hand (see, e.g., Acts 2:34–35; cf. Mark 14:62). Psalm 2:7, likewise, was interpreted by the early Christians as a prophecy regarding Jesus' divine sonship that was decisively fulfilled at his resurrection and exaltation (Acts 13:33; cf. Acts 4:25–26).[17]

In this context, rather than placing Christianity in conflict with first-century Jewish monotheism, "the exclusivist monotheism of ancient Judaism is the crucial religious context in which to view early Christ-devotion," a monotheism that helped shape worship of Jesus as divine "especially in those Christian circles concerned to maintain a fidelity to the biblical tradition of the one God."[18] Thus, "Jesus is not reverenced as another deity of any independent origin or significance; instead, his divine significance is characteristically expressed in terms of his relationship to the one God."[19] For this reason early Christian worship of Jesus as God was binitarian (worship of both God and Jesus) but not ditheistic (worship of two independent deities).[20]

---

[15]Köstenberger and Swain, *Father, Son and Spirit*, 37.
[16]See esp. Aquila H. I. Lee, *From Messiah to Preexistent Son: Jesus' Self-Consciousness and Early Christian Exegesis of Messianic Psalms*, WUNT 2:192 (Tübingen: Mohr-Siebeck, 2005).
[17]For a fuller treatment, see Köstenberger and Swain, *Father, Son and Spirit*, 39–41.
[18]Hurtado, *Lord Jesus Christ*, 56.
[19]Ibid., 51.
[20]Ibid., 52–53.

The results of the above brief survey of the first-century historical setting of Jewish monotheism for the portrayal of Jesus as God in John's Gospel can be summarized as follows.

1) John's presentation of Jesus as divine in his Gospel must be seen within the larger framework of Jewish monotheism. Rather than putting John's Gospel beyond the purview of Jewish monotheistic beliefs, John's treatment, which in turn reflects Jesus' own teaching and the practice of his first followers,[21] expands Jewish categories of the worship of Yahweh and applies these to Jesus, including him in the identity of Yahweh.

2) John's identification of Jesus as God is not primarily predicated upon Second Temple teaching on divine-human intermediaries but flows from a messianic interpretation of important Old Testament passages such as Psalm 110:1 or 2:7. In this regard, the early Christians believed that Jesus did not acquire a new status at the resurrection but that his exaltation merely confirmed the divine status he already possessed.

3) The early church's belief in, and worship of, Jesus as God was not the product of an extended evolution of religious convictions but a function of a virtually instantaneous realization that Jesus was God by virtue of his inclusion in the identity of Yahweh, in keeping with his own claim and consciousness and in line with Old Testament messianic teaching.

The Composition and Historical Setting of John's Gospel

As I have argued more fully elsewhere, John's Gospel was most likely formulated in the context of a crisis of Jewish belief brought on by the destruction of the second temple in AD 70.[22] Specifically, John wrote his Gospel, at least in part, as a response to the religious vacuum left by the temple's destruction, a response that suggests as a permanent solution Jesus' replacement of the temple with himself. Scholars commonly agree that John's Gospel was written in the 80s or early 90s and thus subsequent to the temple's destruction.[23] The demise of the central Jewish sanctuary left a gaping void not only for Palestinian Jews; it also reverberated in the Diaspora.[24] As Philip

---

[21] For a defense of the historical reliability of John, see Craig L. Blomberg, *The Historical Reliability of John's Gospel* (Downers Grove, IL: InterVarsity, 2001). See also Bauckham, *Jesus and the Eyewitnesses* (though Bauckham does not support apostolic authorship).

[22] Andreas J. Köstenberger, "The Destruction of the Second Temple and the Composition of the Fourth Gospel," in *Challenging Perspectives on the Gospel of John*, WUNT 2:219, ed. John Lierman (Tübingen: Mohr-Siebeck, 2006), 69–108.

[23] The (few) exceptions include Daniel B. Wallace, "John 5:2 and the Date of the Fourth Gospel," *Bib* 71 (1990): 177–205; John A. T. Robinson, *Redating the New Testament* (London: SCM, 1976); and John A. T. Robinson, *The Priority of John*, ed. J. F. Croakley (London: SCM, 1985).

[24] See Philip S. Alexander, "'The Parting of the Ways' from the Perspective of Rabbinic Judaism," in *Jews and Christians: The Parting of the Ways A.D. 70 to 135*, ed. James D. G. Dunn (Tübingen:

Alexander notes, the debacle of the Jewish War against the Romans issuing in the destruction of the temple opened for (Jewish) Christians a "window of opportunity," sweeping away the authorities that were hostile to emergent Christianity and removing for the foreseeable future the threat of "being excommunicated from Israel by decree from Jerusalem."[25] The temple's destruction also provided Christians with a propaganda coup, allowing them to point out that this event constituted God's judgment on Israel for her rejection of Jesus as Messiah (cf. Matt. 24:2 par.; cf. Luke 23:28–31).[26]

There are several strategic references to Jesus as the fulfillment and/ or replacement of the temple in John's Gospel.[27] The first is 1:14, where John speaks of Jesus as the Word-made-flesh, who literally "pitched his tent" (*skenoō*) among God's people, a clear allusion to the tabernacle that preceded the temple (cf. Exodus 26–27; 1 Kings 6:13). Later in the first chapter of John's Gospel, Jesus is presented as the place where God is revealed, in keeping with Jacob's vision at Bethel, the "house of God" (cf. Gen. 28:12).[28] Perhaps the two most important references to Jesus as the replacement of the temple are found in the account of Jesus' clearing of the temple (John 2:14–22) and in the context of Jesus' conversation with the Samaritan woman (4:19–24). In the former account, Jesus' clearing of the temple serves as an acted-out parable signifying the temple's forthcoming destruction. With prophetic symbolism, the temple's destruction, in turn, is said to be a sign of the "destruction" of Jesus' body (i.e., the crucifixion) and of its resurrection on the third day (2:18–19).[29] While the Jewish authorities misunderstood the significance of Jesus' teaching in this regard, supposing he was referring to the rebuilding of the literal temple, John makes clear that Jesus "was speaking about the temple of his body" (i.e., the temple *that was* his body, a genitive of apposition; 2:21).[30]

In 4:19–21, Jesus points out that what matters regarding proper worship is not geographical location—whether it is offered on Mount Gerizim or in

---

Mohr-Siebeck, 1992), 1–25. See also Jacob Neusner, "Judaism in a Time of Crisis: Four Responses to the Destruction of the Second Temple," *Judaism* 21 (1972): 313–27.

[25] Alexander, "Parting of the Ways," 20.

[26] For a discussion of other Jewish responses to the loss of the temple, see Köstenberger, "The Destruction of the Second Temple and the Composition of the Fourth Gospel," in *Challenging Perspectives on the Gospel of John*, 82–94.

[27] See ibid., 94–106.

[28] For a commentary on John 1:51, see Andreas J. Köstenberger, *John*, BECNT (Grand Rapids, MI: Baker, 2004), 84–87.

[29] See on this Andreas J. Köstenberger, "The Seventh Johannine Sign: A Study in John's Christology," *BBR* 5 (1995): 87–103.

[30] See Daniel B. Wallace, *Greek Grammar Beyond the Basics* (Grand Rapids, MI: Zondervan, 1996), 98.

Jerusalem (!)—but whether worship is "in spirit and truth" (4:23). As in the previous temple references (1:14, 51; 2:14–22), this passage also presents Jesus as the new temple, where proper worship is to be rendered. In the remainder of the Gospel, Jesus is shown to constitute the replacement of the entire Jewish festal calendar, including the festivals of Tabernacles (chaps. 7–8), Dedication (chaps. 10:22–39), and even Passover.[31] As the Messiah, Jesus gives sight to the man born blind, who in turn worships Jesus after the man is expelled from the synagogue (9:38).[32] Johannine irony is present when the Jewish high priest fears that the Romans will destroy "our place" (i.e., the temple) unless Jesus is crucified (11:48–52). As John's readers were doubtless aware, however, the crucifixion of Jesus did not prevent the temple's destruction by the Romans. Finally, there is a telling silence in the second major section of John's Gospel (i.e., chaps. 13–21) regarding the temple (cf. Rev. 21:22).[33] This provides further indirect evidence that, for John, Jesus is the new temple who, by virtue of his crucifixion and resurrection, replaces the old sanctuary.

As mentioned, the references to Jesus in relation to the temple in John's Gospel do not merely constitute an important Johannine theological theme; they also root the Gospel and its composition in a concrete historical setting, of which the destruction of the temple by the Romans in AD 70 was an important (and then-recent) part. Most likely, the apostle John, himself an eyewitness of Jesus' earthly ministry, wrote subsequent to the temple's destruction in order to make a case to Diaspora Jews and proselytes that Jesus was the new temple and the one to whom worship was to be directed. Just as in Old Testament times the temple was the place where God's glory dwelt, it was now Jesus in whom God's glory was revealed, because Jesus was the preexistent Word (John 1:1); and while "no one has ever seen God," "the only God [i.e., Jesus], who is at the Father's side, he has made him known" (1:18).[34]

Jesus as God in John's Gospel

The Word
At the very beginning of John's story about Jesus, he sets his narrative in the larger context of the Hebrew Scriptures and the creation of the universe: "In

---

[31]See Andreas J. Köstenberger, *A Theology of John's Gospel and Letters*, Biblical Theology of the New Testament (Grand Rapids, MI: Zondervan, 2009), chap. 10.

[32]For another instance of worship of Jesus in John's Gospel, see 20:28, on which see further the discussion below.

[33]See the discussion in Köstenberger, "Destruction of the Second Temple," 106.

[34]See Andreas J. Köstenberger, "The Glory of God in John's Gospel and Revelation," in *The Glory of God*, Theology in Community, vol. 2, ed. Christopher W. Morgan and Robert A. Peterson (Wheaton, IL: Crossway, 2010).

the beginning was the Word" (1:1a; cf. Gen. 1:1). That God created everything that exists by the power of his word follows clearly from a reading of the creation narrative (cf. Heb. 11:2). It follows also that in the beginning, "the Word was *with* God" (John 1:1b). This is similar to the description of wisdom being at God's side at creation in Proverbs 8:22–31. John's third affirmation in the first verse of his Gospel, however, is startling indeed: "The Word *was* God" (1:1c). Not only does John here unequivocally affirm the Word's deity, he does so on par with the Creator: both Yahweh and the Word—Jesus (cf. 1:14, 17–18)—are called *theos*, "God" (see also 20:28, on which see the discussion below).

Later in his introduction, John continues to develop his theology of "the Word" by asserting that, in Jesus, "the Word became flesh and dwelt among us, and we have seen his glory . . . full of grace and truth" (1:14). And while "no one has ever seen God [Yahweh]; the only God [Jesus] . . . has made him known" (1:18).[35] Thus Jesus is presented both as the *preexistent* Word (at creation) and as the *incarnate* Word (at the particular juncture in salvation history at which John [the Baptist] bore witness to Jesus as the one who "was before" him and hence ranked above him [1:15; cf. 1:30]). John therefore presents Jesus as distinct from Yahweh (whom no one has ever seen) and yet at the same time as God—the *incarnate* God—who revealed God *to* humans *in human form*: "Veiled in flesh, the Godhead see; hail, th'incarnate deity." As such, Jesus is also endowed with *glory*, a divine attribute—glory "as of the only Son from the Father" (1:14).[36]

It should probably come as no surprise that the presentation of Jesus as God in John's Gospel has met with significant challenges by those who view Jesus' identity differently, from the patristic era (Arius) to the present (Jehovah's Witnesses). Such detractors maintain that John identifies Jesus merely as *a* god rather than as God, in large part because there is no definite article in front of *theos* in the Greek original of John 1:1. But John, as a monotheistic Jew, would certainly not have referred to another person as "a god." Also, in the context of 1:1, if John had used the definite article before *theos*, this would have so equated God and the Word as to negate the just-established distinction between the two persons in the previous clause ("the Word was *with* God"). What is more, Greek syntax commonly

---

[35]On the textual issues involved in the reading "only God" with reference to Jesus in 1:18, see the additional note in Köstenberger, *John*, 50.

[36]See on this further the discussion of John's "Father-Son" theology below. Mark Stibbe aptly notes that the dynamic in John's introduction significantly revolves around the progressive characterization of the Word-God relationship in terms of a Father-Son relationship. See "Telling the Father's Story: The Gospel of John as Narrative Theology," in *Challenging Perspectives on the Gospel of John*, 175.

requires a definite nominative predicate noun preceded by a finite verb to be without the article. For this reason it is illegitimate to infer from the lack of article before *theos* in John 1:1 that *theos* is therefore indefinite ("a god"). The best understanding of John's affirmations in John 1:1, then, is that Jesus "'shared the *essence* of the Father, though they differed in person.' All that can be said about God can also be said about the Word."[37]

In the end, one may disagree with John's presentation of Jesus as God, or argue that John but constitutes the climax of a prolonged process of elevating Jesus to the status of deity toward the end of the first century. What seems beyond dispute, however, is that in his introduction, John presents Jesus unequivocally and unapologetically as God. "In the beginning was the Word, and the Word was with God, and the Word was God. . . . And the Word became flesh and dwelt among us, and we have seen his glory. . . . No one has ever seen God; the only God, who is at the Father's side, he has made him known" (1:1, 14, 18). With this, the stage is set for John's narrative of Jesus' earthly ministry, culminating in the events surrounding Jesus' crucifixion and resurrection, in the rest of the Gospel.

Father and Son, and the "One and Only Son"
As mentioned, as John's introduction progresses, the Word-God relationship, grounded in the Genesis creation narrative, is gradually transformed into an even more intimate relationship, namely that of Father and Son, what is more, of Father and a "One and Only Son" (Greek *monogenēs*; 1:14, 18; 3:16, 18; cf. 1 John 4:9). This characterization is significant for several reasons. First, it preserves an *appropriate distinction* between the two persons both identified as *theos* in the introduction (see especially 1:1, 18): while sharing the attribute of deity (*theos*), their identity does not constitute undiluted sameness. Rather, the Father is the one who sent the Son, while the Son embarked on his redemptive mission, leading to the cross and his death for the sins of the world.

It is not the Father who died on the cross, but the Son; and it is not the Son who sent the Father, but the Father who sent the Son. And while Jesus could rightfully say, "I and the Father are one" (10:30), he could elsewhere say with equal legitimacy, "The Father is greater than I" (14:28). While the literalistically minded may see here a contradiction, or elevate one truth above the other in order to subsume the "lesser" to the "greater" claim, John equally affirms both, with no apparent sense of tension or

---

[37]Köstenberger and Swain, *Father, Son and Spirit*, 49–50, citing Wallace, *Greek Grammar Beyond the Basics*, 269.

contradiction.[38] The Son, while equally God, nonetheless is called to submit to the Father and to carry out the Father's mission rather than his own, independently conceived.[39] This provides texture and structure to the Father-Son relationship with regard to their respective identities and commensurate authority.[40]

Second, John's introduction presents the relationship between the first and second persons of the Godhead in the *most intimate human terms*, as that of a father and his son, in fact, his one and only son.[41] In the Old Testament, the term *monogenēs* could mean "only child" (Judg. 11:34; cf. *Tob.* 3:15; 8:17). Being an only child, and thus irreplaceable, renders a child of special value to his parents (see, e.g., Luke 7:12; 8:42; 9:39). Thus the Septuagint frequently uses "beloved" (Greek *agapētos*) in the place of *monogenēs* (e.g., Gen. 22:2, 12, 16; Amos 8:10; Jer. 6:26; Zech. 12:10; cf. Prov. 4:3; and Judg. 11:34 [A], where both words are used). The connection between John's reference to Jesus as the Father's *monogenēs* and Old Testament antecedents is particularly pronounced in the seminal event of Abraham's offering his "one and only son," Isaac (cf. Gen. 22:2, 12, 16; cf. John 3:16). While Abraham had earlier fathered Ishmael—so that Isaac was not literally Abraham's *only* son—Isaac was Abraham's son in a *unique way*: he alone was the son God had promised to give Abraham through whom all the nations would be blessed (Gen. 12:1–3; see also Heb. 11:17–19). Later in Old Testament and Second Temple literature, both Israel and the Son of David are called God's "firstborn" or even "only" son (e.g., Ps. 89:27; 2 Esd [*4 Ezra*] 6:58; *Pss. Sol.* 18:4; *Jub.* 18:2, 11, 15). Thus John's portrayal of Jesus as God's "one and only son," unique in the Gospels (though see the comparable epithet "beloved son" in the Synoptics; see especially Mark 1:11; 9:7; 12:6; cf. Luke 20:13), builds on a rich theological trajectory, which, among other antecedents, includes the Abraham-Isaac relationship and the Son of David.[42]

---

[38]Contra Royce C. Gruenler, *The Trinity in the Gospel of John: A Thematic Commentary on the Fourth Gospel* (Grand Rapids, MI: Baker, 1986). See also Kevin Giles, *The Trinity and Subordinationism* (Downers Grove, IL: InterVarsity, 2002); Kevin Giles, *Jesus and the Father: Modern Evangelicals Reinvent the Doctrine of the Trinity* (Downers Grove, IL: InterVarsity, 2006).

[39]See Christopher Cowan, "The Father and Son in the Fourth Gospel: Johannine Subordination Revisited," *JETS* 49 (2006): 115–35.

[40]For an exploration of these and other Trinitarian issues, see Köstenberger and Swain, *Father, Son and Spirit.*

[41]For a discussion of the reference to Jesus as the "one and only Son" in John's Gospel as well as additional bibliographic references, see Köstenberger, *John*, 42–44.

[42]For discussions, and refutations, of the rendering "only begotten" for *monogenēs* in John's Gospel, see Craig Keener, *John* (Peabody, MA: Hendrickson, 2003), 412–14; and G. Pendrick, "*Monogenēs*," *NTS* 41 (1995): 587–600.

What is more, on a human level, depicting Jesus' relationship with Yahweh in terms of a father-son relationship—in fact, as that of father and his one and only son—gives telling expression to the greatest possible intimacy between these two persons of the Godhead, who are equal in essence yet distinct in role, which, in turn, is presented as the basis on which Jesus made God known (John 1:18). As John puts it, Jesus "is at the Father's side," that is, enjoys closest possible intimacy of relationship with Yahweh (1:18; cf. Luke 16:22). In addition, the closeness of the Father-Son relationship also provides the basis for the Son's redemptive mission in keeping with the Jewish messenger or agency model (*shaliach*; e.g., *m. Ber.* 5:5). This is why many have described John's christology as a "sending christology," because "the one who sent me" is Jesus' preferred way of referring to the Father in John's Gospel (see, e.g., John 5:23 in the context of 5:16–47).[43]

Son of God

John's very purpose is bound up with the demonstration that Jesus is "the Christ, the Son of God" (20:31). Rather than a hard and fast distinction existing between the two, "Christ" and "Son of God," it is more likely that both are roughly equivalent and that "Son of God" represents a messianic title with rich Old Testament overtones (see especially Ps. 2:7; 110:1, on which see the discussion above).[44] Jesus is referred to as the "Son of God" eight times in the Gospel: by Nathanael (John 1:49); by the evangelist (3:18; 20:31), whose second reference is anticipated by Martha (11:27); by Jesus as self-references (5:25; 10:36; 11:40); and, negatively, by the Jewish leaders (19:7).[45] As Figure 1 illustrates, the evangelist carefully groups these references to Jesus as the Son of God and develops this theme intentionally as his narrative progresses.

---

[43]On the "mission" theme in John's Gospel, see Andreas J. Köstenberger, *The Mission of Jesus and the Disciples according to the Fourth Gospel* (Grand Rapids, MI: Eerdmans, 1998); Andreas J. Köstenberger, *Theology of John's Gospel and Letters*, chap. 15; and Köstenberger and Swain, *Father, Son and Spirit*, chap. 9.

[44]The following discussion centers on references to Jesus as "Son of God" in John's Gospel. In addition, see references to Jesus as "Christ" or "Messiah" in 1:41; 4:25, 29; 7:26, 27, 31, 41, 42; 9:22; 10:24; 11:27; 12:34; and 20:31, on which see the treatment in Köstenberger, *Theology of John's Gospel*, 311–22.

[45]In addition, John the Baptist may have referred to Jesus as the "Son of God" at 1:34, though perhaps "Chosen One of God" may have a claim to being the more likely original reading there (see the discussion in Köstenberger, *John*, 71, 88). In the Synoptics, the closest Jesus comes to claiming to be the Son of God is when answering the high priest at his Jewish trial (Matt. 26:63 par. Luke 22:70). Elsewhere, it is mostly Satan or his demons (e.g., Matt. 4:3, 6 par. Luke 4:3, 9; Mark 3:11; Luke 4:41; Matt. 8:20 par. Mark 5:7 and Luke 8:28) or those who mock Jesus' messianic claims (Matt. 27:40, 43) who refer to Jesus as the Son of God, while most others fail to recognize Jesus as Messiah (the "misunderstanding theme"). See, however, the notable exceptions of the Twelve (Matt. 14:33), Peter (Matt. 16:16), and the centurion (Matt. 27:54 par. Mark 15:37).

Fig. 1: References to Jesus as "Son of God" in John's Gospel

Character	Section in John's Gospel	Reference	Description
Nathanael	Opening (1:19–50)	1:49	Introduction
Evangelist	Cana Cycle (2–4)	3:18	Anticipates 20:31
Jesus	Festival Cycle (5–10)	5:25	*Inclusio* with 10:36
Jesus	Festival Cycle (5–10)	10:36	*Inclusio* with 5:25
Jesus	Transition (11–12)	11:4	See 11:27
Martha	Transition (11–12)	11:27	Anticipates 20:31
The Jews	Passion Narrative (18–20)	19:7	Culminating charge
Evangelist	Conclusion (20:30–31)	20:31	Purpose statement

The first reference to Jesus as Son of God in John's narrative by Nathanael (1:49) sounds the opening salvo, as it were, as part of an entire series of significant christological references in the opening section of the Gospel. The evangelist's reference to Jesus as Son of God in 3:18, part of an extended commentary spanning 3:16–21, finds its complement in the final purpose statement of the Gospel. At the center of John's portrayal of Jesus as the Son of God are three self-references by Jesus, the first two of which bracket the Festival Cycle in the form of an *inclusio* (5:25 and 10:36). This section is marked by Jesus' escalated controversy with the Jewish leaders and sets the stage for the culminating charge of blasphemy (see 19:7). Jesus' third reference to himself as Son of God follows in 11:4 and is shortly echoed by Martha, whose confession anticipates, almost *verbatim*, John's purpose statement (11:27; cf. 20:31).

While a detailed discussion of the references to Jesus as Son of God in John's Gospel is beyond the scope of this essay,[46] a few implications should be noted. First, John provides an important rationale for why his original disciples chose to follow him: they believed that he was the Messiah and Son of God. Second, John makes clear that Jesus repeatedly claimed to be the Son of God, supplying a plausible rationale for why Jesus was crucified: on account of blasphemy (see especially 10:31–33). It was not because Jesus was a good teacher, or a moral man, or a rabbinic rival, or for some other more innocuous reason that the Jews were adamant that Jesus must be executed. It was because he blatantly, in word and deed, by verbal proclamation and confession, and by active, prophetic, and miraculous demonstration claimed to be God.

Third, the narrative climax of references to Jesus as the Son of God is found in 11:27, where Martha's confession in word culminates John's dem-

---

[46]See, however, Köstenberger and Swain, *Father, Son and Spirit*, 79–84.

onstration that Jesus is the Son of God, just as Jesus' raising of Lazarus in deed crowns the series of "signs" he performs in this Gospel. While in Mark's Gospel it is a Roman centurion who confesses Jesus as Son of God at the end of the Gospel (Mark 15:37), in John it is a woman who acknowledges Jesus in a similar fashion. This is part of the larger witness theme in John, which encompasses women as well as men.[47] Later, in a poignant recognition scene, Mary Magdalene is the first to see the risen Christ (John 20:11–18). Fourth, the purpose of John's entire Gospel centers on the demonstration that Jesus is the Messiah and Son of God (20:30–31; cf. 20:28).

Son of Man

The references to Jesus as the "Son of Man" in John's Gospel span from the opening section (1:51) to the beginning of the Farewell Discourse (13:31). The first reference in 1:51 invokes Daniel's reference to the mysterious figure of one "like a son of man" in Daniel 7:13, in combination with an allusion to Jacob's vision of a ladder "set up on the earth, and the top of it reached to heaven. And behold, the angels of God . . . ascending and descending" (Gen. 28:12). Just as God's sign to Jacob promised God's later revelation and reaffirmation of faithfulness to his covenant, Jesus in John 1:51 promises his followers greater revelation of God in and through his ministry. At this climax of salvation history, Jesus will be the place of much greater divine revelation than that given previously to Abraham, Jacob, Moses, or Isaiah (cf. Heb. 1:1–3).

Most notable is a cluster of references to Jesus as the Son of Man involving the use of the term "to be lifted up" (Greek *hypsoō*) as the narrative progresses (the "lifted up" sayings: John 3:13–14; 8:28; and 12:32; cf. 12:34). By portraying Jesus, in vintage Johannine double entendre, as the "lifted up" Son of Man, John draws on Isaiah's theology, who likewise presented the Messiah as the "lifted up" Servant of Yahweh (Isa. 52:13), who would be both literally raised (as John makes clear, at the crucifixion, John 12:32–34) and figuratively exalted (the resurrection and ascension; cf. 20:17). This is one of many places where John is indebted to Isaiah (see, e.g., 12:38–41).[48] Another notable feature of many of the Johannine "Son of Man" references

---

[47]See Robert G. Maccini, *Her Testimony Is True: Women as Witnesses according to John*, JSNTSup 125 (Sheffield: Sheffield Academic Press, 1996).

[48]See, e.g., Craig A. Evans, "Obduracy and the Lord's Servant: Some Observations on the Use of the Old Testament in the Fourth Gospel," in *Early Jewish and Christian Exegesis: Studies in Memory of William Hugh Brownlee*, ed. Craig A. Evans and William F. Stinespring, Homage Series 10 (Atlanta: Scholars Press, 1987), 221–36; James Hamilton, "The Influence of Isaiah on the Gospel of John," *Perichoresis* 5/2 (2007): 139–62.

Fig. 2: References to Jesus as the "Son of Man" in John's Gospel

Character	Section in John's Gospel	Reference	Description
Jesus	End of opening	1:51	Revelation (see Dan. 7:13)
Jesus	Cana Cycle (2–4)	3:13, 14	First "lifted up" saying
Jesus	Festival Cycle (5–10)	5:27	Authority in judgment
Jesus	Festival Cycle (5–10)	6:27, 53, 62	Bread of Life/descent-ascent
Jesus	Festival Cycle (5–10)	8:28	Second "lifted up" saying
Jesus	Festival Cycle (5–10)	9:35	Self-reference
Jesus	Transition (11–12)	12:23	Glorification/cross
Crowd/Jesus	Transition (11–12)	12:34	Third "lifted up" saying
Jesus	Farewell Discourse (13–17)	13:31	Glorification/cross

is the linkage with the descent-ascent theme in the Gospel (see, e.g., John 3:13–14; 6:62).[49]

Again, it will be helpful to draw some implications from John's depiction of Jesus as the Son of Man.[50] First, the coming of the Son of Man is linked with the notion of divine revelation (1:51; cf. Dan. 7:13; see also John 1:18). Second, in eschatological terms, the Son of Man has been given authority in judgment (5:27). Third, for Jesus, "Son of Man" may simply serve as a term of self-reference (9:35). Fourth, and most significantly, "Son of Man" language clusters around the notion of Jesus' crucifixion (his "lifting up," 3:13–14; 8:28; 12:34; see also 6:27, 53, 62), which, according to John, at the same time constitutes his "glorification" (see especially 12:23; 13:31). In this way, John, in his distinctive theology of the cross, transforms the notion of the cross as a place of shame, humiliation, and suffering into a place of glory and exaltation. The crucifixion culminates the life-giving mission of the obedient Son (19:30; cf. 17:1–5) and serves as the locus of the revelation of God's love for humanity (3:16).

The "I Am"

John features seven "I am" sayings, in which Jesus is presented as the bread of life (6:35, 48, 51); the light of the world (8:12; 9:5); the gate for the sheep (10:7, 9); the good shepherd (10:11, 14); the resurrection and the life (11:25); the way, the truth, and the life (14:6); and the true vine (15:1). He, even

---

[49]Godfrey Carruthers Nicholson, *Death as Departure: The Johannine Descent-Ascent Schema*, SBLDS 63 (Chico, CA: Scholars Press, 1983); and Delbert Burkett, *The Son of Man in the Gospel of John*, JSNTSup 56 (Sheffield: Sheffield Academic Press, 1991); see also Köstenberger, *Missions of Jesus and the Disciples*, 121–30; and Köstenberger, *Theology of John's Gospel and Letters*, chap. 14, esp. 529–31.

[50]It should be noted that this depiction is entirely in keeping with the similar presentation found in the Synoptics.

more strikingly, features several important instances where the phrase "I am" is not accompanied by a descriptive phrase of who Jesus is (absolute "I am" statements). Clearly, these statements are of crucial importance in the present context, since "I am" is the Old Testament name of God (cf. Ex. 3:14–15; see also repeated references to God as "I am" in Isa. 40–66, e.g., 41:4; 43:10–13, 25; 45:18; 51:12; 52:6).

While the phrase may at places constitute a simple self-reference ("It is I," or, in more mundane terms, "It's me"), there are places where references to Jesus in terms of "I am" in John's Gospel almost certainly convey the notion of deity. One such place is Jesus' statement to the Jews in 8:58, "I say to you, before Abraham was, I am." The Jews' reaction—they pick up stones to kill Jesus—makes clear that they took Jesus' pronouncement as involving a claim to deity. Another likely instance is 18:5–6, where Jesus identifies himself to those who would arrest him as "I am he," at which the soldiers drew back and fell to the ground. In this case, *egō eimi* may constitute a self-reference on a literal level and at the same time involve a claim to deity on a secondary, deeper level, as is suggested by the soldiers' response, which is a customary reaction to divine revelation or theophany.[51]

Fig. 3: Absolute "I Am" Sayings in John's Gospel

"I Am" Statement	Reference in John	Description
"I . . . am he."	4:26	Jesus is the Messiah
"It is I."	6:20	Walking on water; implies deity
"Unless you believe that I am he you will die in your sins."	8:24	Likely divine self-reference
"Then you will know that I am he."	8:28	Likely divine self-reference
"Before Abraham was, I am."	8:58	Jesus existed before Abraham
"When it does take place you may believe that I am he."	13:19	Likely divine self-reference
"I am he."	18:5–6	Soldiers' reaction suggests deity

In addition, references where it is highly probable that the use of "I am" involves Jesus' claim to deity include 6:20—Jesus' self-identification to his disciples as "I am" at the occasion of his walking on the water—as well as 8:24, 28 ("For unless you believe that I am he you will die in your sins"; "Then you will know that I am he") and 13:19 ("I am telling you this now, before it takes place, that when it does take place you may believe that I am he"). Other possible instances are 4:26 ("I who speak to you am he" [i.e., the Messiah]) and 8:18 ("I am one who testifies for myself; my other witness

---

[51]See, e.g., Ezek. 1:28; 44:4; Dan. 2:46; 8:18; 10:9; Acts 9:4; 22:7; 26:14; Rev. 1:17; 19:10; 22:8.

is the Father who sent me" NIV).[52] It seems undeniable that John presents Jesus as being taken into the identity of Yahweh, whose Old Testament name, as mentioned, is "I am" in indication of his eternality and by virtue of his being life itself (cf. 5:25–26).

Lord and God

Throughout the Gospel, Jesus is acknowledged as "Lord" (Greek *kurios*) by his disciples and others.[53] At a minimum, this implies respect for Jesus as for a revered rabbi.[54] In light of the fact that *kurios* is regularly applied to Yahweh in the Old Testament, it probably also associates Jesus with the God of Israel and does so certainly in the case of 20:28, where the titles *kurios* and *theos* are juxtaposed.[55] This is perhaps most apparent at 9:38, where the formerly blind man worships Jesus as "Lord" (*kurios*). This scene of worship, in turn, anticipates the even more striking instance when Thomas worships Jesus as "Lord and God" following the resurrection (20:28).

As Murray Harris notes, the reference to Jesus as God in 20:28 forms an *inclusio* with the opening references to Jesus as the Word-made-flesh that was with God in the beginning (1:1, 14, 18).[56] While this is doubtless the case, the correspondence is anything but static. Between the opening and closing references to Jesus as God lie Jesus' earthly ministry, his messianic signs, his gathering of the new messianic community, his "lifting up" at the cross, and his resurrection, resulting in one of Jesus' followers worshiping him in terms unequivocally denoting deity. Placed in John's Gospel immediately preceding the final purpose statement, Thomas's confession of Jesus as Lord and God constitutes the narrative peak of the entire Gospel.[57]

The passage is also remarkable in that Thomas's confession provides a point of reference for John's readers in their own worship of Jesus.[58] While Thomas saw and believed, John's readers will be blessed if they, though not seeing, yet believe on account of John's testimony (20:29; cf. 1 Pet. 1:8). This is even better than faith based on Jesus' messianic signs—faith that

---

[52]For treatments of the "I am" references in John's Gospel, see Harner, *The "I Am" of the Fourth Gospel*; Ball, *"I Am" in John's Gospel*; and Williams, *I Am He*. See also the brief survey in Andreas J. Köstenberger, *Encountering John: The Gospel in Historical, Literary, and Theological Perspective*, Encountering Biblical Studies (Grand Rapids, MI: Baker, 1999), 261.

[53]See, e.g., 6:68; 11:3, 12, 21, 27, 32; 13:6, 9, 25, 36; 14:5, 8, 22; 21:16, 17, 20, 21.

[54]See Andreas J. Köstenberger, "Jesus as Rabbi in the Fourth Gospel," *BBR* 8 (1998): 97–128.

[55]See esp. Wright, *The Mission of God*, chap. 4.

[56]Murray J. Harris, *Jesus as God: The New Testament Use of Theos in Reference to Jesus* (Grand Rapids, MI: Baker, 1992), 284–86.

[57]Köstenberger, *John*, 579.

[58]See John's startling direct address to his readers ("so that *you* may believe") at 20:31; see also 19:35.

receives John's Gospel witness and, like Thomas, worships Jesus as Lord and God. It is hard to think of a more climactic exclamation point to John's presentation of Jesus as God in his Gospel, and hard to imagine a more direct and unequivocal presentation of Jesus as the God to be worshiped. In this, the final worship scene, the Gospel's progressive presentation of Jesus as divine culminates—as the preexistent Word-made-flesh, as God's one and only Son, Son of God, Son of Man, and Messiah.[59]

In a way, worship of Jesus as God even transcends the Gospel's purpose of presenting Jesus as Christ and Son of God: not only is Jesus the heaven-sent Messiah, the obedient Son who faithfully carries out his Father's mission all the way to the cross (see, e.g., John 17:4; 19:30)—he is God in the flesh, and as such is to be worshiped. This final worship scene also culminates the depiction of Jesus as the new temple throughout the Gospel, from the opening reference in 1:14 to the references in 1:51; 2:18–20; 4:19–24, up until 11:50–51.[60] While the recognition scene at 20:16 between Jesus and Mary is striking indeed, Thomas's climactic confession and worship of Jesus at 20:28 is even more striking. While initially resistant—which makes his "second chance" worship all the more credible and remarkable—Thomas sweeps aside all further demands for tangible evidence and steps out in faith, a skeptic-turned-believer, a reluctant convert whose presumptuous and irreverent demand for more evidence is met by Jesus' gracious, cruciform self-disclosure. Like Peter in the epilogue (21:15–19; cf. Luke 22:31–32), and like Paul on the road to Damascus (Acts 9:1–19; cf. 1 Tim. 1:12–16), Thomas is shown grace, and he responds in faith.

What is more, the phrase "Lord and God" was a title attributed to the Roman Emperor Domitian (AD 81–96; cf. Suetonius, *Domitian* 13.2), who was very likely on the throne at the time when John's Gospel was written. In light of that fact, Thomas's confession of Jesus as recorded by John implies a marked contrast between the Roman Emperor's claim to deity and Christians' worship of Jesus as God.[61] As governor Pliny wrote to Emperor Trajan only a couple of decades later, Christians were singing "a hymn to Christ as a god" (*Letters* 10.96–97). The reference to Jesus as "Lord and God" in John's Gospel may therefore "on a secondary level be designed to counter Roman emperor worship."[62]

---

[59] See the discussion of these aspects of John's presentation of Jesus' deity above.

[60] See further the discussion under the next heading below.

[61] See Keener, *John*, 1211–12.

[62] Köstenberger, *John*, 580, with reference to Rudolf Schnackenburg, *The Gospel according to St. John*, trans. C. Hastings et al. (New York: Crossroad, 1990), 3:333; Ben Witherington, *John's Wisdom* (Louisville: Westminster, 1995), 349.

The New Temple and Jesus as Sharing in the Glory of God

The portrayal of Jesus as the new temple and as the fulfillment of Passover symbolism has already been discussed above in conjunction with John's probable historical setting, which most likely included the destruction of the second temple in AD 70. For this reason it will not be necessary to revisit the specific passages involving John's presentation of Jesus as the new temple here. Suffice it to say that in Old Testament theology, the temple was supremely known as the place where God revealed his glory.[63] Glory, in turn, was uniquely Yahweh's divine attribute. For John to testify, therefore, that "the Word became flesh and dwelt [*skenoō*, an allusion to the tabernacle, which preceded the temple in Israel's history] among us, *and we have seen his glory, glory as of the only Son from the Father,* full of grace and truth" (John 1:14), from the very outset identifies Jesus as sharing in Yahweh's identity in terms of his preexistent glory (see also 17:1–5, 24).[64]

In essence, the thrust of John's presentation of Jesus as the new temple is the conviction that instead of the old sanctuary, it is now Jesus who has become the proper place of worship for God's people. This marks all previous places of worship, and all previous manifestations of God's presence and glory with his people, as preliminary anticipations of his final and definitive revelation in the Lord Jesus Christ. Just as Jesus, as the new Israel, is the vine and his followers the branches, he is to be the center of all God's activity and of all worship directed to God. It is readily apparent, then, that John presents Jesus as divine, for worship is to be rendered to no one but God alone.[65] Not that Jesus is conceived of as a deity separate and independent from Yahweh. To the contrary, the deity of Jesus and Yahweh are so closely intertwined as to be inseparable.[66]

Nevertheless, John's point is that Jesus stands at the very center of God's salvation-historical program and purposes and that those who fail to honor him as God also fail to honor Yahweh, Israel's God (the thrust of John's "sending christology"; see, e.g., 5:18–48). Denying this is to accuse Jesus of blasphemy and is tantamount to resisting divinely inspired prophecy

---

[63]See, e.g., Ex. 40:34–35; 1 Kings 8:10–11; 2 Chron. 5:13–14; 7:1–2; Ezek. 10:4; 43:5; 44:4; Hag. 2:7. See Andreas J. Köstenberger, "What Does It Mean to Be Filled with the Spirit? A Biblical Investigation," *JETS* 40 (1997): 229–40, esp. 230. On the "glory" motif in John's writings, see Köstenberger, "The Glory of God in John's Gospel and Revelation," in Morgan and Peterson, *The Glory of God.*
[64]For the implications of this fact for the church's mission, see Wright, *Mission of God,* chap. 4. See also the discussion of John's portrayal of Jesus as the new temple in the context of Jesus' fulfillment of festal symbolism in Köstenberger, *Theology of John's Gospel and Letters,* 403–35.
[65]See esp. Isaiah 40–66, and the discussion of Jesus as "I am" above.
[66]See, e.g., John 5:17: "My Father is working until now, and I am working" and 10:30: "I and the Father are one."

regarding Jesus (see 12:37–41 with reference to Isa. 53:1 and 6:10; cf. John 5:18; 8:59; 10:31–33). Clearly, John stakes his entire purpose for writing on the demonstration that Jesus' deity is the central question on which all must render a verdict. It is impossible not to recall C. S. Lewis's inimitable and highly poignant argument at this point:

> I am trying here to prevent anyone saying the really foolish thing that people often say about Him: I'm ready to accept Jesus as a great moral teacher, but I don't accept his claim to be God. That is the one thing we must not say. A man who was merely a man and said the sort of things Jesus said would not be a great moral teacher. He would either be a lunatic—on the level with the man who says he is a poached egg—or else he would be the Devil of Hell. You must make your choice. Either this man was, and is, the Son of God, or else a madman or something worse. You can shut him up for a fool, you can spit at him and kill him as a demon or you can fall at his feet and call him Lord and God, but let us not come with any patronising nonsense about his being a great human teacher. He has not left that open to us. He did not intend to. . . . Now it seems to me obvious that He was neither a lunatic nor a fiend: and consequently, however strange or terrifying or unlikely it may seem, I have to accept the view that He was and is God.[67]

Not only are Lewis's words memorable and highly dramatic, but also they are in keeping with John's message regarding Jesus. The Pharisees had Jesus crucified because they thought he was blaspheming God, making himself equal to Yahweh, while in fact he was a mere man. Jesus and his followers, however, claimed that Jesus was God and thus must be worshiped as God and be obeyed as Lord. Until the Lord returns, these continue to remain the two stark alternatives with which every person is presented and on the basis of which every person will be judged at the final judgment.[68]

The Resurrection

In John's Gospel, the resurrection of Jesus is part of the larger theme of a new creation.[69] At the outset, Jesus is presented as the agent of God's original creation (1:1–3). As John notes, however, tragically, the world God had made through the Word fails to recognize the Word-made-flesh in Jesus (1:10), including even God's people Israel (1:11). Because of human sin, Jesus must die for his people (11:51–52), as the Lamb of God who takes away the sin of the world (1:29, 36), as the bread from heaven who gives

---

[67]C. S. Lewis, *Mere Christianity* (London: Collins, 1952), 54–56.
[68]See "The Deity of Christ in John's Letters and the Book of Revelation" in this volume.
[69]See Köstenberger, *Theology of John's Gospel and Letters*, chap. 8.

his life for the world (6:31–59), and as the good shepherd who gives his life for his sheep (10:15, 17–18). As God's agent in creation, Jesus is depicted in terms of both "life" and "light" (see especially 1:4–5, 7–9; 3:19–21; 8:12; 9:4–5; 12:35–36, 46).[70] These themes converge and culminate in John's pervasive stream of references to eternal life found in Jesus, and found in him alone (see especially 14:6; 17:2–3; 20:31). This life, in turn, comes to people by believing in the substitutionary, vicarious death of the Son of God who was "lifted up" (i.e., crucified) on behalf of God's people to render atonement for sin.[71]

In keeping with John's creation and new-creation theology, he presents the first week of Jesus' ministry as patterned after the seven days of the original creation (see 1:19–2:11, including the reference to Jesus' attendance of the wedding at Cana "on the third day" [2:1], which strikes possible overtones anticipating Jesus' resurrection; see 2:19).[72] Possible new-creation language is also found in Jesus' reference to a "new birth" in his conversation with Nicodemus (3:3, 5), and later in the Sabbath controversy (see especially 5:17–18). The former passage invokes the prophetic expectation of an end-time renewal and decisive inner transformation in the last days (see, e.g., Isa. 44:3–5; Jer. 31:33–34; Ezek. 11:19–20; 36:25–27; 37), while the latter passage makes the point that, while resting on the seventh day of creation (Gen. 2:2–3), God continued to be at work as he chose to act in his sovereignty and providence. What is more, according to Jesus, not only was God at work, but "I am working" (John 5:17). The fact that Yahweh was at work in the ministry of Jesus the Messiah was vividly demonstrated by his healing of the lame and the blind men in keeping with messianic expectations (5:1–15; 9:1–41). Importantly, aligning Jesus with the Creator presents his ministry from the very outset against a universal backdrop. Just as creation extended to the entire universe, so also the life given by Jesus is universal in scope, extending not only to the Jews but also to Gentiles (10:16; 11:51–52;

---

[70]See ibid., 166–67 and 338–49.

[71]On John's theology of the cross, see chap. 14 in Köstenberger, *Theology of John's Gospel and Letters* (with further bibliographic references). See also Martinus C. de Boer, *Johannine Perspectives on the Death of Jesus*, CBET 17 (Kampen: Kok, 1996); John A. Dennis, *Jesus' Death and the Gathering of True Israel: The Johannine Appropriation of Restoration Theology in the Light of John 11:47–52*, WUNT 2:217 (Tübingen: Mohr-Siebeck, 2006); Wilhelm Thüsing, *Die Erhöhung und Verherrlichung Jesu im Johannesevangelium*, NTAbh 21 (Münster: W. Aschendorff, 1970); and the articles by Leon Morris, "The Atonement in John's Gospel," *CTR* 3 (1988): 49–64; and Max Turner, "Atonement and the Death of Jesus in John: Some Questions to Bultmann and Forestell," *EvQ* 62 (1990): 99–122.

[72]See ibid., 349, with additional bibliographic references.

12:32). Thus while Jesus was a Jew (4:9; cf. 4:22), his messianic ministry transcended ethnic categories.

In the Johannine passion narrative, finally, the Gospel's new-creation theology thickens. Possible instances of the new-creation motif include the following:[73]

- the setting of the passion narrative in a garden, invoking the memory of Eden (18:1, 26; 19:41);
- Pilate's identification of Jesus as "the man" (19:5), which may present Jesus as the new Adam;
- the possible portrayal of Jesus' resurrection as the beginning of a new creation (20:1; cf. 1:3);
- the (albeit mistaken) identification of Jesus as "the gardener" by Mary (20:15), reflecting misunderstanding and possibly also irony;
- Jesus' bodily resurrection and resurrection appearances to his followers in keeping with repeated earlier predictions in the narrative (chap. 20; cf. 2:20–21; 10:17–19);
- Jesus' breathing on his disciples and his giving of the Spirit in the final commissioning scene (20:22), invoking the creation of Adam in Genesis 2:7 (cf. Ezek. 37:9).

In this, the resurrection of the Word-made-flesh climaxes the new-creation theology of John's entire narrative, showing how the lifted-up Son of Man and suffering servant, as creator and sender, "breathes life into his new messianic community and commissions his followers to proclaim the message of forgiveness and eternal life through believing in Jesus (John 20:22)."[74] As I have written elsewhere, therefore, "the Johannine narrative builds inexorably from creation to new creation, spanning the entire range from preexistent, glorious Word to the enfleshed Word's return to its preexistent glory subsequent to its death, burial, and resurrection. Thus the Isaianic pattern of the divine Word's mission has been fulfilled in Jesus, the Messiah and Son of God (Isa. 55:11)."[75] This mission, in turn, is to be continued in the mission of Jesus' followers, so that John's christology seamlessly issues in the Gospel's Trinitarian mission theology.[76]

---

[73]The following list is adapted from Köstenberger, *Theology of John's Gospel and Letters*, 352.

[74]Ibid., 353.

[75]Ibid.

[76]See Köstenberger, *Mission of Jesus and the Disciples*; Köstenberger and Swain, *Father, Son and Spirit*, chap. 9.

Other Elements of John's Theology Involving References to Jesus' Deity

Jesus' Preexistence

Reference has already been made to John's presentation of Jesus as the preexistent Word. In addition, Jesus is also frequently shown to claim preexistence, or others are shown to assert his preexistence (see, e.g., John 1:15, 30; 8:58; 17:5, 24). In addition, Jesus' preexistence is implied in the many references to his "having come" in John's Gospel (e.g., 5:43; 6:14; 7:28; 9:39; 10:10; 11:27; 12:46; 15:22; 18:37), in references to Jesus' "being from God" (e.g., 6:46; 7:29; 9:33; 16:27–28; 17:8) or to his "having been sent" (e.g., 3:17; 4:34; 5:23–24, 30, 36–38). John also implies Jesus' preexistence in certain (already discussed) "I am" sayings (e.g., 8:58) and in the claim that Isaiah saw Jesus' glory (12:41).[77]

Jesus' Foreknowledge

What is more, John's Gospel frequently shows Jesus to possess supernatural knowledge. Jesus saw Nathanael under the fig tree (1:48); he predicted, at the beginning of his ministry, his own demise and resurrection on the third day (2:19; cf. 12:24); and he entrusted himself to no one, cognizant of what was in people's hearts (2:24–25). Jesus also knew the identity of his betrayer long before the actual treacherous act took place (6:64, 71; 12:4; 13:11). Jesus knew, apparently without having been told (11:14), that Lazarus had died. He also evinced foreknowledge of Peter's denials and the manner of that apostle's eventual death (13:38; 21:18–19). Especially in the events immediately preceding and surrounding his crucifixion, Jesus is shown to be completely in command, aided by foreknowledge of what was about to happen (13:1, 3; 18:4; 19:28).[78]

Conclusion

While space does not permit me to develop in full detail all these facets of John's presentation of Jesus as divine, these additional aspects of John's portrayal of the deity of Christ round out an already very full picture. John's Gospel shows Jesus as brilliantly and gloriously divine. Nevertheless, Jesus' deity in no way rivals the deity of Yahweh. To the contrary, Jesus is shown as the humble sent one from the Father who went about his redemptive and revelatory mission as the obedient Son. This son was faithful to the end and, in turn, imparted his Spirit to his followers to equip and empower

---

[77]On Jesus' preexistence, see Robert G. Hamerton-Kelly, *Pre-Existence, Wisdom and the Son of Man*, SNTSMS 21 (Cambridge: Cambridge University Press, 1973). On Jesus as "having come," cf. Gathercole, *Pre-existent Son*.

[78]See the list in Köstenberger, *Theology of John's Gospel and Letters*, 137.

them for their mission (20:22). With this, our investigation of the divinity of Jesus in John's Gospel has come to a close.

In this chapter, we have explored John's exceedingly rich and multifaceted portrayal of the deity of Christ. First, we explored the historical setting of John's Gospel, in the conviction that John's teaching on the divinity of Jesus can be fully appreciated only when understood in the context of Jewish first-century monotheism and the circumstances surrounding the composition of John's Gospel. After this, we looked, in turn, at John's presentation of Jesus as the Word; as the Father's one and only Son; as the Son of God and Son of Man; as the "I am"; as Lord and God; as the new temple and as sharing in the glory of Yahweh; and as the risen Lord whose resurrection comes at the climax of John's creation and new-creation theology. Brief discussions of Jesus' preexistence and supernatural foreknowledge rounded out the discussion.

The above examination has established conclusively that John's Gospel presents Jesus as God and that he is to be worshiped as such. There can be no doubt that the deity of Christ is central to the purpose of John's Gospel. The centrality of Jesus' deity in this Gospel, in turn, is borne out of the conviction that there is no more important issue in the history of humanity than the question of whether Jesus was who he claimed to be—the Christ, the Son of God, God-in-the-flesh. If we, as readers of John's Gospel, want to fulfill John's intended purpose for writing his narrative, we must, with Thomas, exclaim, without reservation and with a radical commitment to obey: "My Lord and my God!" In this way, we will inherit Jesus' parting benediction, "Have you believed because you have seen me? Blessed are those who have not seen and yet have believed" (20:28–29).

5

The Deity of Christ in the Apostolic Witness

STEPHEN J. WELLUM

The Gospels present Jesus as God the Son incarnate, and they do so precisely because this is Jesus' self-identity. If we take the Gospels seriously, we will see that they present a Jesus who is fully aware that he is the Son in relation to his Father, and that this relationship is ultimately rooted in eternity past.[1] Years ago, John Murray noted this fact: "We do not find our Lord speaking or acting in terms of merely human personality. In the various situations reported to us in the Gospel record, it is a striking fact that he identifies himself as one who sustains to the Father his unique relationship as the only-begotten Son, as the one whose self-identity, whose self, is conceived of in such terms."[2] This is not to say that Jesus does not speak and act as a human; rather, it is to say that he first thinks of himself in filial relationship to his Father and of his divine self-identity. In this way, Scripture affirms both the full deity and humanity of Jesus the Christ.

---

[1] For proof of this assertion see the previous chapters on the Gospels' testimony to the deity of Christ.
[2] John Murray, *Collected Writings of John Murray*, 4 vols. (Carlisle, PA: Banner of Truth, 1977), 2:138.

Building on this conclusion, we will now turn to the biblical evidence for the deity of Christ in the apostolic writings. Given the limitations of space and the immensity of the subject, we will do so in two steps. First, we will outline the basic pattern of New Testament christology and illustrate it by discussing four crucial texts. In doing so, we will reinforce the conviction that the New Testament presents us with a unified view of Jesus' identity.[3] As Stephen Clark reminds us, "While the New Testament displays rich diversity in its portrayal of Jesus, underlying this diversity and expressed through it is a uniform conviction that Jesus Christ is God and man."[4] Second, we will outline a potpourri of data that substantiates the claim that Jesus is God the Son incarnate.

Jesus the Christ as God the Son Incarnate: The Basic Pattern of New Testament Christology

As noted in previous chapters, Richard Bauckham has proposed that the category of divine identity better explains New Testament christology. In contrast, he believes the categories of "ontological" and "functional," which have dominated christological discussion in recent years, to be misleading in a number of ways, "not least because they do not reflect an adequate understanding of the way Jewish monotheism understood God."[5] Many have tried often to pit these older categories against each other. So, it is argued, if Jesus exercises the "functions" of deity, he may do so without being regarded as "ontologically" deity. Or, as Oscar Cullmann states, "When it is asked in the New Testament 'Who is Christ?' the question never means exclusively, or even primarily, 'What is his nature?' but first of all, 'What is his function?'"[6] In this vein, a criticism of the early church in its christological formulation (e.g., Chalcedon) is that it uncritically adopted a Greek philosophical mindset that focused on ontology instead of function and thus distorted the New Testament emphasis on function.

Whether the early church actually did this is highly debatable.[7] However, for our purposes, it is crucial to stress that the New Testament does not

---

[3]Contra J. D. G. Dunn, *Christology in the Making: A New Testament Inquiry into the Origins of the Doctrine of the Incarnation*, 2nd ed. (Grand Rapids, MI: Eerdmans, 1996).

[4]Stephen Clark, "Introduction," in *The Forgotten Christ*, ed. S. Clark (Nottingham, UK: Inter-Varsity, 2007), 9.

[5]Richard Bauckham, *Jesus and the God of Israel* (Grand Rapids, MI: Eerdmans, 2008), 30.

[6]Oscar Cullmann, *The Christology of the New Testament*, trans. Shirley C. Guthrie and Charles A. M. Hall (London: SCM, ET 1959), 3–4. Behind this dichotomy of the "ontological" and "functional" is also another debate. Individuals such as Cullmann contend that such ontological considerations were indebted to Greek philosophy and were foreign to a Jewish or Hebrew way of looking at the world. But this will not do. For an excellent critique of this view see, e.g., James Barr, *The Semantics of Biblical Language* (repr. Eugene, OR: Wipf & Stock, 2004).

[7]For a further discussion of this point see Gerald Bray's chapter in this volume. Also cf. Aloys

dichotomize christology this way. Rather, it presents Christ as participating and sharing in the divine rule, which in light of the biblical storyline entails that what Jesus *does* (functional) is intimately tied to *who he is* (ontological) and vice versa. Bauckham states it this way:

> Jesus' participation in the unique divine sovereignty is, therefore, also not just a matter of what Jesus does, but of *who Jesus is* in relation to God. Though not primarily a matter of divine nature or being, it emphatically *is* a matter of divine identity. It includes Jesus in the identity of the one God. When extended to include Jesus in the creative activity of God, and therefore also in the eternal transcendence of God, it becomes unequivocally a matter of regarding Jesus as *intrinsic to* the unique identity of God.[8]

What is crucial to note, especially in light of the unique monotheism of the Old Testament, is that it is Jesus *as a man* who is regarded as intrinsic to the identity of God, thus leading to the conclusion that he is God the Son incarnate. In fact, the overall pattern of New Testament christology is developed in two complementary and intertwined paths, rooted in the storyline of Scripture. The first path accents the Son's deity by including him in the divine identity in a whole host of ways and thus underscoring his utter uniqueness as the Son in relation to the Father and Spirit. In this way Jesus, by virtue of who he has always been as the eternal Son, is Lord. The second path accents the reality of the incarnation and what Jesus achieves as the God-*man*. Thus, the eternal Son, who has always been Lord, now by virtue of his incarnation and cross work becomes Lord and Christ. In his humanity, the eternal Son fulfills the roles of previous sons (e.g., Adam, Israel, David) by inaugurating God's long-awaited kingdom and the promised new-covenant age—and he is able to do so precisely because of who he is. These paths are complementary and should be kept together as they form the basic pattern of New Testament christology. Let us now delve further into this christological pattern by examining four crucial texts, which clearly teach that Jesus is God the Son incarnate.

Romans 1:3–4

Romans 1:3–4 is an important christological text. Some scholars have argued that it is proof that Paul's christology was adoptionistic, i.e., Jesus was not the eternal Son but rather he *became* the Son at his resurrection. Appeal is made to verse 4, where the participle *horisthentos*, the aorist

---

Grillmeier, *Christ in Christian Tradition*, 2nd ed., vol. 1, trans. John Bowden (Atlanta: John Knox Press, 1975).
[8]Bauckham, *Jesus and the God of Israel*, 31.

passive of the verb *horizō*, means "to appoint," and hence the interpretation: Jesus was *appointed* the Son at his resurrection, which assumes that he was not Son prior to this event. For example, James Dunn argues this view by linking Romans 1:3–4 with Acts 13:32–33 and its use of Psalm 2. By appealing to Psalm 2:7—"I will tell of the decree: The LORD said to me, 'You are my Son; today I have begotten you'"—Dunn argues that the "today" was thought by early Christians to teach that Jesus' divine sonship should be viewed "principally as a role and status he had entered upon, been appointed to, at his resurrection"[9] and as such, it was something he gained and did not previously have.

Conversely, Robert Reymond, resisting any hint of adoptionism, translates the participle as "was marked out" or "was designated"[10] and understands "the Spirit of holiness" in verse 4 as a reference to Christ's divine nature. Reymond then argues that it was not at the resurrection that Jesus took on a new role and entered into a new state—i.e., the state of "exaltation" from his previous state of "humiliation"—rather, the resurrection simply marked out Jesus as the Son "in accordance with what he is on his divine side (that is, 'according to the spirit of holiness')."[11] But are these the only two options? Is there no other option that better accounts for the text and underscores the complementary christological paths outlined above? Let us explore a third option by making three observations about the text.

First, the text teaches the Son's preexistence and deity. Placing the phrase "concerning his Son" (*peri tou huiou autou*) before the first of two participial clauses of verses 3 and 4 underscores the Son's preexistence. No doubt, the reference to Jesus as the "Son" recalls Israel's status as God's son (Ex. 4:4),[12] but given the placement of the words before the two participles of verses 3 and 4, it is best to understand that Paul is affirming that the Son who became the seed of David and who was appointed God's Son in power was

---

[9]Dunn, *Christology in the Making*, 36. Dunn states later: "But *the language of the earliest post-Easter confession of Jesus' sonship and the earliest use of Ps. 2:7 certainly seem to have placed the decisive moment on 'becoming' quite clearly in the resurrection of Jesus*" (46; emphasis original). Also see J. A. T. Robinson, *The Human Face of God* (London: SCM Press, 1973), 161, for this same point.

[10]See Robert L. Reymond, *Jesus, Divine Messiah: The New and Old Testament Witness* (Ross-shire, Scotland: Mentor, 2003), 378–79.

[11]Ibid., 382. Reymond also argues the following two points, which are difficult to sustain. First, "flesh," *sarx*, in v. 3 is a reference to Christ's human nature, which is contrasted in v. 4 with "according to the Spirit of holiness," which he understands as a reference to Jesus' divine nature (see 376–81). Second, he rejects vv. 3–4 as teaching "successive stages" in the life of Christ or inserting a contrast between what Jesus was *before* and what he was *after* his resurrection. Thus, the relation between the two participial phrases of vv. 3–4 is one of climax not contrast, so that at the resurrection Jesus was not appointed as Son; rather, he displayed his sonship or demonstrated it in accordance with his divine nature (see 381–84).

[12]See J. D. G. Dunn, *Romans 1–8*, WBC 38A (Dallas: Word, 1988), 11–12.

already the Son before these events.[13] As noted in previous chapters, the title "Son" works at two levels: it designates Jesus as the eternal Son *and* as the Son who is the antitype of previous "sons"—Adam, Israel, and David. Both these truths are found in this text. Thomas Schreiner states this well: "The one who existed eternally as the Son was appointed the Son of God in power as the Son of David. . . . In other words, the Son reigned with the Father from all eternity, but as a result of his incarnation and atoning work he was appointed to be the Son of God as one who was now both God and man."[14] In this way, the preexistence and deity of the Son are stressed while simultaneously emphasizing his appearance on the stage of human history as the incarnate Messiah.

Second, it is best to render the participle, *horisthentos* (v. 4) as "appointed" or "designated" instead of "declared" or "marked out."[15] The emphasis of the verse is on the "appointment" of the Son as Son by God the Father by virtue of his work. This does *not* entail a merely functional christology, as some allege. After all, as Doug Moo reminds us, "we must remember that the Son is the subject of the entire statement in verses 3–4: It is the *Son* who is 'appointed' Son. The tautologous nature of this statement reveals that being appointed Son has to do *not* with a change of essence—as if a person or human messiah becomes Son of God for the first time—but with a change in status or function."[16] This point is tied to Old Testament typological structures rooted in the enthronement of the Davidic king. As the Davidic Son, the Messiah, God the Son *incarnate* comes as the Lord *and* as the antitype of the sons of the Old Testament, and by his work the messianic age has dawned. His work is a work "in power" that "appoints" him, not in terms of his nature, but in terms of his mediatorial role as the God-*man*. By virtue of his entire cross work, a new order is inaugurated in which the Son attains a new, exalted status as the Son. Jesus, then, is Son and Lord from all eternity *and* now Son in power, as Messiah. In him, the two eschatological strands of the Old Testament come together: it is Yahweh who saves in and through his King (Isa. 9:6–7; Ezekiel 34). This is why, as Moo notes, "the transition from v. 3 to v. 4, then, is not a transition

---

[13]See Thomas R. Schreiner, *New Testament Theology* (Grand Rapids, MI: Baker, 2008), 38–39; Douglas Moo, *The Epistle to the Romans*, NICNT (Grand Rapids, MI: Eerdmans, 1996), 46–47; Gordon D. Fee, *Pauline Christology: An Exegetical-Theological Study* (Peabody, MA: Hendrickson, 2007), 240–44.

[14]Thomas R. Schreiner, *Romans*, BECNT (Grand Rapids, MI: Baker, 1998), 38–39.

[15]In its seven other New Testament occurrences, the verb means "to determine" or "to appoint," and there is no compelling reason to think Paul is using the word in a different way. See Moo, *Romans*, 47–48; Schreiner, *Romans*, 42.

[16]Moo, *Romans*, 48.

from a human messiah to a divine Son of God (adoptionism) but from the Son as Messiah to the Son as both Messiah *and* powerful, reigning Lord."[17]

Third, this understanding of the text is confirmed by the antithetical parallel between "according to the Spirit of holiness" and "according to the flesh." Contrary to some who suggest that the "flesh/spirit" contrast is between Jesus' human and divine natures[18] or others who argue that "Spirit of holiness" is a reference to Christ's obedient, consecrated spirit that he manifested throughout his earthly life,[19] a better suggestion, which does justice to Paul's overall redemptive-historical framework, is to interpret the contrast between "flesh/spirit" as referring to eras/ages in redemptive history. In this understanding, the old era is that which is represented by Adam and dominated by sin, death, and the *flesh*, while the new era is represented by Christ and characterized by salvation, life, and the *Spirit*.[20] As applied to Christ, then, the eternal Son has now come and taken on

---

[17]Ibid., 49. This understanding is further grounded in the fact that there is probably an allusion to Ps. 2:7 in this verse: "You are my Son; today I have begotten you." In the New Testament, Psalm 2 is quoted a number of times and in quite diverse ways (see Acts 4:25–26; 13:33; Heb. 1:5; 5:5; Rev. 2:7; 12:5; 19:15). Reymond, *Jesus, Divine Messiah*, 77–81, for example, consistent with his interpretation of Rom. 1:3–4, argues along with many in the early church that Ps. 2:7, in its Old Testament context, does not apply to the Davidic king but rather it should be understood as a direct reference to Christ. In this way, it is an address of the Father to the Son in eternity past, which for many in the early church was used as one of the textual proofs for the doctrine of the eternal generation of the Son. However, it is not necessary to interpret it this way. In fact, in its immediate context, it is difficult *not* to read Psalm 2 as a reference to the Davidic king. A better interpretation is to read Psalm 2 typologically. As each Davidic king was enthroned, so this psalm pointed forward to the day when the Messiah, due to his triumphant cross work and resurrection, will have ushered in God's kingdom and all that it entails, and as such, is now exalted and seated at God's right hand and given a name above every name. In this way, as Schreiner notes, the new dimension that results by virtue of Jesus' work "was not his sonship but his heavenly installation as God's Son by virtue of his Davidic sonship" (Schreiner, *Romans*, 39) and thus fulfills all the hopes and expectations of the Old Testament.

[18]For this interpretation see the discussion in Moo, *Romans*, 49.

[19]See Reymond, *Jesus, Divine Messiah*, 378–81, who argues this point.

[20]See Moo, *Romans*, 49–50; Schreiner, *Romans*, 43–45; Herman Ridderbos, *Paul: An Outline of His Theology* (Grand Rapids, MI: Eerdmans, 1975), 64–68. The use of "flesh" in Paul is diverse but predominately is tied to the old age associated with Adam, sin, and death. Even though one has to be careful in pushing this too far in Rom. 1:3–4 since it could entail that Christ's human nature was fallen, even the more neutral uses of *sarx* (e.g., Rom. 3:20; 4:1; 9:3, 5; 11:14; 1 Cor. 1:26, 29) carry a nuance of weakness. The reason for this, as Schreiner, *Romans*, 43, explains, is "that the flesh participates in the old age of sin and death." Thus, as Paul states elsewhere, Jesus was born "in the likeness of sinful flesh" (Rom. 8:3)—not that he was born fallen but weak and taking on a human nature associated with this old age in order to inaugurate the new age that is characterized by the Holy Spirit. Thus, in the incarnation and state of humiliation, Christ becomes one with us, though without sin, but by his obedience, even obedience to death on a cross and then resurrection from the dead, he who has the Spirit is exalted, and as such, his resurrection marks the beginning of the new age and era. His resurrection signals that the new age has begun and that God's promises from the Old Testament have now become a reality, at least in an inaugurated form.

our humanity. By doing so, in his earthly life, i.e., his life in the realm of the flesh, he is the promised Messiah, and by his powerful work epitomized in the resurrection, he has also brought with him the Spirit. Moo nicely summarizes the thrust of these verses this way: "In Christ the 'new era' of redemptive history has begun, and in this new stage of God's plan Jesus reigns as Son of God, powerfully active to bring salvation to all who believe (cf. 1:16)."[21] So, in the end, the contrast is *not* between the two natures of Christ or even Christ's consecrated spirit, but between the two *states* of Christ—between his state of humiliation and exaltation—so that while Jesus was on earth, "he was the Messiah and the Son of God, but his death and resurrection inaugurated a stage of his messianic existence that was not formerly his. Now he reigns in heaven as Lord and Christ."[22] It is in this sense that Christ's resurrection constitutes him as the messianic Son of God with power—"Jesus Christ our Lord."

In summary, this Romans text is a beautiful illustration of the basic pattern of New Testament christology, stressing both the deity and humanity of our Lord. Jesus is Son and Lord because he is the eternal Son, and he is also Son and Lord because of his work as the God-*man*. Ultimately the kind of Redeemer we need—one who can undo the work of Adam, accomplish our forgiveness, and usher in God's kingdom and the new creation—must be nothing less than God the Son incarnate.

Philippians 2:5–11

This text has been at the center of heated christological discussions for a variety of reasons. In theological studies it has served as an important proof-text for the "Kenotic theory," a phrase rooted in the Greek verb *kenoō*, found in verse 7, that means "to empty." In the nineteenth century, a number of theologians advocated a view of the incarnation which contended that the Son gave up or "emptied" himself of some of his divine attributes in taking on our human nature.[23] The main reason for this view was probably due to the increasing discomfort of many critical scholars in accepting Chalcedonian orthodoxy and trying to make rational sense of the incarnation.

---

[21] Moo, *Romans*, 50.

[22] Schreiner, *Romans*, 42–43.

[23] There are a variety of kenotic views. The most extreme form of the theory teaches that the "relative attributes" of the Son, e.g., omniscience, omnipresence, and omnipotence, were put aside in a voluntary fashion in order for the incarnation to take place. What Christ retained were only the "essential attributes of God," e.g., attributes of holiness, love, and righteousness. See Oliver D. Crisp, *Divinity and Humanity* (Cambridge: University Press, 2007), 122–39; Donald Macleod, *The Person of Christ* (Downers Grove, IL: InterVarsity, 1998), 205–12; Donald G. Dawe, *The Form of a Servant: A Historical Analysis of the Kenotic Motif* (Philadelphia: Westminster, 1963).

In biblical studies, a couple of important discussions have surrounded this text. First, much has been written on whether this text is a pre-Pauline hymn or original to Paul. Regardless of how one resolves this debate, most acknowledge that minimally we must accept it as representing Paul's own view and as such interpret it accordingly.[24] Second, more recently, some, like James Dunn, have proposed that the text is dependent upon an Adam-Christ contrast.[25] If so, then the text is simply contrasting the first Adam, who was in the image of God and wrongly tried to become like God, with the second Adam, who existed in the image of God but never strove to be equal with God. In this way, Dunn argues, the text refers only to the human Jesus and his exaltation to an *earthly* position of glory; it does not refer to the preexistent divine Son who humbles himself by taking upon our humanity.[26] However, the arguments against this view are strong, and the traditional view, which we will assume, is better grounded.[27] Let us look at this important text in five steps.

First, literarily the text is broken into two parts, verses 6–8 and 9–11, with two verbs in each section describing Jesus' self-humbling in connection with his taking our human nature (i.e., the state of humiliation) *and* the Father's action in exalting him due to his victorious work (i.e., the state of exaltation).[28] The thought of the text, then, moves from the preexistent Son, to the state of humiliation, resulting in the exaltation of the Son to a new role due to his obedience to the Father. The text is *not* describing how the Son gained equality with God, but how he effected our salvation by his incarnation and willing submission to the Father on our behalf.

Second, the preexistence and deity of the Son is clearly taught by the phrase "who, though he was in the form of God" (*hos en morphē theou huparchōn*).[29] Even though there has been much debate on the precise meaning of "form of God," and it is true that whatever is said of "form" (*morphē*) in verse 6 must also apply in verse 7 where the same word is used, in recent years, P. T. O'Brien's treatment of the term is most helpful.[30] After

---

[24]See Peter T. O'Brien, *Commentary on Philippians*, NIGTC (Grand Rapids, MI: Eerdmans, 1991), 188–202.

[25]See, e.g., Dunn, *Christology in the Making*, 114–21.

[26]See ibid., 114–21, esp. 119.

[27]See N. T. Wright, *The Climax of the Covenant: Christ and the Law in Pauline Theology* (Minneapolis: Fortress, 1992), 56–98; O'Brien, *Philippians*, 196–98; Fee, *Pauline Christology*, 375–93; Schreiner, *New Testament Theology*, 323–27.

[28]See O'Brien, *Philippians*, 205–32; Schreiner, *New Testament Theology*, 324.

[29]O'Brien, *Philippians*, 206, rightly observes that the relative pronoun *hos* links and identifies the historical Jesus with this Son who existed prior to the incarnation.

[30]See ibid., *Philippians*, 205–11.

surveying the term *morphē*, he concludes that it refers to that "form which truly and fully expresses the being which underlies it."[31]

This conclusion is built off the work of R. P. Martin, who focused on the use of *morphē* in the LXX.[32] There it was discovered that: (1) *morphē* denoted the appearance or form of something by which we describe it; (2) *morphē* and *eikōn* ("image") are used interchangeably; and (3) *eikōn* and *doxa* ("glory") are also equivalent terms. Taken together this entails that *morphē* belongs to a group of words "which describe God not as he is in himself but as he is to an observer."[33] *Morphē*, then, does not describe God's nature per se, but it assumes the nature and is a term that truly and fully expresses the nature that underlies it.[34] As applied to Christ, the assertion is that he has always existed in the *morphē theou*, which is another way of affirming the full deity and equality of the Son with the Father.[35] This text, then, assumes and provides a contrast between two forms of existence and appearance of the Son: the majesty and glory he had from all eternity as he shared in the divine glory as God the Son and what he became by taking to himself the *morphēn doulou* (verse 7), i.e., becoming fully and truly human, now as God the Son incarnate.[36] Macleod captures these points well when he writes:

> The subject of the *kenōsis*, therefore (the one who "emptied himself"), is one who had glory with the Father before the world began (Jn. 17:5). . . . He possessed all the majesty of deity, performed all its functions and enjoyed all its prerogatives. He was adored by his Father and worshiped by the angels. He was invulnerable to pain, frustration and embarrassment. He existed in unclouded serenity. His supremacy was total, his satisfaction complete, his blessedness perfect. Such a condition was not something he had secured by effort. It was the way things were, and had always been; and there was no reason why they should change. But change they did, and they changed because of the second element involved in the *kenōsis*: Christ did not insist on his rights . . . he did not regard being equal with God as a *harpagmos*.[37]

---

[31] Ibid., 210.

[32] See R. P. Martin, *Carmen Christi* (Cambridge: University Press, 1967), 99–120.

[33] Macleod, *Person of Christ*, 213.

[34] So O'Brien, *Philippians*, 207–11, for his helpful survey of the meaning of *morphē*.

[35] Ibid., 211. The use of *morphē* in Phil. 2:6 is very similar to John 17:5 and Heb. 1:3. In John, Jesus says that he shared in the glory of the Father before the world began, and in Hebrews the emphasis is on the Son sharing the radiance of God's glory and the exact representation of his being. All this speaks of the Son—"in the form of God"—as the one who is nothing less than divine.

[36] See Bauckham, *Jesus and the God of Israel*, 41–42.

[37] Macleod, *Person of Christ*, 213–14.

Third, it is best to translate the difficult phrase *ouch harpagmon hēgēsato to einai isa theō* as, "He did not think equality with God something to be used for his own advantage."[38] The issue is *not* whether Jesus gains equality with God or whether he retains it. The text is clear: the Son exists in the "form of God" and thus shares "equality with God" (v. 6).[39] Instead, the issue is one of Jesus' *attitude* in regard to his divine status.[40] As Schreiner rightly points out, "Paul *assumes* that Jesus is equal with God. The verse does not teach that Jesus quit trying to attain equality with God. Rather, Paul emphasizes that Jesus did not take advantage of or exploit the equality with God that he already possessed."[41] In other words, the grasping or advantage-taking does not have "equality with God" as its goal; rather, it begins from it.[42] Thus the emphasis of the text is on the attitude of the preexistent Son who already is fully God—he did not regard equality with God as excusing him from the task of redemptive suffering and death, but actually as uniquely qualifying him for that vocation.[43]

Fourth, we now come to the controversial phrase in verse 7, "but he emptied himself." No doubt a strong contrast is introduced by the voluntary act on the part of the preexistent Son,[44] but what is the precise meaning of the verb *ekenōsen*? Should it be translated "emptied" (e.g., NRSV) or "made himself nothing?" (ESV, NIV). What does this voluntary act consist of? First it is important to note what the text does not say. Contra the extreme

---

[38]Bauckham, *Jesus and the God of Israel*, 41. This translation is dependent upon the work of R. W. Hoover, "The *Harpagmos* Enigma: A Philological Solution," *HTR* 64:95–119, who translates the word *harpagmos* as an idiom to mean "something to use for his own advantage." See the discussion in O'Brien, *Philippians*, 211–16; Wright, *Climax of the Covenant*, 77–82; Schreiner, *New Testament Theology*, 325.

[39]See Schreiner, *New Testament Theology*, 325; O'Brien, *Philippians*, 216; Wright, *Climax of the Covenant*, 72, 75, 80–83, who all rightly argue that to exist in the "form of God" is parallel to being "equal with God."

[40]See Bauckham, *Jesus and the God of Israel*, 41.

[41]Schreiner, *New Testament Theology*, 325.

[42]O'Brien, *Philippians*, 216, reinforces this by following C. F. D. Moule's suggestion that the participial clause in v. 6 should not be viewed as concessive (i.e., who, *though* he was in the form of God), but as causal (i.e., "precisely *because* he was in the form of God he did not regard this equality with God as something to be used for his own advantage").

[43]Macleod, *Person of Christ*, 215, makes a helpful observation when he writes: "The conclusion to which this leads us is that the impulse to serve lies at the very heart of deity. God is not self-centred and self-absorbed. As love, he is pure altruism, looking not on (or at) his own things, but at the things of others. From this point of view the idea of *kenōsis* is revolutionary for our understanding of God. It is his very form to forego his rights."

[44]It should not be missed that this text also implies that Jesus made a self-conscious decision on his part not to take advantage of his position and status, which is only possible for one who actually has consciousness and preexistence before his taking on our humanity. For those who make this same point, see Schreiner, *New Testament Theology*, 325; cf. Simon J. Gathercole, *The Pre-existent Son* (Grand Rapids, MI: Eerdmans, 2006), 25.

kenotic views, there is no hint that the Son emptied himself of his divine attributes or of the "form of God." Such views cannot claim this text as evidence for their position. Not only should the verb be understood in an idiomatic way—"to give up one's rights"—and thus metaphorically (hence the translation of the ESV, NIV), but the nature of the *kenōsis* is explained by two participial phrases which describe the manner in which the Son "emptied" himself:[45] (1) by "taking the form of a servant" (*morphēn doulou labōn*), and (2) by "being born in the likeness of men" (*en homoiōmati anthrōpōn genomenos*).

Thus the context itself interprets the "emptying" as equivalent to "humbling himself" and *taking on* a lowly status and position by becoming human and, wonder of wonders, by choosing to die on a cross for us (v. 8). The nature of the incarnation does not involve the subtraction or reduction of the Son's deity but the addition of a human nature. The stress, then, is *not* on exchanging the "form of God" for the "form of a servant (slave)" but on the Son *manifesting* the "form of God" in the "form of a servant." The text says nothing about Christ's "emptying" as the giving up of divine attributes; rather, it consists in the taking to or the adding to himself a complete human nature and in that human nature willingly undergoing the agony of death for our sake and for our salvation.[46] As Macleod rightly concludes: "It is what Christ *assumes* that humbles and impoverishes him: hence the justice of Augustine's comment that he emptied himself 'not by changing His own divinity but by assuming our changeableness.'"[47]

---

[45]The two aorist participles *labōn* and *genomenos* are both modal and coincident with the verb *ekenōsen*, thus describing the manner in which Christ "emptied himself." That is why the context itself interprets the "emptying" as equivalent to "humbling himself" and taking on our human nature. See O'Brien, *Philippians*, 218–23.

[46]It is not my purpose to discuss the kenotic views at length. However, not only does a proper exegesis of the text not allow for the view, but it is also wrongheaded theologically to think that the divine attributes can be severed from the divine nature. In addition, in vv. 9–11, Paul speaks of Christ's exaltation. Nothing in those verses even slightly hints that this exaltation involved a return of a divine nature lost in the incarnation. Schreiner, *New Testament Theology*, 325, nicely makes this point when he writes, "Paul utilizes paradoxical language by describing Christ's emptying in terms of adding."

[47]Macleod, *Person of Christ*, 216. Space forbids detailed reflection on the nature of the Son's humbling himself. For our purposes it is crucial to stress that there was no loss of deity as a result of the incarnation. However, much more needs to be said regarding the Son's state of humiliation. Macleod argues that the text stresses three movements in terms of the Son's humiliation. First, it began with his taking "the form of a servant/slave." Here we see the parallel with v. 6, the "form of God." Just as truly as he was God the Son, so now he truly became human for us and for our salvation. Second, the incarnation involved the Son's taking on our "human likeness" (*homoiōma*) and "being found in human form" (*kai schēmati heurtheis hōs anthrōpos*), which entails that he became all that we as humans are except without sin (cf. Rom. 8:3). Just as strongly as this text stresses the full deity of Christ, it also, along with the entire New Testament, emphasizes the full humanity of Christ (cf. Luke 2:52; John 1:14; Rom. 8:3; Gal. 4:4; Col. 1:22; Heb. 2:17; 4:15;

Fifth, verses 9–11 stress an incredible, decisive change that occurred in history, theologically referred to as the "state of exaltation." In verses 6–8 Christ is the subject of the verbs and participles and attention has been focused upon his self-humbling and obedience as the eternal Son taking to himself a human nature. Now, in verse 9, the emphasis is on the Father's decisive action to exalt the Son—an action that is directly due to the Son's self-humbling and obedient work climaxed in his death.[48] Thus due to Jesus' obedience, the Father now vindicates him by exalting him to the highest position, the heavenly throne of God. In addition, the Father graciously bestows on him the name above all names, i.e., his own name—Lord—along with all that is entailed in that name, viz., the exercise of universal lordship and receiving the worship of all creation.

There is no way to do justice to this verse, let alone the entire section, without affirming the full deity (and humanity) of the Son. Moreover, Paul's application of Isaiah 45:20–25 to Jesus—a text that refers exclusively to Yahweh—is not an isolated occurrence.[49] It is part of the overall New Testament pattern, whereby Old Testament Yahweh texts, translated "Lord," are repeatedly applied to Christ in the New Testament.[50]

5:7–8; 1 John 4:2–3). One cannot think of the identity of Jesus apart from the affirmation that he is fully God and fully man now and forevermore. Third, the "emptying" of the Son did not end with his incarnation; rather, it ended in "becoming obedient to the point of death, even death on a cross" (v. 8). Having fully identified himself with us in his incarnation—an act of "emptying"—Christ willingly humbled himself in a final, climactic act of obedience—death on a cross! Apart from his "emptying" and "humbling" there would be no salvation, but due to his obedience, climaxing in the cross, he bore our sins, satisfied divine wrath and justice, and secured for us eternal redemption. In him, he is Yahweh who saves, but his glory is hidden, at least for a time. In this sense, then, we can say that *kenōsis* involved an obscuring of the divine glory of Christ, what many have rightly labeled *krypsis* ("hiddenness"), but there is no loss of deity involved. Cf. Crisp, *Divinity and Humanity*, 118–53.

[48]See O'Brien, *Philippians*, 233–34, who makes this point.

[49]In its Old Testament context, Isa. 45:20–25 engages in a polemic against idolatry, insisting that the God of Israel is the only true God. Yahweh declares, "By myself I have sworn; from my mouth has gone out in righteousness a word that shall not return: 'To me every knee shall bow, every tongue shall swear allegiance'" (v. 23). The allusion to this text in Phil. 2:10–11 is impossible to miss. By the use of this text, Paul not only confesses that there is only one true God, but also that Jesus, the crucified and resurrected one, is the Lord—not in the sense that he is the same person as the Father, but that he shares in the divine rule and thus is equal to the Father in every way. As Schreiner, *New Testament Theology*, 326–27, concludes, "Clearly, Paul teaches that Jesus shares in the same divine nature as Yahweh himself, but Paul does this without denying monotheism or the distinctions between the Father and the Son." Cf. Bauckham, *Jesus and the God of Israel*, 41–45; O'Brien, *Philippians*, 241–43; David F. Wells, *The Person of Christ* (Wheaton, IL: Crossway, 1984), 64–65.

[50]It is true that "Lord" (*kurios*) is used in different ways in the New Testament, especially when applied to Jesus. It is used as a polite form of address (e.g., Matt. 8:8, 21; 15:27; 17:15; 18:21), and when done so, it does not necessarily accord Jesus divine status. However, the predominate use of "Lord" as applied to Jesus is to identify him with Yahweh. As Wells, *Person of Christ*, 74–77,

So, for example, what is said of Yahweh in the Old Testament is also said of Christ in terms of his character (Ex. 3:14/John 8:58; Isa. 44:6/Rev. 1:17; Ps. 102:26–27 [LXX]/Heb. 1:11–12; Isa. 28:16/Rom. 9:33; 10:11; 1 Pet. 2:6), holiness (Isa. 8:12–13/1 Pet. 3:14–15), worship (Isa. 45:23/Phil. 2:10–11; Deut. 32:43 [LXX] and Ps. 97:7 [LXX]/Heb. 1:6), prayer (1 Cor. 16:22), and work (creation: Ps. 102:25 [LXX]/Heb. 1:10; salvation: Joel 2:32/Rom. 10:12–13; Acts 2:21; Isa. 40:3/Matt.3:3; judgment: Isa. 8:14/1 Pet. 2:8; cf. Rom. 9:33; and ultimate triumph: Ps. 68:18/Eph. 4:8).[51] On the basis of this evidence, Wells is right to conclude: "To speak of Christ as Lord, then, is to identify him ontologically with Yahweh, to ascribe to him the worship which rightly belongs only to God, to acknowledge him as sovereign in his church and in his creation, and to see him as the vindicator of God's character in the world."[52] A clearer affirmation of Jesus as God the Son incarnate could not be given.

Colossians 1:15–20

This text is "one of the christological high points of the New Testament."[53] Similar to Philippians 2:5–11, many have argued that it is an early Christian hymn that Paul adopted. Regardless of whether this is so, minimally we must affirm that Paul has incorporated it into his letter and thus interpret it as his own. Structurally, the text is divided into two main stanzas (vv. 15–17 and 18b–20) with a transitional stanza between the two (vv. 17–18a).[54] In the first main and transitional stanzas, Jesus is presented as Lord/deity precisely because he is the eternal Son, the agent of creation, and the sustainer of the universe. In the second main stanza, Jesus is presented as becoming Lord due to his work as Redeemer. In this manner, the lordship of Christ is presented in both creation and redemption. Let us consider this text further in four steps.

Step 1. First, this text, set within its larger context, serves as one of the three reasons Paul exhorts believers to give thanks to the Father (vv. 12–14,

---

rightly observes in over 6,000 cases in the LXX, "Lord" is a linguistic substitute for Yahweh and thus, when applied to Jesus, it is an unambiguous affirmation of deity. For a full treatment of Paul's application of *kurios* to Christ see Fee, *Pauline Christology*, and David B. Capes, *Old Testament Yahweh Texts in Paul's Christology*, WUNT 2:47 (Tübingen: Mohr-Siebeck, 1992); John M. Frame, *The Doctrine of God* (Phillipsburg, NJ: P&R, 2002), 650–57.

[51]See Bauckham, *Jesus and the God of Israel*, 182–232, for a nice summary of the data from Fee and Capes.

[52]Wells, *Person of Christ*, 77.

[53]Douglas Moo, *The Letters to the Colossians and to Philemon*, PNTC (Grand Rapids, MI: Eerdmans, 2008), 107. N. T. Wright, *Colossians and Philemon*, TNTC (Grand Rapids, MI: Eerdmans, 1986), 64, agrees that this text is "reckoned among the most important christological passages in the New Testament."

[54]See Moo, *Colossians and Philemon*, 114–16.

15–20, 21–23). The first reason we are to give thanks is that, in Christ, we now share in the "new exodus"—our rescue and transfer from the kingdom of darkness into the kingdom of God's "beloved Son," a kingdom associated with the new-covenant age and the forgiveness of sin. The second reason to give thanks, tied to the third, is that God the Father, in his Son, has revealed himself to be the one God of all the earth, the Creator and Redeemer of all. The Son is not merely another "god" set over against the gods of paganism. Rather, he is the world's creator, sustainer, redeemer, and sovereign Lord. In all things he reigns supreme, and, amazingly, he has given himself to this world in loving self-sacrifice in order to redeem a people and to reverse the effects of the curse through his reconciling work on the cross (vv. 15–20). Paul's viewing Jesus as intimately associated with the Father entails, as Bauckham notes, the inclusion of Jesus in the unique identity of God and hence a claim to deity.[55]

Step 2. Second, the full deity of the Son is strongly taught in the first main stanza (vv. 15–16). Three affirmations ground this assertion. Let us look at each of them in turn.

1) The Son is described as "the image of the invisible God" (*eikōn tou theou tou aoratou*), which strongly suggests that he possesses the very nature of God. "Image" carries the sense of "something that looks like, or represents, something else."[56] As in 2 Corinthians 4:4, the stress is on the Son as the perfect revelation of God. "No one has ever seen God," writes John, but "the only God, who is at the Father's side, he has made him known" (John 1:18). Here Paul makes the same point by stressing that the Son, from all-eternity, has perfectly reflected the Father, and now in his incarnation reveals the invisible God just as perfectly. Only a divine Son can thus justify such an assertion.

In addition, the use of "image" (*eikōn*) also suggests an echo back to the creation of humans. In Genesis 1, humans are created as God's image bearers, designed to represent him in the world. However, we are not to think that we are the original image. Rather, the Son is the original image in accordance with which human beings were created: he is the archetype, and we are the ectype.[57] This is why God the Son, who was the perfect "image of God," is not only the pattern of our creation but in becoming human has

---

[55]See Richard Bauckham, "Where Is Wisdom to Be Found? Colossians 1.15–20 (2)," in *Reading Texts, Seeking Wisdom: Scripture and Theology*, ed. David F. Ford and Graham Stanton (Grand Rapids, MI: Eerdmans, 2003), 133, where he writes: "What the passage does is to include Jesus Christ in God's unique relationship to the whole of created reality and thereby to include Jesus in the unique identity of God as Jewish monotheism understood it."

[56]Moo, *Colossians and Philemon*, 117.

[57]See ibid., 118–19. Also see Schreiner, *New Testament Theology*, 327.

now taken on the role of the last Adam.[58] In this sense, as Wright notes, from all eternity Jesus "held the same relation to the Father that humanity, from its creation, had been intended to bear."[59] Humanity was designed to be a finite representation of God's self-expression within his world and to rule over creation under God's lordship, but sadly, in Adam, we all failed. However, in Jesus, we have one who has eternally borne the Father's image perfectly now completely taking upon our humanity in order to fulfill the purposes that God had marked out both for himself and for us (cf. Heb. 2:5–18). Upon Jesus Christ, then, as God the Son incarnate, has come the role marked out for humanity, an emphasis that is further taught in the next affirmation.

2) The Son is "the firstborn of all creation" (*prōtotokos pasēs ktiseōs*). Since the Arian controversy in the fourth century, much debate has focused on the meaning of this phrase. At first glance it might suggest, as Arius proposed, that Jesus is the first creature in time and thus a created being. However, in the Nicene Creed, the church rejected this understanding and instead affirmed, along with Scripture, that Christ is the "firstborn" in terms of rank and authority.[60] The background to understanding this meaning of "firstborn" is the Old Testament. There the term is closely linked to the right of the primogeniture. Israel is God's "firstborn" son (Ex. 4:22), which entails Israel's status as representative and ruler for God in the world. The Davidic king also receives the title (Ps. 89:27)—"I will make him the first-born, the highest of the kings of the earth."

As Schreiner points out, in the case of David, he "was not the first Isra-elite king. That privilege belonged to Saul. Nor was David the oldest in the family; in fact, he was the youngest. Designating him as the 'firstborn' signals his sovereignty, and this is confirmed by Hebrew parallelism. The word 'firstborn' is elucidated by the phrase 'the highest of the kings of the earth.'"[61] In this way, "firstborn" has the connotation of "supreme over," which is precisely its meaning in Colossians 1:15.[62] This interpretation is confirmed by verse 16—"for (*hoti*) by him all things were created"—which not only explains the fact that the Son existed before creation, and that he

---

[58]Wright, *Colossians and Philemon*, 70, suggests that this emphasis on the Son as the "image of God" shows that the Son is "the climax of the history of creation, and at the same time the starting-point of the new creation."

[59]Ibid.

[60]"Firstborn" (*prōtotokos*) can convey both the idea of priority in time *and* rank. Ultimately it is the context that must determine its use. Cf. Moo, *Colossians and Philemon*, 119–24.

[61]Schreiner, *New Testament Theology*, 327.

[62]See Moo, *Colossians and Philemon*, 119–20. Cf. Peter T. O'Brien, *Colossians, Philemon*, WBC 44 (Nashville, Nelson, 1982), 44–45.

is the agent of creation, but also that he is supreme over creation *because* he is its creator.

(3) Verse 16 contains a third affirmation that further solidifies the deity of the Son. Not only is the divine work of creation attributed to the Son, but the extent of the Son's supremacy is also highlighted by citing three ways the creation is related to him: "*in* him, *through* him, and *for* him." First, "*in* him" (*en autō*) all things were made. Here Paul asserts that all God's creative work was "in terms of" or "in reference to" Christ,[63] which links the Son to the Father in the closest of terms and ties the dependence of creation entirely upon the Son. Second, "*through* him" (*di' autou*) and then, third, "*for* him" (*eis auton*) focus on the beginning and end of creation. The Son stands at the beginning of creation as the one *through* whom all things were created, and he stands at its end as the goal of the universe—"*for* him."[64] The thought of this verse moves from the past (the Son is the agent of creation), to the present (the world owes its allegiance to the Son), and to the future (the Son whose sovereignty will become universal). Again, we would be hard-pressed to find stronger affirmations of the deity of the Son, as Schreiner argues: "Jesus is the goal as well as the agent of all creation. The glory that belongs to the only God also belongs to Jesus as creator and Lord."[65]

Step 3. Third, if the three affirmations of the first stanza (vv. 15–16) underscore the deity of the Son, the intervening stanza (v. 17) continues to do so as it transitions to the glorious work of the incarnate Son (v. 18a). The opening line, "And he is before all things," looks back to verses 15–16 with its focus on the Son's relationship to creation, while the last line, "and he is the head of the body, the church," introduces the focus on Christ's redemptive work that is developed in verses 18b–20. The middle line, "And in him all things hold together," looks both directions, uniting the twofold presentation of New Testament christology, namely, Jesus is Son/Lord because of who he is and by virtue of what he does. In particular, verse 17 teaches the Son's preexistence and supremacy over the entire universe

---

[63]See Moo, *Colossians and Philemon*, 120–21, and O'Brien, *Colossians, Philemon*, 45–46, for a discussion of the preposition *en*. Should it be taken in the instrumental sense: "by him all things were created"? Or, should it be taken in the sense of sphere: "in him all things were created"? Both Moo and O'Brien argue for the latter.

[64]Murray J. Harris, *Three Crucial Questions about Jesus* (Grand Rapids, MI: Baker, 1994), 80–81, rightly notes that in v. 16 the verb "to create" is first used in the aorist tense (*ektisthē*) and then in the perfect tense (*ektistai*). This is more than stylistic. It probably underscores the emphasis that creation not only came to exist by the Son but that it now continues to exist by him. Cf. Moo, *Colossians and Philemon*, 124.

[65]Schreiner, *New Testament Theology*, 327.

as its creator *and* providential Lord. In other words, apart from the Son's continuous sustaining activity, prior to his incarnation *and* as the incarnate Son, the universe would disintegrate[66]—yet another clear and direct affirmation of the Son's deity. Even in the state of humiliation, the New Testament attributes to Jesus of Nazareth divine cosmic functions that underscore his identity as God the Son incarnate, thus making kenotic views nigh impossible.

Step 4. Fourth, turning to the second main stanza (vv. 18b–20), we see Jesus' work accented as God the Son *incarnate.* The same sovereign creator and providential Lord is also head over his people, the church.[67] How has he accomplished this great work of reconciliation (v. 20)? The text is clear: it is due to his crucifixion and resurrection—"he is the beginning, the firstborn from the dead." As Schreiner explains, "Jesus rules over death because he was the first to conquer death."[68] In this way, he is the founder of a new humanity by his incarnation, death, and resurrection, so "that in everything he might be preeminent." Thus, by his resurrection (which is tied to his entire work), he inaugurates a new order, evidenced by the word "beginning" (*archē*),[69] and he becomes the founder of a new humanity. In Christ and his work, the resurrection age has burst forth, and he has set the pattern for all those who have fallen asleep; he is the "firstfruits" who guarantees our future resurrection (1 Cor. 15:20, 23). Thus, what is his by right, namely lordship, has now become *in fact* due to his inauguration of the new creation via his entire cross work for us.[70]

But Paul is not yet finished. In verse 19, he again strongly stresses Jesus' deity as God the Son: "For in him all the fullness of God was pleased to dwell."[71] In other words, the Son, Paul asserts, is the place where God in

---

[66]The verb used, *sunestēken,* is in the perfect tense. As Moo, *Colossians and Philemon,* 125, notes: "The use of the perfect tense suggests a stative idea: the universe owes its continuing coherence to Christ."

[67]Even this statement, as C. F. D. Moule, *The Origin of Christology* (Cambridge: University Press, 1977), has noted, is rich in christological affirmation since it treats the Son as a "corporate person." Moule comments that it is possible to argue that such an idea is commonplace in pantheistic thought, but "it becomes a new and extraordinary phenomenon when it is not a pantheist but a theist who is speaking, and when he speaks of a known individual of recent history as an 'inclusive' or 'corporate Person'. . . which drives us to ask, Who is this; who can be understood in much the same terms as a theist understands God himself—as personal, indeed, but more than individual?" (87). Cf. Moo, *Colossians and Philemon,* 126–28.

[68]Schreiner, *New Testament Theology,* 328.

[69]See ibid.; Moo, *Colossians and Philemon,* 128–29; O'Brien, *Colossians, Philemon,* 50–51.

[70]See N. T. Wright, *Colossians and Philemon,* 73–75.

[71]"For in him all the fullness of God was pleased to dwell" (*hoti en autō eudokēsen pan to plērōma katoikēsai*) is best understood in terms of the Old Testament. In the Old Testament, "fullness" is a reference to God (see O'Brien, *Colossians, Philemon,* 52; Moo, *Colossians and Philemon,* 130–33). In addition, we are repeatedly told that God chooses, or is pleased to display, his glory

all his fullness was pleased to take up his residence and display his glory. As Moo notes, "In typical New Testament emphasis, Christ replaces the temple as the 'place' where God now dwells,"[72] and O'Brien rightly adds, "All the attributes and activities of God—his spirit, word, wisdom and glory—are perfectly displayed in Christ."[73] This is not a temporary dwelling, either, as Colossians later makes clear. In Colossians 2:9, the verb "dwells" or "lives" (*katoikeō*) is not only in the present tense, but the adverb "bodily" (*sōmatikōs*) is separated from the verb, which Harris suggests entails two distinct affirmations: "that the entire fullness of the Godhead dwells in Christ eternally and that this fullness now permanently resides in Christ in bodily form."[74] Thus what is true of God the Son prior to the incarnation is also true of him post-incarnation, namely, that the entire fullness of deity (nature and attributes) resides in him. It is hard to find a higher christology than this. In Jesus the Christ, we have the revelation of the one true God, who reigns supreme over all. There is no sphere of existence over which he is not sovereign and supreme.[75] No wonder, then, that all people are summoned to submit to him in trust, love, worship, and obedience.

Hebrews 1:1–4

It is not an overstatement to say that the entire book of Hebrews is centered in christology. From the opening verses to the close of the book, the main subject matter of the letter is the majesty, supremacy, and glory of the Son, our Lord Jesus Christ. Probably written to Jewish Christians living in Rome (see 13:24), before the fall of Jerusalem, Hebrews seeks to encourage and warn these believers who had seemingly begun well but were now in danger of compromising their commitment to Christ. These believers had been Christians for some time (5:12) and had even experienced persecution for their faith (10:32–34), but they were now drifting away from their faith (2:1–4). As such, the author writes to warn them of their danger.[76] By expounding text after text from the Old Testament, the author seeks to

---

in the universe (see Ps. 72:19; Jer. 23:24; cf. Isa. 6:3; Ezek. 43:5; 44:4), and specifically and uniquely in the temple (see Pss. 68:16; 131:13–14; Isa. 8:18; 49:20). See Moo, *Colossians and Philemon*, 131–32, who rightly argues that the verb "was pleased" is very close to the idea of "choose" or "elect" (cf. Luke 12:32; 1 Cor. 1:21; Gal. 1:15). Thus, in this affirmation we have a strong assertion of the full deity of the Son.

[72]Moo, *Colossians and Philemon*, 133.

[73]O'Brien, *Colossians, Philemon*, 53.

[74]Harris, *Three Crucial Questions about Jesus*, 66; cf. O'Brien, *Colossians, Philemon*, 110–14.

[75]Wright, *Colossians, Philemon*, 79.

[76]For a discussion of some of this background see William L. Lane, *Hebrews 1–8*, WBC 47a (Dallas, TX: Word, 1991), *xlvii–clvii*; George H. Guthrie, *Hebrews*, NIVAC (Grand Rapids, MI: Zondervan, 1998), 17–38.

encourage them with the truth that Jesus is not only the antitypical fulfill-ment of all the hopes and expectations of the Old Testament, but he is also greater precisely because he is God the Son incarnate.[77] In this way, the author simultaneously teaches the full deity and humanity of the Son. As Bauckham notes, the author applies three titles to Jesus—Son, Lord, and High Priest—all of which assume that the Son shares equally the unique identity of God as well as humanity. "In each category Hebrews portrays Jesus as both truly God and truly human, like his Father in every respect and like humans in every respect."[78]

Additionally, in Hebrews the basic pattern of New Testament christol-ogy continues: Jesus is Son and Lord because of who he has always been (1:2–3) *and* by his work of taking on our humanity and fulfilling the role of Adam (2:5–18), David (1:4–14), and the High Priest (4:14–10:39) and thus securing our redemption and inaugurating the promised "age to come." Wells correctly notes that nowhere does the author lay out a theory of the incarnation, yet both the full deity and humanity of Christ are affirmed. Wells writes:

> The author offers no theory as to how the divine became enfleshed. The process of incarnation is referred to (2:9; 10:5), but not explored. Yet it remains clear that for the author this process did not involve diminution of or modification in that Godness which had been the Son's. In the midst of describing Jesus' very human cries and tears, the author insists that it was the same divine Son who was experiencing this pain.[79]

Alongside, then, the unqualified assertions of the Son's deity (e.g., 1:2–3, 4–14) are also the unqualified assertions of his humanity. Jesus is from the tribe of Judah (7:14), he was vulnerable to temptation (but not to sin) as we are (4:15), he learned obedience as we do even though he was the Son (5:8), and he had to be perfected as we do (2:10). But it is crucial to note why these assertions are made. Only as God the Son incarnate is the Son able to inaugurate the promised age associated with the coming of Yahweh and Messiah, undo the work of Adam, and most importantly, fulfill the role of the great High Priest by perfectly representing us and accomplishing for us a full and effective atonement for sin (Hebrews 7–10). Even though Hebrews does not explain how the eternal Son became human, the author is especially

---

[77]In regard to the antitypical fulfillment, Jesus is presented through the book as greater than angels (1:5–2:18), Moses (3:1–6), Joshua (3:7–4:12), the priests (2:17–19; 4:14–10:39), and so on. All this grounds the author's presentation of the supremacy and finality of the Son.

[78]Bauckham, *Jesus and the God of Israel*, 236.

[79]Wells, *Person of Christ*, 55.

concerned to stress the full deity and humanity of the Son in order for us to have an all-sufficient lord and savior. For the Son's sacrifice on the cross to be efficacious, the redeemer had to be both divine and human. That is why, as Wells correctly asserts, for the author an affirmation of Jesus' full humanity as well as sinlessness "was not an incidental matter (4:15; 7:26); it was the sine qua non for the Son's sacrificial mission. His pure humanity was as much necessitated by his pretemporal appointment as was his full divinity, for each was indispensable to his saving work."[80]

These truths are developed throughout the entire book of Hebrews but uniquely begin in the opening verses, which, in many ways, serve as the book's thesis. Unlike typical New Testament letters, the author dispenses with the usual greetings and lays out his thesis in a single, complex sentence, built around the main statement—"God . . . has spoken." As the author looks across the panorama of redemptive history, he speaks both of the "continuity" and "discontinuity" of God's work centered in the Son, which highlights the unique identity of our Lord and which allows him to develop these opening verses throughout the remainder of the book. As he does so, he intertwines the two integral paths of New Testament christology by stressing the identity of Jesus as both God the Son and God the Son incarnate. Let us briefly look at this opening passage, which Schreiner rightly labels as "one of the most beautiful and exalted christological texts in the New Testament."[81] We will examine the verses in two steps.

Step 1. First, the author, through a series of contrasts, asserts that God has spoken finally and definitively in these "last days" in his Son. This first of three contrasts focuses on the eras of God's speaking—"long ago . . . in these last days." Along with the entire New Testament, the author divides redemptive history into two successive ages and views the Son as the one who inaugurates the "last days," i.e., God's sovereign rule and reign.[82] Implicit, if not explicit, in this affirmation is the identification of Jesus with Yahweh.[83]

The second contrast stresses the qualitative superiority of God's speaking in the Son. "Long ago" God spoke "at many times and in many ways" but now, in the Son, God's speaking is complete. This is not to say that Old Testament prophetic revelation was inferior and less authoritative; rather, the point is that the previous revelation was deliberately fragmen-

---

[80]Ibid., 54–55.
[81]Schreiner, *New Testament Theology*, 380.
[82]See Lane, *Hebrews 1–8*, 10–12; Wells, *Person of Christ*, 52–53.
[83]See Wells, *Person of Christ*, 21–66; Bauckham, *Jesus and the God of Israel*, 233–41.

tary, incomplete, and anticipatory.[84] As William Lane comments, "The fragmentary and varied character of God's self-disclosure under the old covenant awakened within the fathers an expectation that he would continue to speak to his people. . . . The ministry of the prophets marked the preparatory phase of that history."[85]

This point is reinforced by the third contrast between the agents of revelation: "by the prophets . . . by his Son," or better, "in Son" (*en huiō*).[86] By this contrast the author presents the Son as more than a prophet; he is in a qualitatively different category. Once again, the purpose is not to downplay the authority of the Old Testament prophets; rather, the point is that the previous revelation was incomplete and intended by God to point beyond itself to its fulfillment in the Son. That is why the Son is greater: he is the one about whom the prophets spoke. Even more, the Son is the one in whom all God's revelation and redemptive purposes culminate (cf. Eph. 1:9–10), which is precisely how the author develops these opening verses throughout the remainder of his letter. Old Testament prophets, priests, and kings all point forward and anticipate the final prophet, priest, and king; the sacrifices and ceremonies of the old covenant point forward to what has now come in Christ and the inauguration of a new-covenant era foretold by the Old Testament.

Step 2. Second, given these incredible assertions, what warrant is given to substantiate the claim that God's speaking in the Son is far greater than anything that has preceded him—even more—that the Son is precisely who the Old Testament prophets spoke of, longed for, and anticipated? The answer is that the author grounds his assertions in the unique identity of the Son as God the Son incarnate (vv. 2b–4). Five crucial identity statements are given. Let us briefly look at each in turn.

1) The Son is first described as the appointed "heir of all things" (v. 2b). It is probably best to understand this appointment as similar to Romans 1:3–4 and in light of such Old Testament texts as Psalm 2, especially given the fact that Psalm 2:7 is quoted in verse 5 as the basis for the argument that Christ is better than angels.[87] In the history of the church, as noted above, some early church fathers understood Psalm 2:7–8 to refer to the Son's appointment in eternity past, or what was called the "eternal generation"

---

[84]This is the meaning of the expression "at many times and in many ways." Not only was the Old Testament revelation repetitive, but by its very nature it was incomplete. In the progress of revelation, more and more of God's plan was disclosed to us, pointing forward to and culminating in the coming of Christ.

[85]Lane, *Hebrews 1–8*, 11.

[86]For a discussion of this point see ibid.; Guthrie, *Hebrews*, 46–47.

[87]See Lane, *Hebrews 1–8*, 12; Guthrie, *Hebrews*, 47; Schreiner, *New Testament Theology*, 380–81.

of the Son.[88] However, it is better to interpret Psalm 2 as a reference to the Davidic king, a type and pattern of the one to come. Accordingly, the entire New Testament applies Psalm 2 to Jesus in terms of his appointment as the antitype of David (Heb. 1:2, 5, 8–9, 13; 5:5; cf. Acts 13:33; Rom. 1:3–4), the one who by virtue of his incarnation, death, and resurrection is now installed at God's right hand as the messianic king.[89] Once again, we see the second path of New Testament christology emphasized as the importance of the incarnation is underscored. However, even though Jesus' appointment to be the "heir of all things" (v. 2b) is directly tied to his incarnation and saving work as a man, the author makes clear that we must not think that the Son is merely another David (1:5; 5:5) or Adam (2:5–9) or Moses (3:1–6) or priest (5:1–10), but that he is also God the Son from all eternity and thus deity. The next three identity statements stress this exact point.

2) The Son is now described as the agent of creation (v. 2b): "through whom also he created the world." Not only is this text consistent with other New Testament texts that attribute the *divine* work of creation to the Son, thus teaching his deity (John 1:1–3; Col. 1:15–17), but it also points to the roles of the Father and Son in creation; it is *through* the Son that the world is made. God's work in creation is ultimately a triune work: the Father through the Son by the Spirit (cf. Gen. 1:2).[90]

3) The Son's full deity is further underscored in verse 3a: "He is the radiance of the glory of God and the exact imprint of his nature." This language so strongly affirms the full deity of the Son that in church history, as Wells reminds us, the Arians refused to recognize the authenticity of Hebrews on the basis of this text alone.[91] Two statements are simultaneously asserted about the Son, evidenced by the fact that they are written in synonymous parallelism: he is "the radiance (*apaugasma*) of the glory of God" and "the exact imprint (*charaktēr*) of his nature (*hupostaseōs*)."[92] Together they make

---

[88] For a defense of this view see Reymond, *Jesus, Divine Messiah*, 77–81.

[89] See Schreiner, *New Testament Theology*, 380–81.

[90] It is also important to note the force of the *kai*—"and through whom . . ." As William Lane, *Hebrews 1–8*, 12, suggests, its purpose is to link this second relative clause with the first, thus underscoring the fact that the appointed Son, whose appointment is no doubt tied to history and his incarnation and entire cross work, is also the same one who preexisted as the Son and through whom God created the universe. Here, once again, we see the two paths of christological reflection converge, forming the basic pattern of New Testament christology.

[91] See Wells, *Person of Christ*, 53. The Arians denied the eternal preexistence and deity of the Son.

[92] It should be noted, especially in light of later church discussion, that the word translated "nature" is *hypostaseōs*. As christological reflection took place in the fourth and fifth centuries, *hypostasis* came to bear the meaning of "person" and not "nature." But early on, as in Hebrews, it is the latter meaning which is in view, demonstrating the point that words can change in their meaning over time. As Macleod, *Person of Christ*, 81, rightly notes, the use of the word *hypostasis* in the sense of person "is much later than the apostolic age." In fact, the word occurs in four other instances

the same point: we cannot understand the identity of Jesus apart from affirming that he is God the Son and thus fully God.[93]

4) Additionally, in verse 3b, similar to Colossians 1:15–17, the Son is presented as the Lord of providence: "He upholds the universe by the word of his power." In speaking of the Son upholding (*pherōn*) the universe, the concept expressed is dynamic, not static. The verb implies the idea of carrying something from one place to another,[94] which tells us that it is the Son through whom the entire created order comes to exist, is sustained, and is carried to its appointed end. In attributing these divine cosmic functions to the Son—even as the incarnate one—his full deity is taught. Is it any wonder that the Son is utterly unique, supreme, and greater? He could be nothing less.

5) After stressing the deity of the Son, the author returns to the second path of christology, i.e., the Son's work as the *incarnate* one. The Son is now presented as the only redeemer of humans, presupposing that he has taken on our humanity and accomplished a work for us as our great High

---

in the New Testament (2 Cor. 9:4; 11:17; Heb. 3:14; 11:1), and none of them require the meaning *person*. But, it may be legitimately asked, in what sense is the Son the image of the Father's nature? Ibid., 82, answers this question: "The primary idea is that the Son is the *charaktēr* of the Father and this is strengthened by introducing the word *hypostasis*. The Son is the exact impression of the very nature of God; of his real being. He is one and the same *hypostasis* repeated. It exists in one form in the Father, in another in the Son." The Son, then, provides a true and trustworthy picture of the Father (see John 14:9), an emphasis which is later picked up by the church in the confession that the Son is of the "same nature" (*homoousios*) as the Father and the Spirit, over against the Arian denial of the full equality and deity of the Son. No stronger statement could be made regarding the full deity of the Son.

[93]The terms *apaugasma* and *charaktēr* are found only here in the New Testament. The former term, *apaugasma*, is best translated "radiance" or "effulgence" and not "reflection" (see Lane, *Hebrews 1–8*, 12–13). The emphasis is that the Son is the one who makes visible the very glory of God, something which only God can do (cf. John 1:14–18). The thought here is very similar to the prologue of John's Gospel (see Philip E. Hughes, *A Commentary on the Epistle to the Hebrews* [Grand Rapids, MI: Eerdmans, 1987], 41–42; D. A. Carson, *The Gospel according to John*, PNTC [Grand Rapids, MI: Eerdmans, 1990], 111–39). As in John, so here in Hebrews, the stress is on this point: as a result of the incarnation, the Son of the Father from all eternity now makes visible to us the Father's glory. Macleod, *Person of Christ*, 80, nicely captures this idea: "He [the Son] is the glory made visible: not a different glory from the Father's but the same glory in another form. The Father is the glory hidden: the Son is the glory revealed. The Son is the Father repeated, but in a different way." The latter term, *charaktēr*, continues this same thought. Originally, the term denoted an instrument used for engraving and later the impression made by such an instrument. Used in this sense, the word "thus speaks of the features of an object or person by which we are able to recognize it for what it is" (Guthrie, *Hebrews*, 48). In the case of coins, for example, the term was used to speak of the exact reproduction of the image on the stamp (Macleod, *Person of Christ*, 80). In this context, then, as this word is applied to the Son, the author is asserting in the strongest of terms that what the Son represents perfectly is the very nature of God. In this way, as Guthrie, *Hebrews*, 48, rightly notes, this expression is parallel to other New Testament texts "that speak of Jesus as the 'form,' 'likeness,' or 'image' of God (e.g., John 1:2; Phil. 2:6; Col. 1:15)."
[94]Hughes, *Hebrews*, 45–46.

Priest—a work which no human (or angel) could achieve. In this way, the Son is presented as the all-sufficient redeemer: "After making purification for sins, he sat down at the right hand of the Majesty on high." The use of the aorist participle, "having made" (*poiēsamenos*) purification for our sins, underscores the once-for-all-time nature of his work.[95] While the Son is ceaselessly the radiance of God's glory and the exact correspondence of his nature; while he continuously upholds the universe; now, due to his glorious work for us as our High Priest, his cross work is finished and complete. Furthermore, the Son's lordship is also emphasized using Psalm 110 in verse 3—a psalm used extensively in Hebrews (see 1:13; 5:6; 6:20; 7:1–8:13). What is significant about this is the fact that the Son is identified with the heavenly throne of God and thus included in the unique identity of Yahweh—further proof of his deity.[96] How is Jesus able to fulfill all these roles? Precisely because he is God the Son incarnate.

In summary, so far we have sought to describe the New Testament's basic christological pattern by investigating four crucial texts. Our conclusion is that the apostolic witness presents Jesus' identity as God the Son incarnate: God the Son from eternity, but now and forevermore, Jesus, the God-man, who fulfills the plan of the Father and accomplishes our redemption. Let

---

[95]See Lane, *Hebrews 1–8*, 15.

[96]See Bauckham, *Jesus and the God of Israel*, 21–23, 233–53. As discussed in Rom. 1:3–4, it is important *not* to interpret this language, as Dunn and others do, as an example of adoptionistic christology. In fact, when it comes to Hebrews, Dunn, *Christology in the Making*, 52, believes that "there is more 'adoptionist' language in Hebrews than in any other New Testament document—that is, language which speaks of Jesus as becoming, or being begotten or being appointed to his status as the decisive intermediary between God and man during his life or in consequence of his death and resurrection: note in particular, 1.4—by his passion and exaltation he *became* superior to angels and has inherited a title superior to that of the angels." Dunn's explanation for this adoptionistic language is that the author has awkwardly merged two incompatible world-views together, namely the Platonic and Hebraic (52–56). But this explanation will not do. First, the thought world of the author is thoroughly Hebraic and not Platonic. The entire presentation of Christ is within the categories and structures of biblical revelation, carefully tracing out the storyline of the Bible and seeing the fulfillment and culmination of the plan of God in the person and work of Christ. Second, as detailed in the opening verses of Hebrews, as well as throughout the entire letter, the deity of the Son is unambiguously affirmed. When God spoke finally and definitively in these last days, he spoke not merely through a prophet but through one who was already a Son—a Son whom the author goes on to proclaim is nothing less than *God the Son*. As Macleod, *Person of Christ*, 85, nicely summarizes the Jesus of Hebrews: "He was the Son of God. This was what distinguished him from the prophets and set him above the angels. He performed the functions of God (creation and providence); he enjoyed the prerogatives of God ('Let all God's angels worship him'); he inherited the titles of God; and he was exclusively related to God as the shining of his glory and the very image of his being. He was, and is, *God* (1:8); which is why to commit apostasy is to commit a sin for which there is no forgiveness (6:6)." Lastly, as argued above, the so-called adoptionist language is better interpreted in light of the entire pattern of New Testament christology. We can only make sense of the entire sweep of New Testament data by maintaining both the full deity and humanity of Christ.

us now explore a number of other texts that further underscore Christ's deity and support the overall pattern of biblical christology.

Jesus the Christ as God the Son: Further Biblical Evidence

We now turn to a potpourri of data that teach the deity of Christ.[97] At the heart of this data, as mentioned in Philippians 2:9–11, is the affirmation that Jesus is Lord and thus takes on the very identity, prerogatives, and role of the covenant Lord of the Old Testament.[98] As John Frame notes, the most concise summary of the Old Testament teaching regarding God who is presented as "the one who controls all things, speaks with absolute authority, and enters creation to draw creatures into covenant relation with him" is "Yahweh is Lord."[99] But, in a similar vein, the New Testament repeatedly presents Jesus as Lord, thus claiming he takes on the very identity of the covenant Lord (Rom. 10:9; 1 Cor. 12:3; Phil. 2:11). We will look at the evidence for these claims in the following categories, each of which affirms the deity of the Son: his divine status and prerogatives, his divine acts and works, and his divine names and titles.

The Divine Status and Prerogatives of the Son

Given the amount of data under this heading, we will organize it in three ways: Jesus' divine attributes, divine rule, and his being worthy of worship.

Divine attributes. The apostolic writings teach that the Son possesses all the divine attributes. We have already noted this point in our brief treatment of Colossians 2:9. Paul stresses that in Christ, "the whole fullness of deity dwells bodily." What is this but another way of saying that every divine attribute is found in the incarnate Son? Paul does not say simply "the plenitude of deity" but "the *entire* fullness of deity."[100] Whatever is characteristic of God as God resides in Christ. In biblical thought this includes both the nature of God and his attributes. As we read the New Testament, this statement is borne out as one divine attribute after another is applied to Christ. Consider what we often label the moral or communicable attributes of God.[101] Scripture defines God's *love* in relation to the Son, particularly

---

[97]Given the space constraints of this chapter we can only sketch out the material. For a more detailed discussion of the material see, e.g., Bauckham, *Jesus and the God of Israel*; Robert M. Bowman Jr. and J. Ed Komoszewski, *Putting Jesus in His Place: The Case for the Deity of Christ* (Grand Rapids, MI: Kregel, 2007); Fee, *Pauline Christology*; Richard N. Longenecker, ed., *Contours of Christology in the New Testament* (Grand Rapids, MI: Eerdmans, 2005); Schreiner, *New Testament Theology*, 305–38, 380–430.

[98]I take the expression the "covenant Lord" from Frame, *Doctrine of God*, 21–35.

[99]Ibid., 650.

[100]Cf. O'Brien, *Colossians, Philemon*, 110–13; Moo, *Colossians and Philemon*, 193–95.

[101]On the classifying of divine attributes see Frame, *Doctrine of God*, 387–401.

his cross (Rom. 8:35–39; Gal. 2:20; Eph. 3:17–19; 5:2, 25; cf. 1 John 3:16; 4:10–12). Jesus is the *righteous* one (Acts 3:14; 7:52; 22:14; James 5:6), the *holy* one (Acts 3:14; 4:27, 30; 2 Cor. 5:21; Heb. 4:15; 7:26; 1 Pet. 2:22),[102] even the one whose *wrath* is God's wrath (Rev. 6:16).

In terms of *truth*, Jesus is uniquely identified with the Lord. Everywhere in the Old Testament the Lord is presented as the God of truth (e.g., Ps. 31:5; Isa. 65:16). This expression implies not only that he is the standard of truth since he is its source, but also that his character is upright, his word is dependable, and his actions are consistent. The New Testament claims the same for Jesus. In John's Gospel he is full of grace and truth (John 1:14)—an allusion to the Lord in Exodus 34—and he is *the* truth (John 14:6). Moreover, because Jesus was God's fully accredited agent (Acts 4:27; 10:38), and the wisdom of God (1 Cor. 1:24, 30; Col. 2:3), and the one who has all authority (Eph. 1:22; Col. 2:10), what he taught about God corresponds to reality and is utterly trustworthy (Matt. 22:16; Luke 20:21; John 8:40, 45).[103] Furthermore, given that Jesus is the truth and is the perfect "form" (Phil. 2:6) and "image" of God (Col. 1:15; cf. 2 Cor. 4:4), exactly corresponding to who God is (Heb. 1:3), he is the perfect revelation of God (Heb. 1:1–3; cf. John 1:18; 14:8–9).

The New Testament authors also ascribe to the Son the incommunicable attributes of God. For example, the Son shares in the Father's eternity. He existed with the Father before the incarnation (John 1:1, he was "with God;" cf. 12:41; 17:5; 1 Cor. 10:4; Heb. 1:2). The Father sent him into the world (Rom. 8:3; Gal. 4:4; cf. John 3:17; 1 John 4:9), or the Son came into the world (2 Cor. 8:9; cf. John 1:9), or he appeared on the earthly scene (Heb. 9:26; 1 Pet. 1:20), which minimally presupposes his prior existence, if not his eternal existence, especially in light of texts that employ the present tense, thus underscoring his eternality (Phil. 2:6; Col. 1:17; Heb. 13:8; cf.

---

[102]No doubt, Jesus' sinlessness in Scripture is presented as a quality of his perfect humanity. However, the righteous, holy sinlessness of the Son has to be viewed in relation to Yahweh as well. Jesus is not merely the perfect man, but he has a quality of perfection that identifies him with God. In this way, he is in a different category than even a perfect human being—he is the Lord. Cf. ibid., 675.

[103]The New Testament clearly teaches that Jesus is the source and standard of truth. See ibid., 676, who summarizes the data this way: "Jesus is God's truth (John 14:6), the one who is true, full of truth (John 1:14), even 'the true God' (1 John 5:20). Like God, Jesus knows all things (Matt. 11:25–27; John 2:24–25; 16:30; 21:17; Col. 2:3). There is no record of his ever having made an error or mistake. He has a supernatural knowledge of events and facts (John 4:16–19, 29). He knows the thoughts, even the hearts, of human beings (Matt. 9:4; 12:25; Mark 2:8; Luke 6:8; 9:47; John 1:47; 2:24–25; 21:17; Rev. 2:23). He knows the future. He knows that he must die at the hands of sinners (Matt. 16:21; Mark 8:31; Luke 9:22). He knows in advance who will betray him (Matt. 26:24), Peter's denial (John 13:38), the kind of death Peter will die (John 21:18–19), and the future of the kingdom (Matt. 8:11). He knows the Father as the Father knows him, and he is sovereign in revealing the Father to human beings (Matt. 11:25–27; Luke 10:22; John 10:15)."

John 1:18; 8:58 with Ex. 3:14). The Son also possesses omnipotence (Matt. 8:26–27; 1 Cor. 1:18, 23–25; Eph. 1:19–20; Phil. 3:21; Col. 2:10), omnipresence (1 Kings 8:27; Ps. 139:7–10 with Matt. 18:20; 28:20; Eph. 4:10), immutability (Num. 23:19; Mal. 3:6; James 1:17 with 2 Cor. 1:20; Heb. 1:10–12; 13:8), and omniscience (Ps. 139:1–3; Isa. 46:8–13; 48:3–6 with Mark 2:8; John 1:48; 2:25; 6:64; 21:17; Acts 1:24; 1 Cor. 4:5; Col. 2:3, 9; Rev. 2:23).

In regard to omniscience, biblical authors, including Jesus himself, also affirm that the Son grew in knowledge and that he did not know certain things (Luke 2:52; Mark 13:32). How one reconciles the tension between an affirmation of the omniscience and ignorance of the Son is one of the most difficult areas in christological reflection. It is no doubt tied to the nature of the incarnation—the relation of the Son to the Father in the state of humiliation as the Son obediently does and knows all that the Father allows him for the purpose of our redemption (John 5:18–47), as well as the Son's relation to the Spirit. For our purposes, it is crucial to note that one cannot do justice to the Scripture's presentation of Christ without acknowledging that it teaches simultaneously the growth of Jesus in wisdom and knowledge in his human nature *and* the omniscience of Jesus as God the Son.

Divine rule. In the apostolic writings Jesus is presented as equally sharing the divine rule and reign and is thus on par with God. One of the constant refrains found throughout the Old Testament celebrating the universal rule and supremacy of the Lord is summed up in the psalmist's words: "For you, O LORD, are most high over all the earth; you are exalted far above all gods" (Ps. 97:9). Significantly, the New Testament also attributes this same universal supremacy to Jesus. He is said to exercise universal rule over "all things" (Rom. 14:9; 1 Cor. 15:27–28; Eph. 1:22; Phil. 2:10; 3:21; Heb. 1:2; 2:8; 1 Pet. 3:22; Rev. 1:5),[104] including all human and angelic authorities (Eph. 1:21; Phil. 2:10; Heb. 1:4–6, 13). Jesus, as a result of his triumphant work, now sits on God's throne (2 Cor. 5:10; Heb. 1:3; 8:1; 12:2; cf. Rev. 22:1) at "God's right hand" thus sharing the sovereign Lord's rule, reign, and supremacy—far above all rule and authority and power and dominion (Rom. 9:5; Eph. 1:20–21; 4:10; Phil. 2:9–11; Heb. 1:3; 7:26). All this teaching presents Jesus "in the place that in the Old Testament and ancient Judaism belonged to God alone. . . . Jesus is utterly unique in this shared position. No one else shares God's throne and rules over all creation. That is because 'he with whom God shares his throne must be equal with God.'"[105]

---

[104]See the discussion of this in Bauckham, *Jesus and the God of Israel*, 18–25.
[105]Bowman and Komoszewski, *Putting Jesus in His Place*, 256. The authors also cite Martin Hengel, *Studies in Early Christology* (Edinburgh: T&T Clark, 1995), 225.

Divine worship. As in the entire New Testament, the apostolic writings teach that Jesus is to receive our worship, devotion, confidence, and trust that God alone demands and deserves. Throughout biblical history, the Jewish people recited the *Shema* (Deut. 6:4) twice daily. This foundational confession affirmed the existence of the one true and living God and entailed that he alone is the proper object of worship; to worship the creature rather than the Creator is blasphemy. The early church also shared this same sense of utter repulsion at the idea that a human being should be worshiped (cf. Acts 14:14–15; Rev. 19:10).

Against this background we must take seriously two astounding points. First, when Jesus was on earth, he received the praise and worship given to him without ever rebuking the persons who acted in this way (Matt. 14:33; 21:15–16; 28:9, 17; John 20:28; cf. 5:22–23). Second, after Jesus returned to heaven as the exalted Lord, praise and worship of him intensified (Eph. 5:19; Phil. 2:9–11; Heb. 1:6; cf. Rev. 5:11–12). John Stott nicely summarizes this evidence when he writes: "Nobody can call himself a Christian who does not worship Jesus. To worship him, if he is not God, is idolatry; to withhold worship from him, if he is, is apostasy."[106] In addition to the worship and devotion Jesus receives, he is also the addressee in prayer (Acts 1:24–25; 7:59–60; 9:10, 13; 22:17–19; 1 Cor. 1:2; 16:22; 2 Cor. 12:8; Rev. 22:20)[107] and the object of saving faith. The Old Testament repeatedly affirms that "salvation belongs to the LORD" (Jonah 2:9); "He only is . . . my salvation" (Ps. 62:2, 6); "On God rests my salvation and my glory" (Ps. 62:7).

However, when we turn to the New Testament, an additional object of saving faith is introduced, namely, the Son (see John 3:15–16; 14:1; Acts 3:16; 4:12; 10:43; 16:31; Rom. 10:12–13; 1 Cor. 1:2).[108] In fact, in the New Testament God the Father is held up somewhat infrequently as the object

---

[106]John R. W. Stott, *The Authentic Jesus* (London: Marshall, Morgan & Scott, 1985), 34. For an extensive treatment of the worship theme applied to Jesus in earliest Christianity see Larry W. Hurtado, *Lord Jesus Christ: Devotion to Jesus in Earliest Christianity* (Grand Rapids, MI: Eerdmans, 2003); cf. Bauckham, *Jesus and the God of Israel*, 127–81.

[107]All the formal prayers recorded in the New Testament are addressed to God the Father. But occasionally prayer was directed to Jesus himself by individuals and groups of Christians. In biblical thought, only if the person addressed in prayer was viewed as God would it be acceptable for human beings to make request of him for salvation, forgiveness, deliverance from evil, healing, providential guidance and protection, and security after death.

[108]Jesus is also presented as the object of the doxologies. A doxology is a formal ascription of praise, honor, glory, or blessings given to a divine person but never to a merely human figure. New Testament doxologies are regularly addressed to God, sometimes through Jesus Christ (Luke 2:14; Rom. 11:36; 2 Cor. 11:31; Gal. 1:5; Eph. 3:21; Phil. 4:20; 1 Tim. 1:17; 1 Pet. 5:11; Jude 24–25; Rev. 5:13; 7:12; Rom. 16:27a; 1 Pet. 4:11; Jude 25). But on at least four occasions a doxology is addressed directly to Christ (2 Tim. 4:18; 2 Pet. 3:18; Rev. 1:5–6; 5:13). This kind of evidence entails that the New Testament authors viewed Jesus as having equal status with God the Father.

of faith.[109] Why is this? As Murray Harris notes, "This is not because Jesus has displaced God the Father as the one we must trust, but because it is in Christ that God meets us in salvation. There are not two competing personal objects of saving faith. Only because Jesus is fully divine, intrinsically sharing God's nature and attributes, does he become a legitimate object of trust."[110] In this same context, it is crucial to note how Paul begins his letters: "Grace to you and peace from (*apo*) God our Father and the Lord Jesus Christ" (Rom. 1:7; 1 Cor. 1:3; 2 Cor. 1:2; Gal. 1:3; Eph. 1:2; Phil. 1:2; 1 Thess. 1:1; 2 Thess. 1:2; Phil. 1:2; 1 Tim. 1:2; 2 Tim. 1:2; Titus 1:4). By the use of the preposition (*apo*) before the Father and Son, Paul is affirming that the Father *and* the Son jointly form a single source of divine grace and peace. Of no mere human being could it be said that, together with God, he is the fount of spiritual blessing. Given Jewish monotheism, only if Paul regards Jesus as fully divine could he have spoken in this way.[111]

The Divine Acts and Works of the Son
As there is a vast amount of evidence in this category, let us divide it into two sections. First, as in our discussion of Colossians 1:15–20 and Hebrews 1:1–3, we discovered that the New Testament makes two incredible claims about the Son: he is the agent of creation and the universe's providential Lord. In biblical thought, it is only God who created the universe and now constantly sustains it (e.g., Genesis 1; Pss. 102:25; 104:24, 27, 30). The New Testament does not deny this (Rom. 1:18–23; 4:17; 11:36; Heb. 2:10; 11:3). However, now in light of Christ's coming, the New Testament presents those divine acts of creation and providence to be acts of the triune God: the Father, in and through the Son, by the Spirit (cf. John 1:3). A stronger affirmation of the deity of the Son would be hard to find.

Second, the New Testament attributes to the Son divine acts and works associated with the "age to come," the inauguration of *God's* kingdom, and the dawning of the new-covenant age.[112] As Wells rightly argues, it is within

---

[109]Harris, *Three Crucial Questions*, 77, 118, lists only twelve places where the Father is held up as the object of faith (see John 12:44; 14:1; Acts 16:34; Rom. 4:3, 5, 17, 24; Gal. 3:6; 1 Thess. 1:8; Titus 3:8; Heb. 6:1; 1 Pet. 1:21).
[110]Ibid., 77.
[111]This is further confirmed in 1 Thess. 3:11 and 2 Thess. 2:16–17. In the former we have two subjects (God and Jesus), yet remarkably the verb ("may . . . clear the way") is singular. In the latter, we have two subjects (God and Jesus), and each of the verbs—"loved, gave, encourage, strengthen" is singular. This does not show that Paul equated God with Jesus, as if they were the same person, but it does indicate that he assumed that Jesus equally shared the divine nature, so he could trace a single action to a single, unified source. Cf. ibid., 75–79.
[112]For a greater development of this point see the chapters in this volume on the deity of Christ in the Gospels.

this conceptual framework, namely, that of the eschatological "age to come," that the New Testament presents and interprets the identity of Jesus.[113] The only one who can usher in and inaugurate God's long-awaited rule and reign must be a divine person. The identity of the agent, instrument, and personifier of God's sovereign, eternal, saving rule is nothing less than the Lord, and in the New Testament, that Lord is Jesus. In this way, all the acts of Jesus associated with the dawning of the kingdom are *divine* acts, and thus are evidence that he is God the Son, now become incarnate. Which divine acts are particularly associated with the coming of the eschatological age, acts that are all attributed to Jesus? Here is a sample list:

1) *Jesus dispenses the promised eschatological Spirit.* The Old Testament is clear: the new-covenant age will be marked by God's giving of his Spirit (Joel 2:28–29; Ezek. 36:25–27; cf. John 3:1–10), which the Gospels say began in the ministry of Jesus, which Peter announces was fulfilled at Pentecost (Acts 2), and which the entire New Testament argues is completely dependent upon Jesus and his entire work (e.g., Acts 2:32–33; Romans 7–8; 1 Corinthians 2; 3:16–17; 2 Cor. 3; Gal. 3:14; 4:6; 4:21–6:10; Eph. 1:13–20; 2:18–22; 3:14–19; 4:1–16). Thus, in Jesus, not only has the rule/reign of God broken into this world, but in the pouring out of the Spirit at Pentecost, this event serves as proof that Jesus is both Christ *and Lord* (Acts 2:36).

2) *Jesus raises the dead and executes final judgment.* The ability to raise the dead and to execute judgment not only rests with God alone (Deut. 1:17; 1 Sam. 2:6; Jer. 25:31; Rom. 14:10) but is also associated with the dawning of the future age (Ezek. 36:25–27; 37; Dan. 12:2). The New Testament not only records three cases in which Jesus restored persons to physical life (Mark 5:21–24, 35–43; Luke 7:11–17; John 11:1–44), but, more importantly, it also presents Jesus as *the* resurrection and the life (John 11:25–26) and assigns to him the unique role of resurrection and judgment on the last day (John 5:21–23, 28–29; cf. 6:39–44, 54; Acts 10:42; 17:31; Rom. 14:10 with 2 Cor. 5:10). Thus, as God's Son, Jesus will raise and judge all persons (Matt. 7:22–23; 16:27) and those on whom he passes a verdict of condemnation will be eternally shut out from his presence (2 Thess. 1:8–9; cf. Matt. 7:23; 25:41).

3) *Jesus grants salvation and eternal life.* Only God can save us and grant eternal life, but in the New Testament these divine actions are done by Jesus (Mark 2:10; Acts 5:31; Col. 3:13). Perhaps this is most clearly seen in each of the three chapters of Titus, where exactly the same expression, "our Savior," is applied first to God (Titus 1:3; 2:10; 3:4) and then almost

---

[113]Wells, *Person of Christ*, 171–75.

immediately to Jesus (Titus 1:4; 2:13; 3:6). In addition, the intimate relationship between the Father and the Son can be seen in terms of these divine acts. For example, God the Father rescues us from the dominion of darkness (Col. 1:13), and the Son rescues us from the coming wrath (1 Thess. 1:10). Whether in John, which ties "eternal life" to Jesus (John 10:28; 17:2), or in the entire New Testament, which proclaims the work of the Son in accomplishing and effecting salvation, all these divine works underscore the utter uniqueness of the Son.

The Divine Names and Titles Applied to the Son

The New Testament attributes numerous titles to our Lord, all of which present him as God the Son incarnate. So, for example, the titles "Son," "Son of Man," and "Messiah" connote both Christ's deity and humanity. Probably the title that identifies Jesus most directly as God is the title "Lord" (*kurios*), but even it is used in the context of underscoring both his deity and humanity (see Phil. 2:6–11). There is one title, however—"God" (*theos*)—which *explicitly* identifies Jesus as God and is applied to him at least seven times in the New Testament (John 1:1, 18; 20:28; Rom. 9:5; Titus 2:13; 1 Pet. 1:1; Heb. 1:8). In John, this title is strategically placed, as it frames the entire prologue (John 1:1, 18) as well as the entire book (1:1; 20:28). In this way, John clearly teaches the deity of the Son which, in fact, explains why he has written the entire Gospel: "so that you may believe that Jesus is the Christ, the Son of God, and that by believing you may have life in his name" (20:31).[114] Much more could be said, but we limit our discussion of the divine names and titles applied to Jesus. Let us then briefly comment on each of the following four texts and see how they affirm in the strongest terms the full deity of the Son.[115]

Romans 9:5. In this text, Paul expresses deep anguish and sorrow for a majority of his fellow Jews because they have failed to embrace their Messiah in saving faith. To explain why his grief is so intense, Paul lists the incredible privileges of the Jewish people: "To them belong the adoption, the glory, the covenants, the giving of the law, the worship, and the promises" (v. 4). However, the consummate privilege, centered in Christ, is described in verse 5: "To them belong the patriarchs, and from their race, according to the flesh, is the Christ who is God over all (*ho ōn epi pantōn*

---

[114]For a discussion of the data in John's Gospel see Andreas Köstenberger's chapter "The Deity of Christ in John's Gospel" in this volume.

[115]For a complete treatment of all these texts see Murray J. Harris, *Jesus as God: The New Testament Use of* Theos *in Reference to Jesus* (Grand Rapids, MI: Baker, 1992).

theos), blessed forever. Amen."[116] Here Paul applies the title *theos*—normally a term that overwhelmingly refers to God the Father—directly to Christ and in doing so affirms at least two things about him—he is "over all" and "blessed forever"—and as such "Christ is a universal sovereign and the object of eternal adoration."[117] All this presents Jesus as sharing the divine name and nature and exercising divine functions.

Titus 2:13 and 2 Peter 1:1. These two texts make a similar claim even though they are written by different authors, namely, that Jesus Christ is "our God and Savior" (*tou theou hēmōn kai sōtēros*). Harris notes that in the first century, the formula "God and Savior" was a common religious expression used by both Palestinian and Diaspora Jews in reference to Yahweh, the one true God, and that the anarthrous *sōtēros* is best explained by viewing "God and Savior" as a title that applies to one person—Jesus Christ.[118] In this way, Paul and Peter both affirm that Jesus as "God and Savior" is more than a human being; he is nothing less than *God* the Son.

Hebrews 1:8–9. The author's overall purpose for the context of verses 4–14 is to demonstrate that Jesus is greater than angels. Angels, as creatures of God, were created to serve Yahweh (Heb. 1:7), but the Son himself is God (vv. 8–9). To ground his argument the author quotes Psalm 45:6–7, a psalm that in its original context celebrates the wedding of the Davidic king. As Hebrews applies the text to Christ, it does so by asserting that Jesus fulfills the promise of the Davidic covenant to be a king who rules forever.[119] In addition, the title "God" (*ho theos*) from the psalm is directly attributed to the Son thus presenting the Son not only as the human antitype of David but also as God himself.[120] In this way, the Son is presented as God the Son

---

[116]It is no doubt the case that the text can be punctuated in various ways. If one puts a semicolon or period after 5a, as do some editors of the Greek text, this has the effect of making the last part of the verse a doxology addressed to God the Father: "God who is over all be blessed for ever. Amen" (RSV). However, as most acknowledge today, this is not correct. The word order in Greek makes it much more natural to regard the final words of the verse as a description of or doxology to the Messiah, Jesus Christ (see NRSV). Importantly, in the most recent Greek New Testament texts (e.g., Nestle-Aland, 26th ed. and UBS, 4th ed.), the editors have punctuated the text in terms of the latter—"the Messiah, who is God over all, blessed forever." See the thorough treatment of these options in Harris, *Jesus as God*, 143–72; cf. Schreiner, *New Testament Theology*, 335–37.

[117]Harris, *Jesus as God*, 165.

[118]Ibid., 178–82, 232–34. In addition, the phrase "God and Savior" was a common formula in the Greco-Roman world, and it regularly refers to one deity in such formulas. There is no reason to think that Paul departs from this standard usage.

[119]It is notoriously difficult to determine how Hebrews reads and applies this text, in its Old Testament context, to Christ. For a full treatment of the issues surrounding Hebrews' use of Psalm 45 see Harris, *Jesus as God*, 205–27; Lane, *Hebrews 1–8*, 29–33.

[120]Once again see Harris, *Jesus as God*, 205–27.

incarnate, whom the Father, as a result of the Son's work, has exalted far above the angels as the exalted Lord.

Given that the title *theos* makes such a strong affirmation of the deity of Christ, some have wondered why it was not used more extensively in the New Testament. Why, for example, do we not find statements such as "Jesus is God" throughout the New Testament writings? Three important points need to be stressed that take us to the heart of New Testament christology. First, the use of *theos* in reference to Jesus *is* widely used in the New Testament and in key places. Not only do four different authors apply the title to Jesus (John, Paul, Peter, the author of Hebrews), but they do so consistently and purposefully.[121] As noted in John's Gospel, the title is strategically placed at the beginning and end of the book to underscore in the strongest terms the divine identity of the Son.

Second, the title is *not* used repeatedly because the identity of Jesus taught by the New Testament is that of God the Son in relation to his Father and the Spirit, thus preserving Trinitarian relations. The God of the Bible is a triune God, and repeated use of the title *theos* could lead to confusion. Normally in the New Testament, *theos* refers to God the Father, and in Trinitarian formulas "God" always denotes the Father, never the Son or the Spirit (e.g., 2 Cor. 13:14). The New Testament repeatedly distinguishes the Father, Son, and Spirit, while also affirming the full equality of each of the persons of the Godhead. That is why, in the salutations of many New Testament letters, "God" is distinguished from "the Lord Jesus." As a result of this distinction, *theos* virtually becomes a proper name for God the Father. Thus, if *theos* were used in reference to the Son as his proper name as well, linguistic ambiguity would emerge. For example, how could one make sense of 2 Corinthians 5:19: "God was in *God*, reconciling the world to himself." In order to preserve the personal distinctions within the Godhead, *theos* predominately denotes the Father and not the Son. Nowhere is this distinction more evident than where the Father is called "the God of our Lord Jesus Christ" (Eph. 1:17), or "his God and Father" (Rev. 1:6), and where Jesus speaks of "my God." The New Testament, then,

---

[121]The use of this title, depending on how we date the New Testament books, begins immediately after the resurrection in AD 30 (John 20:28), continues during the 50s (Rom. 9:5) and 60s (Titus 2:13; Heb. 1:8; 2 Pet. 1:1) and into the 90s (John 1:1, 18). Furthermore, the use of the title was not restricted to Christians who lived in one geographical region or who had a particular theological outlook. It occurs in literature that was written in Asia Minor (John, Titus), Greece (Romans), and possibly Judea (Hebrews) and Rome (2 Peter), and that was addressed to persons living in Asia Minor (John, 2 Peter), Rome (Romans, Hebrews), and Crete (Titus). Additionally, the title is found in a theological setting that is Jewish Christian (John, Hebrews, Peter) and Gentile Christian (Romans, Titus).

is very careful in how *theos* is applied to Jesus in order to underscore Trinitarian relations.

Third, in addition to preserving Trinitarian relations, the New Testament also wants to preserve the fact that Jesus is God the Son *incarnate*, thus safeguarding his humanity and the reality of the incarnation. If "God" had become a personal name for Christ, interchangeable with "Jesus," it is not hard to imagine that the humanity of Christ could be downplayed. For these reasons, we should not be surprised that *theos* is not used more often of Jesus. The very fact that it is used instead—not as a proper name but as a title and description to indicate the category to which he belongs, i.e., deity—is quite staggering and serves as explicit testimony to the divinity of Christ. Murray Harris summarizes the evidence this way:

> Jesus is not only God in revelation, the revealer of God (an official title)—he is God in essence. Not only are the deeds and words of Jesus the deeds and words of God—the nature of Jesus is the nature of God. By nature, as well as by action, Jesus is God. Thus, by nature and by action, Jesus is God. Other New Testament titles of Jesus, such as "Son of God" or "Lord" or "Alpha and Omega," imply the divinity of Jesus, but the title *God* explicitly affirms his deity.[122]

Concluding Reflections

In this chapter, we have sought to summarize some of the data that lead to the conclusion that the Jesus of the apostolic witness is *God* the Son incarnate. As other chapters have emphasized, questions surrounding the identity of the Christ of Scripture must never be reduced merely to academia, things only for exegetes and theologians to ponder. Rather these questions are a matter of urgency—indeed of life-and-death importance—for all. There are many beliefs that distinguish Christianity from other religious and philosophical worldviews but none as obvious and important as the person of Jesus the Christ. The claim of Scripture, whether in the Gospels or the entire apostolic witness, is that Jesus is the eternal Son, the second person of the Godhead, who in time took on our human nature in order

---

[122]Harris, *Three Crucial Questions*, 101. Harris also rightly notes that even though it is appropriate to say that "Jesus is God," it does go beyond the actual New Testament language. The nearest comparable statements are "the Word was God" (John 1:1) or "the only Son, who is God," (John 1:18), and so on. The theological proposition "Jesus is God" is a necessary and true inference from the New Testament evidence, but if we make it without qualification, we are in danger of failing to do justice to the whole truth about Jesus, namely that he is now the incarnate Word and that in his present existence in heaven he retains his humanity, although in a glorified state. Jesus, then, is neither simply "human" nor only "God," but God the Son incarnate, thus preserving Trinitarian relations and the reality of the incarnation.

to redeem a people for himself. This truth cannot be ignored, for in the end, precisely because of who he is and what he has done, Jesus not only deserves all of our commitment, obedience, trust, worship, and affection; he also rightly demands it as our Lord and God.

6

The Deity of Christ in John's Letters and the Book of Revelation

ANDREAS J. KÖSTENBERGER

The chapter on the deity of Christ in John's Gospel has furnished abundant demonstration that Jesus is presented as God in the Gospel John wrote. It is the task of the present chapter to investigate John's letters and the book of Revelation, extending the scope of our investigation to the remaining portions of the Johannine corpus in the New Testament. In our treatment of John's letters, we will focus on 1 John and make passing reference to two relevant passages in 2 John 3 and 7. The discussion of the deity of Christ in the book of Revelation will focus on the depiction of Jesus in terms of deity within the larger context of the christology of Revelation. As will be seen, the portrayal of Jesus in John's letters is predicated upon John's message regarding Jesus in the Gospel, while Revelation extends the scope from Jesus' first coming to his future glorious return.[1]

---

[1] It will not be possible here to discuss matters of authorship related to John's letters and Revelation. For detailed treatments see Andreas J. Köstenberger, L. Scott Kellum, and Charles L. Quarles, *The Cradle, the Cross, and the Crown: An Introduction to the New Testament* (Nashville, TN: Broadman, 2009), chaps. 19–20.

151

The Deity of Christ in John's Letters

Occasion and Purpose

Most likely, John's first letter was written because of a concern that some in the congregation(s) to which the letter is addressed had departed from the apostolic message that they had heard "from the beginning" (2:24; cf. 1:1–4). Consequently, John reiterated the importance of remaining in the original teaching regarding Jesus rather than "going on ahead" and failing to "abide in the teaching of Christ" (2 John 9; cf. 1 John 2:24). Apparently, some false teachers had arisen from within the congregation, challenging John's original message regarding Christ, and these false teachers had only recently left the church (1 John 2:19).

In the wake of the departure of these secessionists, John's purpose seems to have been to reassure those remaining in the congregation of their standing in Christ. Believers are assured that they had "been anointed by the Holy One" (2:20; cf. 2:27), i.e., they had received the Holy Spirit. They are also assured that they "all have knowledge" (2:20), contrary to the false teachers' claim that they alone had special knowledge pertaining to God and how to experience fullness of spiritual communion with him with no need for anyone to teach them (i.e., teach them a message that was different from the original apostolic message; 2:27). John's reassuring message in the book culminates at the end of his letter where the recipients are told, "I write these things to you who believe in the name of the Son of God that you may know that you have eternal life" (5:13).

Scholarship on the likely background of John's first letter has frequently focused on rather conjectural reconstructions of the setting based on an alleged Gnostic backdrop, often by way of "mirror-reading" certain passages in 1 John. While full-fledged Gnosticism is now widely acknowledged as having coalesced only at some point in the second century of the Christian era, some have contended that an earlier form of gnostic thought was already present at the time 1 John was written and that this incipient Gnosticism led to a distortion of the apostolic teaching regarding Christ. These efforts, for their part, were frequently grounded in references to affirmations or denials of Jesus "having come in the flesh" (4:2; cf. 2 John 7). However, it may be preferable to see John's first letter as standing in essential continuity with John's Gospel, whose purpose was bound up with the demonstration that "Jesus is the Christ, the Son of God" (20:31).[2]

---

[2]See Daniel R. Streett, "'They Went Out from Us': The Identity of the Opponents in First John," PhD dissertation, Wake Forest, NC: Southeastern Baptist Theological Seminary (2008).

If so, John's concern in 1 and 2 John would likewise have been to affirm that Jesus was the Christ, the Son of God (1 John 2:22; 4:15; 5:1, 5, 10, 13), assuring believers of their possession of eternal life in Jesus. References to confessing—or denying—Jesus as "having come in the flesh," for their part, would then constitute a mere shorthand for confessing Jesus and the totality of his earthly, messianic ministry as narrated in the Gospel.[3] If this reading of the evidence is at least approximately on target, John's letters should be understood as calling believers back to the essential message of the Gospel regarding Jesus.

Relevant References to Christ's Deity in John's Letters

The prologue of 1 John. In keeping with the sketch of the occasion and purpose for John's writing of 1 John, the following brief discussion of references to Christ's deity in John's letters will have to suffice. To begin with, the prologue of 1 John makes reference to Jesus as "the word of life" (1:1) that "was with the Father"—asserting Jesus' preexistence in terms similar to the introduction to the Gospel—and that "was made manifest to us" (1:2). The prologue of 1 John also links Jesus with God the Father and includes Father-Son language familiar to us from the Gospel (1:3–4; cf. 2 John 3).

The occasion: the departure of the secessionists (1:5–2:27). In what follows, John initially focuses on the cleansing power of Jesus, God's Son (1:7), and his role as believers' advocate (*paraklētos*) with God the Father, referring to Jesus as "Jesus Christ the righteous" (2:1–2). Jesus' atoning work is described as rendering propitiation for the sins of the whole world (2:2), presumably a polemic reference against the false teachers who construed the scope of God's saving activity more narrowly.[4] In additional sharp polemical references to the secessionists, John links a proper confession of the Son to a confession of the Father (2:23); stresses the importance of remaining in the Son and in the Father (2:24); and identifies the denial of Jesus as the Christ as prompted by the spirit of the antichrist (2:22), which characterized the false teachers who had by then departed (2:18–19; see also 4:2–3). In this application of the message of John's Gospel, and in defense against misrepresentation by the secessionists, John drove home even more strongly

---

[3]See in this context the reference to Jesus as having come "by the water and the blood" in 1 John 5:6, most likely a reference to Jesus' baptism and crucifixion, respectively, encompassing as the beginning and end points the totality of Jesus' earthly ministry. See Robert W. Yarbrough, *1–3 John*, BECNT (Grand Rapids, MI: Baker, 2008), 282–83.

[4]For a thorough discussion of 1 John 2:2, see Yarbrough, *1–3 John*, 77–81.

the inextricable unity between God the Father and Jesus Christ his Son as indispensable for true believers' orthodox confession.[5]

The message: love one another (2:28–3:24). The second major unit of 1 John starts out with a reference to Jesus' second coming, exhorting believers to "abide in him, so that when he appears we may have confidence and not shrink from him in shame at his coming" (2:28). Obviously, the expectation of Jesus' return is predicated upon the belief that Jesus rose from the dead subsequent to his crucifixion. Thus this reference entails belief in Jesus' deity as amply asserted in the Gospel and prepares the way for the message of the book of Revelation, which is taken up largely with the circumstances surrounding Jesus' return.

The remaining references to the purpose and nature of Jesus' first coming in this section almost entirely reiterate similar statements in the Gospel. Thus, it is said that Jesus the Son of God appeared in order to destroy the Devil's works, who sinned "from the beginning" (3:8; cf. John 8:39–47).[6] In this 1 John shares in the worldview underlying John's Gospel, portraying Jesus' coming as part of a cosmic drama and cosmic conflict between God and Jesus on the one hand and Satan or the Devil on the other.[7] The Devil, in turn, is behind the spirit of the antichrist (2:16, 22; 4:3) and the spirit of error (4:6) leading John's opponents to deny that Jesus is the Christ and Son of God.

Also, John told his readers that Jesus laid down his life for believers (3:16), again echoing similar language in the Gospel (see esp. John 15:13). This invokes the image of Jesus as the good shepherd who lays down his life for his sheep (cf. John 10), which, in turn, brings into play the messianic notion of Jesus as the Son of David (cf. Ezekiel 35–36). Thus, for John, Jesus' identity and work cannot be separated. As the Christ and Son of God, Jesus offered vicarious, substitutionary atonement for believers, so that by believing in Jesus they can have their sins forgiven and receive eternal life.

Testing the spirits and overcoming the world (4:1–5:12). In this third and final major section of his first letter, John enjoins believers to "test the spirits to see whether they are from God" (1 John 4:1). The simple test is

---

[5]Note that 1 John 2:22 states the converse of John's purpose as articulated in John 20:31. On the notion of orthodoxy in first-century Christianity, see Andreas J. Köstenberger and Michael J. Kruger, *The Heresy of Orthodoxy: How Contemporary Culture's Fascination with Diversity Has Reshaped Our Understanding of Early Christianity* (Wheaton, IL: Crossway, 2010).

[6]Note the possible implied contrast between the Devil, who sinned "from the beginning," and "that which was from the beginning"—i.e., Jesus Christ (1:1)—and the apostolic message concerning him that the congregation had heard "from the beginning" (2:24). See Yarbrough, *1–3 John*, 33–36.

[7]See chap. 11 in Andreas J. Köstenberger, *The Theology of John's Gospel and Letters*, BTNT (Grand Rapids, MI: Zondervan, 2009).

that every spirit that confesses that "Jesus Christ has come in the flesh" is from God, while every spirit that denies Jesus is not from God (4:2–3). As mentioned, this confession of Jesus "come in the flesh" seems equivalent to the acknowledgment of Jesus as the Christ, the Son of God (cf. 4:15; 5:1, 5, 10; cf. John 20:31).

Again, John's assertion that the Father sent the Son to be the Savior of the world in 1 John 4:14 echoes similar language in John's Gospel (4:42). The reference to Jesus as having come by water and blood, as noted, likewise focuses on the totality of Jesus' earthly ministry, from his baptism to his crucifixion (1 John 5:6–8). The section closes with an affirmation that eternal life is exclusively found in God's Son, Jesus Christ (5:11–12).

Purpose statement and conclusion (5:13–21). John closes his letter by, first, stating his purpose, that is, assuring those who believe in the name of the Son of God that they have eternal life (5:13). The most direct assertion of Jesus' deity is in all probability found in the penultimate verse of 1 John where "the Son of God," "his Son Jesus Christ," is said to be "the true God and eternal life" (5:20).[8] While some have disputed that reference is here made to the deity of Christ, the Greek syntax of the passage seems not only to allow for this but to make it likely.[9] In particular, as Daniel Wallace points out, of the approximately seventy instances in John's Gospel and letters in which *houtos* has a personal referent, at least two-thirds refer to the Son, while not a single one refers to the Father.[10] Thus the consistent linkage between God the Father and Jesus the Son culminates in a striking affirmation that not only God the Father, but also Jesus his Son, is "the true God."[11]

---

[8]Yarbrough, *1–3 John*, 329, citing Westcott, here speaks of John "striving for effect that is elegant and doxological in substance if not in literary form."

[9]See Daniel B. Wallace, *Granville Sharp's Canon and Its Kin: Semantics and Significance*, Studies in Biblical Greek 14 (New York: Lang, 2009), chap. 13, who after sustained technical discussion concludes that "1 John ends with an affirmation of Jesus Christ as the true God and eternal life" (277). See also Daniel B. Wallace, *Greek Grammar Beyond the Basics* (Grand Rapids, MI: Zondervan, 1996), 327; and Yarbrough, *1–3 John*, 320, with reference to Rudolf Schnackenburg, *The Johannine Epistles*, trans. Reginald and Ilse Fuller (New York: Crossroad, 1992), 262; and Gerald S. Sloyan, *Walking in the Truth: Perseverers and Deserters: The First, Second, and Third Letters of John* (Valley Forge, PA: Trinity, 1995), 59. Contra Murray J. Harris, *Jesus as God: The New Testament Use of* Theos *in Reference to Jesus* (Grand Rapids, MI: Baker, 1992), 239–53, who concludes that while "it is certainly possible that ou-toj refers back to Jesus Christ, several converging lines of evidence point to 'the true one,' God the Father, as the probable antecedent."

[10]Wallace, *Granville Sharp's Canon*, 277.

[11]The language echoes John 17:3, where Jesus in his final prayer refers to God the Father as "the only true God." Remarkably, in 1 John, the same language is applied to Jesus. A similar climax is

The Deity of Christ in the Book of Revelation

The Nature of the Book: Its Genre, Historical Setting, and Literary Structure

The book of Revelation was written in the form of a prophetic-apocalyptic letter.[12] Apocalyptic involves the frequent use of symbolism,[13] while the prophetic component entails speaking both to the present state of the churches and to future events that will ensue at the end of time.[14] The book's content is conveyed within an epistolary framework where the seer, John, is identified as the author (1:4; cf. 1:9–10) and the seven churches in Asia Minor as the primary recipients of the work (1:4; cf. chaps. 2–3). In light of this, the interpretation of Revelation must take into account the late first-century setting of the book and understand its contents in terms that would have made sense to its original recipients.

One major aspect of the historical backdrop for the book is the Roman emperor cult.[15] While initially deity was ascribed to a given emperor subsequent to his death,[16] in due course some emperors demanded they be worshiped as divine even while they were still living. Most likely, Revelation was written during the reign of Domitian (AD 81–96), who arrogated the title *dominus et deus noster* ("our Lord and God"; Suetonius, *Dom.* 13.2). Apart from Caligula's excessive claims to deity, Domitian was the first Roman emperor to use, and even require, the title *deus*, a practice denounced by his critics. Against this backdrop, it is profoundly countercultural when God is worshiped in 4:11 as "our Lord and God."

---

found in John's Gospel, where Jesus' deity is affirmed at its literary peak in 20:28 (see the discussion of this passage in the chapter in this volume on John's Gospel).

[12]See George E. Ladd, "Why Not Prophetic-Apocalyptic?" *JBL* 76 (1957): 192–200.

[13]See the classic definition in John J. Collins, "Introduction: Towards the Morphology of a Genre," *Semeia* 14 (1979): 9, and the amended definition in Adela Yarbro Collins, "Introduction: Early Christian Apocalypticism," *Semeia* 36 (1986): 7 (both reproduced in Köstenberger et al., *Cradle, the Cross, and the Crown*, 831–32).

[14]Note the global references to revelation in terms of "the words of this prophecy" at the beginning and the end of the book (1:3; 22:7, 10, 18–19).

[15]See esp. J. Nelson Kraybill, *Imperial Cult and Commerce in John's Apocalypse*, JSNTSup 132 (Sheffield: Sheffield Academic Press, 1996); and Colin J. Hemer, *The Letters to the Seven Churches of Asia in Their Local Setting*, JSNTSup 11 (Sheffield: Sheffield Academic Press, 1986). For a brief description, with additional bibliographic references, see Köstenberger et al., *The Cradle, the Cross, and the Crown*, 85, 817. See also David A. deSilva, "Ruler Cult," in *Dictionary of New Testament Background*, ed. Craig A. Evans and Stanley E. Porter (Downers Grove, IL: InterVarsity, 2000), 1026–30; and Everett Ferguson, *Backgrounds of Early Christianity*, 2nd ed. (Grand Rapids, MI: Eerdmans, 1993), 30–39.

[16]Thus, in 42 BC, the Roman senate declared Julius Caesar, who had been assassinated in 44 BC, *divius Iulius* ("divine Julius"). Octavian, his successor, was called *divi filius* ("son of a divine being"). See David E. Aune, *Revelation*, 3 vols., WBC 52 (Nashville, TN: Nelson, 1997–1998), 1.310.

In keeping with its apocalyptic genre, Revelation contains four visions John saw, each of which is introduced by the phrase "in the Spirit" (*en pneumatic*; 1:10; 4:2; 17:3; 21:10).[17] Each vision sets the seer in a different location. The scene shifts from Patmos (1:9) to the heavenly throne room (4:1–2), to a desert (17:3), and to a high mountain (21:10).[18] In the first vision, John beholds images of the glorified Christ examining his churches (1:10–3:22). In the second vision, he witnesses the divine court proceedings against, and judgment of, the nations (chaps. 4–16). In the third vision, he sees the sentencing and destruction of "Babylon" (17:1–21:8). The fourth vision presents the vindication and reward of believers in the new heaven and new earth (21:9–22:4).

The Depiction of Christ in Terms Suggesting Deity

The Trinitarian framework of Revelation. Jesus Christ is the primary subject of John's revelation (1:1), and his return to earth as the victorious messianic king is the main message of the book.[19] From the very beginning, the glorified Jesus is presented within a Trinitarian framework:

> Grace to you and peace
> from him who is and who was and who is to come,
> and from the seven Spirits who are before his throne,
> and from Jesus Christ the faithful witness, the firstborn
> of the dead,
> and the ruler of kings on earth. (1:4–5)

As Richard Bauckham observes, this opening salutation "places Jesus Christ with God on the divine side of the distinction between the divine Giver of blessings and the creaturely recipients of blessings. It shows how naturally early Christians implicitly included Jesus in the divine, because he was the source of the salvation that comes from God to humans, even if they had no way of conceptualizing in ontological terms the relation of Jesus to God."[20] As Bauckham continues:

---

[17]See Richard Bauckham, *The Theology of the Book of Revelation*, New Testament Theology (Cambridge: Cambridge University Press, 1993), chap. 5. Note also the phrase "I will show you" (*deixō soi*) three times in close proximity to *en pneumati* (4:1; 17:1; 21:9).

[18]Merrill C. Tenney, *Interpreting Revelation* (Grand Rapids, MI: Eerdmans, 1957), 33. See also George E. Ladd, *A Commentary on the Revelation of John* (Grand Rapids, MI: Eerdmans, 1972), 14.

[19]For a helpful summary of the major theological themes in the book of Revelation, see Grant R. Osborne, *Revelation*, BECNT (Grand Rapids, MI: Baker, 2002), 31–49.

[20]Bauckham, *Theology*, 23.

John has reflected creatively on the Christian understanding of the divine. Far from taking over unreflectively conventional early Christian ways of speaking of God, Christ and the Spirit, he has forged his own distinctive forms of God-language, not, of course, *de novo*, but by creative use of the resources of Jewish and Jewish Christian tradition. His book is the product of a highly reflective consciousness of God.[21]

Jesus as the "one who was pierced" and as the glorious Son of Man. In a highly programmatic passage in the opening christological section of the book, Christ is identified as the one who, in keeping with eschatological expectations, will return at the end of time to bring both salvation and judgment (1:7, a conflation of Dan. 7:13 and Zech. 12:10).[22] Against the backdrop of these passages, John identifies Jesus as the glorious Son of Man who receives authority to judge the nations (Dan. 7:13) and as the pierced Son whose appearance will strike terror among God's enemies (Zech. 12:10).[23]

Remarkably, in the original context of Zechariah 12:10, it is none other than Yahweh himself who is pierced ("they look on me, on him whom they have pierced"), not by the nations but by "the house of David and the inhabitants of Jerusalem."[24] The piercing is in all likelihood a literal, actual killing, resulting in extraordinary grief owing to the uniqueness of the individual ("as one mourns for an only child . . . as one weeps over a firstborn"). In the depiction of Jesus as the one who was pierced, John closely associates him with Yahweh, revealing that he conceived of Christ's identity as sharing in the identity of God. As I have written elsewhere:

The notion of the "piercing of Yahweh" in Zech. 12:10 suggests that the suffering is not an unfamiliar experience to God, but that he knows it firsthand. This clearly constitutes a mystery that can be understood more fully only in light of the incarnation and crucifixion of the Word-become-flesh, Jesus, who, as the God-man, was pierced for our transgressions as the messianic

---

[21] Ibid., 24.

[22] G. K. Beale, *The Book of Revelation*, NIGTC (Grand Rapids, MI: Eerdmans, 1999), 196; cf. Robert H. Mounce, *The Book of Revelation*, rev. ed., NICNT (Grand Rapids, MI: Eerdmans, 1997), 73. For a major study of the christology of the Apocalypse, see Traugott Holtz, *Die Christologie der Apokalypse des Johannes*, TUGAL 85 (Berlin: Akademie, 1962).

[23] See the depiction of Jesus as the Son of Man in John's Gospel and the quotation of Zech. 12:10 in John 19:37, on which see Andreas J. Köstenberger, "John," in *Commentary on the New Testament Use of the Old Testament*, ed. G. K. Beale and D. A. Carson (Grand Rapids, MI: Baker, 2007), 504–6. See also G. K. Beale and Sean M. McDonough, "Revelation," in ibid., 1090–91.

[24] In context, the phrase "on me" can refer only to Yahweh himself. See, e.g., Thomas E. McComiskey, "Zechariah," in *The Minor Prophets: An Exegetical and Expository Commentary* (Grand Rapids, MI: Baker, 1998), 3.1214. See the discussion in Köstenberger, "John," 504.

shepherd and the suffering servant in keeping with the pattern of Old Testament prophecy regarding a suffering Savior.[25]

The first and the last. Another major way in which deity is attributed to Christ in the book of Revelation is by the epithet "the first and the last."[26] Both at the beginning and the end of the book, there is a striking parallelism between the descriptions of Christ and Yahweh.

**Fig. 6.1: The Depictions of Christ and Yahweh
as "The First and the Last" in Revelation**

Person	Self-Identification	Reference
Introduction:		
Yahweh:	"I am the Alpha and the Omega."	1:8
Christ:	"I am the first and the last."	1:17
Conclusion:		
Yahweh:	"I am the Alpha and the Omega, the beginning and the end."	21:6
Christ:	"I am the Alpha and the Omega, the first and the last, the beginning and the end."	22:13

The designation "the first and the last" itself is drawn from Isaiah 44:6 and 48:12, where Yahweh is identified as the creator and redeemer. As "the first and the last," God is shown to be the one who "precedes and originates all things as their Creator" and who "will bring all things to their eschatological fulfillment."[27] As Bauckham observes, "The titles cannot mean anything else when they are used of Christ in 22:13." He continues:

Although it might initially seem that God and Christ are in some way distinguished by the two different self-declarations in 1:8 and 1:17, in 22:13 the placing of the title which is used only of Christ ("the first and the last") between those which have hitherto been used only of God seems deliberately to align all three as equivalent. Moreover, since the title, "the first and the last," is the one that occurs in divine self-declarations in Deutero-Isaiah (Isa. 44:6; 48:12), with very much the significance that the other two titles have in Revelation, it would be very odd if precisely this one meant something different from the others in Revelation.[28]

Bauckham also demonstrates that these interrelated portrayals of Christ and Yahweh are part of a chiastic pattern that is almost certainly deliberate (*Fig. 6.2*).

[25]Köstenberger, "John," 504.
[26]See Bauckham, *Theology*, 25–26.
[27]Ibid., 55.
[28]Ibid.

Fig. 6.2: The Chiastic Pattern of the Portrayals of Christ and Yahweh in Revelation as "First and Last"[29]

A	B	B'	A
1:8	1:17	21:6	22:13
End of prologue	Beginning of vision	End of vision	Beginning of epilogue
Yahweh	Christ	Yahweh	Christ
Alpha and Omega		Alpha and Omega	Alpha and Omega
	First and last		First and last
		Beginning and end	Beginning and end
Parousia	New life	New life	Parousia

As Bauckham observes, the significance of this pattern is that according to John, "it is in Christ's parousia that God who is the beginning of all things will also become the end of all things. It is the eschatological life that Christ entered at his resurrection that all the redeemed creation will share in God's new creation."[30] Yet "the identification of Christ with Yahweh implied by the titles is not the result of an adoptionist christology, in which the mere man Jesus is exalted at his resurrection to divine status. Important as the resurrection is for Christ's participation in God's lordship (cf. 2:28; 3:21), these titles he shares with God indicate that he shared the eternal being of God from before creation."[31]

In light of these observations, the application of the title "the first and the last" to Christ in the book of Revelation is indicative of a very high christology and presents Jesus unequivocally as taken up into the identity of none other than Yahweh himself.[32] By using the very epithet applied to Yahweh in Isaiah 44:6, where he declares, "I am the first and I am the last; besides me there is no god," and applying it to the glorified Christ in Revelation, John "does not designate him a second god, but includes him in the eternal being of the one God of Israel who is the only source and god of all things."[33]

The eschatological king and judge and the divine warrior. The book of Revelation prophetically portrays the glorified and exalted Christ as the eschatological judge and king by way of three christophanies (1:12–18; 5:1–14; 19:11–21).[34] The first of these in chapter 1 presents Jesus as the

---

[29]Adapted from ibid., 57. See Bauckham's entire discussion on pp. 55–58.
[30]Ibid., 58.
[31]Ibid.
[32]See the section "John's Teaching on Jesus as God and First-Century Jewish Monotheism" in the chapter "The Deity of Christ in John's Gospel" in this volume, pp. 92.
[33]Bauckham, *Theology*, 58.
[34]I am indebted to Alan S. Bandy for a few of the observations in the discussion below.

faithful witness; the paradigmatic martyr; the firstborn from the dead who is preeminent in his church; and the ruler of the kings of the earth, fulfilling Jewish messianic expectations (cf. 1:5). John's ensuing visionary description of the Son of Man highlights certain characteristics of Christ's appearance, borrowing images from a variety of Old Testament texts, all of which emphasize his role in judgment.[35]

The christophany of chapter 5 portrays Jesus as the lion-turned-lamb (*to arnion*; see 1:5–7; 5:5; 12:11; 13:8; etc.; cf. Gen. 49:9), an image that combines paschal imagery with the notion of the warrior-lamb prominent in apocalyptic literature.[36] The purpose of this scene is to depict the appointment of Christ as the Davidic king and end-time judge who alone is worthy to pronounce God's judgment upon humanity. The scene represents the inauguration of Jesus' eternal reign at the right hand of God.[37]

Apart from the christophany of chapter 1 and the image of the lion-turned-lamb, perhaps the most powerful depiction of Christ in Revelation is that of the rider on a white horse who is called "faithful" and "true" (chap. 19). In the christological culmination of the book, Jesus returns as the rightful king and divine warrior.[38] The imagery of riding a white horse was the common Roman symbol for the emperor who had triumphed over his enemies.[39] The diadems on Christ's head signify that his cosmic sovereignty surpasses all other earthly claims to authority (cf. 12:3; 13:1).[40]

At his return, Christ is accompanied by an army of believers whom he has redeemed to constitute his kingdom (cf. 1:6).[41] The fact that he will rule over his domain with an iron scepter authenticates him as the true messianic king (cf. Ps. 2:9; Isa. 11:4). The name engraved on his thigh attests that he is king and Lord over all (cf. 1:5; 17:14). Christ comes to wage a just war

---

[35] As George B. Caird, *The Revelation of St. John*, BNTC (Peabody, MA: Hendrickson, 1966), 25–26, rightly notes, one must not simply compile a list of allusions so as to "unweave the rainbow," because John paints a composite portrait rather than a piecemeal collage.

[36] Compare the reference to Jesus as the "Lamb (*amnos*) of God" in John 1:29, 36, on which see the discussion in Andreas J. Köstenberger, *John*, BECNT (Grand Rapids, MI: Baker, 2004), 66–68. For a helpful study of Jesus as the Lamb in the Apocalypse, see Peter Stuhlmacher, "Das Lamm Gottes—eine Skizze," in *Geschichte–Tradition–Reflexion: Festschrift für Martin Hengel zum 70. Geburtstag*, vol. 3: *Frühes Christentum*, ed. Hermann Lichtenberger (Tübingen: Mohr-Siebeck, 1996), 529–42.

[37] On the enthronement of Christ, see Holtz, *Christologie der Apokalypse*, 27–54; Aune, *Revelation*, 1.332–35; Ranko Stefanović, *The Background and Meaning of the Sealed Book of Revelation 5*, AUSS Doctoral Dissertation Series 22 (Berrien Springs, MI: Andrews University Press, 1996), 206–17.

[38] Osborne, *Revelation*, 678–79.

[39] Aune, *Revelation*, 3.1050–51.

[40] Caird, *Revelation of St. John*, 241; Gerhard A. Krodel, *Revelation* (Minneapolis: Augsburg, 1989), 321; Beale, *Book of Revelation*, 954.

[41] Although believers come as a messianic army, Christ alone is the one who executes the battle.

against the beast's kingdom in order to exact vengeance for the unjust war the beast waged against believers (13:7). Two images from the inaugural vision of Christ reappear: blazing eyes, denoting judicial insight, and a sword proceeding from Jesus' mouth, conveying the penetrating nature of his pronouncements (cf. *4 Ezra* 13:9–13).

Finally, Jesus is depicted as the divine warrior whose robe is soaked with blood from treading the winepress of the fury of God's wrath (see 19:13, 15; cf. 14:19–20).[42] The blood on Jesus' robe is that of his victims (cf. Isa. 63:2–6). The great and final battle constitutes a slaughter that ends as soon as it begins (19:17–21). The beast and the earth's kings amass their forces in a deluded attempt to attack the coming messianic king (cf. 16:13–16).[43] Despite the boasts of the beast and the false prophet, they are quickly captured and thrown into the fiery lake (19:20); the rest die instantly at the spoken word of Christ (19:21). Christ thus effectively conquers all the kingdoms of the earth and subjects them to his rule.

The worship of Jesus. The book of Revelation is supremely concerned with the difference between true and false worship.[44] When dealing with other religions, the book is highly relevant with regard to the nature and proper object of worship and concerning the meaning of martyrdom and believers' future hope. According to the theology of Revelation, it is ultimately Satan himself who stands behind the forces conspiring against Christians.[45] Worship occupies a place at the center of the struggle between believers and Satan as it is played out in the arena of the imperial cult versus faithful allegiance to Christ.[46]

---

[42]Cf. Joel 3:12–13; *1 En.* 100:3; *4 Ezra* 15:35–36. See Aune, *Revelation*, 2.847; Richard Bauckham, *The Climax of Prophecy: Studies on the Book of Revelation* (London: T&T Clark, 1993), 40–48.

[43]See Ps. 2:1–3; Ezek. 38:14–16; 39:1–6; Joel 3:2; Zech. 12:1–9; 14:2; cf. *1 Enoch* 56:5–6; 90:13–19; 99:4; *2 Bar.* 48:37; 70:7; *4 Ezra* 13:33–38; *Jub.* 23:23; *Sib. Or.* 3.663–68; *Pss. Sol.* 2:1–2; 17:22–23; 1QM 1:10–11. See Aune, *Revelation*, 3.1064.

[44]See Andreas J. Köstenberger, "The Contribution of the General Epistles and Revelation," in *Christianity and the Religions: A Biblical Theology of World Religions*, Evangelical Missiological Society Series 2, ed. Edward Rommen and Harold Netland (Pasadena, CA: William Carey Library, 1995), 133–35. On the worship of Jesus in Revelation, see Richard Bauckham, "The Worship of Jesus in Apocalyptic Christianity," *NTS* 27 (1980–81): 322–41; revised as chap. 4: "The Worship of Jesus" in Richard Bauckham, *Climax of Prophecy*; Richard Bauckham, *Theology*, 58–63; Richard Bauckham, "Jesus, Worship of," in David Noel Freedman, ed., *ABD* (Garden City, NY: Doubleday, 1992), 3.812–19; Larry W. Hurtado, *Lord Jesus Christ: Devotion to Jesus in Earliest Christianity* (Grand Rapids, MI: Eerdmans, 2003); and Osborne, *Revelation*, 46–49.

[45]See the discussion of the cosmic conflict motif in John's Gospel in the chapter "The Deity of Christ in John's Gospel" in this volume.

[46]Except for Hebrews, the Apocalypse is perhaps the most liturgical book of the New Testament. See J. Massyngberde Ford, "The Christological Function of the Hymns in the Apocalypse of John," *AUSS* 36 (1998): 207.

John's assertion of the deity of Christ in the context of the worship motif in Revelation comes to the fore most clearly in the scene of heavenly worship in chapters 4 and 5. In chapter 4, the center and object of worship is Yahweh, the creator (see esp. 4:11), who is paid homage by the heavenly court. In chapter 5, it is the Lamb, that is, Christ, the one who has conquered on account of his death and resurrection and who is depicted as standing on the divine throne (see 5:6; cf. 7:17), who becomes the center of heavenly worship by the living creatures and the elders (5:8). In addition, myriads of angels and all of creation join in and worship the Lamb (5:12–13).

The import of these parallel scenes of worship of Yahweh and Christ is clear: "John does not wish to represent Jesus as an alternative object of worship alongside God, but as one who shares in the glory due to God. He is worthy of divine worship because his worship can be included in the worship of the one God."[47] What is more, as Bauckham keenly observes, while John presents both Christ and Yahweh as proper objects of worship, John avoids referring to them as a plurality.[48] While placing Christ on the divine side of the God-creation divide, John is careful not to speak of Christ and Yahweh in a way that seems to advocate polytheism.

Another remarkable instance of John's portrayal of Christ in terms of deity deserving to be worshiped is the doxology with reference to Jesus, which is part of the greeting to the seven churches at the outset of the entire book of Revelation:

> To him who loves us and has freed us from our sins by his blood and made us a kingdom, priests to his God and Father, to him be glory and dominion forever and ever. Amen. (1:5b–6; cf. 2 Tim. 4:18; 2 Pet. 3:18)

Doxologies, by their very nature, were addressed to the one God who alone is worthy of eternal glory and worship. Bauckham draws the only possible conclusion: "There could be no clearer way of ascribing to Jesus the worship due to God."[49]

Also, especially in John's fourth and final vision (21:10–22:5), worship of Yahweh and of the Lamb is repeatedly mentioned in a turn of phrase in which the two figures, in the context of worship, are inextricably intertwined. John notes that he saw no temple in the heavenly city, "for its temple is the

---

[47]Bauckham, *Theology*, 60. See also Andreas J. Köstenberger, "The Glory of God in John's Gospel and Revelation," in *The Glory of God*, Theology in Community 2, ed. Christopher W. Morgan and Robert A. Peterson (Wheaton, IL: Crossway, 2010).

[48]Bauckham, *Theology*, 60–61.

[49]Ibid., 61.

Lord God the Almighty and the Lamb" (21:22).[50] He elaborates that it is the glory of God that illumines the city, "and its lamp is the Lamb" (21:23). Then John is shown by the angel the river of the water of life "flowing from the throne of God and of the Lamb" (22:1). Finally, it is said that "the throne of God and of the Lamb" will be in the city, "and his servants will worship him" (22:3).[51] Thus for John, in the eternal state, worship of Yahweh and Christ will be all but indistinguishable.

The worship of Yahweh and Christ, in turn, is set within the larger framework of the imperial cult, allusions to which occur frequently especially in the latter half of the second vision.[52] John envisions a time when the imperial cult escalates to the point of mandatory participation by all inhabitants of earth.[53] The term *proskyneō* ("worship"), used in direct connection with the beast (13:4, 8, 12, 15), was commonly employed in conjunction with the imperial cult.[54] Christians refusing to bow down in worship to the beast incur his wrath and are summarily executed (13:15). They are exhorted to remain faithful and true to Christ even if their witness results in martyrdom (2:10, 13; 13:10; 14:12; 17:14) and are assured that at the end of time God will vindicate them by judging those who chose to worship the beast (14:9, 11; 16:2).[55]

The book of Revelation strongly urges abstaining from all forms of idolatry because God is the only one worthy of worship (4:11; 5:2, 4, 9, 12). Exclusive worship of God constitutes the major theological imperative for Christians, indeed, for all of humanity (9:20; 14:7; 15:4; 19:10; 22:9). The command in 19:10 anticipates 22:8–9, where the angel who refuses to receive worship identifies himself as John's "fellow servant" and, aligning himself with John's "brothers the prophets, and with those who keep the words of this book," exhorts the seer, "Worship God."[56] As Bauckham points out:

---

[50]For the temple motif in the book of Revelation, see esp. Peter W. L. Walker, *Jesus and the Holy City: New Testament Perspectives on Jerusalem* (Grand Rapids, MI: Eerdmans, 1996), 235–65. See also the treatment of the temple and its destruction in the year 70 as part of the historical setting in "The Deity of Christ in John's Gospel" in this volume. Clearly, the destruction of the temple is also an important historical datum for the writing of the book of Revelation.

[51]Regarding the theological significance of John's use of a singular personal pronoun with reference to a plural subject (Yahweh and Christ), see Bauckham, *Theology*, 60–61.

[52]See 13:4, 15–16; 14:9–11; 15:2; 16:2; cf. 20:4.

[53]Cf. David A. deSilva, "The 'Image of the Beast' and the Christians in Asia Minor: Escalation of Sectarian Tension in Revelation 13," *Trinity Journal* new series 12 (1991): 197–201.

[54]Dio Cassius, *Hist.* 59.24.4; Philo, *Leg.* 116; Aune, *Revelation*, 2.741.

[55]Thus the assurance of believers is an important theme in Revelation.

[56]Bauckham, *Theology*, 120, notes the parallel with Moses' encounter with Pharaoh and his magicians and Elijah's conflict with Jezebel and the prophets of Baal. See Bauckham's entire detailed discussion on pp. 120–40. See also C. H. Giblin, "Structural and Thematic Correlations in the Theology of Revelation 16–22," *Bib* 55 (1974): 487–504.

The point is that the angel who shows the vision to John is not the source of revelation, but only the instrument for communicating it to John. Jesus, however, is represented as the source of revelation (22:16). The implication would seem to be that he is not, like the angel, excluded from monotheistic worship, but included in it. This implication is confirmed by the explicit worship of Jesus elsewhere in Revelation.[57]

In the end, the dragon and all his followers will face God's righteous wrath because of their sin, their mistreatment of God's people, and their failure to worship God (18:19–24; 19:1–3, 22:9).

The two final visions, then, serve to contrast the fate of those who worship the beast with the glory awaiting the followers of the Lamb.[58] Christian commitment is not merely a system of beliefs to be affirmed but an allegiance to be maintained in the face of constant pressure to compromise one's convictions. In the post-Christian West at the beginning of the third millennium after Christ, where, in keeping with Francis Schaeffer's prophetic words, personal peace and affluence reign almost supreme, even in large segments of the evangelical subculture, this message is timely indeed.

Christ's coming and divine presence in judgment and salvation. Bauckham poignantly expresses the contention under the present heading: "What Christ does, God does."[59] The hope and expectation of Christ's coming pervades the entire book (1:7; 2:5, 16; 3:3, 11; 16:15; 22:7, 20, 22), and seven times Christ himself announces, "I am coming" (*erchomai*; 2:5, 16; 3:11; 16:15; 22:6, 12, 20). In keeping with Old Testament passages regarding God's coming in judgment (e.g., Isa. 40:10; 62:11), "coming" terminology with reference to Christ in the book of Revelation is clearly predicated upon Old Testament prediction whose fulfillment in Christ is said to be imminent. God's coming—the visitation of "him who is and who was and who is to come" (1:4, 8; cf. 4:8)—at the end of time will take place emphatically *in and through Christ.*

Not only is God's judgment executed through Christ, but also the glorified Son of Man, his sacrificial death, which is likewise at the heart of the message of Revelation, is cast as God's action in and through Christ. As Bauckham perceptively notes, when the slain Lamb appears in the midst of the divine throne in heaven (5:6; cf. 7:17), this signifies that "Christ's sacrificial death *belongs to the way God rules the world.*"[60] Indeed, "the

---

[57]Ibid., 59.
[58]Barbara R. Rossing, *The Choice between Two Cities: Whore, Bride, and Empire in the Apocalypse,* HTS 48 (Harrisburg, PA: Trinity, 1999), 14–15.
[59]Bauckham, *Theology,* 63; see his entire discussion on pp. 63–65.
[60]Ibid., 64; emphasis original.

symbol of the Lamb is no less a divine symbol than the symbol of 'the One who sits on the throne.'"[61]

While God is not present in the world directly but is depicted as enthroned in heaven, "he *is* present as the Lamb who conquers by suffering," and "Christ's suffering witness and sacrificial death are, in fact, . . . the key event in God's conquest of evil and establishment of his kingdom on earth," and Christ's presence—moving among the lampstands (1:13; 2:1)—with those who follow him in witness and sacrifice is in fact God's presence among them. In this, too, the theology of Revelation builds on the Gospel where Jesus is presented as the manifestation of God's glory among his people (John 1:14) and as the one who has made him definitively known (John 1:18).

Conclusion

Not only is Christ presented in terms of deity in John's Gospel, but also the same characterization continues in John's letters and in the book of Revelation. John's first letter was essentially written to defend the apostolic message as set forth in John's Gospel against misrepresentation, reaffirming that Jesus is the Christ and Son of God. Similar to the Gospel, John's first letter contains a startling concluding reference to Jesus in terms of deity (1 John 5:20; cf. John 20:28). Also similar to the Gospel, 1 John ties Jesus to God by using the language of "Father" and "Son" and identifies Jesus as the preexistent Word.

The book of Revelation continues the Gospel portrait of Jesus as the pierced Son who will return as the glorified Son of Man to exercise his God-given role in salvation and judgment. Also in continuity with John's Gospel, where Jesus is presented as the "Lamb of God," Revelation depicts Jesus as the lion-turned-lamb. In keeping with the image of the conquering Roman emperor, and against the backdrop of the imperial cult, John also portrays Jesus as the rider on a white horse who comes to vanquish all God's foes and to establish his eternal kingdom.

What is more, the author of Revelation clearly places Jesus within a Trinitarian framework and depicts him as "the first and the last"—that is, as eternal and preexistent—in keeping with Old Testament descriptions of Yahweh (see esp. Isa. 44:6). While not obliterating the personal distinctions between Yahweh and Christ, the latter is clearly taken up into the identity of the former, and the return of the risen, exalted, and glorified Christ is presented as the ultimate, eschatological demonstration of God's sover-

---

[61]Ibid.

eignty over all of human history. This assertion of God's all-encompassing sovereignty puts believers' present suffering in proper perspective.

I close with a pertinent comment by Bauckham, who well illumines the reason why the early Christians worshiped Jesus, and why Christians today, and in the future, should still worship him until he returns:

> In the language of the doxology to Christ (1:5b–6) and of the heavenly hymn to the Lamb, which closely resembles it (5:9–10), we can recognize at least part of the impetus that must originally have led to the worship of Jesus. He is there praised for his work of redemption. *It was because Christians owed salvation to Jesus Christ that he was worshipped.* An overwhelming religious debt to one who was regarded as living in heaven and indeed an experienced presence in the Christian community was naturally expressed in worship. The salvation was too closely connected with Jesus himself for Jesus to be bypassed in worship offered to God for it, but at the same time it was salvation *from God* that Jesus gave and so Jesus was not treated as an alternative object of worship alongside God. He was included in [the] worship of God.[62]

---

[62]Ibid., 62; emphasis added.

7

. . . .

The Deity of Christ in Church History

GERALD BRAY

. . . .

How far back into the origins of Christianity can belief in the deity of Christ be traced? There is no question that it was proclaimed as orthodoxy in the fourth century and even a good deal before that. The issues debated during the decades of classical creedal formation were more about how belief in his divinity should be expressed and harmonized with monotheism than about whether he was divine at all.

The Question
But the fact that the New Testament does not appear to express this belief with the same unambiguous conviction that is found in the later creeds has led many scholars and theologians, particularly since the eighteenth-century Enlightenment, to doubt whether the first Christians ever held it. Skepticism concerning the value of the Gospels as source material for the life and teaching of Jesus has made it almost impossible to use them as evidence, since modern critics tend to assume that the closer they get to affirming Christ's deity, the further away they are from the authentic message of the historical Jesus. This is a circular argument, but the prevalence, not to say dominance, that it exercises in so much modern scholarship makes it imperative for us to determine whether the fathers of the church,

who formulated the classical christological statements of the fourth and fifth centuries, were expressing the faith taught by Jesus and validated by his resurrection from the dead, or simply elaborating an understanding of him that suited them but bore little relation to historical truth. In other words, did the Jews, pagans, and heretics who objected to the orthodox Christian formulas have a more accurate understanding of Jesus than the leaders and defenders of the church had?

It can hardly be doubted that whatever we think the historical Jesus really said and did, he stands out in the Jewish world as a unique figure. There had been prophets long before him who had attracted a following, and it is possible that a great one like Isaiah created a school that outlived him by some centuries, though the evidence for that is sparse and controversial.[1] But none of the prophets founded a lasting movement, and Jewish sectarianism, which was alive and well in the time of Jesus, was never dependent on, or associated with, charismatic founder figures.

The only person in Jesus' day who can be compared with him is John the Baptist, but the contrasts between Jesus and John are at least as important as the similarities. Like Jesus, John had an itinerant teaching and preaching ministry that attracted disciples, but they left no written record, and any movement he might have founded fizzled out, probably even before his death. The circumstances of his beheading were such that it would not have been surprising if there had been a protest movement against King Herod's rule, but that does not seem to have happened, and whatever was left of John's legacy was integrated into the ministry of Jesus. Those who are skeptical of the Gospel record will naturally see this as early Christian propaganda, but nothing can detract from the fact that Jesus left a movement behind him of a kind unparalleled by anyone else. Even the false messiahs who appeared from time to time left nothing to posterity, and when the leaders of the Jewish revolts of AD 66–73 and AD 135–138 failed, they also disappeared from the historical record. How was it possible that Jesus should not only have bucked the universal trend but gone on to be worshiped as God?

The implausibility of the Christian claim was such that its early apologists used it as proof that it was true—Tertullian's famous *credo, quia absurdum est* ("I believe because it is absurd") being the outstanding example of this.[2] Particularly significant was the fact that the claims were not made about some remote figure of ancient legend, like Enoch for example, but about an

---

[1] For a discussion of this issue, see Brevard S. Childs, *Isaiah* (Louisville: Westminster, 2001).
[2] *De carne Christi*, 5.4.

obscure man who had died an ignominious and very public death in recent times. Tertullian did not hesitate to direct doubters to the Roman archives, where they would find the report sent back by Pontius Pilate, which would confirm the Gospel accounts of the resurrection of Jesus.[3] How Tertullian knew that (or whether he was correct) does not matter very much; the fact is that nobody refuted his claim, which would have been fairly easy to do if the archives had *not* contained the relevant material.

Something very strange had clearly happened in Judea in the first half of the first century, and its repercussions had a ripple effect that grew, rather than diminished, with the passage of time. Given that there was no encouragement for the new belief from any religious or secular authority—quite the contrary—there must be some explanation for this widespread growth that goes beyond such absurdities as collective self-delusion in the minds of Jesus' erstwhile disciples, or other such theories. One must also ask why no rival cults appeared. There were certainly a large number of Gnostic sects that competed with the early church, but these sects tried to appropriate Jesus and interpret him to suit themselves. It never seems to have occurred to anyone to find an alternative figure who might have been more acceptable to the Gentile world. Why not? Clearly there was something about Jesus that kept attention focused on him in spite of everything, and it is this fact which demands an explanation.

There are two possible lines of approach. The first is to ask whether Jesus taught his disciples that he was God. If he did, then the origins of belief in his divinity are solved. Even if he was mistaken in that belief, there were clearly enough people who accepted what he had to say about himself and who were prepared to stick to their convictions despite the catastrophic failure that led to his death. The other possibility is that it was only later reflection on his life and career that led his disciples, or possibly *their* disciples, to focus their devotion on him, a devotion that in time led to his divinization. That is the standard approach taken by most liberal New Testament scholarship today. The details of how, when, and why it happened vary from one scholar to the next, but the essential point is that the worship of Jesus as the Son of God did not derive from Jesus himself but was the product of what any objective observer must regard as an excessive adoration of the man who gave the Christian movement its name. What scholars say is basically that a Jewish sect, devoted to the teaching of a somewhat eccentric rabbi, turned itself into a semi-pagan cult and finally into a distinct religion that tried to purge itself of pagan ideas and claim as

---

[3] *Apologeticum*, 5.21.

much of its monotheistic Jewish heritage as it could, but without denying its newly fashioned doctrine of the deity of Christ.

Is that what really happened? Is such a scenario more plausible than the traditional Christian account? These are the most fundamental questions about belief in the deity of Christ, and we must try to answer them on the basis of the information and sources available to us.

The Evidence

What the early Christians believed and taught about Jesus has been the subject of intense scholarly debate for many decades and has gone through a number of phases, which have been demarcated and chronicled as quests for the "historical Jesus." It is not necessary to retrace all these steps, except to say that the extreme theories about Jesus that circulated in the nineteenth century and that can still be found at the popular level have long since been discredited.

Since the appearance of Albert Schweitzer's *The Quest for the Historical Jesus* in 1906, it has not been possible to maintain that Jesus was no more than a scholarly rabbi who preached moral regeneration, which got him into trouble with the establishment and led to his crucifixion. Such a bourgeois conception of Christ may tally with the expectations of liberal Protestant academics in imperial Germany, but it hardly reflects the atmosphere of first-century Palestine, where the Jews were an oppressed minority, desperate and prepared to adopt extreme measures for their national freedom. Schweitzer's proposal that Jesus was an apocalyptic figure who was later domesticated for general consumption by his surviving disciples was preferable to the view that Jesus was a moralistic rabbi, but it was still implausible, since figures of that kind were usually shunned during their lifetime and abandoned after their death, not least by the relatively few zealots who had been taken in by them. It is much more likely that Jesus appeared to his contemporaries as unusual but not so peculiar as to be completely beyond the pale of respectable society. This is the view of the historical Jesus that has prevailed in recent times and that has led to an intense study of contemporary Judaism in an effort to understand where he may have fitted into it and what his thought world was like.

No one has pursued this study with greater determination or with more compelling results than Larry Hurtado (b. 1943), professor of New Testament at the University of Edinburgh, who has written a number of important books on the subject.[4] Professor Hurtado operates within the critical assumptions of modern liberal scholarship, which means that he gives priority to the evidence found in the letters which most people agree come from the hand of the apostle Paul.[5] While this restricts him to a relatively small slice of the New Testament, these letters contain material that is universally agreed to be among the earliest Christian writings. If they can be shown to proclaim the deity of Christ, as Hurtado believes they can, then we have come as close as we can to the origins of Christianity, and the probability that belief in Christ's divinity goes back to the beginning of the church is substantially increased. Whatever one thinks about his conclusions, Hurtado has taken the debate about Christian origins to a new level and made much of what went before obsolete.

To make his case that the earliest Christians believed in the divinity of Jesus, Hurtado concentrates on the pattern of their worship and compares it with the norms of contemporary Judaism. His method assumes that worship presupposes belief, whether or not the latter was explicitly formulated. Fundamental to his approach is the fact of Jewish monotheism, which by the time of Jesus had become so integral to Jewish identity that the slightest departure from it would have been regarded as apostasy and entailed ostracism from that community of faith. Given that the earliest Christians were Jews, this was an issue that they could hardly ignore. It is virtually impossible to imagine how a group of Jews could ever have recommended prayer and devotion to Jesus without the most compelling reasons to do so. The consequences for them were so serious that they could hardly have committed themselves to it if they had not been thoroughly convinced that Jesus was divine.

In his analysis of Jewish monotheism, Hurtado singles out two of its features that seem to characterize it overall. First, there was what he calls "a remarkable ability to combine a genuine concern for God's uniqueness with an interest in other figures with transcendent attributes which are described in the most exalted terms and which we may call 'principal agent' figures who are even likened to God in some cases."[6] These are angels or angelic beings, who formed part of the divine entourage and in that capac-

---

[4] See esp. his *Lord Jesus Christ: Devotion to Jesus in Earliest Christianity* (Grand Rapids, MI: Eerdmans, 2003). He refers readers to his earlier work, *One God, One Lord: Early Christian Devotion and Ancient Jewish Monotheism* (1988; repr. London: T&T Clark, 2003). There is also a series of lectures that distill his main ideas and present them in easily digestible form: *How on Earth Did Jesus Become a God? Historical Questions about Earliest Devotion to Jesus* (Grand Rapids, MI: Eerdmans, 2005).

[5] Romans; 1 and 2 Corinthians; Galatians; Philippians; 1 Thessalonians; and Philemon.

[6] Hurtado, *How on Earth Did Jesus Become a God?*, 111.

ity served to underline the greatness of God, but who were never confused with or assimilated to God himself.

Could the early Christians too have turned Jesus into one of these beings? Almost certainly not, for several reasons. First, although angelic beings occasionally revealed themselves on earth in human form, when they did so it was for a specific purpose, and they soon left again. This was certainly not the case with Jesus. He may have been miraculously conceived by the Holy Spirit in the womb of the Virgin Mary, but he was born as a human baby and lived an ordinary life for thirty years before starting his ministry. During that time, no one thought that he was any different from them, and despite the miracles he performed in the company of his disciples, none of them ever suggested that he was not a human being. Furthermore, he died a terrible death, which no angel would have been capable of doing, since angels are immortal. Everything we know about the life of Jesus works against identifying him with an angel, and so it is not surprising that the idea was never put forward by any large number of Christians.[7]

Next, there was "an exhibition of monotheistic scruples, particularly and most distinctively in public cultic/liturgical behavior."[8] There is no doubt that some Jewish writers loved to speculate on the existence and powers of heavenly beings, and on occasion they came close to seeing them as sharing at least some of the attributes of God. But however exalted these beings might be, they were always ancillary to God himself, whom the Jews regarded as both sovereign and unique. These were not merely characteristics of God that had been revealed in their sacred Scriptures; they were also vital ingredients in their own battle for survival in a pagan world where religious syncretism was rife and where there was a readiness to assimilate the gods of one nation to others. It seems that the Romans were prepared to acknowledge Yahweh as Saturn, because the Jews worshiped him on Saturn's day—to the Romans, such a connection would have seemed obvious and even complimentary! But no Jew could accept that the God he worshiped was merely one deity among others, and it was this conviction that set Jews apart as a nation. Still less could a Jew have accepted the pagan concept of deification, by which great human beings were assimilated into the heavenly pantheon. The distinction between the Creator and his creation was absolute and could not be relaxed without falling into the idolatry that Jews condemned as among the very worst of sins.

---

[7]It can be found in works such as *The Shepherd of Hermas*, but the references tend to be vague and controversial.

[8]Hurtado, *How on Earth Did Jesus Become a God?*, 111.

Jewish worship was the chief means by which this message was communicated, and, if anything, the message grew stronger in the Diaspora, where the temptation of syncretism was obviously greater. But in the Judaism of Jesus' day, there was no tolerance on this score. The Samaritans were thought to have mixed their Judaism with pagan cults and practices, and no group was more consistently vilified by Jews and shunned by them. The uniqueness of the God of Israel was jealously protected from even the slightest attempt to compromise it, and the followers of Jesus fully accepted that only Jewish religious observances had any validity in the sight of God.[9]

The evidence of Judaism in the time of Jesus forces us to conclude that belief in the deity of Christ could not have emerged within it. Anyone who might have moved in that direction would have been cut off from the community, and very few others would have followed him. The unique place accorded to Jesus in early Christian worship, and the willingness of his followers to stand up for it in the face of persecution and death, can be adequately explained only by saying that Jesus not only taught that he was God but demonstrated that fact by what he did. Ultimately, it was his resurrection from the dead that persuaded the disciples that he was who he said he was. And although they certainly emphasize this fact, the Gospel writers generally downplay miracles in their accounts of the life of Jesus. In their eyes, the proofs of his divinity could be found in many other things that were ultimately more significant. First, he was tempted by the Devil to do things that only God could do.[10] Second, he claimed the power to forgive sins, which again, only God could do.[11] Third, he claimed the power to interpret the Scriptures as referring to himself, although everyone knew that they referred primarily to God and his covenant with Israel.[12] The miracles, and especially his resurrection from the dead, backed up these things, but they were not his sole claim to divinity, and the early church always had a bigger picture of him than that.

If human beings had invented the deity of Jesus, we would expect them to emphasize his miraculous deeds as the main evidence for this, and the more improbable the miracles were, the better. There would have been little reason for them to have added the more mundane details found in the Gospels if they had not been part of Jesus' claims about himself. The conclusion must be that Jesus taught these things about himself, and it was for that reason that his disciples worshiped him as God. For all their

---

[9]See John 4:20–22, where Jesus tells the Samaritan woman that "salvation is from the Jews."
[10]Matt. 4:1–11; Luke 4:1–13.
[11]Mark 2:1–12.
[12]Luke 24:37; John 5:39.

reflection on the person and natures of Jesus Christ, none of the fathers of the church ever believed that, in confessing the deity of Christ, he was adding anything to the teaching of Jesus himself. Their aim was to explain the evidence that had been set before them in the historical events of the life, death, and resurrection of the man whose claims they believed and whose teachings they followed. What that explanation was is the substance of the development of the doctrine of Christ in the history of the church.

The Explanation

The first major attempt to express the divinity of Christ after the close of the apostolic age was the so-called *logos* christology of the second-century apologists. This they derived primarily from the prologue to John's Gospel, where Jesus is described as the eternal Word (*logos*) of God.[13] This concept appealed to them because it was already familiar from the writings of the Greek philosophers, who called the ruling principle of the universe the *logos*. But John went much further than this and proclaimed that the *logos* had become flesh (*sarx*), a concept that was utterly alien to the ancient Greek mind.[14] To the Greeks, the *logos* was an impersonal force that belonged to the spiritual world, which was good, whereas the flesh was a material object, and therefore evil. For the *logos* to become flesh, good would have to be personal and make common cause with something that was evil, both of which ideas were absurd in their eyes. But although the philosophers rejected these ideas, they did believe that something of the transcendent *logos* had entered the world of matter and created human beings, who possessed a rationality that was linked to the transcendent Reason (*logos*) but was at the same time trapped in matter, which dragged that rationality down and compromised its purity. If there was such a thing as salvation, it would be achieved by separating the sparks of the *logos* from the flesh into which they had fallen and reabsorbing them into the eternal *logos* from which they had come.

In contrast to this, the Christian claim was that when the Word (*logos*) became flesh, "we have seen his glory."[15] In other words, when it entered the created order, the *logos* was not diminished, fragmented, or compromised in any way but revealed in its fullness and power. How could this have been? One solution was to say that God had his Word (and his Spirit) in him from eternity, but that he produced them when he wanted to create the world. This production could be justified by saying that the Word

---

[13]John 1:1.
[14]John 1:14.
[15]Ibid.

was "begotten" and that the Holy Spirit "proceeded" from God, who thus became identified as the Father, in the sense that he was the source of the other two. The difficulty with this solution was that if the Word and the Spirit became distinct beings at some point in time, was God the Father thereby deprived of his rationality and his spirituality? Obviously not! It was therefore necessary to think of the divine Word in a different way, not as a function or attribute of God but as an eternally existing, distinct being within the Godhead.

How was this being to be described? There was only one God, so anything that suggested an increase in the number of divine beings was ruled out from the start. The suggestion that God appeared in different guises at different times, depending on what he was doing, was also put forward but was quickly ridiculed and dismissed as untenable. God could not have been crucified in Jesus Christ, if by that we are meant to understand that he had no other existence. Who would have been ruling the universe while he lay dead in the tomb? How could the impassible and immortal God become subject to suffering and death, when these things are alien to his nature? This was clearly absurd, so a way had to be found by which it would be possible to maintain both monotheism and the deity of Christ without diminishing the being of the one God or making the incarnation of the divine Word an impossibility.

It was this dilemma that pushed the church fathers to develop their doctrine of the Trinity. That doctrine can be traced back to the New Testament, and so we cannot say that it developed as belief in the divinity of Christ grew. If that had been the case, there would have been no need to include the Holy Spirit, who was always part of the Christian doctrine of God, even if little was said specifically about him before the fourth century. Christians did not have to invent a new Trinitarian doctrine to explain what they were starting to believe about Jesus, but they had to expound their existing doctrine more fully in order to harmonize what they had to say about him with what they believed about the essential unity of God.

The conceptual vocabulary that was needed to do this adequately emerged in the second century. In the Greek-speaking world, a distinction was made between the one being (*ousia*) of God and the three *hypostases* in which that one being was manifested. It was impossible to gain access to the one being, or even to contemplate it, other than in and through one of the *hypostases*, since that was the way God revealed himself to his people. Each *hypostasis* revealed the fullness of God and therefore also revealed the other *hypostases* as well. To put it simply, it was not possible to know God the Father without also knowing the Son and the Holy Spirit, and vice versa. To know one was to know all three. By this means it was possible to affirm the eternal deity of the Son without compromising the integrity of the one Godhead.

In the Latin-speaking world, *ousia* was translated as *substantia*, which made it difficult to find a good translation for *hypostasis*, since (strictly speaking) *substantia* was its Latin equivalent. Unable to say that God was three substances in one substance, Tertullian came up with the word *persona*, which he borrowed from the theater (by way of the Roman law courts). Originally, this word had meant "mask," something which was to cause confusion when Greek-speakers understood the Romans to be saying that God wore different masks when performing different roles. But in Roman law it had come to be used to denote an "agent," someone who could sue and be sued in court, and in this sense, it was a superior term to *hypostasis*, which denoted identity but without necessarily including the concept of agency.

The doctrine of the Trinity would require further elaboration later on, but by the year AD 200 its main elements were already in place. The next question was how to integrate the doctrine of the incarnation of the Son into the doctrine of the Trinity. Christianity was not just belief in three divine persons dwelling in eternity but also in the incarnation of the second of those persons—and only the second of them—in the man Jesus of Nazareth. It is not always properly appreciated that the doctrine of Christ forced Christians to restate not only their understanding of God but also their understanding of humanity. In becoming a man, the Son of God not only revealed what God was like but also what a human being is. Jesus had to be fully human if he was to become sin for us and take our place on the cross, but how could he do this and be God at the same time? Would his divinity not clash at some point with his humanity? Was he best described as some mixture of the two, partly God and partly man but not wholly either?

To resolve this problem of dual natures, various solutions were put forward. The most notorious and influential of them was that of Arius, who claimed that the Son of God was not divine in the absolute sense but the most God-like of the creatures. Arius worked with the notion of a hierarchy of being, according to which the angels are higher than we are, and God is the highest of all. But somewhere between God and the angels, he found room for this extraordinary creature, a being who was so close to God that he could call him "Father" yet was not encumbered by divine attributes that would prevent him from becoming human. Unlike the Father, the Son was not impassible, and therefore it made sense to say that he could come to earth and suffer death for us without denying that he was as close to

God, and therefore as like God, as it was possible to get without actually being God.

To many people, this seemed to resolve the problem of Christ's divinity, and although Arianism was eventually defeated, it has left an enduring legacy in the history of the church. Nobody today would call himself "Arian" in the historical sense, but a great many people find it difficult to say that Jesus was God without qualification. If asked about this, they are liable to hesitate and reply that he was the *Son* of God, implying that there is some ontological distinction to be made between him and the eternal Father, who is (in their eyes) the only true God. This is not the official teaching of any Christian church, but it is a widespread popular perception and shows us why Arianism was so attractive to so many people. It appeared to offer a viable solution to the difficulty of having to reconcile Christ's divinity, which Arius did not want to deny, with the need to maintain monotheism and the sovereignty of God over suffering and death.

Many people were fooled by Arianism, but from the very beginning there were church leaders prepared to suffer exile and death to resist what they rightly saw as a complete denial of the Christian faith. What Arius had done was to offer a solution to the problem of Christ's divinity that destroyed the very essence of our salvation. If Christ was the being whom Arius claimed he was, then he was not God. And if he was not God, he was as far away from him as we are and therefore totally unable to do anything for us. There may be gradations of being within the created order, but whatever they are and however much they matter to us, they are as nothing to God. The chasm separating creatures from their Creator makes everything else pale in significance by comparison. It is simply not possible to be divine without being God, just as it is not possible for something relative to be "like" something absolute. You are either one thing or the other; any resemblance between them is illusory.

Arianism lasted a long time but its fundamental flaws were spotted early on. It was condemned at the first council of Nicaea in AD 325, less than a decade after Arius had first preached it at Alexandria and while he was still alive. Political support for a compromise prevented the Nicene solution from being universally accepted at first, although it prevailed in the end and has remained standard orthodoxy ever since. The key teaching at Nicaea was that the Son is "consubstantial" (*homoousios*) with the Father, that is to say, that he shares the same being. For a time some people tried to pretend that it was possible to have more than one divine being and that the Son had a being similar (*homoiousios*) to that of the Father but not identical to his. However, that false solution was soon exposed for what it was and never got very far. If the church was going to confess that Christ is God, then he must be fully God for the simple reason that anything less than that is not God at all.

Having established that point, the next step was to work out how someone who is fully God could also be a man. It was not long before Apollinarius (a disciple of Athanasius of Alexandria, who had led so much of the fight against Arianism) proposed that the incarnate Christ was a man only to the extent that this did not interfere with his divinity. In other words, Jesus had a divine mind but not a human one, since he did not need something that could serve no purpose. Similarly, he did not have a human soul or a human will, since these things were only pale copies of their divine archetypes and therefore redundant in someone who was God incarnate. Indeed, the only thing that Jesus Christ possessed that he did not already have by virtue of his deity was his flesh. He needed that in order to be able to suffer and die on the cross, but that was all. It was not difficult to see why Apollinarianism was unsatisfactory. The divinity of Christ was so overemphasized that there was no room left for him to be a proper human being. He could not have been tempted, nor could he have become sin for us, because those parts of the human being that can respond to sin were lacking in him. But mere skin and bones could not rebel against God, and human sinfulness was not a material thing, as the doctrine of Apollinarius implied. By seeking to do justice to Christ's divinity, Apollinarius had diminished his humanity almost to a vanishing point, and in doing so had made it practically impossible for Jesus to be or to become our Savior. It is hardly surprising, therefore, that Apollinarius was swiftly condemned, and his disgrace was to have momentous consequences for the reputation of the Alexandrian church, the theology of which he claimed to represent.

The reaction against Apollinarianism spawned the next stage of christological reflection, which swung first to the opposite extreme and then settled down in the classical formula of the Council of Chalcedon (AD 451). The first thing that happened was that a number of theologians from Antioch reacted against the devaluing of Christ's humanity that they perceived as typical of Alexandria; to their minds, Apollinarius was merely the most obvious exponent of a tendency that they thought permeated the whole church there. Theodore of Mopsuestia (d. 428), and later Nestorius (d. c. 451) responded to this by emphasizing the humanity of Jesus, insisting that unless he was a complete human being he could not have taken our place on the cross. That was true, of course, and there have been many people in modern times who have questioned Nestorius's subsequent condemnation for heresy, because to their minds he was merely defending the obvious

against the spiritualizing tendencies of the Alexandrians.[16] But the Antio-
chene school went so far as to claim that the baby in Mary's womb was a
human child independently of his conception by the Holy Spirit. To them
it was wrong to say that Mary gave birth to God; as a human being herself,
she could only give birth to another human being. The union of God and
man in Jesus was one of conjunction between an autonomous divine being
(the Son of God) and an equally autonomous human one (Jesus of Nazareth). In combination they produced the Christ figure whom we worship
as God and man. Nestorius called this conjunction a *person* (*prosopon*
in Greek), which he understood as the manifestation of the union of two
self-contained *hypostases.*

It was this formulation that the church could not accept. Cyril of Alexandria (d. 444) insisted that the Son of God must be understood as having
been the agent of the incarnation. After he took on humanity in Mary's
womb, he united it to himself in a single nature, by which Cyril meant that
Jesus was what we would now call a single person. Cyril did not use the
term *person*, but if he had, he would not have accepted that it was not a
conjunction of two *hypostases* effected in the womb of Mary. Most likely
he would have applied the word to the hypostatic agent who brought about
the incarnation in the first place, what we now call the divine person of the
Son of God. As formulated at the Council of Chalcedon, what happened in
the incarnation is that this divine hypostasis or person took on a second
nature without giving up or diminishing the first one.[17] The incarnate Christ
was therefore one divine hypostasis or person in two natures, one of which
was divine and the other human. Cyril's claim that the two had become one
was rejected; they were united in the person of Christ but not merged. This
Chalcedonian formula completely inverted the understanding of reality,
human and divine, that had prevailed until that time, forced the church
to come to terms with an entirely new way of thinking, and remains the
standard of orthodoxy in most Christian churches to this day.

To put it simply, before Chalcedon, most people had thought of "God"
and "man" in terms of being, or nature. To say that Christ was fully God
and fully man meant that he was fully divine and fully human. One nature
interacted with the other, which in practice meant that the human was
more or less absorbed by the divine, since the divine was by far the more
powerful of the two. For example, when Jesus spat on the ground to create mud in order to heal the blind man, it was stated that his saliva had

---

[16]See Alois Grillmeier, *Christ in Christian Tradition* (London: Mowbray, 1975), 559–68.
[17]It was at Chalcedon that the terms *hypostasis* and *person* (as used in the Western church) were
declared to be synonymous.

divine properties, communicated to it by the presence of the divine nature within him. Similar explanations were found for Jesus' walking on water and so on. When he claimed to be thirsty, or told his disciples that he did not know the date of his return at the end of time, he was feigning these things. Even as orthodox a theologian as Athanasius was prone to this kind of reasoning because he could not see any other way in which the divine and the human could interact.[18]

Chalcedon solved this problem by stating that the two natures of Christ do not engage directly with one another. His divine nature keeps its divinity and acts according to it, and his human nature does the same. The union between them is effected by his person, which is now understood as an agent that is not bound by his divine nature and thereby prevented from becoming anything else. Thus, on the cross, it was the divine person of the Son of God who suffered and died in his human nature, which was capable of suffering and dying, but not in his divine nature, which was not. In terms of church politics, Chalcedon expressed the doctrine of Alexandria in the language of Antioch, a solution that convinced most of the church but unfortunately alienated both the followers of Cyril of Alexandria and those of Nestorius at Antioch. To this day there are non-Chalcedonian churches of Middle Eastern origin that have not been fully reconciled with the rest of the Christian world, though in recent times it has been increasingly recognized that the differences that keep them apart are more terminological than substantial. The Alexandrians in particular are nowadays generally thought to confess the same doctrine as the rest of the church but in different words, a recognition which, if it has not healed the breach, has gone a long way to making it less divisive in the wider Christian world.

The Defense

Because the Chalcedonian definition of the divinity of Christ remains the touchstone of orthodoxy for most of the Christian church, the history of that doctrine since 451 is largely one of defending and elaborating it as required by the emergence of later controversies and perspectives. Even in 451, the council was thought to have laid down the main lines of development while at the same time leaving a number of questions unanswered, most of them to do with drawing the line between aspects of Christ's natures. For example, where did the will belong? Was it a function of the person or of the nature? In other words, did Christ have one will or two? Basing themselves on what

---

[18]This was called the "transfer of properties" or *communicatio idiomatum* in Latin.

Jesus said in the garden of Gethsemane ("Not as I will, but as you will"),[19] the Chalcedonian churches eventually decided that the incarnate Christ must have had two wills, one human and the other divine. As a human being, he could not have desired his own death, since it is abnormal for a human being to want to die. However, as the Son of God he knew that he had come into the world to do the will of his Father, and that he and the Father were one. In christological terms, the will therefore belonged to the nature, not to the person. This means that in God there is only one will, although there are three persons, whereas in human beings the will is part of our human nature and therefore subject to the desires of the flesh. The human will is free to do what the flesh wants it to do, but it cannot play any part in our salvation, because it is not a function of our personhood.

To the objection that Jesus could not be fully human without being a human person, the response must be that personhood is not part of our human nature but a gift of God, in whose image and likeness we are made. Because we have been created in his image, we have the same capacity for relationship that he has and already enjoy an eternal relationship with him. That relationship was broken by the fall of Adam and Eve, but it has not disappeared. On the contrary, the ongoing presence of that relationship and its indelible character is what makes us guilty before God. Had the relationship been destroyed or removed, we would now be in the same condition as animals. The fact that God holds us responsible for our sin shows that we are still persons in relationship with him and will have to answer for that sin when we are judged at the end of time.

It is precisely because personhood is something of divine origin that Jesus could be a divine person yet still be fully human. Moreover, it is because he is a divine person that he can take our place before the judgment seat of the Father, and because we are persons that we can be united with him for our salvation. Personhood is the channel by which God communicates with man and man is redeemed by God. It was the achievement of Chalcedon to realize this and to put into words a concept that can be used and adapted, as indeed it has been, by subsequent generations of believers down to the present time.

Another question, one that surfaced in the eighth century, concerned the visibility of the divinity of Christ. This sounds odd to us today, but this issue had lain dormant within the church for many centuries and became a pressing matter after the rapid spread of Islam. Muslims rejected any depiction of God as blasphemous. In theory, Christians might be said to agree

---

[19]Matt. 26:39.

with this, not least because the second of the Ten Commandments forbids the making of any images of the divine. But Christian churches were full of pictures of Christ, which led to criticism from Muslims. To them, a picture of Christ was either blasphemous, because God could not be depicted, or else proof that Christ was not divine. Christians were apparently trying to have it both ways, by claiming that Christ is God and at the same time making pictures of the one who is by nature invisible.

Controversy over this erupted in Constantinople in 726, when the reigning emperor (Leo III) decreed that all pictures of Christ and the saints should be destroyed. This was strongly resisted and led to a lengthy dispute that was not finally resolved until 843, when the erection of images in churches was officially permitted. Before that, however, theologians had gone to work, and in 787, at the second Council of Nicaea, they declared that it was perfectly in order to make pictures of Christ because he had been a genuine human being and therefore just as visible as anyone else. That seems reasonable enough, and if there were no more to it, the controversy might have died out sooner than it did. But the real issue was (and is) whether Christ's divine person could be portrayed in the image, and if it could be, whether it deserved the same respect and devotion as Christ in the flesh would have received. To those questions the council also replied in the affirmative, and the result was the rapid development of iconography, which continues to play a central role in the life of the Eastern Orthodox churches to this day. The Western church at first resisted the decisions of the council, partly for political reasons, but eventually accepted their theological orthodoxy, although the veneration of icons was never fully established in the West. On the other hand, it must be said that iconography was replaced by something arguably even more controversial—the veneration of three-dimensional statues, which were "idols" in a way that two-dimensional icons were not.

The theological issues at stake in this controversy seem arcane to us today, but they were closely tied to the deity of Christ and must be judged in that context. To ban pictures of Jesus would be to deny his humanity, but what should we do with them once they are made? Clearly we ought to treat them with respect, but should we push that to the point where we regard them as equivalent to the person himself? We might perhaps compare this to the images of great figures on stamps, coins, and banknotes. Do we venerate them? Here the answer must surely be no. The image cannot take the place of the person it represents, particularly when he is present among us and in us by the power of his Holy Spirit. We do not deny that it is possible to make pictures of Jesus or that the Jesus so depicted is a divine person, but we also do not mistake the image for the reality it represents. Roman Catholics and Eastern Orthodox officially deny that they do this, but it has to be said that unhealthy devotions to "wonder-working" images have grown up in their churches, with varying degrees of approval from the authorities. Such devotions are little more than baptized forms of paganism and very far indeed from their stated desire to give due worship to the incarnate Son of God.

After the eighth century there was little further dispute about the deity of Christ within the Christian church for at least a thousand years. The great quarrels of the Reformation era, especially those to do with the nature of the church and the sacraments, had a christological dimension and were occasionally interpreted in those terms, but claims that Martin Luther was a Nestorian or that John Calvin was an Arian were easily scotched and never became serious matters of debate.[20]

In the Reformation era, the most important group to deny the divinity of Christ was the movement that followed Lelio Sozzini and his nephew Fausto, two Italians who rejected the doctrine of the Trinity. The Socinians, as their followers were called, based themselves at Raków in Poland, where they took advantage of the climate of relative religious tolerance; from there they issued the notorious Racovian Catechism, a short statement of their beliefs, which spread widely across Europe. Eventually the Socinians became what we now know as Unitarians, and they became very influential, especially in what had once been Puritan circles. New England was particularly affected, and many famous old churches in Boston defected to the Unitarian cause, even taking Harvard University along with them. But despite these prominent victories, Unitarianism never became the official belief of the major Protestant denominations, all of which have continued to affirm the deity of Christ in modern times.

Official statements of belief, however, do not tell the whole story. For at least two (and perhaps three) centuries now, the deity of Christ has been challenged from within the Christian churches by a wave of skepticism loosely, but not inaccurately, associated with the Enlightenment. It is difficult to say precisely when the challenge began, because it started indirectly. Unable to criticize Christian orthodoxy openly, a number of freethinkers in the late seventeenth and early eighteenth centuries instead challenged the presuppositions on which it was based.

---

[20]These criticisms arose in the context of debates about the real presence of Christ in the Eucharist and not about his deity as such.

The most important of these presuppositions concerned the possibility of miracles. If the scientific laws governing the universe were as unalterable as most natural scientists of the time said they were, then miracles were logically impossible because they involved a "violation" of those laws. This had not been a problem for earlier generations, which had relied on the concept of divine providence governing the universe. As long as God was seen as being directly involved in everything that happened, miracles were understandable; the so-called scientific laws were only a record of what he normally did, not a limitation on what he was able to do. But once it came to be believed that the Creator established his creation along rational lines (in accordance with his own nature) and then allowed it to run according to an internal system of cause and effect, interference with the mechanism became a problem. Neither a virgin birth nor a resurrection from the dead was conceivable, and so the question of Christ's identity was once more thrown into the melting pot.

The result was a long series of alternative "lives of Jesus" that characterized the nineteenth century and which Albert Schweitzer comprehensively debunked in his book. The main difficulty faced by the would-be revisers of traditional Christian orthodoxy was the problem of reconciling what they continued to believe was the elevated moral teaching of Jesus, which they accepted, with his claims to divinity, which they rejected. His moral teaching could be regarded as a divine gift to him personally, and essentially no different from what has been given to other great historical figures like Socrates or the Buddha. However, it is only fair to add that before 1914 it was not uncommon for educated Europeans and North Americans to believe that the teaching of Jesus was superior to that of other religious leaders, and that Christianity was the highest form of religion that had yet emerged on earth. Conversion to Christianity could therefore be encouraged as a form of cultural development analogous to the spread of Western civilization, which was its natural counterpart, and many liberal theologians supported Christian missionary efforts for that reason.

Jesus' claims to divinity, on the other hand, were regarded as absurd and even immoral. Who in his right mind would presume to equate himself with God? Only someone who was self-deluded, or who was intent on deluding others, would even think of such a thing, but Jesus does not come across as that kind of person in Scripture. The only alternative therefore was to argue that his followers were responsible for his divinization after his death. Some scholars even purported to discover evidence that there had been a conflict over this in the early church, with conservatives fighting against the divinization process, which was only imposed after a long and bitter struggle in the course of which "orthodoxy" and "heresy" came to be defined.[21] This kind of thinking was backed up by the claims of scholars like Rudolf Bultmann (1884–1976), who argued that the portrait of Jesus presented in the Gospels was a myth that needed to be deconstructed for a modern audience. Bultmann believed that the moral teaching of Jesus, contained in the so-called *kerygma* ("proclamation"), must be retained, and some of his followers even thought that it should be recast in modern forms, including myths geared to the thought processes of our own contemporaries. However, any suggestion that Jesus might really be God in human flesh was anathema to them and had to be rejected.

Two world wars and the end of European hegemony in Africa and Asia virtually destroyed the world in which these men lived and wrote, but their influence lives on. It is significant that Walter Bauer's work was written in 1934 but not translated into English until 1972, long after it had been convincingly refuted, by H. E. W. Turner and J. N. D. Kelly in particular.[22] Astonishingly, these refutations have largely been ignored, and Bauer's original thesis has been recycled as if it were beyond dispute. Today even respectable academic presses will often publish books purporting to reveal the "hidden" Jesus or to tell us what the early Christians censored out of the Scriptures.[23]

Orthodoxy still exists, to be sure, but in most mainline Protestant churches it has become no more than one option among many, and often becomes harder to find the further up the hierarchy of a denomination one goes. Smear words like *fundamentalist* and *traditionalist* are used to characterize the orthodox, as if believing what the church has always believed is somehow the sign of an inferior intellect. Unfortunately, we live in a world where novelty is highly prized, and any defense of orthodoxy is bound to sound old-fashioned to some degree, which puts the orthodox at a considerable disadvantage when faced with the sensationalist media. Yet in a very important sense and precisely because of these problems, Christians today have been brought back to the foundations of their faith in a

---

[21] The chief exponent of this viewpoint is Walter Bauer, *Orthodoxy and Heresy in Earliest Christianity* (London: SCM, 1972), originally published in German, 1934.

[22] H. E. W. Turner, *The Pattern of Christian Truth: A Study in the Relations between Orthodoxy and Heresy in the Early Church* (London: Mowbray, 1954) and J. N. D. Kelly, *Early Christian Doctrines*, 2nd ed. (New York: Harper & Row, 1960).

[23] A good example of this is the way in which Oxford University Press has been prepared to publish the works of Bart Ehrman, whose declared aim is to discredit orthodox Christianity. Ehrman's books have been widely criticized for their obvious bias, but this has not deterred his publishers.

way that has not happened since the early days of the church. The defense of Chalcedon now has to go back to the New Testament and to its basic principles in a way that has not happened before, and, painful though that may be for some, we must hope that the long-term benefit for the church will be worth the effort expended.

Confessing the Deity of Christ Today

Opposition to the extreme liberalism of the nineteenth century was never lacking at the time, but in most cases it involved little more than a stock defense of the traditional teaching of the church. Occasionally, however, an attempt would be made to recast that teaching in a way that might answer the critics and offer a better solution to the problem of the deity of Christ than that given in the Chalcedonian definition. One of the more successful of these attempts was the so-called kenotic theory, based on Philippians 2:7. That verse says that Jesus "emptied" (*ekenose* NASB) himself to become a servant of God the Father, and because of that he became a man. Traditionally, this word has been understood to mean that the Son of God humbled himself, forgoing the prerogatives of his divinity and accepting the role of a servant so as to accomplish the will of the Father for the salvation of mankind.

But in the mid-nineteenth century a German theologian called Gott-fried Thomasius (1802–1875) proposed that the incarnation of Christ could best be understood as a surrender, not merely of the prerogatives but of the substance of divinity on the part of the Son, who became a man by abandoning his divine nature for the duration of his incarnation. This idea was then picked up and developed by Charles Gore (1853–1932) and by Peter Taylor Forsyth (1848–1921) into a full-blown christology of *kenosis*. Gore and Forsyth had different emphases, in that the former was actively trying to bolster the Chalcedonian position by modifying it slightly in order to remove some of the more obvious difficulties, whereas Forsyth was presenting his understanding as a replacement for the traditional doctrine and not just a modification of it. As far as the bigger picture is concerned, however, this difference does not really matter. Both men believed that the best way to explain the humanity of Christ and its obvious limitations was to say that he had given up the use of his divinity.

The difficulty with this explanation, and one that has proved fatal to kenotic theology as a lasting explanation of christology, is that it takes us back (by another route) to the problems encountered in ancient times. If the Son of God really did abandon his divinity during his earthly incarnation, what does this say about the Trinity? Are we to think that during that time, the Father and the Holy Spirit were left to constitute the Godhead on their own? This was the fundamental weakness of second-century *logos* christology, which was abandoned precisely because of its inadequacy on this point. If Jesus of Nazareth was not fully God in human flesh, then what was he? How far did his *kenosis* extend? He could hardly have given up his divine attributes without ceasing to be God, because the divine attributes are coterminous with his divinity. Take one of them away and his divinity disappears!

Chalcedonian orthodoxy says that the incarnate Son of God was a divine person acting in and through a human nature in order to do and achieve things that could not be done in a divine nature alone, but his divine person was not detached from his divine nature when it became incarnate. How indeed could the person of the Son remain divine if his divine nature was separated from it? Although neither Gore nor Forsyth would have agreed, what they came up with was perilously close to a form of Arianism, in which the Son of God was somehow "divine" and yet a creature at the same time. This makes no sense, as orthodox Athanasians long ago recognized, and so the kenotic theory was bound to be found wanting as an interpretation of the deity of the incarnate Christ that might supplement or replace the Chalcedonian definition.

Since the collapse of kenoticism, defenders of orthodox christology have been much more cautious about trying to find viable alternatives to Chalcedon. Instead, they have preferred to concentrate on examining some of the problems raised by modern thinking about the nature of man. Ours is an age of psychology, in which a human being's inner life is perhaps more important than the outward behavior that we observe. There is not much about this in the New Testament because the ancient world rarely explored the psychological dimensions of humanity, although the Gospel writers do mention the spiritual struggles of Jesus and tell us that he "had compassion" and so on.[24] Moreover, the writer to the Hebrews tells us that he was tempted in every way just as we are,[25] which must mean that he had a normal human psychology, but beyond that we cannot go. How it felt to be God in human flesh is something the ancients did not ask and the New Testament does not reveal.

These, however, are the very questions that modern people ask. Just as we sometimes wonder what language a perfectly bilingual person dreams

---

[24]E.g., Matt. 9:36; 14:14.
[25]Heb. 4:15.

in, so we also ask how Jesus thought about himself. When he came up against a situation, did he react to it as a man or as God? Since so much of modern psychology revolves around the concept of the person, how can we say that Jesus was a normal human being if he was not a human person? What sort of personality did he have, or could he have had, if he was God in human flesh? If he had been psychoanalyzed, what would the results have been?

Questions like these raise the problem of our theological vocabulary, and notably our use of the word *person*. Many modern theologians are at pains to point out that our current use of this word differs from the classical one, but if that is so, is it not necessary to change the ancient formulation so as to express what we mean in today's language? While many people would agree, finding that language is a much more difficult proposition and has to face an uphill battle against an established tradition with all its many nuances and interpretations. The future is impossible to predict, and it will doubtless be some centuries before we will be able to say for sure whether a new formulation of the traditional doctrine of the deity of Christ can displace the Chalcedonian definition as the touchstone of orthodoxy.

For the present, suffice it to say that the concerns expressed in recent years can be accommodated within the traditional structure without too much difficulty. Once we realize that what the modern mind understands as "personality" belongs to the human nature of Christ, we can begin to integrate psychologically based concerns into our understanding of the deity and humanity of Jesus. In his incarnation he was a divine person with a human psychology, with all that that implies. Just as he worked in and through his human mind and will, so he operated within the constraints of a human psychological makeup as well. That is not to imply that he abandoned or compromised his divinity in any way—his divinity functioned in a different dimension and was revealed to his disciples only partially and at specific times in his life.

The defense of Chalcedonian christology today demands an understanding of its fundamental principles and a realization that it can and must be developed to deal with the problems raised by a new generation. This does not mean denying the past, or even restating it in any significant way, but rather extending the past to answer questions that were not raised in earlier times. If, instead of doing that, we give in to the skeptics, we shall have abandoned our faith, and Christianity might as well disappear altogether because it will be seen to have been built on a lie. But if we are determined to defend the deity of Christ and all that

that entails, then we must be prepared to face the basic questions just as the first generation of Christians had to face them—and to pay the price, if need be, that they were forced to pay for their temerity. Now, as then, we are called to answer the question that Jesus posed to Peter: "Who do you say that I am?"[26] And now, as then, we are expected to answer as Peter answered: "You are the Christ, the Son of the Living God." From there, it is simply a question of working out the consequences of that confession for our life as Christians today.

---

[26]Matt. 16:15–16.

8

Toward a Systematic Theology
of the Deity of Christ

ROBERT A. PETERSON

The early church believed Jesus Christ to be divine. It applied to him the highest conceivable designations (Son of God, Son of Man, Lord, God); it saw him as possessing the full range of divine attributes, performing the full range of divine functions and enjoying the full range of divine prerogatives; it worshipped him and prayed to him and broke out in doxology at the mere mention of his name. . . .

The extraordinary thing is that there is no trace of any controversy on this issue in the early church. There was fierce argument over many things, notably Gentile mission, the nature of justification and the place of the law in the Christian life. There was obviously also fierce debate between the church and the outside world as to the identity of Christ. But within the church itself there was no such debate.

Considering the implications of belief in the deity of Christ, this unembarrassed, un-selfconscious, unhesitating belief is quite remarkable. They believed God to be invisible, yet worshipped one they had seen, heard and embraced. They believed in a God of almost absolute transcendence, yet worshipped a man. They believed God to be one, yet worshipped him *and* his Son. *A priori*, all such developments were inconceivable. Yet the evidence that this is what actually happened is overwhelming.[1]

The preceding essays have laid a firm biblical and historical foundation for this one. They have surveyed the contemporary significance of the deity of Christ, explored it in both the Old and New Testaments, and considered its place in the history of doctrine. This essay will build upon this solid foundation and work toward a systematic theology of Christ's deity.

Various methods have been used to study the person of Christ and to demonstrate his deity. Oscar Cullmann famously studied christology by way of titles, and many have followed his approach.[2] Others have employed a method from biblical theology—tracing the witness to Christ's deity through the various corpora of the New Testament.[3] Still others have used categories from systematic theology, such as Robert M. Bowman Jr. and J. Ed Komoszewski, who, aiming at a lay audience, employ the acronym HANDS: Honors: Jesus shares the *honors* due to God; Attributes: Jesus shares the *attributes* of God; Names: Jesus shares the *names* of God; Deeds: Jesus shares in the *deeds* that God does; Seat: Jesus shares the *seat* of God's throne.[4] In the following I use systematic categories based on exegetical theology.

Recently Richard Bauckham and Larry Hurtado have breathed new life into the study of New Testament christology. Hurtado for years has maintained in essays that the earliest Christian communities expressed devotion to Christ that is fitting only for God.[5] His *Lord Jesus Christ: Devotion to Jesus in Earliest Christianity* was published in 2003. Bauckham's *Jesus and the God of Israel* (2008, which incorporates *God Crucified: Monotheism and Christology in the New Testament*, 1999) has changed the way many study christology.[6]

---

[1]Donald Macleod, *The Person of Christ*, Contours of Christian Theology (Downers Grove, IL: InterVarsity, 1998), 109–10.

[2]Oscar Cullmann, *The Christology of the New Testament*, trans. S. C. Guthrie and C. A. M. Hall (Philadelphia: Westminster, 1959).

[3]So Robert L. Reymond, *Jesus, Divine Messiah: The New Testament Witness* (Phillipsburg, NJ: P&R, 1990).

[4]Robert M. Bowman Jr. and J. Ed Komoszewski, *Putting Jesus in His Place: The Case for the Deity of Christ* (Grand Rapids, MI: Kregel), 2007.

[5]Larry W. Hurtado, *Lord Jesus Christ: Devotion to Jesus in Earliest Christianity* (Grand Rapids, MI: Eerdmans, 2003).

[6]Richard Bauckham, *Jesus and the God of Israel* (Grand Rapids, MI: Eerdmans, 2008); *God Crucified: Monotheism and Christology in the New Testament* (Grand Rapids, MI: Eerdmans, 1999).

Bauckham challenged traditional notions of ontological and functional christology for not being consonant with early Jewish thinking about God. Second Temple Judaism did not think primarily in terms of God's essence or roles but instead emphasized God's identity. He argued that "early Judaism had clear and consistent ways of characterizing the unique identity of the one God and, thus, distinguishing the one God absolutely from all other reality."[7] Bauckham studied the New Testament's witness to Jesus in this light and concluded:

> From the earliest post-Easter beginnings of Christology onwards, early Christians included Jesus, precisely and unambiguously, within the unique identity of the one God of Israel. They did so by including Jesus in the unique, defining characteristics by which Jewish monotheism identified God as unique.[8]

In what follows, I acknowledge a debt to the pioneering work of Hurtado and Bauckham, especially in my first argument.

Jesus Is Identified with God

Following the path blazed by Hurtado and Bauckham leads to strong evidence for the deity of Christ. The New Testament, which continues to affirm monotheism, identifies Jesus with the one true God in a number of ways, including the way his name is used, the fact that Old Testament passages that use Yahweh are applied to him, the interchangeability of Jesus and God in the New Testament, and the fact that he is called "God."

Jesus' Name Is Divine

In a number of passages Jesus' name is used in a way that befits only the name of God. This is true in the Synoptic Gospels. Simon Gathercole points to two places in Matthew where religious events occur in the name of Jesus:

> For where two or three are gathered in my name, there am I among them. (Matt. 18:20)

> Go therefore and make disciples of all nations, baptizing them in the name of the Father and of the Son and of the Holy Spirit. (Matt. 28:19)

Gathercole cites the valuable work of Adelheid Ruck-Schröder on Jewish-rabbinic use of the expression "into the name" where that expression is used in contexts pertaining to religious rites. In such cases, "rites are performed

---

[7] Bauckham, *Jesus and the God of Israel*, ix.
[8] Ibid.

'into the name' of the god. . . . This god is the fundamental referent of the rite; he/she is the one whom the worshipper 'has in mind' or 'with respect to' whom the rite is performed and who thus makes it meaningful."[9] In the two passages cited above, "gathering" in Jesus' name and "baptizing" in his name "are the two ritual acts of worship that have Jesus as their ultimate reference point and object."[10] In Matthew 18:20 and 28:19, then, the religious rites involved take place for the honor of Jesus, who occupies the place of God. We note that arguments based on the "name" of Jesus support Bauckham's thesis that the New Testament *identifies* Jesus as God. Names concern identity.

Some texts in the New Testament use Jesus' name similarly to how Yahweh's name is used in the Old Testament. Gathercole discusses three, each of which reflects an Old Testament antecedent. I will cite his first two, giving the New Testament passage first and then its Old Testament antecedent:

Many will come in my name, saying, "I am he!" and they will lead many astray. (Mark 13:6)

Blessed is he who comes in the name of the LORD! (Ps. 118:26)

On that day many will say to me, "Lord, Lord, did we not prophesy in your name, and cast out demons in your name, and do many mighty works in your name?" (Matt. 7:22)

The prophet who presumes to speak a word in my name that I have not commanded him to speak, or who speaks in the name of other gods, that same prophet shall die. (Deut. 18:20)

These passages also demonstrate the New Testament's high view of Christ. In Mark's version of Jesus' eschatological discourse, Jesus warns of false christs who will deceive many by claiming to come in his name and to be the Christ. When this saying is viewed against its background in the Psalms, the conclusion is irresistible: Jesus "is clearly drawing an analogy between coming in his own name and the coming in the name of Yahweh mentioned in the Psalm."[11] Mark identifies Jesus with Yahweh.

Toward the end of the Sermon on the Mount, Jesus warns of and condemns false disciples who profess his lordship but whose deeds belie that

---

[9]Simon J. Gathercole, *The Pre-existent Son: Recovering the Christologies of Matthew, Mark, and Luke* (Grand Rapids, MI: Eerdmans, 2006), 65.
[10]Ibid., 66.
[11]Ibid., 67.

profession (Matt. 7:21–23). They perform three kinds of miraculous deeds in the name of Jesus, only one of which concerns us here—prophecy. Viewed against its background in the law, the words "prophesy in your name" in Matthew 7:22 identify Jesus with the God of the Old Testament. "Since prophecy in Deuteronomy here should be speaking 'in the name of Yahweh,' the move made in Matt. 7:22 is unmistakable."[12] The name of Jesus is used in place of the name of Yahweh.

We find the same phenomenon in Paul's epistles. Here are two Pauline texts with Old Testament antecedents:

For "everyone who calls on the name of the Lord will be saved." (Rom. 10:13)

And it shall come to pass that everyone who calls on the name of the LORD shall be saved. (Joel 2:32)

Therefore God has highly exalted him . . . so that at the name of Jesus every knee should bow. . . and every tongue confess that Jesus Christ is Lord, to the glory of God the Father. (Phil. 2:9–11)

By myself I have sworn; from my mouth has gone out in righteousness a word that shall not return: "To me every knee shall bow, every tongue shall swear allegiance." (Isa. 45:23)

In the Romans passage, Paul proclaims that the message of salvation in Jesus is for all who believe, including Jews and Gentiles. When the apostle urges, "everyone who calls on the name of the Lord will be saved" (Rom. 10:13), he quotes Joel 2:32, which uses "Yahweh." There is no doubt as to the identity of the Lord on whom Paul wants people to call. Verse 9 speaks of confessing "Jesus is Lord" as the way to "be saved."

It is the same in Philippians 2. There Paul, after speaking of Christ's great condescension, tells of his magnificent exaltation. When the Father brings the Son to heaven he gives him the name of exalted "Lord." God's purpose? "That at the name of Jesus every knee should bow" (v. 10). This is a quotation of Isaiah 45:23. There Yahweh mocks idols: "I am God, and there is no other" (v. 22; cf. vv. 18, 21), and declares: "To me every knee shall bow, every tongue shall swear allegiance" (v. 23). Paul applies the words of Yahweh directly to the exalted Lord Jesus. So Paul as well as the Gospels identifies Jesus with Yahweh.

---

[12]Ibid., 68.

Yahweh Passages Are Applied to Jesus

New Testament passages that do not use the word "name" also apply Old Testament Yahweh texts to Jesus. We will consider passages in the Gospels, Acts, the Epistles, and Revelation.

Mark's Gospel begins with quotations from the Old Testament. One of these is Malachi 3:1: "Behold, I send my messenger, and he will prepare the way before me . . . says the LORD of hosts." Mark cites the passage thus: "Behold, I send my messenger before your face, who will prepare your way" (Mark 1:2). Donald Macleod brings out the significance of Mark's quotation of Malachi: "Old Testament passages which in their original context clearly applied to Jahweh are in the New Testament applied unequivocally to Christ. . . . Mark 1:2 applies this passage, without comment, to Christ. He is the Lord and John the Baptist is *his* Messenger."[13]

Peter does the same on the day of Pentecost. He cites the prophet Joel to explain that the ascended Lord Jesus poured out the Holy Spirit on the church. Part of Peter's quotation is: "And it shall come to pass that everyone who calls upon the name of the LORD shall be saved," which is Joel 2:32 almost verbatim (Peter changes "on" to "upon"). In the same sermon, fifteen verses later, he identifies the "Lord" whom his hearers must call upon to be saved—"God has made him both Lord and Christ, this Jesus whom you crucified" (Acts 2:36).

Paul cites Jeremiah 9:24: "Let him who boasts boast in this, that he understands and knows me, that I am the LORD," when he writes: "so that, as it is written, 'Let the one who boasts, boast in the Lord'" (1 Cor. 1:31). Eight verses later he identifies the "Lord" in whom believers are to boast—he is "the Lord of glory" whom the foolish rulers of this age "crucified" (2:8).

Peter relies on Isaiah 8:12–13: "Do not fear what they fear, nor be in dread. But the LORD of hosts, him you shall honor as holy," when he says, "Have no fear of them, nor be troubled, but in your hearts honor Christ the Lord as holy" (1 Pet. 3:14–15). Clearly Peter substitutes "Christ the Lord" for the prophet's "LORD of hosts."

Jesus' words in Revelation 1 are reminiscent of Yahweh's words in Isaiah:

> I, the LORD, the first,
> and with the last; I am he. (Isa. 41:4)

---

[13]Donald Macleod, *Jesus Is Lord: Christology Yesterday and Today* (Geanies House, UK: Mentor, 2000), 52.

I am the first and I am the last; besides me there is no god. (Isa. 44:6)

I am he; I am the first,
and I am the last. (Isa. 48:12)

Echoing the prophet's words where Yahweh alone speaks, Jesus says: "Fear not, *I am the first and the last*, and the living one. I died, and behold I am alive forevermore, and I have the keys of Death and Hades" (Rev. 1:17–18). Isaiah's eternal Yahweh is Revelation's eternal Christ.

We have chosen five passages, and there are more.[14] It is plain to see that all parts of the New Testament apply to the Lord Jesus Old Testament texts that spoke of Yahweh. Once more the New Testament identifies Jesus with Yahweh. Of course, this is more evidence that he is divine.

Jesus Is Interchangeable with God

Not only do New Testament writers use Jesus' name in ways fitting only for God, and not only do they attribute Old Testament Yahweh texts to Jesus, but within the New Testament itself, they also identify Jesus with God. This is especially evident in Paul, whom, David Wells says, "moves easily into a complete linguistic identification of Christ and Yahweh."[15] I cannot improve upon Wells's impressive list and here quote it in full:

> If the gospel is God's (1 Thess. 2:2, 6–9; Gal. 3:8), then that same gospel is also Christ's (1 Thess. 3:2; Gal. 1:7). If the church is God's (Gal. 1:13; 1 Cor. 15:9), then that same church is also Christ's (Rom. 16:16). God's Kingdom (1 Thess. 2:12) is Christ's (Eph. 5:5); God's love (Eph. 1:3–5) is Christ's (Rom. 8:35); God's Word (Col. 1:25; 1 Thess. 2:13) is Christ's (1 Thess. 1:8; 4:15); God's Spirit (1 Thess. 4:8) is Christ's (Phil. 1:19); God's peace (Gal. 5:22; Phil. 4:9) is Christ's (Col. 3:15; cf. Col. 1:2; Phil. 1:2; 4:7); God's "Day" of judgment (Isa. 13:6) is Christ's "Day" of judgment (Phil. 1:6, 10; 2:16; 1 Cor. 1:8); God's grace (Eph. 2:8, 9; Col. 1:6; Gal. 1:15) is Christ's grace (1 Thess. 5:28; Gal. 1:6; 6:18); God's salvation (Col. 1:13) is Christ's salvation (1 Thess. 1:10); and God's will (Eph. 1:11; 1 Thess. 4:3; Gal. 1:4) is Christ's will (Eph. 5:17; cf. 1 Thess. 5:18). So it is no surprise to hear Paul say that he is both God's slave (Rom. 1:9) and Christ's (Rom. 1:1; Gal. 1:10), that he lives for that glory which is both God's (Rom. 5:2; Gal. 1:24) and Christ's (2 Cor. 8:19, 23; cf. 2 Cor. 4:6), that his faith is in God (1 Thess. 1:8, 9; Rom. 4:1–5) and in Christ Jesus (Gal.

---

[14]See Bowman and Komoszewski, *Putting Jesus in His Place*, 157–70.
[15]David F. Wells, *The Person of Christ: A Biblical and Historical Analysis of the Incarnation* (Wheaton, IL: Crossway, 1984), 64.

3:22), and that to know God, which is salvation (Gal. 4:8; 1 Thess. 4:5), is to know Christ (2 Cor. 4:6).[16]

Jesus Is Called God

Murray Harris has conducted a painstaking study of New Testament passages that call Jesus "God."[17] He concludes that the following six passages do that very thing: John 1:1; John 20:28; Romans 9:5; Titus 2:13; Hebrews 1:8; and 2 Peter 1:1. Harris's general conclusion is worthy of full quotation:

> While the NT customarily reserves the term θεος [*theos*] for the Father, occasionally it is applied to Jesus in his preincarnate, incarnate, or postresurrection state. As used of the Father, θεος [*theos*] is virtually a proper name. As used of Jesus, θεος [*theos*] is a generic title, being an appellation descriptive of his *genus* as one who inherently belongs to the category of Deity. In this usage θεος [*theos*] points not to Christ's function or office but to his nature. When this title is anarthrous (John 1:1, 18; Rom. 9:5), the generic element is emphasized. When it is articular (John 20:28; Titus 2:13; Heb. 1:8; 2 Pet. 1:1), the titular aspect is prominent.[18]

Harris's investigation underscores the importance of repeatedly going to Scripture to test theological method. Bauckham has changed the way we do christology by emphasizing identity over ontology or function. But that does not preclude our appealing to ontology or function if the New Testament does, as in this case. Harris draws out the christological implications of his study:

> In the christological use of θεος [*theos*] we find both the basis and the zenith of NT Christology: the basis, since θεος [*theos*] is a christological title that is primarily ontological in character and because the presupposiconclusiontion of the predominantly functional Christology of the NT is ontological Christology; the zenith, because θεος [*theos*] is a christological title that explicitly and unequivocally asserts the deity of Christ.[19]

Jesus Receives Devotion Due God Alone

Against its Old Testament monotheistic background, where worship of the one true and living God alone was commanded and all other worship condemned, the New Testament's practice is amazing. It continues to affirm monotheism but also affirms another truth—it is proper and necessary to

---

[16]Ibid., 65.
[17]Murray J. Harris, *Jesus as God: The New Testament Use of* Theos *in Reference to Jesus* (Grand Rapids, MI: Baker, 1992).
[18]Ibid., 298.
[19]Ibid., 299.

offer religious devotion to Jesus. He is worshiped, honored in baptism and the Lord's Supper, praised in doxologies, adored in hymns, and the object of prayers.

Worship

Religious devotion to Jesus includes worship. This is evident in the Gospel of John, the Epistles, and Revelation. After healing a man who had been lame for thirty-eight years, Jesus preaches a powerful sermon in which he puts his deeds on a par with the Father's. This includes the work of judgment: "The Father judges no one, but has given all judgment to the Son, that all may honor the Son, just as they honor the Father" (John 5:22–23). Not only does the Son perform the work of judgment done by God alone, but also he is worthy of the same honor as the Father. To prevent any misunderstanding of his words, Jesus drives home his point: "Whoever does not honor the Son does not honor the Father who sent him" (v. 23). Jesus deserves and wants divine honor for himself.

Such honor is given in John 9 by a man born blind. Jesus gives him sight and asks him if he believes in the Son of Man. When Jesus identifies himself as that Son of Man, the man replies: "'Lord, I believe,' and he worshiped him" (John 9:38). Perhaps the most famous example of worship in the Gospels is that of Thomas. Previously skeptical, when the resurrected Christ appears to him he exclaims: "My Lord and my God!" (20:28).

We already saw that Paul taught that all will bow before the exalted Jesus and confess that he is Lord (Phil. 2:9–11). It is important to note that although "all" here is universal in scope, it does not entail universalism— the view that everyone will be saved. The background in Isaiah 45 makes that clear. All will bow and swear allegiance to Yahweh, who according to Paul is Jesus (Isa. 45:23; Phil. 2:10–11). But that includes those who "shall come and be ashamed" even "all who were incensed against him" (v. 24). By contrast, "In the LORD all the offspring of Israel shall be justified and shall glory" (v. 25). So, all will come and bow in acknowledgment of Jesus' lordship. But those who hate God will be condemned while only spiritual Israelites will be saved.

Hebrews 1, a powerful passage on Christ's deity, teaches that the Father tells the angels to worship the Son: "When he brings the firstborn into the world, he says, 'Let all God's angels worship him'" (Heb. 1:6). When did this occur? At Bethlehem? No, but at Christ's session at God's right hand, as the preceding and following contexts in Hebrews 1 demonstrate. When the victorious Son returned to God's presence, there was much worship in heaven. The angels relate to Christ not as to a peer but as creatures relate to their Maker—they worship him.

Revelation also speaks of worship of Christ. John introduces his favorite designation for Christ—the Lamb—in chapter 5 and immediately speaks of worship. He is "a Lamb standing, as though it had been slain," before whom "the four living creatures and the twenty-four elders fell down" in worship (Rev. 5:6, 8; cf. 4:10). They sing a song of worship to him after which, accompanied by "myriads of myriads and thousands of thousands" they say "with a loud voice" a doxology to the Lamb. Indeed, they repeat the worship and ascribe to the Father and Son "blessing and honor and glory and might forever and ever!" (vv. 11–13). John then explicitly says: "And the four living creatures said, 'Amen!' and the elders fell down and worshiped" (v. 14).

Peter Carrell, who wrote a dissertation on Jesus and the angels in Revelation, aptly says:

> Jesus is bound with God in such a manner that together they form a single object of worship. . . . No encouragement is given to those inclined to believe Jesus to be a second god. Rather, there is a strict adherence to monotheism—but a monotheism which allows for Jesus to be included with God as the object of worship and which envisages Jesus sharing the divine throne with God.[20]

It is important to contrast what we have just seen with the fact that good human beings refuse worship, as Paul and Barnabas do in Acts 14:11–16, and that good angels do the same, as Revelation 19:10; 22:8–9 testifies. But the Lamb accepts worship from human beings and angels. He is not a mere man or an angel but God himself incarnate.

Baptism and the Lord's Supper

Religious devotion to Jesus includes baptism and the Lord's Supper. First, we consider Christian baptism. Previously, we learned from Simon Gathercole that gathering in Jesus' name, in Matthew 18:20, and baptizing in his name, in Matthew 28:19, were two religious rites that occur for Jesus' honor, so that he assumes the place of God. Gathercole draws additional implications from the latter passage. He admits that it would be possible (though he rejects the idea) to understand the name of Jesus as merely an extension of the name of Yahweh in most passages in the Synoptics. But not so in Matthew 28:19. Rather, this text "can only be understood as referring to an explanation or 'trifurcation' of the single divine name which has

---

[20]Cited in Bowman and Komoszewski, *Putting Jesus in His Place*, 43.

been revealed by the risen Jesus."[21] Jesus, alive from the dead, tells us what the name of the only God is—it is Father, Son, and Holy Spirit. "Jesus is an interpretation of the name of God in the last days."[22]

Gordon Fee brilliantly draws out implications for devotion to Christ from Paul's teaching concerning the Lord's Supper in 1 Corinthians 10–11.[23] Fee agrees with Hurtado and Gathercole that "this is *the Christian version of a meal in honor of a deity*"[24] and gives four reasons why this is so. First, Paul calls this meal "the Lord's supper," indicating that it pertains to "the Lord" in whose name and honor it is eaten (1 Cor. 11:20). Second, amazingly, "as with the Passover in Israel, which this meal replaces, this is the only singularly Christian meal, and the focus and honor belong to the 'Lord,' not to God the Father."[25] Third, Paul in 1 Corinthians 10 contrasts the Lord's Supper with meals in pagan temples that he labels "the table of demons" (1 Cor. 10:14–22). "Thus Paul's clear setting out of the Lord's Table as the Christian alternative to these pagan meals assumes that Christ is the Christian deity who is honored at his meal."[26] Fourth, Paul's severe words of correction put the abuse of the Corinthians in a strong christological framework. Make no mistake: a meal in honor of the Lord brings the Lord's temporal judgment on abusers (1 Cor. 11:29–32). "In Paul's Jewish worldview, such prerogatives belong to God alone."[27] The passage as a whole, therefore, teaches a very high christology, where Christ is presented as divine Savior and Lord.

Doxologies

Religious devotion to Jesus includes doxologies. We find these in the Epistles and Revelation:

> Now may the God of peace who brought again from the dead our Lord Jesus, the great shepherd of the sheep, by the blood of the eternal covenant, equip you with everything good that you may do his will, working in us that which is pleasing in his sight, through Jesus Christ, to whom be glory forever and ever. Amen. (Heb. 13:20–21)

---

[21]Gathercole, *The Pre-existent Son*, 68.
[22]Ibid., quoting Ruck-Schröder.
[23]Gordon D. Fee, *Pauline Christology: An Exegetical-Theological Study* (Peabody, MA: Hendrickson, 2007), 490–92. Fee points to Larry Hurtado for more thorough analysis than he can give: *Lord Jesus Christ*, 134–53.
[24]Fee, *Pauline Christology*, 491; emphasis original.
[25]Ibid.
[26]Ibid., 492.
[27]Ibid.

> But grow in the grace and knowledge of our Lord and Savior Jesus Christ. To him be the glory both now and to the day of eternity. Amen. (2 Pet. 3:18)

> Then I looked, and I heard around the throne and the living creatures and the elders the voice of many angels, numbering myriads of myriads and thousands of thousands, saying with a loud voice, "Worthy is the Lamb who was slain, to receive power and wealth and wisdom and might and honor and glory and blessing!" (Rev. 5:11–12)

In Revelation 5:12, the Lamb is praised, then the Father and Son together (v. 13). This shows that Christ is worthy to receive the worship due God the Father. Matthias Hoffmann, who wrote a dissertation on the Lamb in Revelation, deserves quotation: "Most of the predicates within the doxologies do not seem to distinguish God and the Lamb from each other, but rather express an equal status of both of them in general."[28]

Remarkably, in Hebrews 13:20–21 and 2 Peter 3:18 Jesus Christ alone is praised! He does not crowd out the Father but sometimes takes roles that we are accustomed to seeing the Father play. Bowman and Komoszewski sum up matters nicely: "By constructing such doxologies to God and Christ together, or even to Christ alone, the New Testament writers were exalting Jesus Christ to the very level of God."[29]

The Singing of Hymns
Religious devotion to Jesus includes the singing of hymns. This is evident in two Pauline texts:

> Let the word of Christ dwell in you richly, teaching and admonishing one another in all wisdom, singing psalms and hymns and spiritual songs, with thankfulness in your hearts to God. (Col. 3:16)

> Be filled with the Spirit, addressing one another in psalms and hymns and spiritual songs, singing and making melody to the Lord with your heart, giving thanks always and for everything to God the Father in the name of our Lord Jesus Christ, submitting to one another out of reverence for Christ. (Eph. 5:18–21)

We learn from the first text that the singing of Christian hymns focused on "the word of Christ," that is, the message about Christ. This message centered in his death and resurrection, as was explained in Colossians 1:15–23.

---

[28]Cited in Bowman and Komoszewski, *Putting Jesus in His Place*, 34.
[29]Ibid., 34.

We learn from the second text that such singing was to be done "to the Lord." Gordon Fee, who wrote a seven-hundred-page book on Pauline christology, explains, "Paul uses κύριος [*kurios*, "Lord"] exclusively to refer to Christ."[30] Fee effectively shows the significance of these two incidental references to singing: "For our purposes, the significance lies in the fact that in the Pauline churches Christ often assumes the dual role of being sung to and sung about—precisely as in the Psalter, whose hymns are both addressed to and inform about God."[31] Here again is evidence for Christ's deity.

Prayers

Religious devotion to Jesus includes prayers. We see this in the Gospel of John, Acts, Paul's letters, and Revelation. Though there is some manuscript variation, the best texts of John 14:13–14 include prayer addressed to Jesus: "Whatever you ask in my name, this I will do, that the Father may be glorified in the Son. If you ask me anything in my name, I will do it." To ask in Jesus' name is to approach the Father confidently based on the mediatorial work of Jesus (cf. John 16:23–24). Thus the disciples could not yet ask in Jesus' name because he had not returned to the Father (v. 24). After he returns they are to ask the Father on the basis of the Son's person and finished work. They are also to ask the Son himself: "If you ask me anything in my name, I will do it." Father and Son alike are the objects of Christian prayer.

This is vividly portrayed in Acts 7. There the martyr Stephen, as he was being stoned to death, "called out, 'Lord Jesus, receive my spirit'" (Acts 7:59). Here, combined with a use of "Lord" indicating divinity, is an urgent prayer directed to Jesus just as one would direct such a prayer to God. And that is the point. Praying to Jesus is praying to God.

The Bible ends with a prayer to Jesus. John begins Revelation thus: "The revelation of Jesus Christ, which God gave him to show to his servants the things that must *soon* take place" (Rev. 1:1). John ends his book on the same note when he records Jesus' words: "He who testifies to these things says, 'Surely I am coming *soon*'" (22:20). What follows is a prayer to Christ: "Amen. Come, Lord Jesus!"

It is too easy to take praying to Jesus for granted. But it is not to be taken for granted, as Bowman and Komoszewski remind us: "There is a close, natural link in biblical thought between prayer and salvation. . . . *God* is the Savior; *God* is the one who answers prayer. He is therefore the only one to whom we should turn in prayer."[32] That is exactly right, and in the New

[30] Fee, *Pauline Christology*, 525.
[31] Ibid., 493.
[32] Bowman and Komoszewski, *Putting Jesus in His Place*, 47; emphasis original.

Testament that great God, who alone saves and answers prayer, is named Father, Son (and Holy Spirit).

Conclusion

I cannot improve upon Gordon Fee's summary of Paul, which serves as a summary for the whole New Testament:

> The point of all this is that Christ as Savior is not just the *mediator of salvation*: he also emerges as the *object of devotion and worship* in the Pauline corpus, both for Paul and for his churches. And the worship is both because of *what* he did for us and especially of *who* he is as divine Savior. And what becomes clear in Paul's letters is that Christ's significance as divine Savior did not *begin* with his earthly life as Jesus of Nazareth; rather, that earthly life was an expression of an incarnation of the preexistent Son of God.[33]

Jesus Brings the Age to Come

The New Testament contrasts "the present age" and "the age to come." "The present age," the one in between Christ's advents, looks back on the Old Testament and ahead to "the age to come," the *eschaton*. "The present age" is characterized by evil (Gal. 1:4), spiritual blindness (2 Cor. 4:4), and spiritual death (Eph. 2:1–2). "The age to come" is characterized by the resurrection (Luke 20:3–36), eternal life (Luke 18:30), and the riches of God's grace (Eph. 2:7). From an Old Testament perspective, the fulfillment of the ages has come already (1 Cor. 10:11; Heb. 1:2; 9:26). Amazingly, believers living in "the present age" experience "the powers of the age to come" (Heb. 6:5). Although this is often explained as involving the overlapping of the future with the present, it better accords with New Testament theology to regard it as a present foretaste of greater future blessings.[34]

Biblical studies greatly aided eschatology by making another distinction—that between "the already" and "the not yet." Popularized by Oscar Cullmann, the ideas were already present in the writings of Geerhardus Vos.[35] Viewed from an Old Testament perspective the New Testament presents "the already," the fulfillment of prophetic predictions and hopes of the people of God. "In the New Testament we find the realization that the great

---

[33]Ibid., 494–95; emphasis original. Due to space constraints I exclude christological titles. For capable treatments see Stephen Wellum's chapter in this volume, "The Deity of Christ in the Synoptic Gospels," and Wells, *The Person of Christ*, 67–81.

[34]I thank David Clyde Jones, professor emeritus of systematic theology and ethics at Covenant Theological Seminary, for this insight.

[35]Oscar Cullmann, *Salvation in History*, trans. S. G. Sowers (New York: Harper & Row, 1967); Geerhardus Vos, *The Pauline Eschatology* (Grand Rapids, MI: Eerdmans, 1953).

eschatological event predicted in the Old Testament has happened."[36] This, of course, is the coming of Jesus Christ. Nevertheless, side by side with "the already" in the New Testament is "the not yet," the fact that many prophecies are yet to be fulfilled. The tension between "the already" and "the not yet" permeates the New Testament and contributes to its special character.

The significance of all this for our present purposes is this. The transitions from the Old Testament to "the present age" and from "the present age" to "the age to come" are solely the works of Almighty God. Human beings and angels do not cause these momentous transitions. Rather, only God himself establishes "the already" and "the not yet." Now it is evident that in the New Testament Jesus Christ brings both "the already" and "the not yet." This is powerful evidence that Scripture identifies Jesus with God.

It is Jesus Christ who brings both "ages." We see this in the Gospels, Acts, the Epistles, and Revelation. In the Gospels "the already" and "the not yet" are primarily presented as the coming of the kingdom of God, present and future. Jesus inaugurates the kingdom in his preaching, for he tells his disciples: "To you it has been given to know the secrets of the kingdom of heaven" (Matt. 13:11). Jesus brings the kingdom in his exorcisms: "But if it is by the Spirit of God that I cast out demons, then the kingdom of God has come upon you" (Matt. 12:28). "In and with the person of the incarnate Son has come the promised Messianic age, and this identification is so close that the age or Kingdom can only be entered by believing in Jesus," as Wells reminds us.[37]

And it is the same Jesus, the Son of Man, who will yet bring the consummated kingdom. He will return in great glory, sit on his glorious throne, judge the nations, and assign eternal destinies:

> Then the King will say to those on his right, "Come, you who are blessed by my Father, inherit the kingdom prepared for you from the foundation of the world." . . . Then he will say to those on his left, "Depart from me, you cursed, into the eternal fire prepared for the devil and his angels." (Matt. 25:34, 41)

It is the same in Acts. There the exalted Lord Jesus from his heavenly throne gives gifts of repentance and forgiveness now, as Peter declared: "God exalted him at his right hand as Leader and Savior, to give repentance to Israel and forgiveness of sins" (Acts 5:31). But "times of refreshing . . . from the presence of the Lord" have not yet come. When will they arrive? Only when the Father sends again "the Christ appointed for you, Jesus, whom

---

[36]Anthony A. Hoekema, *The Bible and the Future* (Grand Rapids, MI: Eerdmans, 1979), 15.
[37]Wells, *The Person of Christ*, 66.

heaven must receive until the time for restoring all the things about which God spoke by the mouth of his holy prophets long ago" (Acts 3:20–21).

It should not surprise us, then, that in the Epistles too Jesus brings "the already" and "the not yet." As believers our sins have been forgiven by Christ because we have become a part of his kingdom. God the Father already "has delivered us from the domain of darkness and transferred us to the kingdom of his beloved Son, in whom we have redemption, the forgiveness of sins" (Col. 1:13–14). But the day has not yet appeared when we will be resurrected and God will be all in all. That will happen only when the risen one, Jesus Christ, returns and transfers the kingdom to the Father:

> For as in Adam all die, so also in Christ shall all be made alive. But each in his own order: Christ the firstfruits, then at his coming those who belong to Christ. Then comes the end, when he delivers the kingdom to God the Father after destroying every rule and every authority and power. For he must reign until he has put all his enemies under his feet. (1 Cor. 15:22–25)

Finally, Revelation testifies to the same truths. Already Christ is the one "who loves us and has freed us from our sins by his blood and made us a kingdom, priests to his God and Father" (Rev. 1:5–6). But that day is still to come when his kingdom on earth will be outwardly and eternally established in the new heaven and new earth. Believers long for the day when "the kingdom of the world has become the kingdom of our Lord and of his Christ, and he shall reign forever and ever" (Rev. 11:15).

Here is a demonstration of Christ's deity as big as the New Testament itself. David Wells captures the point: "Jesus was the one in whom this 'age to come' was realized, through whom it is redemptively present in the church, and by whom it will be made cosmically effective at its consummation. He is the agent, the instrument, and the personifier of God's sovereign, eternal, saving rule."[38] Surely such divine roles can be played only by God himself—in this case God the Son incarnate.

Jesus Saves Us When We Are Spiritually United to Him

Salvation is God's work from beginning to end. He plans, accomplishes, applies, and consummates it. The Father planned salvation before the beginning of the world when he gave grace to a people whom he chose for himself (Eph. 1:4–5; 2 Tim. 1:9). The Son accomplished salvation when he died and arose to rescue sinners (Rom. 4:25; 1 Cor. 15:3–4). The Holy Spirit applies salvation when he opens hearts to the gospel (Acts 16:14; 1 Cor. 12:3). The

---

[38]Ibid., 172.

triune God consummates salvation when he raises the dead and brings final salvation (Rom. 8:11; Heb. 9:28).

Paul's favorite way of speaking of the application of salvation is union with Christ. In fact, union with Christ *is* the application of salvation. Union with Christ is the Holy Spirit's joining believers spiritually to Christ and to all his saving benefits. Paul speaks of union with Christ in two main ways. First, many times Paul speaks of being "in Christ," and although not every one of these occurrences pertains to union with Christ, the big majority does. Second, the apostle speaks of believers' being united with him in his death and resurrection. In fact, the Spirit joins believers to *all* Christ's saving deeds. We are joined to:

> Christ's death (Rom. 6:2–6, 8; Col. 2:20)
> Christ's resurrection (Rom. 6:4, 5, 8, 11; Eph. 2:5–6; Col. 3:1)
> Christ's ascension (Col. 3:3)
> Christ's session (Eph. 2:6)
> Christ's second coming (Rom. 8:19; Col. 3:4).

The last of these calls for special comment. What sense does it make to speak of our union with Christ's second coming? It is important to see that this is what Scripture teaches: "For the creation waits with eager longing for the revealing of the sons of God" (Rom. 8:19). Literally, it is "the *revelation* (Greek, *apokalypsis*) of the sons of God." "Revelation" speaks here of Christ's return even as it does in the first words of the last book of the Bible: "The revelation of Jesus Christ" (Rev. 1:1). Colossians 3:4 also teaches that we have been united to Christ in his return: "When Christ who is your life appears, then you also will appear with him in glory." It is obvious that "to appear" speaks of the second coming here because Paul uses it of Christ— "When Christ . . . appears." But believers also have a "second coming" of sorts—"then you also will appear with him in glory."

But what does it mean to say that we have a "revelation" and that we "will appear" with Christ? Paul means that we as Christians are so bound to Christ in saving union that our true identity will be manifested only when he comes again. Only then will it be revealed what spiritually beautiful daughters or handsome sons of God we are. In the meantime, we see only glimpses of our full identity as God's children.

To say that we have been united to Christ's saving deeds is to say that his deeds count for us; they are ours. With him we died to sin and with him we were raised to life (Rom. 6:2–11). Indeed, our union with him is so intimate and permanent that suffering (Rom. 8:17) and even death cannot separate us from him. For this reason John writes: "Blessed are the dead who die *in the Lord* from now on" (Rev. 14:13).

"Union with Christ is in itself a very broad and embracive subject. . . . Union with Christ is the central truth of the whole doctrine of salvation."[39] John Murray is right—union is very broad and embracive; in fact, it is the most comprehensive way of speaking of God's applying salvation to us. This is demonstrated by showing that the subsets of the application of salvation all involve union with Christ. Being joined to Christ, we receive:

> regeneration (Eph. 2:4–5)
> justification (2 Cor. 5:21; Phil. 3:9)
> adoption (Gal. 3:26–29)
> perseverance (Rom. 8:1, 38–39)
> resurrection (1 Cor. 15:22)
> glorification (Col. 3:4)

We are not regenerated, justified, and adopted apart from Christ, nor do we persevere apart from him, and we are not resurrected and glorified apart from Christ, but in spiritual union with him. Indeed, union with Christ *is* the application of salvation, as the list of constituents shows.

We have seen that union with Christ, as an aspect of salvation, is the work of God alone. In it the Holy Spirit joins believers to all of Christ's spiritual accomplishments. And this union is comprehensive, including all the various elements that comprise the application of salvation. But how does this union constitute an argument for Christ's deity? David Wells answers definitively: "To speak of being 'in' a teacher, and of participating at an ontological and ethical level in that teacher's capacities, would be preposterous if that teacher were not divine."[40]

It is difficult to overemphasize the importance of union with Christ in Paul's theology, as Hoekema reminds us: "This union underlies and makes possible the entire process of salvation. From beginning to end, we are saved only in Christ."[41] And the prominence of union highlights Christ's deity by underlining the fact that union casts him in a divine role, a role that only God could play.

It helps to understand this argument for Christ's deity by putting other beings in his place in the equation. What sense does it make to say we are "in the archangel Michael" or that "we died, were buried, and raised with the apostle Peter"? To ask these absurd questions is to answer them. It

---

[39] John Murray, *Redemption Accomplished and Applied* (Grand Rapids, MI: Eerdmans, 1955), 161, 170.
[40] Wells, *The Person of Christ*, 61.
[41] Anthony A. Hoekema, *Saved By Grace* (Grand Rapids, MI: Eerdmans, 1989), 59.

makes no sense at all to say that we are spiritually joined to mere creatures, whether angelic or human. It is, to use Wells's apt word, *preposterous.* Why? Because Christ's place in saving union is surely the place that only God occupies! Only union with the *God*-man in his death, resurrection, ascension, session, and second coming brings salvation. Only union with God himself brings regeneration, justification, adoption, perseverance, resurrection, and glorification. Union with Christ, then, is a sweeping and powerful demonstration of our Lord's deity.

Jesus Performs the Works of God

A prominent biblical argument for Christ's deity is that he performs many works that only God can perform. These include the works of creation, providence, judgment, and salvation.

The Son of God and Creation

Both Testaments abundantly testify to the fact that God alone does the work of creation.

In the beginning, God created the heavens and the earth. (Gen. 1:1)

Know that the Lord, he is God!
    It is he who made us, and we are his. (Ps. 100:3)

To whom then will you compare me,
    that I should be like him? says the Holy One.
Lift up your eyes on high and see:
    who created these? (Isa. 40:25–26)

And when they heard it, they lifted their voices together to God and said, "Sovereign Lord, who made the heaven and the earth and the sea and everything in them." (Acts 4:24)

To me . . . this grace was given, to preach to the Gentiles the unsearchable riches of Christ, and to bring to light for everyone what is the plan of the mystery hidden for ages in God who created all things. (Eph. 3:8–9)

Worthy are you, our Lord and God,
    to receive glory and honor and power,
for you created all things,
    and by your will they existed and were created. (Rev. 4:11)

The New Testament does not hesitate to ascribe the work of creation to the Son of God:

All things were made through him, and without him was not any thing made that was made. (John 1:3)

Yet for us there is one God, the Father, from whom are all things and for whom we exist, and one Lord, Jesus Christ, through whom are all things and through whom we exist. (1 Cor. 8:6)

For by him all things were created, in heaven and on earth, visible and invisible, whether thrones or dominions or rulers or authorities—all things were created through him and for him. (Col. 1:16)

But in these last days he has spoken to us by his Son, whom he appointed the heir of all things, through whom also he created the world. (Heb. 1:2)

> You, Lord, laid the foundation of the earth in the beginning,
> and the heavens are the work of your hands."(Heb. 1:10)

A few comments are in order. John 1:3 speaks comprehensively by affirming the positive—"All things were made through him"—and denying the negative—"and without him was not any thing made that was made." The eternal Word, who was God, was the Father's agent in creating *everything*.

First Corinthians 8:6 parallels the creative work of the Father and Son. "The Father" is the one "from whom are all things and for whom we exist," and the "Lord, Jesus Christ" is the one "through whom are all things and through whom we exist." Father and Son alike perform the divine work of creation.

Similar to John 1:3, Colossians 1:16 comprehensively ascribes creation to the Son. It does so in three ways. First by echoing Genesis 1:1: "By him all things were created, in heaven and on earth." The words "the heavens and the earth" in the Bible's first verse comprehensively designate creative reality and so do "all things . . . in heaven and on earth" in Colossians 1:16. Second, when Paul says, "By him all things were created . . . visible and invisible," he speaks comprehensively. There is no third category; all creatures are either "visible" or "invisible" (the angels, "whether thrones or dominions or rulers or authorities"). Third, by repetition, thus creating an inclusion: "all things were created through him." It is difficult to conceive how Paul could more emphatically say that the Son of God created everything that has been created.

Twice in his first chapter, the author to the Hebrews teaches that the divine Son was the Father's agent in creation. First, he speaks of "his

Son . . . through whom also he created the world" (Heb. 1:2). Second, he quotes Psalm 102, ascribing to Christ what was there said of God: "You, Lord, laid the foundation of the earth in the beginning, and the heavens are the work of your hands" (Heb. 1:10). This too is an allusion to Genesis 1:1 and God's universal work of creation.

The argument is powerful: the Old Testament consistently assigns the work of creation to Almighty God. The New Testament does the same to Jesus Christ.

The Son of God and Providence

Both Testaments abundantly testify to the fact that God alone does the work of providence. God not only creates all things but he alone sustains and directs them to his appointed ends:

> O LORD, how manifold are your works!
>> In wisdom have you made them all;
>> the earth is full of your creatures.
> Here is the sea, great and wide,
>> which teems with creatures innumerable,
>> living things both small and great.
>
> There go the ships,
>> and Leviathan, which you formed to play in it.
>
> These all look to you,
>> to give them their food in due season.
> When you give it to them, they gather it up;
>> when you open your hand, they are filled with good things.
> When you hide your face, they are dismayed;
>> when you take away their breath, they die
>> and return to their dust.
> When you send forth your Spirit, they are created,
>> and you renew the face of the ground. (Ps. 104:24–30)

The God who made the world and everything in it, being Lord of heaven and earth, does not live in temples made by man, nor is he served by human hands, as though he needed anything, since he himself gives to all mankind life and breath and everything. And he made from one man every nation of mankind to live on all the face of the earth, having determined allotted periods and the boundaries of their dwelling place, that they should seek God, in the hope that they might feel their way toward him and find him. Yet he is actually not far from each one of us, for "In him we live and move and have our being." (Acts 17:24–28)

The New Testament does not hesitate to ascribe the work of providence to the Son of God:

> And he is before all things, and in him all things hold together. (Col. 1:17)

> He is the radiance of the glory of God and the exact imprint of his nature, and he upholds the universe by the word of his power. After making purification for sins, he sat down at the right hand of the Majesty on high. (Heb. 1:3)

The divine work of providence has two aspects, preservation and government. Preservation is God's work of sustaining his creation. Government is his work of directing his creation toward his ends. The first aspect of providence is highlighted in these two New Testament texts. In Christ "all things hold together" (Col. 1:17). In context it refers to all created reality, as we showed above. The Son holds together all created reality.

Among other great things, Hebrews 1:3 says that the Son "upholds the universe by the word of his power." The English Standard Version renders "all things" as "universe." The Son upholds all things by his powerful word. This is another unanswerable argument for Christ's deity. Because he performs the divine work of providence he is God.

The Son of God and Judgment

Both Testaments abundantly testify to the fact that God alone does the work of judgment:

> Far be it from you to do such a thing, to put the righteous to death with the wicked, so that the righteous fare as the wicked! Far be that from you! Shall not the Judge of all the earth do what is just? (Gen. 18:25)

> The heavens declare his righteousness,
>   for God himself is judge! (Ps. 50:6)

> Then shall all the trees of the forest sing for joy
>   before the LORD, for he comes,
>   for he comes to judge the earth.
>   He will judge the world in righteousness,
>   and the peoples in his faithfulness. (Ps. 96:12–13)

> Why do you pass judgment on your brother? Or you, why do you despise your brother? For we will all stand before the judgment seat of God. (Rom. 14:10)

And if you call on him as Father who judges impartially according to each one's deeds, conduct yourselves with fear throughout the time of your exile. (1 Pet. 1:17)

The New Testament does not hesitate to ascribe the work of judgment to the Son of God:

For the Son of Man is going to come with his angels in the glory of his Father, and then he will repay each person according to what he has done. (Matt. 16:27)

The Father judges no one, but has given all judgment to the Son, that all may honor the Son, just as they honor the Father. Whoever does not honor the Son does not honor the Father who sent him. (John 5:22–23)

And he commanded us to preach to the people and to testify that he is the one appointed by God to be judge of the living and the dead. (Acts 10:42)

. . . when the Lord Jesus is revealed from heaven with his mighty angels in flaming fire, inflicting vengeance on those who do not know God and on those who do not obey the gospel of our Lord Jesus. (2 Thess. 1:7–8)

Jesus Christ, according to the New Testament, will execute all judgment. The reason that John gives for this is particularly instructive: "that all may honor the Son, just as they honor the Father. Whoever does not honor the Son does not honor the Father who sent him" (John 5:23). Because he performs the divine work of judgment, Jesus is worthy of the worship due only God. The conclusion is irresistible: the Son too is God.

In fact, a corollary of the fact that in the New Testament Jesus shares the work of judgment with the Father is a change in familiar Old Testament terminology. The Old Testament speaks of "the day of the Lord" as the time when God would visit his people in judgment. Usually this refers to events near to the time of the prophets (Isa. 13:6; Ezek. 13:5; Joel 1:15; Amos 5:18). But sometimes, it refers to events far off (Joel 2:31; Obad. 15).

Sometimes the New Testament uses the Old Testament expression in a way similar to that of the Old Testament (1 Cor. 5:5; 1 Thess. 5:2; 2 Pet. 3:10). But at other times, in the New Testament "the day of the Lord" becomes "the day of our Lord Jesus Christ" (1 Cor. 1:8), "the day of our Lord Jesus" (2 Cor. 1:14), "the day of Jesus Christ" (Phil. 1:6), or "the day of Christ" (Phil. 1:10; 2:16). At least once, the very Old Testament expression "the day of the Lord" is used in the New Testament with reference to Jesus:

Now concerning the coming of our Lord Jesus Christ and our being gathered together to him, we ask you, brothers, not to be quickly shaken in mind or alarmed, either by a spirit or a spoken word, or a letter seeming to be from us, to the effect that the day of the Lord has come. (2 Thess. 2:1–2)

Bowman and Komoszewski highlight the inescapable conclusion of such evidence:

New Testament affirmations of Jesus as the eschatological Judge not only assign him that role but often do so (once again) in language that appears to be deliberately echoing Old Testament affirmations about the Lord God. . . . The use of such a familiar Old Testament idiom ["the day of the LORD"] in reference to the Lord Jesus' exercising the same function of judgment strongly identifies the Lord Jesus with the Lord YHWH.[42]

The Son of God and Salvation

Perhaps the strongest argument for the deity of Christ is that he is the Savior. Both Testaments abundantly testify to the fact that God alone does the work of salvation. He alone is the Savior:

The LORD is my strength and my song,
    and he has become my salvation;
this is my God, and I will praise him,
    my father's God, and I will exalt him. (Ex. 15:2)

For God alone my soul waits in silence;
    from him comes my salvation.
He only is my rock and my salvation,
    my fortress; I shall not be greatly shaken. . . .
On God rests my salvation and my glory;
    my mighty rock, my refuge is God. (Ps. 62:1–2, 7)

But I with the voice of thanksgiving
    will sacrifice to you;
what I have vowed I will pay.
    Salvation belongs to the LORD! (Jonah 2:9)

And Mary said,
    "My soul magnifies the Lord,
    and my spirit rejoices in God my Savior." (Luke 1:46–47)

---

[42]Bowman and Komoszewski, *Putting Jesus in His Place*, 229–30.

> Paul, an apostle of Christ Jesus by command of God our Savior and
> of Christ Jesus our hope . . . (1 Tim. 1:1)

The New Testament does not hesitate to ascribe the work of salvation to the Son of God. It does so in at least seven ways.

1) Jesus is called "Savior." As the above quotations show, God is called "savior" in the Old Testament. The quotations of Luke 1:47 and 1 Timothy 1:1 above also show that sometimes the New Testament calls God the Father "Savior" (see also 1 Tim. 2:3; 4:10). But the New Testament calls Jesus "Savior" as well. In fact, three times Titus refers to both the Father and Son as "Savior" in short compass:

> Paul . . . in hope of eternal life, which God . . . manifested in his word through the preaching with which I have been entrusted by the command of God our Savior; To Titus, my true child in a common faith: Grace and peace from God the Father and Christ Jesus our Savior. (Titus 1:1–4)

> . . . not pilfering, but showing all good faith, so that in everything they may adorn the doctrine of God our Savior. . . . Waiting for our blessed hope, the appearing of the glory of our great God and Savior Jesus Christ. (Titus 2:10, 13)

> But when the goodness and loving kindness of God our Savior appeared, he saved us, not because of works done by us in righteousness, but according to his own mercy, by the washing of regeneration and renewal of the Holy Spirit, whom he poured out on us richly through Jesus Christ our Savior. (Titus 3:4–6)

In many other places Jesus is called "Savior," including Luke 2:11; John 4:42; Acts 5:31; 13:23; Ephesians 5:23; Philippians 3:20; 2 Peter 3:2; and 1 John 4:14. And in many other places Scripture presents Jesus as the only Savior, without using the word "Savior." An angel of the Lord announces to Joseph: "She will bear a son, and you shall call his name Jesus, for he will save his people from their sins" (Matt. 1:21). Jesus is the unique mediator of the knowledge of God the Father: "And no one knows the Father except the Son and anyone to whom the Son chooses to reveal him" (Matt. 11:27). Jesus himself declared: "I am the way, and the truth, and the life. No one comes to the Father except through me" (John 14:6). How do people gain eternal life? The apostles answer unambiguously: "Believe in the Lord Jesus, and you will be saved, you and your household" (Acts 16:31). He is "the source of eternal salvation to all who obey him" (Heb. 5:9). Paul's summary of his saving message is: "Christ died for our sins in accordance with the Scriptures, that he was buried, that he was raised on the third day in accordance with the Scriptures" (1 Cor. 15:3–4).

Scripture says and shows that Jesus Christ is the Savior of the world. And because only God saves, this means that Jesus is identified with God.

2) Jesus forgives sins. In every section the Old Testament teaches that forgiving sins is a divine prerogative:

> The LORD, the LORD, a God merciful and gracious, slow to anger, and abounding in steadfast love and faithfulness, keeping steadfast love for thousands, forgiving iniquity and transgression and sin. (Ex. 34:6–7)

> He does not deal with us according to our sins,
>   nor repay us according to our iniquities. . . .
> as far as the east is from the west,
>   so far does he remove our transgressions from us. (Ps. 103:10, 12)

> I, I am he who blots out your transgressions for my own sake,
>   and I will not remember your sins. (Isa. 43:25)

In every section of the New Testament forgiving sins is also Jesus' divine prerogative:

> "Therefore I tell you, her sins, which are many, are forgiven—for she loved much. But he who is forgiven little, loves little." And he said to her, "Your sins are forgiven." Then those who were at table with him began to say among themselves, "Who is this, who even forgives sins?" (Luke 7:47–49)

> The God of our fathers raised Jesus, whom you killed by hanging him on a tree. God exalted him at his right hand as Leader and Savior, to give repentance to Israel and forgiveness of sins. (Acts 5:30–31)

> He has delivered us from the domain of darkness and transferred us to the kingdom of his beloved Son, in whom we have redemption, the forgiveness of sins. (Col. 1:13–14)

> To him who loves us and has freed us from our sins by his blood and made us a kingdom, priests to his God and Father, to him be glory and dominion forever and ever. Amen. (Rev. 1:5–6)

Only God forgives sins. And Jesus forgives sins.

3) Jesus does the work that saves human beings forever. Sometimes we take for granted the magnificent work that the Son of God performed to save us. Of course, this theme is predicted in the Old Testament and reverberates throughout the New Testament. I will focus on what only one New Testament document—the letter to the Hebrews—teaches about the grandeur of Christ's saving accomplishment:

> After making purification for sins, he sat down at the right hand of the Majesty on high. (Heb. 1:3)

> Since therefore the children share in flesh and blood, he himself likewise partook of the same things, that through death he might destroy the one who has the power of death, that is, the devil, and deliver all those who through fear of death were subject to lifelong slavery. (Heb. 2:14–15)

> But when Christ appeared as a high priest of the good things that have come, then through the greater and more perfect tent (not made with hands, that is, not of this creation) he entered once for all into the holy places, not by means of the blood of goats and calves but by means of his own blood, thus securing an eternal redemption. (Heb. 9:11–12)

> And every priest stands daily at his service, offering repeatedly the same sacrifices, which can never take away sins. But when Christ had offered for all time a single sacrifice for sins, he sat down at the right hand of God, waiting from that time until his enemies should be made a footstool for his feet. For by a single offering he has perfected for all time those who are being sanctified. (Heb. 10:11–14)

Unlike the Old Testament priests, who offered a million sacrifices, Christ made one sacrifice (Heb. 10:12). But what a sacrifice it was! Unlike the Old Testament priests, who never sat down while serving in tabernacle or temple, Christ sat down at God's right hand (Heb. 1:3; 10:12). How is it possible for one sacrifice to make "purification," "destroy . . . the devil," and secure "an eternal redemption" (Heb. 1:3; 2:15; 9:12)? How can "a single offering" perfect "for all time those who are being sanctified" (Heb. 10:14)? We cannot explain these things fully. But there is one important fact that can help us understand in part—the identity of the one who died (and arose). This sacrifice is monumental because of the one who made it—the God-man Jesus Christ. The death of no mere human being or angel could accomplish the things that Jesus' death did. The fact that he performed a work that saves believers forever, then, points to his divine identity.

4) Jesus raises himself from the dead. When Paul sums up the gospel that he preached, he does not stop with the crucifixion: "For I delivered to you as of first importance what I also received: that Christ died for our sins in accordance with the Scriptures, that he was buried, that he was raised on the third day in accordance with the Scriptures" (1 Cor. 15:3–4). Jesus' resurrection is an essential part of the gospel. His resurrection saves, as he explains: "Because I live, you also will live" (John 14:19). The apostle Paul affirms: "Jesus our Lord . . . was delivered up for our trespasses and raised for our justification," and, "As in Adam all die, so also in Christ shall all be made alive" (Rom. 4:24–25; 1 Cor. 15:22). And the writer to the Hebrews adds: "Consequently, he is able to save to the uttermost those who draw near to God through him, since he always lives to make intercession for them" (Heb. 7:25).

Jesus' resurrection saves, but who raises him from the dead? Both Peter and Paul point to Psalm 16 as an Old Testament passage that predicts the Messiah's resurrection (Acts 2:24–32; 13:32–35). Peter specifically cites these verses:

> I have set the LORD always before me;
>> because he is at my right hand, I shall not be shaken.
> Therefore my heart is glad, and my whole being rejoices;
>> my flesh also dwells secure.
> For you will not abandon my soul to Sheol,
>> or let your holy one see corruption.
> You make known to me the path of life;
>> in your presence there is fullness of joy;
>> at your right hand are pleasures forevermore. (vv. 8–11)

It is plain that God will raise his Messiah.

Whom does the New Testament credit with raising Jesus? Most often it attributes this mighty deed to God the Father: "If you confess with your mouth that Jesus is Lord and believe in your heart that God raised him from the dead, you will be saved" (Rom. 10:9). "He . . . was made manifest in the last times for the sake of you who through him are believers in God, who raised him from the dead and gave him glory, so that your faith and hope are in God" (1 Pet. 1:20–21). A few times it appears to attribute Jesus' resurrection to the Holy Spirit—Romans 1:4; 1 Peter 3:18.

Amazingly, twice in John's Gospel Jesus raises himself from the dead:

> Jesus answered them, "Destroy this temple, and in three days I will raise it up." The Jews then said, "It has taken forty-six years to build this temple, and will you raise it up in three days?" But he was speaking about the temple of his body. When therefore he was raised from the dead, his disciples remembered that he had said this, and they believed the Scripture and the word that Jesus had spoken. (John 2:19–22)

> For this reason the Father loves me, because I lay down my life that I may take it up again. No one takes it from me, but I lay it down of my own accord. I have authority to lay it down, and I have authority to take it up again. This charge I have received from my Father. (John 10:17–18)

Resurrecting the Son of God is a divine work, predicted in the Old Testament and performed by the Father, Holy Spirit, and even the Son himself.

5) Jesus is the object of saving faith. In the Old Testament God alone is the proper object of his people's faith. This is evident in the life of Abraham, the father of the Jews: "He believed the LORD, and he counted it to him as righteousness" (Gen. 15:6). Later, when the Red Sea swallowed the Egyptian army, "Israel saw the great power that the LORD used against the Egyptians, so the people feared the LORD, and they believed in the LORD" (Ex. 14:31). Bowman and Komoszewski remind us, "In the New Testament, God is still the primary object of faith. Jesus himself told his disciples, 'Have faith in God' (Mark 11:22). One of the fundamentals of the Christian religion is 'faith toward God' (Heb. 6:1)."[43]

But the New Testament proclaims an additional message. Repeatedly, it presents Jesus as the proper object of saving faith. Here is a sampling:

> For God so loved the world, that he gave his only Son, that whoever believes in him should not perish but have eternal life. (John 3:16)

> Whoever believes in the Son has eternal life; whoever does not obey the Son shall not see life, but the wrath of God remains on him. (John 3:36)

> And I said, "Who are you, Lord?" And the Lord said, "I am Jesus whom you are persecuting. . . . I am sending you to open their eyes, so that they may turn from darkness to light and from the power of Satan to God, that they may receive forgiveness of sins and a place among those who are sanctified by faith in me." (Acts 26:15–18)

> But now the righteousness of God has been manifested apart from the law, although the Law and the Prophets bear witness to it—the righteousness of God through faith in Jesus Christ for all who believe. (Rom. 3:21–22)

> Yet we know that a person is not justified by works of the law but through faith in Jesus Christ, so we also have believed in Christ Jesus, in order to be justified by faith in Christ and not by works of the law. (Gal. 2:16)

---

[43] Ibid., *Putting Jesus in His Place*, 62.

And this is his commandment, that we believe in the name of his Son Jesus Christ and love one another, just as he has commanded us. (1 John 3:23)

Scripture is unequivocal: "There is no other name under heaven given among men by which we must be saved" (Acts 4:12). John Frame speaks truth:

> As J. Gresham Machen argued so eloquently against the theological liberalism of his day, Scripture presents Jesus, not primarily as a model or example of faith, but as the object of faith. . . . The commitment of the biblical writers to Christ as the ultimate object of faith and worship led them often to speak of Christ and the Father in interchangeable terms. . . . So we see again the pervasiveness of the biblical teaching concerning the deity of Christ.[44]

6) Jesus gives the Holy Spirit to his church. It is not always appreciated that Pentecost is as much a part of Jesus' saving work as his death and resurrection. Here we emphasize that it is a *divine* saving work. The prophet Joel predicts that in the last days God himself would pour out his Spirit on all flesh:

> And it shall come to pass afterward, that I will pour out my Spirit on all flesh; your sons and your daughters shall prophesy, your old men shall dream dreams, and your young men shall see visions. Even on the male and female servants in those days I will pour out my Spirit. . . . And it shall come to pass that everyone who calls on the name of the LORD shall be saved. (Joel 2:28–32; cf. Ezek. 36:25–27)

John the Baptist in all four Gospels predicts that the Messiah will baptize the church with the Holy Spirit: "After me comes he who is mightier than I, the strap of whose sandals I am not worthy to stoop down and untie. I have baptized you with water, but he will baptize you with the Holy Spirit" (Mark 1:7–8; cf. Matt. 3:11; Luke 3:16; John 1:32–34).

In his farewell discourses in the fourth Gospel, Jesus predicts that the Father and he will send the Spirit to perform vital ministries. Here is one example: "I will ask the Father, and he will give you another Helper, to be with you forever, even the Spirit of truth, whom the world cannot receive, because it neither sees him nor knows him. You know him, for he dwells with you and will be in you" (John 14:16–17; cf. 14:25–26; 15:26–27; 16:7–11; 16:12–15).

The coming of the Spirit at Pentecost is so important in Acts that immediately after his introduction, Luke records Jesus' words to his disciples:

---

[44]John M. Frame, *The Doctrine of God: A Theology of Lordship* (Phillipsburg, NJ: P&R, 2002), 679, 680.

he "ordered them . . . to wait for the promise of the Father, which, he said, 'you heard from me; for John baptized with water, but you will be baptized with the Holy Spirit not many days from now'" (Acts 1:4–5). The Baptist predicted that the Messiah would baptize the church with the Holy Spirit, and in Acts 2 he does just that. The coming of the Holy Spirit at Pentecost is the work of the Messiah, Jesus.

The Jewish feast of Pentecost after Jesus' death and resurrection is like none other. The Jewish pilgrims, who came to Jerusalem from across the Roman Empire, had no idea of the special thing God would do. He works through wind and fire, both of which symbolize the coming of the Holy Spirit. The word translated "spirit" (*pneuma*) means "breath," "wind," or "spirit." God sends a mighty wind to indicate that he was about to pour out his Holy Wind upon the apostles. God does this to proclaim the mighty works of Jesus in order to bring many people into his kingdom. He accomplishes this by filling the apostles with the Holy Spirit and giving them the ability to speak in languages they do not know, the very languages of the Pentecost pilgrims. In response to the Jewish pilgrims' astonishment that they each hear the apostles telling of God's mighty works of God in their own languages (vv. 7–8), Peter explains: "This is what was uttered through the prophet Joel" (v. 16). Peter then quotes the entire prophecy of Joel cited above.

Peter proceeds to preach Jesus to them—crucified and risen from the dead, in fulfillment of Old Testament prophecies: "This Jesus God raised up, and of that we all are witnesses. Being therefore exalted at the right hand of God, and having received from the Father the promise of the Holy Spirit, he has poured out this that you yourselves are seeing and hearing" (vv. 32–33).

It is crucial to understand that *Jesus* pours out the Spirit on the church on the day of Pentecost. He is the Messiah, the Christ, the anointed one. He received the Spirit at his baptism in order eventually to give the Spirit to the church. The four Gospels record the most important of Jesus' saving deeds—his death and resurrection. But the Gospels do not record Jesus' pouring out the Spirit upon the church. That would wait until Acts 2, where Jesus performs the divine work of sending the Spirit to the church in a new and powerful way. This is a work of God, according to Joel; indeed it was a work of the Lord Jesus. As Peter explained, this event serves as proof that Jesus is both Christ and *Lord* (Acts 2:36).

7) Jesus consummates salvation. The Old Testament ascribes to God alone the prerogatives of putting people to death and making them alive:

> The LORD kills and brings to life;
>> he brings down to Sheol and raises up. (1 Sam. 2:6)

> See now that I, even I, am he,
>> and there is no god beside me;
> I kill and I make alive;
>> I wound and I heal;
>> and there is none that can deliver out of my hand. (Deut. 32:39)[45]

The New Testament continues to speak of God in similar terms, although transposing them to a higher key. Jesus warns: "Do not fear those who kill the body but cannot kill the soul. Rather fear him who can destroy both soul and body in hell" (Matt. 10:28). His brother James affirms: "There is only one lawgiver and judge, he who is able to save and to destroy" (James 4:12). The New Testament applies the Old Testament principle of God's killing and making alive to eternal destinies.

And the New Testament ascribes these same divine prerogatives to the returning Christ. It is he who will "make alive" the dead, assign eternal destinies, and bring final salvation, including the new heavens and new earth.

Jesus will raise the dead. The Gospel of John teaches that Jesus will perform the divine work of raising the dead:

> Do not marvel at this, for an hour is coming when all who are in the tombs will hear his voice and come out, those who have done good to the resurrection of life, and those who have done evil to the resurrection of judgment. (John 5:28–29)

> For this is the will of my Father, that everyone who looks on the Son and believes in him should have eternal life, and I will raise him up on the last day. (John 6:40)

> No one can come to me unless the Father who sent me draws him. And I will raise him up on the last day. (John 6:44)

> Whoever feeds on my flesh and drinks my blood has eternal life, and I will raise him up on the last day. (John 6:54)

Raising the dead is a job for God alone; no mere human being or angel raises the dead. Because Christ performs this role, he is God. Jesus also performs the divine role of assigning saints and sinners their final destinies:

---

[45] I credit Bowman and Komoszewski, *Putting Jesus in His Place*, 228, for pointing me to these texts.

Then the King will say to those on his right, "Come, you who are blessed by my Father, inherit the kingdom prepared for you from the foundation of the world." (Matt. 25:34)

Then he will say to those on his left, "Depart from me, you cursed, into the eternal fire prepared for the devil and his angels." (Matt. 25:41)

Surely this is a divine work! Who but God will assign human beings to heaven or hell?

Jesus will bring final salvation. The New Testament casts Jesus in the role of consummating salvation when he returns. In his first coming Jesus, our great High Priest, offered himself as an atoning sacrifice. In his second coming he will bring salvation: "And just as it is appointed for man to die once, and after that comes judgment, so Christ, having been offered once to bear the sins of many, will appear a second time, not to deal with sin but to save those who are eagerly waiting for him" (Heb. 9:27–28).

Although we live on earth, "our citizenship is in heaven." From there "we await a Savior, the Lord Jesus Christ, who will transform our lowly body to be like his glorious body, by the power that enables him even to subject all things to himself" (Phil. 3:20–21). Our mortal bodies are lowly because they are subject to illness and death. At his return Christ will exert his almighty power and cause our lowly bodies to share his resurrection glory. His second coming will mean great glory for all the redeemed.

Jesus will bring cosmic restoration. Through Jesus "God was pleased . . . to reconcile to himself all things, whether on earth or in heaven, making peace by the blood of his cross" (Col. 1:19–20). Jesus' death and resurrection not only save all the people of God of all ages but are the reason why there will be a new heaven and a new earth (Isa. 65:17; 66:22–23). His saving work has cosmic consequences.

When will those cosmic consequences be manifested? After speaking of Jesus' sufferings, Peter invites his hearers in Jerusalem to repent that "times of refreshing may come from the presence of the Lord, and that he may send the Christ appointed for you, Jesus, whom heaven must receive until the time for restoring all the things" (Acts 3:20–21). Jesus' return will bring many blessings for his people, including God's "restoring all things" according to Old Testament prediction. This cosmic restoration, a work of God himself, is accomplished by the returning Son of God.

In all of these ways, Jesus will bring consummate salvation, and here again Scripture identifies him with God.

Conclusion

I have marshaled five arguments for the deity of Christ:

1) Jesus is identified with God.
2) Jesus receives devotion due God alone.
3) Jesus brings the age to come.
4) Jesus saves us when we are spiritually united to him.
5) Jesus performs the works of God.

It is difficult to overemphasize the significance of Christ's deity. It has huge ramifications for Christian theology and life.

Christianity stands if Christ's deity is true. If Jesus is divine, then his claims are true "and there is salvation in no one else, for there is no other name under heaven given among men by which we must be saved," as Peter preached (Acts 4:12). G. C. Berkouwer understands well that Christ's deity is essential to Christianity:

> The heart of the Christian religion pulsates in the confession that in Jesus Christ, in the Incarnation of the Word, God truly came down to us. . . . The practice of the ancient church, to speak of Christ "as of God," goes directly back to the New Testament itself where we hear adoring voices addressing Christ as truly God and not as quasi-God.[46]

Robert L. Reymond underscores the importance of that subject for the other topics in systematic theology:

> Whatever else one may think of Karl Barth's total theological edifice (and I find much in it with which I must disagree), he was absolutely right when he declared that what a man thinks about Christ will determine what he ultimately thinks about everything else. Jesus even declared that a man's eternal destiny would be determined by his thoughts about Him (John 8:24).[47]

Reymond is right on both counts. The affirmation or denial of Christ's deity affects every other locus for christology and for systematic theology in general. It is also true that one's estimation of Jesus has consequences beyond this life, as Jesus himself says: "Unless you believe that I am he you will die in your sins" (John 8:24). Indeed, Jesus claims: "I am the way, and

---

[46]G. C. Berkouwer, *The Person of Christ*, Studies in Dogmatics (Grand Rapids, MI: Eerdmans, 1954), 156–57, 161–62.
[47]Reymond, *Jesus, Divine Messiah*, 323.

the truth, and the life. No one comes to the Father except through me" (John 14:6).

Bernard Ramm communicates this truth in a pithy manner: "Christology is so central to Christian theology that to alter Christology is to alter all else."[48] David Wells elaborates on this statement and laments the disastrous effects for those who deny the deity of Christ:

> Their christs might be admired, but they cannot be worshiped. They might inspire religious devotion, but they cannot sustain or explain Christian faith. They tell us very much about their authors and very little about Jesus. They are, inevitably, half-breed christs. They are half ancient and half modern. . . . These christs are impotent, and their appeal is superficial. Their appeal is not that of the biblical Christ.[49]

The true Christ of Scripture deserves more than our admiration. That is because he is the eternal Word become incarnate in Jesus of Nazareth. He is God and man in one person and deserves worship as the only mediator between God and human beings. Because he is God, "he is able to save to the uttermost those who draw near to God through him" (Heb. 7:25). As Wells reminds us, the biblical Christ is "the One who was God with us, the means of forgiveness for our sin, and the agent of our reconciliation. Forgiveness and reconciliation are what we need centrally. We need to know there is someone there to forgive us, someone who can forgive and heal us, and that was why the Word was incarnate."[50]

---

[48]Bernard Ramm, *An Evangelical Christology: Ecumenic and Historic* (Nashville: Nelson, 1985), 16.
[49]Wells, *The Person of Christ*, 172
[50]Ibid.

9

The Deity of Christ and the Cults

ALAN W. GOMES

W ho do people say that the Son of Man is?" The question that Jesus asked his disciples in Matthew 16:13 is just as relevant today as when he first asked it over two thousand years ago. If anything, one now finds an even greater diversity of answers than when Jesus originally posed this query.

The typical "man on the street" views Jesus as a benign moral teacher who taught a sublime system of ethics, captured in aphorisms like the Golden Rule. Some may toss in the idea that he was a prophet for good measure. But ask the average person whether he or she believes that Jesus is God come in the flesh and you will likely receive a blank stare.

Nowhere is the diversity of opinion about Jesus—or "chaos," to use Van Baalen's pointed description—more evident than in the cults.[1] The Jesus of the cults not only includes the "man on the street" view described above but many other positions besides. Some cults describe Jesus as a kind of guru, dispensing nuggets of arcane, theosophical wisdom,[2] while others see him as a kind of quasi-divine being—less than God but more than a mere

---

[1] J. K. Van Baalen, *The Chaos of the Cults* (Grand Rapids, MI: Eerdmans, 1962).
[2] "Theosophy" refers to a system of esoteric, mystical insights into the being of God. Only initiates, or those "in the know," possess these special insights.

man. Still other cultists believe that he attained divine status by obedience to the same commands and precepts that they themselves follow. And then there are those who regard Jesus to be God in the literal and full sense of the word but identify him as the same person as the Father and the Holy Spirit, thus denying that the one God exists as three eternal persons. If Jesus' words are as relevant today as they were over two thousand years ago, then so are the apostle Paul's, who warned against believing in "another Jesus," "a different spirit," and "a different gospel" (2 Cor. 11:4).

This chapter examines what the cults say about the deity of Christ and also considers the crucial practical implications of these views. It is fair to say that *all* the cults have an incorrect view of Jesus, i.e., they advance "another Jesus" than the Jesus of the Bible. But this does not mean that all cults are cut out of the same cloth. History shows us that the ways in which one may go wrong about Jesus are legion, and so it is with the cults. As a practical matter, we cannot respond adequately to the Jesus of the cults without attending to the important differences that one finds in the variety of cultic teaching; a "one-size-fits-all" approach simply will not work. Fortunately, there is little new in the teaching about Jesus that one finds in the modern cults. The church has faced the same type of errors in the past and dealt with them effectively. Therefore, there is much we can learn from how the Christians of ages past dealt with these false views, which we can draw upon profitably for today.

Our approach to the topic is as follows. First, since we are considering what the cults say about the deity of Christ, it is first necessary to define what is a cult. That way, we will know which groups we are considering and which ones we are not. Next, we shall take a brief historical tour to look at the different sorts of views of Jesus that arose in the life of the church. This will provide us with a grid that will help us to classify the teaching of today's cults. In doing so we shall focus specifically on what these different teachers and movements said about the deity of Christ, and for each we shall note some contemporary cults that teach the same type of error. Third, we shall consider some scriptural arguments for the deity of Christ that could be useful in witnessing to someone in the cults. (The arguments here will be brief because other chapters in this same book provide much more detailed information on this doctrine from both the Old and New Testaments.) Fourth, we shall consider the impact that the cultic view of Christ's deity has on other doctrines in their theological system. For example, does their position on Christ have implications for how they see his work of atonement and salvation? And what, if any, are the real life effects of these errors? Do these faulty theological views "cash out" somehow in practical, day-to-day living? Finally, I shall conclude with some overall conclusions and principles to keep in mind as we consider the Jesus of the cults.

What Is a Cult?

Among researchers who study religious cults, one finds a variety of approaches and definitions.[3] Some engage the subject from a behavioral science perspective, focusing on the psychological or sociological characteristics of cultic groups. Those who take the behavioral approach frequently define cults according to such criteria as the group's authority structure (e.g., hierarchical, with a strong "prophetic" cultic leader), proselytizing techniques, mechanisms for maintaining commitment to the group, methods for dealing with behavior that deviates from the cult's established norms, etc.[4] Proponents of the behavioral approach also tend to emphasize how cults deviate religiously and behaviorally from the norms of the society in which they are situated.[5]

Whatever the merits or problems associated with behavioral definitions of cults,[6] the approach taken in this chapter is *theological*. That is, we shall focus particularly on the religious truth claims made by the group and use these to determine whether it is a cult. This is not to deny that faulty theology will have a negative result in one's life, behaviorally speaking: in fact, we shall make a few observations on the bad "fruits" of cultic belief toward the end of this chapter. Nevertheless, for our purposes here it is the belief system that will be central to our consideration. Accordingly, I have defined a cult as follows:

---

[3]I discuss these different approaches in my book *Unmasking the Cults*, The Zondervan Guide to Cults and Religious Movements, ed. Alan W. Gomes (Grand Rapids, MI: Zondervan, 1995), esp. 12–16, 47–80.

[4]E.g., Ruth A. Tucker gives this definition: "A 'cult' is a religious group that has a 'prophet'-founder called of God to give a special message not found in the Bible itself, often apocalyptic in nature and often set forth in 'inspired' writing. In deference to this charismatic figure or these 'inspired' writings the style of leadership is authoritarian and there is frequently an exclusivistic outlook supported by a legalistic lifestyle and persecution mentality. . . . It is the attribute of a prophet-founder that very distinctly separates cults from denominations." See Ruth A. Tucker, *Another Gospel* (Grand Rapids, MI: Zondervan, 1989), 16, 24.

[5]E.g., Charles Braden's definition includes the idea that a cult is "any religious group which differs significantly in some one or more respects as to belief or practice, from those religious groups which are regarded as the normative expressions of religion in our total culture." See Braden, quoted in Walter R. Martin, *Kingdom of the Cults* (Minneapolis: Bethany Fellowship, 1965), 11. Similarly, Ronald Enroth defines cults as "religious organizations that tend to be outside the mainstream of the dominant religious forms of any given society." See Ronald Enroth, *Youth, Brainwashing, and the Extremist Cults* (Grand Rapids, MI: Zondervan, 1977), 168.

[6]I discuss both the strengths and weaknesses of the behavioral approach to cults in my book *Unmasking the Cults*, 12–16.

A cult of Christianity is a group of people claiming to be Christian, which embraces a particular doctrinal system taught by an individual leader, group of leaders, or organization, which (system) denies (either explicitly or implicitly) one or more of the central doctrines of the Christian faith as taught in the sixty-six books of the Bible.[7]

While there are several important elements contained in this definition, let us note two important features in particular. First, in order for a group to be a "cult of Christianity" it must claim to be Christian. Accordingly, we distinguish cults of Christianity from world religions, which make no claim to be Christian and actually deny vigorously that they are such. Second, a cult is a group that denies one or more of the central doctrines of the Christian faith. A "central" doctrine is one that is foundational to the Christian faith, such that if one were to remove it, the belief system would no longer be Christian. This is different from peripheral doctrines, which do not define the essence of the Christian faith and about which genuine Christian groups sometimes agree to disagree. An example of a central doctrine would be Christ's bodily resurrection, as Paul himself states in 1 Corinthians 15:17. Salvation by grace through faith and Christ's deity (the subject of this chapter) are likewise central doctrines. Examples of peripheral doctrines are the timing and nature of certain end-time events (such as the exact nature of the millennial kingdom mentioned in Revelation 20) and the mode of baptism (e.g., whether by immersion, sprinkling, pouring, etc.). Thus, cults differ from legitimate Christian denominations in that they deny the core, central teachings that make the Christian faith Christian. And these core beliefs are the teachings that all Christians of every denominational (and nondenominational) stripe hold in common.

Therefore, in applying this definition to the present chapter, we shall consider groups that claim to be Christian but which have faulty teaching on the deity of Christ. Consequently, for our purposes here we shall not consider world religions such as Islam—though Islam (and other world religions) has a defective view of Jesus as well.

Types of Christologies

The various views of Jesus tend to fall into certain clear and distinct categories or christological types. This is true whether one looks at the various christologies that arose at different times in the church's history or whether one considers the christologies that one finds on the modern scene. By identifying the different historical christological types, we shall have a basis

---

[7]Ibid., 7.

for classifying contemporary movements and then for responding to them, just as the early church had to do.

Polytheism

As is well known both from the Bible (e.g., Acts 17:16, 23) and from secular history, polytheism permeated the Greco-Roman world. Though to the pagans there were "many 'gods' and many 'lords'" (1 Cor. 8:5), to the Christians there was but one God the Father, and Jesus Christ his Son, "from whom are all things" (1 Cor. 8:6).

The Roman state placed great importance on the worship of the various pagan deities, for they saw this as crucial both for the civic and the religious life of the Republic. The outcome of wars, the fertility of crops, and the general prosperity of the nation depended on keeping these deities appeased through sacrifice and proper religious observance. The Romans actually had a rather tolerant view of religion, so long as one was careful to give the Roman gods their due. That is, they permitted a great deal of "extracurricular" religious activity provided that this was over and above the proper religious obeisance owed to Rome's own gods. And it is precisely here that the early Christians ran afoul of the Roman state. Had the Christians agreed to offer sacrifice to the Roman gods, their worship of Jesus as a deity *in addition to* the Roman pantheon likely would not have generated any controversy. The Christians, however, were unwavering in their affirmation of divine oneness and in asserting the utter uniqueness of Jesus Christ. They absolutely refused to share with another the glory due to him alone. They, like Paul, regarded the Roman gods as mere pretenders or so-called gods. It was to Jesus alone that they would bow the knee, even at the cost of their lives.

When we evaluate the polytheistic Roman religion in light of the Christian position, the root problem was not an opposition to the deity of Christ as such. As noted, if the Christians wanted to consider Christ to be a deity alongside of all the other Roman deities, that probably would not have raised an eyebrow. No, the problem from a Christian perspective was that the Roman religion actually denied "the deity of deity," so to speak. The Roman deities were figments of their own imagination. The Roman gods did not create heaven and earth and did not possess the attributes of the biblical God. They often manifested the same passions and foibles as men. Indeed, there were men, such as the emperors, who achieved godhood after their deaths and sometimes even before. Thus, the Romans erred both in worshiping more than one god and also in their faulty view of deity itself.

Mormonism is a latter-day example of a polytheistic cult of Christianity.[8] Joseph Smith, the founder of Mormonism, taught clearly and unequivocally the "plurality of Gods":

> I will preach on the plurality of Gods . . . I wish to declare I have always and in all congregations when I have preached on the subject of Deity, it has been the plurality of Gods.[9]

In the creation story according to Smith, we find a polytheistic account that would rival the worst of pagan mythology: "The head God called together the Gods and sat in grand council to bring forth the world. . . . In the beginning, the head of the Gods called a council of the Gods; and they came together and concocted a plan to create the world and people it."[10]

So, then, Mormonism is clearly a polytheistic religion and for that reason alone cannot be considered Christian. But notice also that, just as in ancient paganism, Mormonism does not really believe in "the deity of deity." According to Mormonism, the gods were once men who attained exaltation to godhood through what they call a law of eternal progression. The gods, who are exalted men existing on their own planets, procreate spirit children. These spirit children come to have physical, earthly existence when they inhabit earthly bodies provided them through an earthly mother and father.[11] Then, by obedience to the principles of the gospel (such as repentance, baptism, faith, and good works, as set forth in Mormon teaching), one may attain exaltation to godhood and rule over a planet, producing spirit offspring that will in turn inhabit earthly bodies, etc. Thus, there is an endless, eternal progression of spirit children inhabiting earthly bodies

---

[8]The LDS strongly eschew the label "polytheism" to describe their doctrine of God, with some insisting that their position should be labeled "henotheism." But this argument is fallacious, granting that henotheism is but one kind of polytheism in which the existence of many gods is acknowledged even though only one is worshiped. LDS apologist David Paulson rejects the label of henotheism, though the contortions he puts himself through to do so are enlightening (http://maxwellinstitute. byu.edu/publications/review/?vol=13&num=2&id=392). Whatever semantic games Mormons may wish to play in describing their view, it most assuredly is *not* monotheism—the belief in the existence of only one God by nature—as the citation from their "prophet, seer, and revelator" Joseph Smith that follows demonstrates clearly.

[9]Joseph Smith Jr., *History of the Church of Jesus Christ of Latter-day Saints*, 6 vols. (Salt Lake City: Deseret, 1912), 6:474.

[10]*Journal of Discourses*, 26 vols. (Liverpool: The Church of Jesus Christ of Latter-day Saints, 1854–1886), 6:5. Note that although the *Journal of Discourses* is not one of the so-called Mormon standard works, it contains the utterances of Mormonism's main apostles and prophets, such as Joseph Smith (the founder of Mormonism) and Brigham Young. As the key leaders of the movement, their teaching represents authoritative Mormon doctrine.

[11]That is, these spirit children *preexist* before their earthly birth and come to inhabit physical bodies provided for them through their earthly parents in the process of procreation.

and—for those who are faithful during their probationary time on earth—achieving exaltation to godhood after their deaths. As Joseph Smith taught, this is true even for God the Father:

> I will go back to the beginning, before the world was, to show what kind of a being God is. What sort of a being was God in the beginning? . . . God himself was once as we are now, and is an exalted Man, and sits enthroned in yonder heavens. That is the great secret. . . . I say, if you were to see him to-day, you would see him like a man in form—like yourselves, in all the person, image, and very form as a man. . . . I am going to tell you how God came to be God. We have imagined and supposed that God was God from all eternity. I will refute that idea, and will take away and do away the vail [sic], so that you may see. . . . God himself, the Father of us all, dwelt on an earth, the same as Jesus Christ himself did.[12]

And just as God the Father attained his godhood, even so may observant Mormons, as Brigham Young explains:

> After men have got their exaltations and their crowns—have become Gods, even the sons of God—are made Kings of kings and Lords of lords, they have the power then of propagating their species in spirit.[13]

What, then, do the Latter-Day Saints teach about Jesus? Mormons teach that Jesus Christ preexisted as a spirit being, one of the offspring of a heavenly father and mother. Lucifer was also the offspring of this same heavenly father and mother, making Jesus the spirit brother of Lucifer (who became the Devil) according to official Mormon teaching.[14] As for his coming to earth, Mormons deny the virginal conception of Jesus. Instead, they promote the blasphemous idea that God the Father and Mary had literal sexual intercourse in order to prepare Jesus' physical body (or "tabernacle," as they refer to it).[15] But what about Christ's deity? Here their teaching is inconsistent. Though LDS doctrine holds that the law of eternal progression applies to all—even to God the Father (as the preceding quotes make clear)—the Mormons *also teach* that Jesus was *already* a god even while he was on earth. So in that regard he might seem to be different from other gods, who did not attain

---

[12]*Journal of Discourses*, 6:3.
[13]Ibid., 6:275.
[14]See Milton Hunter, *Gospel through the Ages* (Salt Lake City: Steven & Wallis, 1945), 15; cited in Kurt Van Gorden, *Mormonism*, Zondervan Guide to Cults and Religious Movements, 45.
[15]See *Journal of Discourses*, 1:50–51; 11:268. Remember that according to Mormon teaching, God the Father "has a body, with parts the same as you and I have" (*Journal of Discourses* 1:50). This is true not only of God the Father but of all who achieve exaltation to godhood.

godhood until being exalted to it after their deaths. Yet, they also teach, somewhat confusingly, that Jesus did not attain the *completeness* or *fullness* of his godhood until after his resurrection.[16]

Can it be said, then, that Mormonism affirms the deity of Christ? As with the ancient pagan polytheism, the answer is much the same: Mormons believe in the "deity" of Christ, but they do not believe in the deity of deity! That is, in the Mormon view, God (or, more correctly, "the gods") and man are of the same species, the former being merely an exalted instance of the latter. So, while it is true that the Mormons regard Jesus to be "God" in the same sense that they believe the Father to be God—a sentiment which might sound orthodox—on further consideration one discovers that even God the Father is not really "God" in the biblical understanding of the word.

Dynamic Monarchianism and Gnosticism

Another view of Jesus that plagued the church, particularly in the late second and third centuries, is known as "dynamic monarchianism." One of the main early proponents of this view was Paul of Samosata, Bishop of Antioch (in Syria) from c. 260–272. The impetus behind this view was the desire to safeguard monotheism while at the same time maintaining some kind of special status for Jesus of Nazareth. According to this teaching, Jesus was by nature a mere man but one whom God specially empowered. The advocates of this teaching felt that it safeguarded the divine monarchy (i.e., the sole rulership of God) while at the same time acknowledging that a special divine power (Greek: *dunamis*) rested on the man Jesus in a degree that exceeds any man before or since.

The dynamic monarchians claimed to believe that Jesus is "God," but by this they meant that he participated in the divine *dunamis* and exercised divine prerogatives, such as ruling, reigning, and judging. They denied, however, that Jesus was God in the sense of literal deity, or that he was literally God by nature. In other words, they averred that the word "God" could be used both in a figurative and in a literal sense. Jesus was "God" according to the former but certainly not according to the latter usage.

Another teaching that functionally amounted to the same thing, although coming from a very different perspective and worldview, was Gnosticism. Particularly active in the second century, Gnosticism was a kind of

---

[16]Joseph Fielding Smith, *Doctrines of Salvation*, 3 vols. (Salt Lake City, UT: Bookcraft, 1956), 1:33; cited in Van Gorden, *Mormonism*, 48–49. (Note that Joseph Fielding Smith was the tenth president of the Mormon Church and should not be confused with Joseph Smith Jr., the founder of Mormonism.)

"theosophy."[17] The Gnostics taught that God differentiates into or emanates from himself lesser spiritual beings called "aeons." The Gnostics referred to these aeons collectively as the "pleroma" or "fullness." One of these lesser spiritual beings or aeons is an evil, inferior deity who, among his other misdeeds, created the physical universe, which the Gnostics regarded as inherently evil. They refer to this wicked creator aeon as the Demiurge, whom they also identify with the God of the Old Testament. Due to a supposed fall in the pleroma, certain spirit beings became cruelly imprisoned in matter, forgetting their true, original identities as divine spirit beings in the process. These imprisoned spirits are, of course, human beings. In order to liberate these trapped souls, the good God of the New Testament sent the Christ on a rescue mission, in which the Christ provides the secret knowledge needed to enlighten the Gnostic about his or her true spiritual identity and provenance. The secret teachings also provide the information necessary to enable the Gnostic Christian to escape the cycle of reincarnation after his or her physical death and ascend directly to this good God.

The Gnostic views of Jesus varied but a common version saw Jesus as a mere man with whom the "Christ" aeon associated, providing Jesus with special insight in order to equip and enlighten him to function as a purveyor of arcane Gnostic truths. "The Christ" refers to a kind of heightened spiritual consciousness, which enlightened the man Jesus of Nazareth. Again, we should note that dynamic monarchianism and Gnosticism are actually very different theological systems, arising from radically different worldviews and motivated by vastly divergent concerns. But in one key particular respect they intersect:[18] the "deity" of the man Jesus—whether in the form of divine *dunamis* or of "Christ consciousness"—was something that empowered or rested upon him; Jesus was not God incarnate but a God-inspired man. It is worth noting that the early church fathers who combated dynamic monarchianism observed the similarity with Gnosticism at this point and used it in their polemic against it (granting that the dynamic monarchians did not want to be tarred with a Gnostic brush).

In what forms do we see dynamic monarchian and Gnostic views of Christ on today's scene?

Consider Unitarianism, now known as Unitarian Universalism.[19] The Unitarians are so called because of their denial of the Trinity; historically

---

[17]See n. 2.

[18]Or at least the version of Gnosticism presented here. Recall that Gnostic systems were diverse.

[19]In 1961 the American Unitarian Association merged with the Universalist Church of America to form the Unitarian Universalist Association. See Alan W. Gomes, *Unitarian Universalism*, Zondervan Guide to Cults and Religious Movements, 20.

they argued for the unipersonality of God. The modern Unitarian movement traces its origin to the period of the Protestant Reformation. Unitarianism's most famous teacher—their theological brain, as it were—was Faustus Socinus (1539–1604), an Italian who migrated to Poland and defended the Unitarian position both in writing and in oral debate. Socinus was a convinced dynamic monarchian.[20] Modern Unitarians pretty much followed suit, at least until the early part of the twentieth century. For these Unitarians, as for Socinus, Jesus was a man, sent and empowered by God to teach obedience to God's truths, through which we may attain salvation. However, a shift took place in the movement in the early 1900s away from Christianity and in the direction of humanism.[21] An increasing number of Unitarians disavowed any Christian allegiance whatsoever, and a significant percentage of modern Unitarians do not believe in God at all, much less in Christianity. Today, Unitarians who even claim Christian allegiance represent somewhere between 10 and 20 percent of the total movement.[22] Among the minority of Unitarians who still consider themselves Christians, the dynamic monarchian view of Christ would predominate.

The "mind science" cults present an obviously Gnostic take on the question of Jesus' deity. The three main mind science cults are Christian Science, Religious Science, and Unity School of Christianity.[23] Like ancient Gnosticism, these groups place a premium on arcane theosophical insights, involving the notion that we must be freed from the "errors of mortal mind" in order to recognize our "true divine sonship." They also distinguish Jesus from the Christ, teaching that the Christ is a kind of spiritual anointing or knowledge operative in him (and in others), consisting especially of the consciousness of one's own divine nature or "sonship." Consider the following representative quotations:

> JESUS—the name of a man. Distinguished from the Christ. The man Jesus became the embodiment of the Christ, as the human gave way to the Divine Idea of Sonship.[24]

---

[20]See, e.g., Alan W. Gomes, "The Rapture of the Christ: The 'Pre-Ascension Ascension' of Jesus in the Theology of Faustus Socinus (1539–1604)," *HTR* 102:1 (2009): 79-81; and Alan W. Gomes, "Faustus Socinus's *A Tract Concerning God, Christ, and the Holy Spirit*," *Journal of the International Society of Christian Apologetics* 1:1 (2008): 40–41.

[21]Gomes, *Unitarian Universalism*, 18–20.

[22]Ibid., 33.

[23]For a concise overview of these three movements I recommend Todd Ehrenborg, *The Mind Sciences*, Zondervan Guide to Cults and Religious Movements.

[24]Ernest Holmes, *The Science of Mind* (New York: Dodd, Mead, 1965), 603.

This Christ, or perfect-man idea existing eternally in Divine Mind is the true, spiritual, higher self of every individual. Each of us has within him the Christ, just as Jesus had, and we must look within to recognize and realize our sonship, our divine origin and birth, even as He did.[25]

Christ, meaning "messiah" or "anointed," designates one who had received a spiritual quickening from God, while Jesus is the name of the personality. To the metaphysical Christian—that is, to him who studies the spiritual man—Christ is the name of the supermind and Jesus is the name of the personal consciousness. The spiritual man is God's Son; the personal man is man's son.[26]

We should note that the mind science cults do not, strictly speaking, deny the deity of Christ so much as his *unique* deity. As Religious Science puts it, "Mental Science does not deny the divinity of Jesus; but it does affirm the divinity of all people. It does not deny that Jesus was the son of God; but it affirms that all men are the sons of God."[27] Of course, as we saw with Mormonism, their very notion of deity itself is defective.

Arianism

The term "Arianism" refers to the christological and anti-Trinitarian teaching of a fourth-century presbyter from Alexandria, Egypt, named Arius. In AD 325 Emperor Constantine convened a council at Nicaea (in modern-day Turkey) specifically to address this error. The council produced the famous Nicene Creed, which is a direct repudiation of Arianism.

Like the dynamic monarchians who preceded him, Arius took great pains to safeguard monotheism as he understood it. It seemed to him that granting Jesus a divine status equal to the Father ran directly counter to it. Though Arius's teaching and that of the Nicene Council centered on the deity of Christ, when we examine Arius's teaching in detail it becomes clear that he did not affirm the true humanity of Christ either. In this respect Arius's teaching was even worse than the dynamic monarchianism that preceded him, for at least they had a fully human Jesus.

According to Arius, God originally created Jesus as an angel-like spirit creature known also as the "Son Logos." (The word "Logos," or "Word," is the title given to Jesus in John 1:1ff.) We are not here talking about Christ's birth as a man roughly two thousand years ago but rather about a creation

---

[25] *The Metaphysical Bible Dictionary* (Kansas City, MO: Unity School of Christianity, 1942), 150.
[26] Charles Fillmore, *Jesus Christ Heals* (Unity Village, MO: Unity School of Christianity, 1939), 10; cited in Ehrenborg, *Mind Sciences*, 69.
[27] Holmes, *Science of Mind*, 161–62.

that took place in the heavenly realm aeons ago, even before the visible created universe existed. After creating the Son Logos, God inspired him with his *dunamis* (sound familiar?) and then commanded him to create our entire universe. Thus, Jesus (in his role as the Son Logos, i.e., before his earthly birth) created all things after he himself was first created by God.

When the fullness of time came, God sent the Son Logos to earth to become incarnate through Mary in the virginal conception. Before the incarnation, the Son Logos existed merely as a disembodied spirit creature, like an angel. After the incarnation, the Son Logos existed in and operated through a physical body of flesh and bones. Jesus, the incarnated Son Logos, walked the earth among men, died, and rose bodily from the grave.

Just as the dynamic monarchians before him, Arius taught that the word *god* can be used both literally and figuratively, asserting that Jesus can be called "god" in the sense of one who participates in divine power and prerogatives. In other words, Jesus is "god" but only in a manner of speaking. As to his actual nature, literally considered, Jesus is not God but is an altogether different essence (*heteroousios*) from the Father.

The Arian christology did have a certain advantage over the earlier dynamic monarchian position. For the dynamic monarchians, Jesus of Nazareth had no existence before his earthly birth. But the Arians could give at least some accounting of the biblical texts that speak of Christ's existence before his earthly sojourn. For example, they used texts such as John 3:13 and 6:33, which speak of the Son of Man coming down from heaven, to refer to his existence in heaven before his birth in Bethlehem. They could also give some explanation of those texts that spoke of all things coming into existence through him (John 1:3; Col. 1:16), which clearly point to activities that antedate his appearance on earth.

Nevertheless, the church rejected the Arian christology as fatally flawed. For one thing, it could not *truly* account for those texts that speak of Christ's antemundane creative activity, for these demonstrate clearly that Christ is not in the class of created things. Indeed, if Christ created *all* things, as John 1:3 and Colossians 1:16 declare, then he cannot himself be a created thing. Additionally, Arian protestations notwithstanding, if Christ is not God by nature, then the church is worshiping a creature, which is idolatry, however much *dunamis* we ascribe to that creature. And if Jesus were himself a creature, then he would not have the power to atone for our sins and reconcile us to God. In short, the Christian faith would be but another pagan variant, worshiping the creature rather than the creator.

We should also observe that the Arian Jesus is not fully human, either. Their Jesus is an angel-like spirit creature animating a body. But an embodied angel is not a human, for to be human requires a human soul. Be that as it may, the Nicene Council, under the theological leadership of Athanasius of Alexandria (c. 296–373), trained its guns on the question of Christ's deity in relation to that of the Father. The Council firmly declared that Jesus is "true [i.e., literal] God" and "of the same essence" (*homoousios*) as the Father. He is the creator of all things and is not himself the product of creative activity.

The modern cult that most closely approximates the ancient Arian teaching is the Jehovah's Witnesses (JWs), the organization of which is known as the Watchtower Bible and Tract Society. According to the JWs, before the incarnation Jesus was Michael the Archangel, the first and greatest creation of Jehovah God.[28] Jehovah commissioned and empowered him to create the universe, including the realm of angels and men.[29] In the incarnation, they say, Michael the Archangel became human, taking on a literal physical body in the virgin birth. After his death on a "torture stake,"[30] Jehovah raised him from the dead: not bodily but as Michael the Archangel again, in the form of an invisible spirit creature. Jehovah did not revivify Christ's body but "whether it was dissolved into gases or whether it is still preserved somewhere as the grand memorial of God's love, of Christ's obedience, and of our redemption, no one knows."[31] The King Christ Jesus now rules as a disembodied angel over the 144,000, a special class of Jehovah's Witness, who also experienced resurrection in a disembodied form. The rest of the Jehovah's Witnesses faithful—the vast majority of them, in fact—ultimately hope to escape the coming judgment of Armageddon, achieve a bodily resurrection, and live forever on a paradise earth.

The JWs use many of the same arguments offered by Arius, together with some novel ones of their own. The Watchtower has produced its own translation of the Bible, called *The New World Translation.* Among the more creative renderings in this translation is John 1:1, the latter part of which reads, ". . . and the Word was a god."[32] From this they argue that Jesus was not literally God, but was "a god" in the sense of "a mighty one." Psalm 82:6 is an example of the word *god* used in this "lesser" sense of the term.[33]

---

[28]See the Watchtower's official website: http://www.watchtower.org/e/bh/appendix_11.htm.

[29]*Let God Be True* (Brooklyn, NY: Watchtower Bible and Tract Society, 1946), 35.

[30]The JWs wrongly teach that Christ was not put to death on a cross consisting of a vertical pole and a crossbeam, as commonly depicted, but instead was nailed to a single upright pole. Their view is historically incorrect. Note that their *New World Translation* renders "cross" as "torture stake" (e.g., John 19:17).

[31]Charles Taze Russell, *Studies in the Scriptures,* Series 2 (Brooklyn, NY: International Bible Students Association, 1915), 129.

[32]Wayne Grudem, who is both a New Testament scholar and a noted systematic theologian, provides an outstanding discussion of John 1:1 and the Watchtower's faulty handling of it. See Wayne Grudem, *Systematic Theology* (Grand Rapids, MI: Zondervan, 1994), 233–35, esp. nn. 12 and 13.

[33]See *Reasoning from the Scriptures* (New York: Watchtower Bible and Tract Society, 1985), 213.

Modalistic Monarchianism

We have already examined dynamic monarchianism, a theological position that attempted to maintain the sole monarchy of God (i.e., monotheism) by relegating Jesus to the status of a kind of super-prophet, specially inspired by God's *dunamis*. But there is another attempted solution to the same problem that achieved some popularity in the late second through fourth centuries: modalistic monarchianism, known more simply as "modalism." The modalists also wished to safeguard monotheism but at the same time they wanted to do full justice to the genuine, literal deity of Christ. So the modalists thought they could solve the problem as follows. They taught that there is only one God but that this one God simply *reveals* himself in three different ways or "modes." For example, in the Old Testament he reveals himself as Father, in the New Testament as Son, and in the church age as the Holy Spirit. In other words, there is only one God (monarchianism/monotheism), but this one God is also only one person; Father, Son, and Spirit are simply the *modes of manifestation* in which this one person, God, expresses himself. Put another way, God is not in himself three persons any more than Clark Kent and Superman are two different persons. But just as Clark Kent can slip into a nearby phone booth and reveal himself according to his Superman manifestation, even so God can reveal himself in a variety of ways.

At first glance modalism would seem to offer some formidable advantages over dynamic monarchianism and Arianism. For one thing, the modalist can truly affirm the deity of Christ without equivocation or verbal sleight of hand. Jesus *is* God, and he is so by nature. And modalism does indeed safeguard monotheism, since Jesus is not another God alongside God the Father and God the Holy Spirit. But does this solution really work?

Its "higher" christology notwithstanding, modalism had some serious defects that the church recognized. For one thing, it simply could not make sense of those texts that show the Father and the Son relating to one another in a subject-object ("I-thou") relationship. A relationship requires at least *two* persons; one cannot be in a relationship with oneself. The baptism of Jesus in Matthew 3:16–17 is a very clear case in point. Here we see Jesus receiving baptism, the Father declaring him to be his beloved Son in whom he is well pleased, and the Holy Spirit descending like a dove. Note that all three are present *simultaneously*. Again, as Tertullian (a late second-/early third-century theologian from North Africa) pointed out to his modalist opponent Praxeas, what is one to make of Psalm 2:7 on modalistic terms: "Thou art my Son; this day have I begotten thee"? If modalism were true, chided Tertullian, the text ought to read, "I am my own Son; this day have

I begotten myself."[34] Stated simply, the distinction in pronouns shows a distinction of persons who interact with one another in genuine relationship.

In modern times, the single largest modalist group is the United Pentecostal Church (UPC), which boasts somewhere around one million members.[35] So-called oneness Pentecostalism split off from the mainstream Pentecostal body, the Assemblies of God, beginning as early as 1914. One of the main reasons for the split was over the modalistic doctrine. This original split spawned a number of different mergers and schisms, some dividing along racial lines.[36] The UPC, the largest and most actively proselytizing of the oneness cults, formed in 1945. In addition to their modalistic teaching, which they propagate aggressively, the UPC deviates from mainstream Christianity (including also mainstream Pentecostalism) in teaching that one must speak in tongues in order to be saved. They also observe a detailed, legalistic "holiness" code and teach that water baptism is necessary for salvation. Along those same lines, the UPC, as is true for other "oneness" groups, baptizes in the name of Jesus only and not in the name of the Father, Son, and Holy Spirit, in keeping with their modalistic beliefs. For this reason they, and groups like them, are known as "Jesus only" Pentecostals. As we have already noted, they are also called "oneness Pentecostals" because of their identification of the Father, Son, and Spirit as one and the same person.

Some Brief Arguments for the Deity of Christ

Elsewhere in this volume appear detailed treatments of the deity of Christ from the Old and New Testaments. Those chapters may be studied profitably to assist in answering the cultic errors concerning the deity of Christ. What follows is merely a quick recap of some of the most common and obvious verses that one might use to argue for the true deity of Christ to a cultist.

Verses That Explicitly Call Jesus "God"

The Old and New Testaments furnish numerous passages that apply the title "God" to Jesus. Consider first of all Isaiah 9:6. This text, which is clearly a prophetic reference to the Messiah, calls him "the Mighty God" (Heb. *El Gibbor*). Similarly, Isaiah 7:14 calls him *Immanuel*, which is Hebrew for "God with us."

In the New Testament, John 1:1 directly calls Jesus "God" (Gk. *theos*). The "Word," which obviously refers to Jesus (see v. 14), was "God." Note that this

---

[34]Tertullian, *Prax.* 11.
[35]E. Calvin Beisner, *"Jesus Only" Churches*, Zondervan Guide to Cults and Religious Movements (Grand Rapids, MI: Zondervan, 1995), 9.
[36]Ibid., 7–8.

verse rules out both Arianism and modalism. It excludes Arianism because the verse declares Jesus to be "God," or *theos*—not in any supposed figurative sense but literally God by nature. In fact, the grammar of this verse in the original Greek highlights the *qualitative* nature of Christ's Godhood; he is *theos* in the sense that he is of the nature, essence, or quality of deity. A fair rendering of this verse therefore might be, "The Word [Jesus] was *deity*."[37] The verse also refutes modalism, because John says that the Word "was with God" (*pros ton theon*), i.e., with God the Father. Note that if the Word is *with* the Father then he cannot *be* the Father; it makes no sense to speak of a person "being with" himself. Therefore, this verse is useful when speaking to those in Arian cults (such as JWs) and modalistic cults (such as the UPC).

Titus 2:13 is another New Testament verse that explicitly calls Jesus "God." This verse speaks of "the appearing of the glory of our great God and Savior Jesus Christ." Thus, Paul identifies Jesus not only as "our savior" but also as "our great God."[38] Likewise, Thomas calls Jesus "God" in John 20:28. On seeing the resurrected Christ, Thomas exclaims, "My Lord and my God!" (*ho kurios mou kai ho theos mou*) and then proceeds to worship him. Note well that Jesus did not rebuke Thomas for calling him God nor for worshiping him, as Jesus would have had to do were he not actually God in the flesh. (Consider, e.g., Paul and Barnabas's reaction when the Lycaonians mistakenly identified them as deity in Acts 14:8–18, esp. vv. 14–15.) Instead, Jesus received both the divine name and Thomas's worship.[39] Consider

---

[37] Again, refer to Grudem's fine treatment in his *Systematic Theology*, 233–35. On the use of anarthrous predicate nouns (the grammatical construction we find in John 1:1) see the classic work of Philip B. Harner, "Qualitative Anarthrous Predicate Nouns: Mark 15:39 and John 1:1," *JBL* 92 (1973): 75–87. See also Murray J. Harris, *Jesus as God* (Grand Rapids, MI: Zondervan, 1992), 310–13.

[38] That "great God" and "savior" refer to the same person is supported by the grammar of the passage, specifically by the Granville Sharp rule. According to Granville Sharp's Rule 1, "When the copulative *kai* [and] connects two nouns of the same case . . . if the article *ho* [the] . . . precedes the first . . . and is not repeated before the second . . . the latter always relates to the same person that is expressed or described by the first." The construction that one finds in Titus 2:13 corresponds directly to this rule. For more discussion on this see Harris, *Jesus as God*, 173–85 (esp. 179–82); 307–10. For a much more detailed analysis of this rule see Daniel B. Wallace, *Greek Grammar beyond the Basics* (Grand Rapids, MI: Zondervan, 1996), 270–90.

[39] The JW evasions of this verse are singularly unconvincing. In one version they say that Thomas was startled and blurted out, "Oh my God!"—essentially taking the Lord's name in vain. As Walter Martin pointed out, if this were so, then Jesus, being a rabbi, ought to have censured Thomas for blasphemy, which he does not do. Another ad hoc response says that when this event took place, Thomas looked at Jesus and said, "My Lord," and then turned his eyes heavenward and said, "and my God." This "argument" is eisegesis at its worst. Grudem discusses these in *Systematic Theology*, 235n14. A third version takes Thomas's ascription of the title "God" to Jesus in the figurative, "a god" sense in which they wrongly interpret John 1:1. See *Reasoning from the Scriptures*, 213.

also Hebrews 1:8, in which the Father applies the title "God" (*theos*) to the Son: "But of the Son he says, 'Your throne, O God, is forever and ever.'"[40]

Indirect Proofs for Christ's Deity

Besides the verses that apply the title "God" (*theos*) to Jesus, there are other clear scriptural indications that Jesus is God. Jesus' true deity is shown by his eternal preexistence, by divine titles he shares in common with God, and by the ascription of divine attributes to him. There are many verses that one could produce for each of these three categories, but we shall look at but a few for our present purpose.

First, consider some of the verses that teach Christ's eternal preexistence. In Isaiah 9:6 the prophet applies the adjective "everlasting" to Christ. The New Testament's teaching about Christ's eternal preexistence is even more explicit. John 1:1–3, 10; 1 Corinthians 8:6; and Colossians 1:16–17 teach that *all things* came into being (i.e., were created) through Christ. The salient point here is that the Word preexisted before all created things and created them. Consequently, he himself cannot be in the class of created things. And if he is not in the class of created things, then he must be uncreated, which means he did not come into existence as created things did. Therefore, he must have always existed, and so he must be God (Isa. 44:24).[41]

Next, we see a number of divine titles that Christ shares in common with God the Father. There are at least a dozen such titles, including "I Am" (Ex. 3:14; John 8:58; 18:5–6), "First and Last" (Isa. 41:4; 44:6; 48:12; Rev. 1:17; 2:8; 22:13), "Redeemer" (Hos. 13:14; Ps. 130:7; Titus 2:13; Gal. 3:13; Rev. 5:9), "Savior" (Isa. 43:3; Ezek. 34:22; 2 Pet. 1:1, 11), and "Judge" (Joel 3:12; 2 Tim. 4:1; 2 Cor. 5:10).

Finally, consider the texts that ascribe divine attributes to Christ. Christ is said to share the same substance as God (Heb. 1:3), enabling him to be a perfect expression of it.[42] We have already noted that he shares the attribute of eternality (e.g., Isa. 9:6; John 1:1–2). He possesses the attribute

---

[40]The JWs attempt to get around this passage by mistranslating it in the *New World Translation*, "God is your throne forever and ever." This rendering makes absolutely no sense in the context, which is an argument for the superiority of the Son's nature over that of angels. How would the fact that God is the throne of Jesus (whatever that is supposed to mean) demonstrate Jesus' superiority to angels?

[41]The JWs recognize that if Christ did indeed create *all* things, then he must be God. This explains why they mistranslate Col. 1:16 in their *New World Translation*. They insert the word "other" into the text, making it read, "For by him all *other* things were created . . . all *other* things were created through him and for him." There is absolutely no textual basis in any extant Greek manuscript for inserting the word "other" here; the Watchtower has done this purely in an attempt to escape the clear theological implications of this text.

[42]Heb. 1:3 employs the word *hypostasis*, which, in this particular context, translates as "substance."

of omnipotence, being called "Almighty" (Rev. 1:8) and "the Mighty God" (Isa. 9:6). Accordingly, Jesus is able to "uphold the universe by the word of his power" (Heb. 1:3). We see his claim to omniscience in John 13:19: Jesus cites his knowledge of Judas's future betrayal as proof of his deity, ascribing the divine title "I Am" to himself on this basis. And Hebrews 13:8 predicates the attribute of immutability to him.

The Theological Implications of Cultic Views on Christ's Deity

To this point we have trained our focus on one doctrine only: the deity of Christ. But now it is important for us to understand how the doctrines of the Christian faith interrelate and to chart some of these interrelations. It is critical to realize that the core teachings of Christianity stand or fall together. It is not possible to deny one central doctrine but then be correct about everything else; it simply does not work like that. It is like a one-piece knit sweater: if you unravel one part of the sweater you eventually wind up with a tangle of yarn at your feet. And so it is with the cultic errors on the deity of Christ. Their faulty view of Christ's deity has implications for other parts of their theological system.

Consider modalism. Besides the clear difficulty that modalism has in accounting for texts that speak of the Father and the Son as having a distinct personal relationship,[43] modalism has theological problems on a much deeper, systemic level. Modalism renders meaningless the entire "economy of salvation." When we speak of the economy of salvation we mean that there is what theologian Louis Berkhof has termed a "division of labor," so to speak, among the members of the Godhead in accomplishing human redemption.[44] For example, the Bible says that it is the Father who sends the Son to take on flesh and to pay the penalty owed for our sins. The Spirit, sent by the Son, applies the Son's work—regenerating, adopting, and sealing the believer.[45] Note that the Bible never teaches that the Son sends the Father to become incarnate or to pay the penalty for our sins on the cross, or that the Holy Spirit sends the Son as another comforter. But in a modalistic schema, what is one to make of such activities, which clearly require a Trinitarian Godhead? So, a faulty view of the *person* of Christ has direct implications for his *work* as a distinct person in the Godhead.

Furthermore, consider the religious life of the incarnate Christ. As a man, Christ relates to the Father as a man relates to his God. For instance,

---

[43]See pages 242–43 above.
[44]Louis Berkhof, *Systematic Theology* (Grand Rapids, MI: Eerdmans, 1941), 266.
[45]See, e.g., John 10:36; 14:26; 15:26; Rom. 8:15, 23; 2 Cor. 1:22; Eph. 1:13; 4:30; Titus 3:5; 1 John 4:14.

the Scriptures show him praying frequently and fervently to his Father.[46] Now, if Jesus *is* the Father, as modalists claim, then how and to whom can he pray? Modern modalists, at least, attempt to answer this by saying that Jesus' human nature is praying to his divine nature.[47] But is that really a solution? In fact, it may be paying such an answer too high a compliment to declare it false: it is actually meaningless. That is because *natures* do not pray but rather *persons* do. Praying is a *personal* act, specifically the act of a person with a human nature, such as Jesus had and still has. And the object of his prayers must also be a *personal* object, namely, the divine *person* of the Father. Thus, the modalist Jesus cannot serve as our substitute to provide payment for our sins to the Father, nor can he serve as an example of our own religious life, as the Bible clearly says he is (Heb. 2:14–18; 4:15; John 13:12; 1 Pet. 2:21). This is no small defect in the position, with devastating theological and practical consequences for the Christian life.

As another test case, let us examine the theological implications of the Mormon view of Christ's deity. While Mormons claim to believe in the deity of Christ, we have already observed that they do not believe in the true "deity of deity"; for the Mormon, God and man are of the same species. Consequently, at the end of the day, Jesus—and even God the Father, for that matter—is but an exalted man, different from us in degree but not in kind. However exalted they may say Jesus is, he remains *finite*, just like his Father and like all the other gods who ever have and ever will exist in an endless series of gods.[48] He, like all the other gods, is growing in his god-hood and will continue to grow, just as faithful Mormons believe that they will grow in their own exaltation in godhood. The Mormon Jesus, having a considerable head start, would most probably continue to keep ahead of the faithful Mormon of today. Nevertheless, it absolutely follows from the logic of their position that, given enough time, there will be Mormons of today who will attain the degree of exaltation that Jesus currently pos-

---

[46]There are too many Scriptures here to list. To cite but one of many, see Matt. 26:39.

[47]Beisner, *"Jesus Only" Churches*, 15–18.

[48]The Mormons deny the charge that they hold to a finite God, because, as Kurt Van Gorden relates, they state, "Jesus' existence began as organized intelligence, a spirit-element that eternally exists with matter." However, this Mormon argument proves too much, for as Mormon apostle Bruce McConkie points out, "It might be said that he [Jesus] is eternal, *as all men are,* meaning that spirit element—the intelligence which was organized into intelligences—has always existed and is therefore eternal" (*The Promised Messiah,* 165; emphasis added). Regardless of Mormon protestations, according to their doctrine Jesus *progresses* in his deity, which ipso facto precludes him being infinite in any orthodox sense. For a good critique of the Mormon concept of God that deals with "finite godism" from a philosophical point of view, see Francis J. Beckwith, "Philosophical Problems with the Mormon Concept of God," http://www.equip.org/articles/philosophical-problems-with-the-mormon-concept-of-god.

sesses. (By then, presumably, he'll have attained even more exaltation than he possesses now.[49])

Is it any wonder, then, that the finite Jesus of the Mormons cannot and does not make a complete and sufficient atonement for our sins? We are not surprised, then, when we observe that in Mormon theology Christ's atonement is thoroughly sufficient only for Adam's sin. As Mormon apostle LeGrand Richards put it, "Jesus Christ redeemed all from the fall; he paid the price; he offered himself as a ransom; he atoned for Adam's sin, leaving us responsible only for our own sins."[50] In atoning for Adam's sin, Christ's death procures what they call "general salvation," which means that all people, believers and unbelievers alike, will be resurrected. However, his atonement does not secure "specific salvation," which one attains only through following the precepts of Mormonism, most particularly baptism, repentance, faith, and good works. Brigham Young took their teaching to its logical conclusion. He stated clearly that there are sins so serious that the blood of Christ could not possibly atone for these. He even went so far as to say that the sinner must atone for such sins by shedding his or her own blood!

> It is true that the blood of the Son of God was shed for sins . . . yet men can commit sins which it can never remit.[51]

> There is not a man or woman, who violates the covenants made with their God, that will not be required to pay the debt. The blood of Christ will never wipe that out, your own blood must atone for it.[52]

Although we have been speaking of the *theological* implications of a faulty view of Christ's deity, I hope these two cases make clear that the doctrinal fallout of these errors has profound practical implications for one's life. In the two instances we have examined—modalism and the finite god teach-

---

[49]We should note that some Mormon scholars, such as apostle Bruce McConkie, are unwilling to admit this conclusion, even though it follows inexorably from the logic of their system.

[50]LeGrand Richards, *A Marvelous Work and a Wonder* (Salt Lake City: Deseret, 1976), 98.

[51]*Journal of Discourses*, 4:54. Of course, Young's statement highlights one of the myriad of inconsistencies in Mormon doctrine. Apostle Richards appeared to teach that Christ's death was for Adam's sin alone (as we already observed), yet here Young states that Christ's death does atone for our personal sins, just not for the most serious of them.

[52]*Journal of Discourses*, 3:247. In this same context Young presents the following hypothetical example: "Let me suppose a case. Suppose you found your brother in bed with your wife, and put a javelin through both of them, you would be justified, and they would atone for their sins, and be received into the kingdom of God. I would at once do so in such a case; and under such circumstances, I have no wife whom I love so well that I would not put a javelin through her heart, and I would do it with clean hands."

ing of Mormonism—the bad fruit they yield is clear. The modalist Jesus is not one who can make an atonement for our sins to the Father. He is not a Jesus who can serve as a high priest for us. He cannot set an example for our own religious life, whether in terms of his prayer life or in any other way. Similarly, the Mormon Jesus is not a Jesus who can truly save anyone. He cannot and does not make a full atonement for all of our sins, leaving the Mormon to earn his or her salvation through works; in the Mormon understanding, "we are saved by grace *after all we can do.*"[53] This, of course, leads to the bondage of legalism and self-effort, with either self-doubt or presumptuous pride as the necessary result. The Mormon faithful cannot know the true peace of Christ, which has as its basis the "canceling the record of debt that stood against us with its legal demands," which God removed by "nailing it to the cross" (Col. 2:14). Consequently, we are not engaging in mere theological hairsplitting when we criticize the false view of Christ's deity held by the cults. The issues at stake literally make the difference between life and death, bondage and peace.

Some Concluding Thoughts and Principles

Now that we have seen the many ways in which the cults go astray in their understanding of the deity of Christ, we should consider some practical principles that follow from our study. These issues become especially relevant when one must speak to a cultist, be it a relative, coworker, or a total stranger who comes proselytizing at the door. Therefore, I shall focus my remarks on the implications of what we have learned as applied to hands-on dialogue with a cultist.

Treat the Cultist as an Individual

While it is safe to say that all the cults have a defective view of Christ's deity (and of a whole lot of other doctrines as well), we have noted that there are a variety of ways in which they depart from the truth. Not only that, but I have many times encountered cultists who are unclear on their own official teaching and hold something about the deity of Christ that doesn't exactly toe the party line. (I am not suggesting that the view held is more orthodox than the group's official teaching, just that it is different.) So my advice is that you take the time to establish just what the person you are talking to believes about the person of Christ. This way, you will know what type of error you are dealing with (e.g., polytheism, Arianism, modalism, etc.) and can respond appropriately.

---

[53]2 Nephi 25:23; emphasis added.

Focus on the Key Issues

As we have noted throughout this chapter, the deity of Christ is at the heart of the Christian faith; it is no minor subpoint of Christian theology. It is important in its own right and also because, as we have seen, the person and work of Christ go together. Stated simply, if Christ is not God, then he does not have the power to save. This being the case, it is critical to steer any discussion with the cultist to the question of who Jesus is, what he did, and what we must do to be saved (Acts 16:30–31).

Sometimes cultists like to "major on the minors."[54] For instance, the JWs often obsess on issues like the celebration of birthdays, religious holidays (such as Christmas), and saluting the flag; they oppose all these as pagan. They also love to engage in speculation about end-times events. On the one hand, you may need to discuss these to some degree with the JWs because they are big issues *to them.* But in the big scheme of things, such issues as celebrating birthdays are not of eternal significance. A person can go to heaven without ever exchanging a birthday present, but one who rejects Christ's true deity, and accordingly his saving work, is lost for eternity. Try to move the discussion to the person and work of Christ as sensitively and expeditiously as you are able.

Watch Out for the "Bait and Switch" in the Use of Terms

Some cults, such as the JWs, explicitly deny the deity of Christ. In their case there is no doubt about what they really believe. In other cases, a group may profess *verbally* that it believes in the deity of Christ, even trying to convince you that they believe the same thing you do. Yet, they redefine what they mean by "the deity of Christ" so that it bears no resemblance to the biblical view. We observed this clearly in the mind science cults and also in the case of Mormonism. This redefinition of terminology holds true for other concepts as well, including words such as *God, salvation,* and *sin.* It is therefore critical that you establish the meaning of key terms when you engage a cultist in discussion. Again, let me stress: *do not assume that the cultist means the same thing as you do by basic theological terms.* Otherwise, you may fool yourself (or they may fool you, sometimes deliberately) into thinking that agreement exists where there is none. This can have fatal consequences for the cultist you are trying to win.

Be Prepared to Demonstrate the Deity of Christ from the Scriptures

While it is not realistic to expect every Christian to have a working knowledge of the myriad of cults peppering today's religious landscape, all Chris-

---

[54]Gomes, *Unmasking the Cults,* 45–46.

tians should know the Scriptures and be able to establish such a fundamental teaching as the deity of Christ. In this chapter I have provided a few of the key texts that are sufficient for this purpose, and other chapters in this volume flesh out the biblical basis for this doctrine in even greater detail. Now, even if you know little about Mormon doctrine, for example, you can still witness to the Mormon by asking him or her to describe what he or she believes about the deity of Christ (as suggested in my first principle given above) and then applying the appropriate Scriptures.

Walter Martin, arguably the father of modern cult apologetics, used to give the following illustration. He said that banks train their tellers to detect counterfeit money by having them carefully study real money. They become so familiar with the genuine article that when a fake bill comes through they can detect it instantly. Similarly, the single most important thing a Christian can do to deal with cultic error is to know the truth thoroughly—and that means knowing the Bible. While God does specially call some to a cult apologetics ministry, it is not necessary for every Christian to master the details of every cult under the sun (though some knowledge of specific cultic beliefs can certainly prove helpful for anyone). But *all* Christians need to know their Bible. When churches or individuals spend all (or even most) of their time teaching on recovery, self-esteem, codependency, or other such self-focused issues, then we should not be surprised when a cultist wreaks havoc with some members' faith. Christians need to know the Scriptures if they are to lead effective lives of service for their Master. And this applies to sharing one's faith with cultists as much as to any other activity in the Christian life.

Some Final Remarks

Earlier in this chapter we observed that Athanasius of Alexandria led the charge at the Council of Nicaea in the defense of Christ's deity. Unfortunately, turmoil continued over this doctrine over a span of about thirty years, and through various political machinations and maneuvering the Arian party managed to prevail at certain times. Depending upon the sensibilities of the emperor at the time, Athanasius was variously exiled and recalled, sometimes having to dodge assassins and hide out in the desert until a more favorable climate made it safe for him to return. His homecoming was often short-lived: Athanasius suffered banishment and recall five times!

What are we to make of such a man, willing to suffer such indignities over—of all things—a *doctrine?* Was this a mark of heroism or of mental instability?

A soul such as Athanasius may prove enigmatic to modern sensibilities, even among many Christians. The tendency in our day is to see those who contend for doctrinal beliefs as narrow, divisive, and given to hairsplitting. Now, let us admit that it *is* possible to be all of these things, and when Christians behave in an unseemly way, particularly over minor issues, they are not honoring their Lord or advancing his cause. But what we should not admit is that contending for the truths of the Christian faith *automatically* entails these negative traits. Indeed, Jude 3 tells us to "contend earnestly for the faith which was once for all handed down to the saints" (NASB). It is possible to *contend* without being *contentious,* i.e., hostile, unloving, and argumentative.

In all this Christians need to maintain a sense of proportion. While there are some issues about which we may agree to disagree, the question of the deity of Christ is not one of them. When Athanasius contended earnestly for this doctrine, he was not splitting hairs or merely wrangling about words. No, he understood that the entire faith hung in the balance, for a Jesus who is not God is a Jesus who cannot save.

How about us? Do we have the sense of proportion that Athanasius had? Are we convinced of the importance of knowing and being able to defend this truth? Are we willing to share it with others? Or do we clam up out of fear of being thought contentious or from a desire to avoid conflict at all costs?

We may well suffer the ill will of cultists when we tell them that they believe in a false Jesus who cannot save. We may not wish to tell them this, because it sounds so harsh. But tell them we must, for to allow the cultic view of Jesus to go unchallenged is not loving, given the literally life-and-death issues that hang in the balance.

So, when we find ourselves reticent to speak, we should think of Athanasius, who literally took his life in his hands to defend the doctrine of Christ's deity. Perhaps this will help us keep matters in perspective and give us the courage that we sometimes lack as we strive to fulfill our calling as "a worker who has no need to be ashamed, rightly handling the word of truth" (2 Tim. 2:15).

10

The Deity of Christ for Missions, World Religions, and Pluralism

J. NELSON JENNINGS

J esus is God." For better or for worse, that provocative declaration thrusts us straightaway into the explosive, nuanced, and interrelated worlds of Christian missions, multiple religious traditions, and religious pluralism.

Navigation Guidelines

We need to chart our course for the daunting task before us of considering Christ's deity in relation to missions, world religions, and pluralism. While our task is a complicated one, it is helpful to note at the outset that, on one hand, our Christian confession that Jesus is God is a straightforward claim. As other chapters in this book explain, the Bible definitely reveals that Jesus of Nazareth was—and still is—the incarnate creator-redeemer, the God of old-covenant Israel, God the Son. To be sure, many people don't agree with the Bible's claims about the divinity of Jesus Christ,[1] and we Christians have often struggled to explain how Jesus is in fact God. Even so, it is clear enough how God the Holy Spirit inspired the biblical writers to explain

---

[1] In this chapter, I will use "divinity" and "deity" practically interchangeably (especially since they seemingly have identical etymological roots).

Jesus Christ's deity in categories understandable to themselves and to their intended audience. It is also clear enough how subsequent generations of Jesus' followers, after wrestling over how to do so, have articulated with full conviction—both for their own sakes and for others'—how a man and God could be united in one historical, risen, and ascended figure. Despite regular challenges, then, confessing the deity of Christ has always been the church's clear stance.

We Christians therefore can and indeed must believe in our hearts and declare to others with full, unshakeable confidence that "Jesus is God." My hope and prayer is that this chapter will coalesce with the rest of this book in strengthening your assurance of, and your capacity to articulate to others, the deity of Jesus Christ. If you are reading these words and do not yet believe that Jesus is God—that he is the world's creator and king as well as your own personal king and savior—I pray this discussion will help to birth in you a newfound trust in the carpenter of Galilee, the one who clearly demonstrated himself to be the God who made you and came into this world to free you to know, love, and serve him.

Challenges

Yes, the man Jesus is most assuredly the world's divine creator-redeemer. At the same time, as already noted, Jesus' followers have repeatedly faced the challenge of understanding and explaining how it is that a man could be God, as well as how it could be that God became a man. Throughout history and in numerous cultural-linguistic settings, the fact of Christ's divinity has required fresh articulation and witness. Explaining Jesus' divinity has at times involved tremendous struggle, likely the most widely known of which were those resulting in the fourth-century Nicene Creed and the fifth-century Chalcedonian Creed (more on those later). Suffice it to note for now that fresh contexts—such as our globally interactive world today—require Christians to make fresh affirmation, articulation, and witness of their faith in Christ's deity.

In addition to our varied and ever-changing contexts, the interpersonal challenge of communicating well to their contemporaries faces Christians of any generation. We who have written this book have sought God's help in explaining various biblical, historical, and contemporary facets of the Christian confession of Christ's deity for an early twenty-first-century, English-language audience. We have sought to be faithful, particularly to the Scriptures but also to the historical witness of the church. Our explanations should be appropriate in terms of how they communicate information, most of which originated in earlier historical periods and in cultural-linguistic situations different from our own. What you find here also needs to be relevant to concerns and issues that you and others face today. Understanding and communicating the divinity of Christ faithfully, appropriately, and in relevant fashion is no small task.[2]

Moreover, it is by no means the case that the totality of our early twenty-first-century, English-language audience heartily confesses that "Jesus is God." Members of that audience raise all sorts of objections and alternative confessions with which a book like this must deal evangelistically and apologetically. Add the objections and alternative confessions made by people among the majority, non-English-speaking portion of planet earth's human population, and our evangelistic-apologetic task here is daunting indeed.

Approaches

Taken as a whole, then, the challenges presented by our present contexts, the need to communicate well within those contexts, and the burden of testifying effectively to various unbelievers around us are major. In fact, the more one thinks about those challenges, the more one can become rattled and confused. In order to steady ourselves to navigate our challenging course effectively, we will take two overriding approaches.

First, we will proceed in consecutive fashion through the areas of missions, world religions, and religious pluralism. We noted earlier how these areas are very much interrelated, but they have their distinctive themes that can best be addressed in turn. Doing so should at least help keep us on track.

Second, our mind-set will need to bear some marks that might seem new to some readers. Namely, we are intentionally going to have to think in multilingual and global as well as biblical and bold ways. What those intertwined marks mean practically will become clearer along the way. But as a taste of what lies ahead, I submit that one cannot think "biblically" about anything—certainly the topic of Christ's deity—without also thinking explicitly in a multilingual, global, and bold manner. After all, the Bible's message of Christ's divinity originally came in languages different from contemporary English. That message has been understood, believed, and confessed throughout the world in a plethora of socio-political and cultural-linguistic contexts; yet there always have been to this day all sorts of potent arguments against (and often derogatory mocking of) the necessarily bold Christian confession that "Jesus is God."

---

[2]These three categories about communicating God's Word—faithful, appropriate, and relevant—come from R. Daniel Shaw and Charles E. Van Engen, *Communicating God's Word in a Complex World: God's Truth or Hocus Pocus?* (Lanham, MD: Rowman & Littlefield, 2003).

Having thus charted our course, it is time to enter first the world of relating Christ's deity to missions. This will be the longest of our three main sections. Since the three topics of missions, religions, and pluralism are interrelated, sections two and three can be more streamlined by drawing on some of what is covered in the first section.

Jesus and Missions

I believe many evangelical readers will latently assume the following four realities to undergird and provide a framework for this section.

First, many peoples throughout the world resist the exclusivity associated with declaring that Jesus is the one true and living God.[3] While those peoples—Hindus, for example—might be happy enough to incorporate Jesus into their limitless pantheon of deities, the claim that he alone is the creator-redeemer is unacceptable. Missionaries must therefore stand firm and patiently insist that Jesus Christ alone is God, along with the Father and Holy Spirit.

Second, Muslims in particular, along with Jewish people and others, find Christians' claim that Jesus is divine both unthinkable and offensive. Allah (or Yahweh) alone is God, period. This basic difference is a major stumbling block to missions among Muslims and Jewish people.

Third, animists (assumed to be those primitive peoples who believe that the natural world is infused or "animated" with spirits) need first to understand that there is one God who has created all things, and second that he has come into the world as Jesus Christ. Missionaries must patiently and wisely explain monotheism to these peoples, then demonstrate that Jesus was the Creator-God incarnate among us.

Fourth, in general, whether the people to whom missionaries go are Buddhists, animists, Muslims, Hindus, or something else, the missionaries will need to use the Bible to explain God and Christ's deity with patience, wisdom, clarity, and love. Ultimately the Holy Spirit must reveal Jesus to people and convince them that he is God the Son.

As we will discuss shortly, these assumptions about approaching the relationship between Christ's divinity and missions lead primarily into strategic matters: how do missionaries, in reliance on the Holy Spirit, demonstrate to various non-Christian peoples that Jesus is divine? Moreover, collectively these assumptions support the notion that preaching the deity of Christ among the nations—part and parcel of missions—is indeed a challenging

---

[3] I will use the plural "peoples" in reference to the biblical-Greek *ethne*, translated into English as "nations," "ethnic groups," and "people groups."

task. And for evangelicals aware of worldwide religious developments, the growth of Christian cults that deny the deity of Christ—Jehovah's Witnesses and Latter-Day Saints (Mormons) in particular—is cause for great concern.

What these assumptions also have in common with respect to content is the theme of world religions, our next section. That is, the four points above are concerned with how to explain Christ's divinity to people who are Buddhists, animists, Muslims, Hindus, or something else. Given that common theme, we are going to suspend treatment of these assumptions until the section on world religions.

As for the rest of this section on Jesus and missions, we will examine Jesus' relationship to both the process and the content of missions. First, though, we need to consider the operative term here that evangelicals use freely and often, but one they practically never define: "missions." By taking what appears to be a side path to investigate our assumed understandings of Christian missions, our overall discussion will avoid unwittingly sinking into the quicksand of failing to make constructive progress.

What Is (Are) "Missions"?

While evangelicals speak with a shared sense of certainty about what missions is,[4] the last one hundred years have seen spirited discussion over the nature of Christian missions. By way of synopsis, the much-celebrated Edinburgh Missionary Conference of 1910 was upbeat (some would pejoratively say triumphalistic) in its strategizing over Christianity's seemingly inexorable expansion across the globe. However, two world wars, the breakup of European empires in the 1950s and 1960s, and the persistence and even resurgence of non-Christian religions—all against the backdrop of disconcerting theological currents flowing out of nineteenth-century Germany (and Enlightenment thought before that)—raised probing questions for many Christian leaders.

That questioning ferment involved, for example, a thirty-five-member "Laymen's Foreign Missions Inquiry" in the early 1930s representing seven Protestant denominations. That influential group offered an "objective review of the presuppositions of the entire [missions] enterprise,"[5] generating widespread, soul-searching discussion. Almost two decades later, soon after the war-delayed but much-anticipated formation of the World Council of Churches in 1948, the Maoist takeover of China—long the "crown jewel"

---

[4]Note the singular verb "is," commonly used by evangelicals with the plural noun "missions." I will observe that usage throughout these few paragraphs that describe common evangelical understandings of missions.

[5]William Ernest Hocking, *Re-thinking Missions: A Laymen's Inquiry after One Hundred Years* (New York and London: Harper & Brothers, 1932), x.

of many missions efforts—had a devastating ripple effect throughout missions circles. The Barthian-informed *missio Dei* ("mission of God") quickly emerged as a compelling framework that many embraced to believe in God's ongoing work throughout the world. However, when some churchmen drifted increasingly in the 1960s toward seeing God's mission as focused on political and economic liberation movements, other Christian leaders decided to organize what became the evangelical Lausanne Movement, starting in 1974.

Since that time, for its part the Lausanne Movement has stayed the course on proclaiming salvation by faith alone in Christ alone as its central message. Evangelism and church planting have also remained fundamental emphases for evangelicals. Various social concerns have been evident as well, the relative importance of which (in relation to evangelism and church planting) has been often hotly discussed.[6] A primary focus of reaching the unreached peoples of the world came to the fore in the AD 2000 Movement.[7] "Finishing the task of the Great Commission," the proclaimed goal and assumed essence of "missions," came to be seen as reaching the world's unreached peoples.[8] In the early years of the twenty-first century, church-planting movements and "insider movements" have become prominent rubrics through which the missions enterprise is seen to be progressing.[9] Throughout—and directly related to our overall topic here—the deity of Christ has remained an unquestioned conviction and confession of evangelicals.[10]

"Missions," then, is largely understood among evangelicals as proclaiming salvation in Christ to those who have not heard of him, the unreached; social ministries often need to accompany (and are sometimes seen as necessary preparation for) gospel proclamation. For many US evangelicals,[11] the unreached are peoples scattered throughout the world in need of gospel

---

[6]J. Nelson Jennings, *God the Real Superpower: Rethinking Our Role in Missions* (Phillipsburg, NJ: P&R, 2007), 203–6.

[7]See ibid., 171–74.

[8]Ibid., 194–95.

[9]A visit to almost any evangelical missions agency's website will confirm that "church-planting movements" are a central focus; see, e.g., http://www.mtw.org (Mission to the World, the agency of my own denomination, the Presbyterian Church in America), http://www.imb.org (Southern Baptist International Mission Board).

[10]As the statement of faith of almost any evangelical missions agency will confirm; see, e.g., websites linked to The Mission Station website at http://www.missionaries.org/Organizations_and_Boards/Evangelical_Mission_Agencies/index.html.

[11]I realize the generalizations I am making here are by nature suspect. I am basing these claims on extensive visits to US evangelical churches, various interactions with US evangelicals (including hundreds of seminary students), and reading of US evangelical materials.

messengers sent "out" there to "the mission field."[12] As Paul's oft-(mis) applied words state the matter: "How then will they call on him in whom they have not believed? And how are they to believe in him of whom they have never heard? And how are they to hear without someone preaching? And how are they to preach unless they are sent?" (Rom. 10:14–15). Missions involvement thus means some Christians going as missionaries to Buddhists, animists, Muslims, Hindus, or people of some other religion, other Christians sending the missionaries who go, and all Christians praying for the missionaries. Part of the good news of forgiveness of sin, or the gospel, that missionaries are to proclaim to the unreached is necessarily the deity of Christ—since only a divine Savior can save people from their sins. The methods and strategies associated with presenting Jesus as divine to various peoples have already been noted.

For reasons that will emerge more fully in what immediately follows, I suggest that this framework for understanding "missions"—and thus for understanding Christ's deity in relation to missions in a largely strategic (sometimes mechanical) way—is truncated. Consider, for example, common missions-conference themes such as "Declaring Christ among the Nations." Such a slogan effectively means something like, "Caucasian Americans going to other parts of the world and preaching Jesus." That type of understanding would never be stated so explicitly, but US Caucasians going, sending, and praying for the gospel's progress "out there" among "the nations" at "the end of the earth" (à la Acts 1:8) is the pervasive operative paradigm for "missions" across the landscape of US evangelicals.[13]

In order to appreciate the scope of Christ's divinity in relation to Christian missions in a more full-orbed, comprehensive manner, we need a more full-orbed, comprehensive, and I believe biblical notion of "missions." While spirited discussions continue regarding the nature of "missions,"[14] and while we necessarily can only summarize matters here, the basic framework from which to develop that notion involves distinguishing between the inseparable realities of God's (singular) mission and Christians' (plural) missions.[15] God's mission involves his decisive commitment and acts to redeem his world gone awry; Christians' missions efforts involve cross- and intercultural participation with God in his mission.[16] God is at work

---

[12]I have discussed the ideas within quotation marks, as well as the assumptions undergirding those ideas, in Jennings, *God the Real Superpower*.

[13]This description of missions includes the increasingly asserted statement, "The nations have come to us." These matters are all discussed more extensively in ibid., 181.

[14]Ibid.

[15]Ibid., esp. 16–19 and 217–25.

[16]Ibid., esp. 183–84.

throughout the world, and he includes (but does not restrict himself to) Christians' initiatives in how he carries out his work.

Having taken the side path of briefly investigating our notions of "missions," we can now proceed down our main road of considering Jesus and missions.

Jesus the Divine Orchestrator of Missions (Process Point 1)

A broader historical view of God's mission, Christian missions, and Christ's deity in relation to mission(s) will help us here. Much of the prevailing, contemporary evangelical notion of "missions" comes out of the last two centuries of the activist, strategizing "Modern Missions Movement." [17] That movement is largely understood to have begun with William Carey and other pioneers associated with the formation of Protestant mission societies in the 1790s and early 1800s. With respect to being "modern," however, the Modern Missions Movement actually began about five hundred years ago, when Western powers fueled by modernity's scientific discoveries began expanding throughout the world.[18] To expand our horizons even further, Christian missions actually have been taking place for two millennia—and arguably since God created the world.[19] Taking our lead from the full historical scope of the divine Jesus Christ's relationship with God's mission/Christian missions can help us break out of the confining, largely strategic notions of that relationship associated with the last few hundred years of Christian missions.

The risen Jesus' words recorded by Luke and found in Acts 1:8, oft-cited as they are, provide a crucial paradigm for understanding the relationship between Jesus the God-man and the process of Christian missions: "But you will receive power when the Holy Spirit has come upon you, and you will be my witnesses in Jerusalem and in all Judea and Samaria, and to the end of the earth." Typically, evangelicals take Jesus' words here as a concentric-circle imperative directed toward each local church's "comprehensive missions strategy in their community (Jerusalem), state (Judea), continent (Samaria), and world (ends of the earth)."[20] Truer, however, to what unfolds throughout the rest of Acts and Christian history is to hear Jesus foretelling what

---

[17]Wilbert R. Shenk, *Changing Frontiers of Mission*, American Society of Missiology Series 28 (Maryknoll, NY: Orbis, 1999), 33.

[18]Ibid., 153–58.

[19]Jennings, *God the Real Superpower*, 24–27.

[20]This particular quotation is from the first website that came up from an Internet search for "Acts 1:8 churches" on February 22, 2010. I could have chosen any other listed website for an equivalent description. In my experience of visiting various evangelical churches (usually to speak at missions conferences), I have yet to visit one that has not seen itself as Jerusalem within a concentric-circle strategy.

he, by his Spirit, will bring to pass through his followers. Grammatically, either an imperative or an indicative/predictive interpretation would fit. But within the overall flow of the book of Acts' early transition from Luke's first-volume account of "all that Jesus began to do and teach" (Acts 1:1) to the rest of volume two's record of Jesus' continuing work of miracles and opening people's hearts (e.g., 3:6; 14:27; 16:14), understanding Acts 1:8 as Jesus' prediction that the Holy Spirit would come and empower his disciples to witness throughout history "to the end of the earth" makes better sense.[21]

Throughout Acts, Luke follows the outline of Jesus' prediction, recounting Jesus' work from Jerusalem to Judea and Samaria (8:1ff.), then on to Ethiopia (8:27ff.), Phoenicia, Cyprus, Cyrene, Antioch (11:19ff.), Asia Minor (13:4ff.), Europe (16:12ff.), and beyond. Luke includes explicit references to divine intervention within the missions process Jesus is orchestrating, perhaps most famously in leading Paul and his team to Macedonia:

> Having been forbidden by the Holy Spirit to speak the word in Asia. . . . They attempted to go into Bithynia, but the Spirit of Jesus did not allow them. . . . And a vision appeared to Paul in the night: a man of Macedonia was standing there, urging him and saying, "Come over to Macedonia and help us." And when Paul had seen the vision, immediately we sought to go on into Macedonia, concluding that God had called us to preach the gospel to them. (Acts 16:6–10)

Along with Luke's description here of divine guidance and the corresponding discernment of Paul's missions team, the Trinitarian character of that divine guidance ("the Holy Spirit," "the Spirit of Jesus," "God") is yet another pointer to the divine, risen, and exalted Jesus' orchestration of Christians' missions efforts.

There is not space here to recount even just an outline of the entire scope of the history of Christian missions. The relevant point is to recognize the divine Jesus orchestrating the ongoing movement of his people as he has empowered them as his witnesses. To appreciate the full biblical sweep of Christ's presence among his followers, it is worth at least mentioning the triune God's leading of his people during earlier, old-covenant days, for example in the Sinai wilderness:

> I want you to know, brothers, that our fathers were all under the cloud, and all passed through the sea, and all were baptized into Moses in the cloud

---

[21] I discuss more extensively these interpretations of Acts 1:8 in Jennings, *God the Real Superpower*, particularly 87ff.

and in the sea, and all ate the same spiritual food, and all drank the same spiritual drink. For they drank from the spiritual Rock that followed them, and the Rock was Christ. (1 Cor. 10:1–4)

Later, the risen Jesus, to whom "all authority in heaven and on earth" had been given, promised his ongoing presence with his followers "to the end of the age," even as they were to minister in the Father's, the Son's, and the Holy Spirit's divine, triune name (Matt. 28:18–20).

The glorified Jesus continues that presence and empowerment through and beyond Luke's open-ended conclusion of Acts, whereby Paul was "proclaiming the kingdom of God and teaching about the Lord Jesus Christ with all boldness and without hindrance" (Acts 28:31). Jesus, the ascended Son of God and eternal God the Son, has continued for two millennia to orchestrate his people's witness—in earlier centuries into Western Asia, India, Europe, Northeast Africa, and Central Asia, then in modern centuries into other parts of Africa, Southeast and East Asia, and the Americas.

Jesus the Divine Intruder (Content Point 1)
Throughout Christian missions, the Holy Spirit has empowered Christ's witnesses to preach "the Lord Jesus" (Acts 11:20). Having just sketched the process of the divine Jesus' orchestration of Christian missions, next we need to explore the message brought to people by empowered witnesses of "the Lord Jesus." It is timely here to remind ourselves to keep thinking in a multilingual, global, biblical, and bold manner. It is also timely to remind ourselves of how Jesus' witnesses, empowered as they have been by the Spirit of God the Son, have communicated "the Lord Jesus" faithfully, appropriately, and in relevant terms.

Returning to Acts 11, Luke does not fully explain why some believers scattered by persecution "as far as Phoenicia and Cyprus and Antioch" witnessed "to no one except Jews," but other witnesses, "men of Cyprus and Cyrene," spoke in Antioch "to the Hellenists [Greeks, i.e., Greek-speaking non-Jews] also, preaching the Lord Jesus" (Acts 11:19–20). Luke's account continues, "And the hand of the Lord was with them, and a great number who believed turned to the Lord" (v. 21). The significance of this groundbreaking addition of non-Jews to the Christian community was not lost either on the leaders in Jerusalem or on the Spirit-inspired Luke: "The report of this came to the ears of the church in Jerusalem, and they sent Barnabas to Antioch" (11:22) to examine and test the legitimacy of what was happening. The explosive intra-Christian, Jew-Gentile dynamic had been launched, a central topic throughout much of the New Testament.

The question on which we will focus here is more expressly theological, or perhaps vertical: what was happening between Jesus and the Hellenists in Antioch? Those Greek-speaking non-Jews heard Jesus' followers from Cyprus and Cyrene speaking, presumably in Greek, about a Jewish rabbi who had lived to the south and, according to these witnesses, had risen from the dead. "Well, sounds interesting but no way on the rising from the dead part," those Hellenists must have thought (in Greek, of course). But the reality was that the risen Jesus was speaking through these witnesses who were using not only Greek but also the key designation *Kurios*. The Hellenists' Creator was actually addressing them in their heart language and in a relevant conceptual category that demanded some sort of reaction.

Unless the non-Jewish, Greek-speaking hearers in Antioch were closely familiar with the Septuagint's use of *Kurios* for the Hebrew *Yahweh*, they would not have heard in Old Testament terms (at least initially) the witnesses' claim that the allegedly risen rabbi was *Kurios*, the creator and God of Israel. Rather, those hearers would have been jolted by the audacious assignment to the obscure man Jesus of the title that belonged exclusively to the Roman Caesar, who alone was *kurios*, the one above whom there was to be no authority and the one to whom ultimate loyalty was to be given. As for Jesus' active part in the interaction, he was speaking through his empowered witnesses to the Hellenists in Antioch as their creator, the one above whom there was in fact no authority and to whom their ultimate loyalty was to be given. In other words Jesus, while ever the Hellenist's creator to whom they (consciously or not) were ever responsible, was shouldering his way into their linguistic, religio-political world and demanding their conscious, ultimate allegiance.[22]

For those first-century non-Jewish Greeks, an ascription of ultimate authority to Jesus, accompanied by a commitment of ultimate loyalty to Jesus, was functionally on the same trajectory as a confession of Jesus' deity. After all, they "turned to the Lord [and away from any other ultimate *kurios*, including Caesar or a Greco-Roman religious deity]." Jesus the God-man was pressing into those Hellenists' Greco-Roman religio-political world as their sovereign creator. Further instruction was needed for them to equate Jesus as the Greco-Roman *Kurios* with Israel's *Kurios*. Generations of questions, discussions, and decisions were needed to articulate, in Latin and Greek philosophical and theological terms, how God could be triune and how Jesus could be both God and man (hence the Nicene and Chalcedonian Creeds). But with respect to what those first-century Greeks in

---

[22]Ibid., 46.

Antioch believed through the Christians' witness, they were confronted by the missions-orchestrating Jesus coming to them as their ultimate *Kurios*, challenging the Roman Caesar who claimed that place of honor. As an initial intrusion into that religio-political world, Jesus was staking his claim as their ultimate, unique, and only true (to use the Greco-Latin term familiar to English speakers) deity.

That type of intrusion into peoples' particular linguistic-cultural, religio-political worlds is what Jesus has been doing throughout missions history. As the creator of all peoples, the triune God—including God the Son, of course—has always overseen peoples' historical development, including geographically, religiously, culturally, socio-economically, politically, and otherwise (Acts 17:26–27). We should thus understand the triune God to have brought—not just sent out from somewhere else—his human emissaries to peoples to bring the good news of Jesus' life, death, and resurrection. As God has done that throughout missions history, Jesus the God-man has intruded into peoples' lives, individually and collectively, offering them life in his own divine name. Hence he invaded peoples' lives in the Indian subcontinent when he brought Thomas there in the first century, northeast Africans' lives in the fourth century (through two Syrian boys, Aedisius and Frumentius), Chinese peoples' lives in the seventh century (through Alopen and others), Slavic peoples' lives in the ninth century (through Cyril and Methodius), and thousands of other peoples' lives down to the present. History testifies that "a great number [of those people have] believed [and] turned to the Lord" in their own languages and contexts.

To summarize, Jesus has been using Christian missions to become the divine Intruder into peoples' lives, individually and collectively. Those people who, upon Jesus' initial intrusion into their midst, have acknowledged him as their supreme authority to whom they owe their ultimate allegiance, and who have trusted in the crucified and risen Jesus' offer of himself for life, thereby effectively have confessed the equivalent of the English-language claim, "Jesus is God." Just like the first-century Hellenists in Antioch, new believers within each cultural-linguistic people have thus begun a trajectory of working out the meaning and implications of their confession.

We will examine such trajectories further after examining another missions-process matter.

Jesus the Divine Orchestrator of Multidirectional Missions (Process Point 2)
Jesus predicted the multidirectional movement of his witnesses from Jerusalem to Judea, Samaria, and beyond. Jesus did not—at least directly in his pre-ascension words recorded in Acts 1:8—prescribe a concentric-circle

movement outward from one or any local church. As we have already sketched very briefly, a macro-historical view of the past two millennia confirms the multidirectional movement of the Christian gospel into all areas of the world. Contrary to some of our engrained instincts about the movement of Christian history, Jesus did not orchestrate the gospel's preaching in a unidirectional manner from Jerusalem into Europe, then to North America, then from the North Atlantic to the rest of the world. The divine Jesus has directed his witnesses much more along varied paths than along a straight line through the Western world.[23]

What can keep us from appreciating the worldwide, multidirectional spread of Christian missions is our immediate background (i.e., the last few centuries) of Western development and expansion. For most US-born Americans,[24] our educational training, whether in school, church, or families, understandably has focused on American and Western European history. Our resulting sense of Christian history, theology, and missions initiatives is thus in large part limited to American and Western European settings. With specific regard to Christian missions, then, our unexamined sense is that all missionaries have gone from the US (or perhaps Britain) to the non-Western world. That sense is buttressed by the fact that many missionaries have indeed gone from the US (and Britain) over the last few centuries throughout the non-Western world. Nineteenth-century British military and economic power, joined (then eclipsed) by twentieth-century US power, has enabled that recent, large flow of English-speaking missionaries.[25]

The entirety of Christian missions history, however, demonstrates that the recent, dominant outflow of European and North American missionaries is only part of Jesus' multidirectional orchestration of his worldwide mission.[26] Especially in the early twenty-first century, the fact that missions initiatives are originating all around the world needs to be understood. As is increasingly documented and publicized,[27] missionaries are going out from North America, Latin America, Africa, Europe, the Pacific Islands,

---

[23]A helpful online map, entitled "World Distribution of Christians, 1997," that illustrates the multidirectional movement of the Christian gospel is available at http://www.wadsworth.com/religion_d/special_features/popups/maps/schmidt_patterns/content/map_49.html.

[24]Once again, I am forced here to run the risk of overgeneralizing.

[25]Jennings, God the Real Superpower, 20–21.

[26]The nineteenth- and twentieth-century prominence of Roman Catholic missionaries—particularly from France—as well as of Russian Orthodox missionaries (at least until the Communist revolutions) must be included in a representative picture of modern European (and North American) missions, in association with European and North American economic and military expansion.

[27]See, e.g., the online prayer guide "Operation World" at http://www.operationworld.org that notes a variety of country-by-country statistics, including missionaries to and from each country.

and various sectors of the vast continent of Asia. Both the Christian church and the flow of Christian missions are more worldwide and international than ever before.

For this overall discussion, one crucial implication of recognizing the worldwide, multidirectional origins and destinations of Christian missions concerns an inherent aspect of Christ's deity: his global rule over, as well as his intimate familiarity with, the entire world that he has created and worked to redeem. The cultural-linguistic limitations that people all have necessarily limit our notions of who God is and how he relates to people—even if we might intellectually believe that God is multilingual and the God of all peoples. Without realizing it or intending to do so, we can limit Jesus to a tribal, linguistically limited deity. That subconscious reality certainly has been my personal experience.[28]

The confession "Jesus is God," however, entails that he knows and relates to all people of all languages. He made all people and, according to the apostle Paul, has guided them "in the hope that they might feel their way toward him and find him. Yet he is actually not far from each one of us" (Acts 17:27). Related are the apostle John's words: "The true light, which enlightens everyone, was coming into the world" (John 1:9). Jesus the creator God is intimately acquainted with all those whom he has created. He is "omnilingual" and is the divine orchestrator of what essentially has always been a multidirectional missions enterprise.

Continuing Missions (Content Point 2)
To help us get our bearings, here is a freshly worded summary of our discussion so far about Jesus and missions:

- It might be assumed that "missions," particularly including defending Christ's deity, primarily entails presenting Jesus to adherents of other religions.
- "Missions" are Christians' cross-cultural and intercultural initiatives that are empowered and guided by the triune God (including, of course, the divine Jesus) as part of his redemptive mission.
- Jesus uses his witnesses to intrude into peoples' collective and individual lives, eliciting from his newly reclaimed creatures an indigenous confession of both his ultimate authority and their ultimate loyalty to him—the double-door entrance to articulating his full divinity.

---

[28] In my own case, growing up a monolingual US-American, learning Japanese and relating to God in Japanese with no internal English translation was revolutionary with respect to knowing God to be the God of all peoples. I chronicle that experience in Jennings, *God the Real Superpower*, 27, 78.

- As the God of the whole earth, Jesus first orchestrated the movement of his emissaries out of Jerusalem in multiple directions, such that today there are more origin and destination points than ever before.

The entire discussion has been conducted within the framework of Christ's divinity. The tack we have taken has been to see Jesus as in fact both the divine leader and the divine message of Christian missions. Our multilingual, global, biblical, and bold posture has maintained that the relationship between Christ's deity and Christian missions is not primarily a matter of missionaries' determining how to convince others that Jesus is God. Rather, the relationship between Christ's deity and Christian missions consists primarily in Jesus Christ the ascended God-man orchestrating, empowering, and intruding into peoples' lives through his followers' cross-/intercultural witness.

Jesus' initial intrusion that elicits acknowledgment of and allegiance to him as the ultimate authority (as well as conscious rejection and unbelief) accompanies his divinely empowered witnesses who communicate to people faithfully, appropriately, and in relevant terms. Hence people can make an honest, indigenous confession of faith in the one, true, and living Jesus Christ. But missions among a people do not stop with the initial communication of the gospel and confession of faith in Christ. So-called Christianization is not a one-time step.[29] Rather, learning to "observe all that I have commanded you" (Matt. 28:20) involves an ongoing, daily walk of faith. The cross-/intercultural input into that walk is also ongoing; in other words, missions among a people—any people—continue.

Jesus the God-man persistently presses his authority among peoples from among whom he has begun to call together his followers. One of the primary ways he persists in pressing his authority is through outside, expatriate witness. If a people and Christians among them are exclusively cultural insiders, the centripetal pull of the contexts can choke, squelch, and defang the Christians' prophetic voice. Christian history is rife with countless examples of movements that gradually acquiesce to their surroundings, freeze their traditions and language (e.g., Latin, Ge'ez,[30] Slavic, Syriac), and become defenders of the socio-political status quo (e.g., the Orthodox Church in Russia, churches established in the North American colonies). Thankfully, however, Jesus graciously persists in bringing out-

---

[29]Regarding the relationship between the notion that "Christianization" is a one-time step and a now bygone European Christendom, see Shenk, *Changing Frontiers of Mission*, 122–24.
[30]An ancient language used in the liturgy of Ethiopian Orthodoxy.

siders—missionaries, whether organized or unorganized[31]—into contexts to give fresh insight, perspective, and gospel witness. Missions continue within all contexts within which they have begun.

Part of the fresh insight, perspective, and gospel witness from ongoing missions input involves further coming to grips with who Jesus is as a people's ultimate authority. That identity and place of Jesus needs to be articulated in indigenous terms: he is the creator of all peoples, but he is not a foreign deity. In Greco-Roman terms, that meant calling Jesus *Kurios* and *Theos*, all the while understanding those designations both to counteract any political or religious rival and to equate Jesus with *Yahweh* of Israel.

"Jesus is God" and "Jesus is Lord" are perhaps the supreme examples of how English speakers have articulated Jesus' ultimate authority and place in indigenous terms. Both phrases connote divinity, as other chapters in this book explain. Please note as well that both God and Lord, as linguistic terms, have particular etymological backgrounds, as does the label "deity."[32] That means that the confessions "Jesus is God" and "Jesus is Lord" and the expression "Christ's deity" all have particular contextual meanings. None of the three expressions is either eternal or static. What each means (and meant in the past) to the believers who confess them, as well as what each communicates to others who hear those confessions as witness, needs to be faithful to the Bible's original meanings, appropriate with respect to the meaning and communication conveyed, and relevant to contemporary contexts.

It is thus worth asking, for example, if "Jesus is Lord" is a biblical confession, namely with respect to the communicative relationship between the original, first-century Greco-Roman context and today's English-speaking contexts. (Please note again that what "Lord" meant several centuries ago in feudal England, when Tyndale translated the Scriptures in English, and what the term means in twenty-first-century US-American circles, are of course not the same.) That is, does confessing Jesus as "Lord" *faithfully* represent what the Bible's first-century, Greco-Roman confession of Jesus as *Kurios* meant? Does the "Lord" Jesus *appropriately* carry the same ultimate authority as *Kurios* Jesus in New Testament times? Is calling Jesus "Lord" *relevant* in contemporary US circles? Since "lord" is used only sparingly

---

[31] Jennings, *God the Real Superpower*, 117–22, 138–39.

[32] "God" is from the Germanic designation for deities, *Gott*; "Lord" is apparently from an Old English term for a household master or, going further back, "guard of the loaves," referring to a Germanic tribal custom of a chieftain providing food for his followers; "deity" (and "divinity"), by contrast, comes from an Old French and Latin line that goes back to the supreme Greek god *Zeus* (a name based, perhaps, on the Persian *daiva*).

and in limited, obscure ways (e.g., in video games), other designations, e.g., "commander-in-chief," "champion," or "hero," might be more "biblical" in terms of faithfulness, appropriateness, and relevancy.[33]

The question about the biblical character of "Jesus is Lord" is at the very heart of this "Jesus and missions" section, specifically in reference to Christ's deity. How do missions relate to today's English-speaking context? How is Jesus pressing home his divinity in today's ever-changing, English-speaking context? How is he orchestrating Christian missions into and within today's US context? Such questions are part and parcel of considering Christ's deity in relation to the Christian missions that he continues to orchestrate throughout the entire world. Those considerations necessarily spill over into the ensuing section.

Jesus and Religions

We are now ready to consider Jesus' divinity in relation to the world's religious traditions. We have discussed Jesus' continual claim to authority within ever-changing contexts into which he has intruded through bringing his witnesses to those same contexts that he has actually superintended since he created the world and all peoples within it. The peoples of the world have thus always been under God's authority and rule. They have also been responsible to serve and honor him as their creator king, especially since that triune creator has continually taken the initiative to reveal himself to all people, his covenantal subjects, through his creation (Ps. 19:1–7), their consciences (Rom. 2:15), and his inescapable presence (Job 38:4ff.; Ps. 139:7–12).

The Nature of Religion(s)

How have people responded to God, or exhibited their (ir)responsibility to him? Speaking in general terms, the world's peoples have responded to God's authority and rule in mixed ways, that is, both constructively and destructively, in positive and negative ways, with truth and error intermingled. Insofar as people have "suppress[ed] the truth" and "became futile in their thinking, and their foolish hearts were darkened" (Rom. 1:18, 21), clearly they have reacted to God destructively, negatively, and in error. At the same time, insofar as people have—according to God's image with which everyone is created, and per God's divine superintendence over their lives—moved to "seek God . . . [and] feel their way toward him and find him" (Acts 17:27), they have reacted to God constructively, positively, and with at least a measure of truth. Yes, "all have sinned and fall short of the

---

[33]Jennings, *God the Real Superpower*, 45–49.

glory of God" (Rom. 3:23). But just as "all" types of people (Jew and Gentile alike) have fallen short, so have "all" peoples been sustained by God's gracious word (Heb. 1:2–3[34]) and received his ongoing blessings that come "on the just and on the unjust" (Matt. 5:45). The Evil One has been ruling in deception throughout the whole world (1 John 5:20), but his power is limited and "his doom is sure; one little word shall fell him."[35]

As they have taken shape throughout the world's varying contexts, peoples' responses to God's gracious, covenantal initiatives of revelation, sustenance, and blessings essentially comprise the world's various religious traditions.[36] A helpful working definition of religion in general is people's reaction to God's inescapable presence. We never find religion in general, but only particular instances of it. Furthermore, particular religions are both inexorably intertwined with particular socio-cultural contexts and identifiably distinguishable from those contexts. Thus, for example, Hinduism and India are closely connected, as are Islam and things Arab,[37] Judaism and Israel, Buddhism and East Asia, and the people in Lystra's religious sensibilities and first-century Asia Minor (Acts 14:11–18). At the same time, the religious aspects of Hinduism, Islam, Judaism, Buddhism, and first-century Lycaonian religion—in terms of how those adherents have reacted to God—can be identified and examined on their own terms.

One helpful image for identifying and examining the various constructive-destructive, positive-negative, true-false traits of peoples' responses to God—that is, of the world's various religious traditions—is that of a three-legged stool.[38] The three legs represent sin, Satan, and searching. Just like a

---

[34]The Ghanaian theologian Kwame Bediako describes how the Twi (an Akan language of southern Ghana) rendering of Heb. 1:2 helps more than the English "world" in conveying the original Greek *aionas*. Instead of pointing to "the world" geographically, the Twi term *mmeresanten*, like the Greek, connotes the world's historical unfolding and development. Indeed the term "conveys the sense of not only the stages . . . in time of the generations of human society stretching into the past and the future, but also the notion of the total cultural, social, political and religious structures that inform and determine individual and collective human existence within these stages of time and history." According to Heb. 1:2, then, Christ has created and provided for "all these elements necessary for the unfolding of human history and for the development of our individual and collective existence." Kwame Bediako, "Facing the Challenge: Africa in World Christianity in the 21st Century—A Vision of the African Christian Future," *Journal of African Christian Thought*, vol. 1 (June 1998): 54–56.

[35]Martin Luther, "A Mighty Fortress Is Our God."

[36]Hisakazu Inagaki and J. Nelson Jennings, *Philosophical Theology and East-West Dialogue*, vol. 15, Currents of Encounter Series, ed. Rein Fernhout et al. (Amsterdam, Netherlands, and Atlanta, GA: Rodopi, 2000), 141–42.

[37]At least in terms of Islam's origins and ongoing characteristics—even though the vast majority of Muslims today are not Arabs.

[38]J. Nelson Jennings, "God's Zeal for His World," in *Faith Comes By Hearing: A Response to Inclusivism*, ed. Christopher W. Morgan and Robert A. Peterson (Downers Grove, IL: IVP Academic,

stool needs all three legs to stay upright, so do our views of religions need to keep all three types of traits in view. Analyses that reduce a religion to having only one or two types of traits thereby have a truncated view. So, for example, one must not view Islam as simply sinful and satanic. Similarly, one must not view Islam simply as Muslims searching for (and perhaps adhering to) the truth. Islam, like all religious traditions, evidences morally sinful, deceptively satanic, and genuinely searching (and true) aspects. Keeping all three types of traits in view is needed to view religions accurately and fairly.

Applications of this three-trait view of religion are practically limit-less. For illustrative purposes here, note Siddhartha Gautama's ("the Bud-dha's") first "Noble Truth," namely that life is full of suffering. On one hand, a skeptic might claim that such an assertion is simply obvious and that Gautama exhibited little insight or searching for truth in this, his bedrock teaching. Moreover, that teaching sprang out of Prince Siddhartha's leav-ing his secluded palace as a young man and meeting people suffering from what are indisputably common maladies of old age, sickness, and death. However, Gautama's teaching that suffering presents to human beings the fundamental problem of life—an insight realized after years of rigorous, ascetic meditation—suggests more than a simple claim about the obvious. Rather, did not Siddhartha Gautama catch at least a glimpse of the truth of humanity's dilemma of seemingly endless and helpless entrapment in a world full of pain and agony?

If we are willing to grant at least a measure of true insight on Gautama's part, we should be quick to add the accompanying error in his teaching about the nature of and solution for that suffering. The Buddha taught that the problem of suffering is our (unfulfilled) desire, and that the solution to suffering is thus the elimination of desire through the Eightfold Path.[39] This solution is ultimately irreconcilable with the Christian gospel, efforts to bring the two teachings together notwithstanding.[40] The main point is the combination of truth and genuine human searching together with sin- and even satanically induced falsehood. Exclusive emphasis on either the positive or the negative side (or legs of our three-legged stool) does not yield a fair, Christian picture of what is happening in people's religious reactions to God's covenantal initiatives.

2008), 237. Cf. Harold A. Netland, *Encountering Religious Pluralism: The Challenge to Christian Faith and Mission* (Downers Grove, IL: InterVarsity, 2001), 308–10.

[39]It is practically impossible to do justice to Buddhism's teachings in such a brief way. My sugges-tion to seminary students is that if they think they understand those teachings after only a limited exposure to them, then most certainly they do not understand.

[40]More than attempting to reconcile Christian and Buddhist teachings have been attempts to reconcile the religious traditions' practices, particularly meditation.

The same pattern follows for all religious traditions. Zoroastrianism's stress on right thoughts, words, and actions overlaps with biblical teaching, but that religion's teaching of an eternal dualism between good and evil, or of how one is to produce right thoughts, words, and deeds, goes awry. Islam's stress on God's transcendence and justice rings true with God's revelation of himself in the Bible, but sin's and Satan's deceptions pull Muslims away from God's tri-unity, covenant grace, and incarnation in Jesus. Even some primal religions' horrific practice of human sacrifice at least evidences a true sense of the price to be paid to appease divine wrath.[41] Paul rightly condemned the people of Lystra's misdirected, ill-informed worship of Barnabas and him as Zeus and Hermes, but he pointed those people to their true experience of their Creator's revelatory witness to them "by giving you rains from heaven and fruitful seasons, satisfying your hearts with food and gladness." The people's sense of the gods having "come down to us," as well as the attempt by the priest of Zeus to offer sacrifices to Paul and Barnabas, clearly were "vain things." Nevertheless, even though the situation was compounded by the particularity of the people's understanding of matters in their own Lycaonian language (thus they all the more misunderstood Paul and Barnabas), Paul connected with the people of Lystra's *Divinitatis sensum* that gave them the right instinct to worship, including through sacrifice, and urged them to "turn from these vain things to a living God," namely their Creator (Acts 14:11–17).[42] On and on the list of examples goes of religious traditions' adherents' mixed responses to the God who made everyone and holds us all responsible.

Christ's Deity

The divinity of Jesus Christ enters the picture precisely at this point in our discussion. The creator covenant God who graciously and continuously has taken the initiatives of revelation, sustenance, and blessings toward the world is of course the triune God: Father, Son, and Holy Spirit. As discussed earlier, Jesus, God the Son, superintends all peoples, and in turn all peoples religiously respond to his inescapable presence. As the omnipresent creator-sustainer of all things, Jesus the redeemer directs Christian missions throughout his world. That dynamic therefore includes God the Son, the one to whom all people are responding through their religious traditions in a mixed, searching-sinful-satanic manner, pressing home his ultimate authority, the one to whom ultimate loyalty is to be committed.

---

[41]I am indebted to Kwame Bediako for this insight.

[42]John Calvin, *Institutes of the Christian Religion*, ed. John T. McNeill, trans. Ford Lewis Battles (Philadelphia: Westminster, 1960), 1:43.

Some readers will, for various reasons, immediately think here of so-called Christian inclusivism: members of various religions unwittingly but actually worship Jesus Christ and are "included" by his saving work as they believe and practice their own religious traditions.[43] However, God the Son revealing himself, sustaining peoples, and indiscriminately blessing the just and unjust—as well as bringing gospel messengers to those people so they might hear, believe, and then continue to have Jesus' claims on their lives clarified and deepened—is different from an inclusivist understanding of how God deals with people salvifically. Saying that all peoples respond to the one, true, and living God of the Bible does not imply that all peoples are thereby redeemed, forgiven, and adopted by the God to whom they are responding. People's responses are mixed and, apart from explicit faith in the Jesus Christ proclaimed in the good news of the gospel, inadequate.[44]

Now we can bring back (in slightly abbreviated form) those four stated assumptions we laid out at the beginning of the first section on Jesus and missions:

1) Many peoples throughout the world resist the exclusivity associated with declaring that Jesus is the one true and living God. Missionaries must therefore stand firm and patiently insist that Jesus Christ alone is God, along with the Father and Holy Spirit.

2) Muslims in particular, along with Jewish people and others, find Christians' claim that Jesus is divine both unthinkable and offensive. This basic difference is a major stumbling block to missions among Muslims and Jewish people.

3) Animists need first to understand that there is one God who has created all things and, second, that he has come into the world as Jesus Christ. Missionaries must patiently and wisely explain monotheism to these peoples, then demonstrate that Jesus was the Creator-God incarnate among us.

4) In general, missionaries will need to use the Bible to explain God and Christ's deity with patience, wisdom, clarity, and love. Ultimately the Holy Spirit will need to reveal Jesus to people and convince them that he is God the Son.

If we had discussed these assumptions, I dare say our focus would have been on Western missionaries' strategies for convincing non-Western

---

[43]Cf., e.g., Raimundo Panikkar, *The Unknown Christ of Hinduism*, rev. ed. (London: Darton, Longman & Todd, 1981).

[44]Morgan and Peterson, *Faith Comes by Hearing*.

people (assumed to be non-Christians) about Jesus' divinity. But we have worked through how the divine Son of God orchestrates Christian missions by bringing gospel witnesses to peoples who are responding to him inadequately via their own religious traditions (as well as to Christian believers who are ever working through the implications, within their ever-changing contexts, of Jesus' ultimate authority and place of honor). Now our focus can be on the triune God (1) pressing in on people who resist Jesus' exclusive claims; (2) patiently instructing unitarian monotheists, using their own categories of thought,[45] in ways resembling the patient instruction and, if need be, confrontation between Jesus and the apostles and the fierce monotheists they encountered; (3) God utilizing the name of the high deity of primal peoples to assure them that he is their God, not a foreign deity;[46] and (4) God the Holy Spirit, speaking through translated Scriptures in people's heart languages and thought patterns, convincing people that the Jesus to whom the Bible testifies is in fact their divine creator and redeemer.

In other words, our framework for understanding Christ's deity in relation to the world's religions is not primarily one of missionary strategy. Rather, our framework focuses on the divine Jesus ever at work among people's lives, pressing home his claims of ultimate authority through his witnesses whom he brings into the world's socio-political, cultural-linguistic contexts. How Jesus goes about that work of pressing home his ultimate authority and demand for loyalty, specifically through his gospel messengers, involves a vast tapestry of particular situations. Interwoven throughout that worldwide tapestry are thousands of nuanced, religious confessions of Christ's deity, all of which are scrambled together with various examples of the world's thousands of socio-political and cultural-linguistic contexts.

As we stated at the outset, "Jesus is God" is a provocative declaration inexorably interconnected with the explosive, nuanced, and interrelated worlds of Christian missions, multiple religious traditions, and—as we shall examine next—religious pluralism.

Jesus and Pluralism

The ending of the previous section could, for some readers, lend itself to a pluralistic scenario for confessing Jesus' divinity. After all, the reasoning could go, asserting "thousands of nuanced, religious confessions of Christ's deity" sounds like some sort of creedal free-for-all, within which there

---

[45]Cf., e.g., numerous articles through the 2007 and 2008 issues (vols. 24–25) of the *International Journal of Frontier Missions*. Available online at http://www.ijfm.org.

[46]For reasons beyond what our available space here can include, "primal people" is a better description than "animists" to describe those relatively unaffected by outside contact and influence.

are no standards for determining whether English speakers' confessing that "Jesus is God" means the same as ninth-century Saxons' confessing that Jesus is the greatest chieftain or eighth-century Persian missionaries' declaring in China that Jesus is the Buddha.[47] Who can say what is true in all of these situations?

It is the triune God himself who not only can but in fact does say what is true in the wide tapestry of religious confessions of Christ's deity throughout the world's socio-political and cultural-linguistic contexts. As the Bible is faithfully, appropriately, and relevantly articulated in vernacular languages within the world's contexts, the one, true, and living God speaks his one, true, and living Word—including about the divine Son, Jesus Christ.

So is Jesus the most powerful Saxon chieftain ever born, as declared in the anonymous ninth-century Saxon poem "Heiland" ("Savior")? Is he "the Buddha," as carved in AD 781 on the Nestorian Monument in China?[48] At face value, and speaking and thinking within contemporary English-language biblical categories, the answer to both questions is a clear no. However, if we take seriously the implications of the Bible's translatability,[49] including the need for cultural-linguistic insiders (as led by God the Holy Spirit and aided by cultural-linguistic outsiders) to determine how most faithfully, appropriately, and relevantly to express in their vernacular tongue the intended meanings of the Scriptures as originally given—unless we have some sort of competency or trustworthy connection with those historically, socially, politically, culturally, and linguistically distant contexts—we must hold any opinion at arm's length. God knows what is true, and those believers of the day thought they knew what was true, but we today do not know.

To turn the tables on ourselves, we may believe today that "Jesus is God," but distant Bible believers may, for example, look askance at identifying their divine Savior with Germanic deities (even if we protested that we are not doing that). I confess wholeheartedly, 「イエス・キリストは神である, 主である (Iesu Kirisuto ha Kami de aru, Shu de aru), but unless you know Japanese you will have to plead total ignorance, question my faith, or trust me and other Japanese-speaking Christians when I tell you that I am confessing Jesus Christ's ultimate authority and that I am pledging ultimate allegiance to him—that I am confessing the deity of Christ. Even if I were to give you

---

[47]Cf. Dale T. Irvin, "The Gift of Mission," *Christianity Today*, December 6, 1999, 58.

[48]Ibid.

[49]The seminal and still pivotal contemporary examination of such implications of the Bible's translatability remains Lamin Sanneh's widely influential *Translating the Message: The Missionary Impact on Culture*, American Society of Missiology Series 13, ed. James A. Sherer (Maryknoll, NY: Orbis, 1989).

the corresponding English-language confession, "Jesus Christ is God and Lord," as well as explain in English the indigenous meanings of 「 神」 and of 「 主」, while you could no longer plead total ignorance you still might question my faith, or you could choose to trust my assurance to you that the confession is "just as biblical" as "Jesus is God and Lord."

Plurality

There is thus a built-in *plurality* to Christian belief in general, and to Christian belief in Christ's deity in particular. That is, due to Christianity's contextual translatability—a trait stemming from how Jesus orchestrates Christian missions among the world's multitude of religious contexts—there are in fact many different, expressed confessions of the deity of Jesus Christ. Simultaneously, however, there is one Christian faith in the one Jesus Christ, or in New Testament language "one body and one Spirit . . . one Lord, one faith, one baptism, one God and Father of all, who is over all and through all and in all" (Eph. 4:4–6). Christian faith has both a unifying, universal side and a diversifying, particular side.[50] Similarly, Jesus is the one God-man who intrudes into the multitude of human contexts and is thereby confessed to be the one God-man in a multitude of ways.

Such an acknowledgment of Christian plurality-in-unity does not, as might be supposed, paint one into a paradoxical corner, escape from which can only be achieved through some manufactured distinction between different formulations of Christ's deity, in particular "functional" (pluralistic) and "ontological" (unified) christologies. As explained elsewhere in this volume,[51] that type of disingenuous distinction is foreign to the Bible's revelation of Jesus' identity with God and as God. And while Greco-Roman ecumenical councils necessarily (per our overall discussion here) used Greek and Latin conceptual and philosophical categories to articulate Jesus' deity, to claim that those councils' early creeds fell into Greek ontological concepts in such a way as to impose Christ's identity onto the Bible's supposed presentation of Jesus' exhibition of only divine functions fails to recognize both Jesus the God-man in the Bible and the Bible's original articulation within, and legitimate translatability into, particular philosophical-linguistic settings.[52]

---

[50]Andrew Walls has expounded on these twin traits of the Christian faith throughout his many writings.

[51]Stephen J. Wellum, "The Deity of Christ in the Apostolic Witness."

[52]The related matter of the christology of churches further to the east, e.g., the so-called Nestorian church, is a discussion beyond our present scope. Suffice it to note that contextual differences had a great deal to do with the christological differences confessed within the Chalcedonian discussions.

To move the discussion wider, a plurality of the world's religious traditions is undeniable. That is, there is the obvious fact or reality of people's various reactions to God's inescapable presence, of people's religions. Christians should thus freely acknowledge religious plurality, see God at work in relation to people's searching-sinful-satanic religious groping, and co-labor with God in seeing the gospel brought to all people—including the message of Jesus' divinity.

Pluralism

The ground shifts, however, when the discussion moves from the fact of plurality to the ideology of *pluralism*. The plurality of religions is nothing new; religious pluralism, by contrast, is "a new theological understanding of the relationship between Christian faith and other faiths."[53] Various religious traditions, intertwined with various historical contexts, as reactions to the triune Creator's rule and presence are to be expected from communities of divine image bearers enchained by sin and blinded by the Evil One; a framework that insists on the equally truthful and salvific viability of all religions is an aberrant religio-philosophical ideology into which Jesus the God-man rightfully intrudes and presses his ultimate authority and calls for all peoples' ultimate allegiance.[54]

John Hick has long been recognized as a seminal and representative proponent of religious pluralism. In Hick's words, pluralism "holds that there is not just one and only one point of salvific contact between the divine reality and humanity, namely, in the person of Jesus Christ, but that there is a plurality of independently valid contacts, and independently authentic spheres of salvation, which include both Christianity and the other great world faiths."[55] With specific reference to Christ's deity, then, Jesus does not uniquely hold the place of ultimate authority and of the one to whom all people are to pledge their ultimate allegiance.[56]

---

[53]Vinoth Ramachandra, *The Recovery of Mission: Beyond the Pluralist Paradigm* (Grand Rapids, MI: Eerdmans, 1997), *ix*.

[54]One could, and perhaps should, therefore classify the ideology of religious pluralism as a new religious tradition in its own right. Hence our discussion about Christ's deity in relation to pluralism necessarily will have a combined religio-philosophical flavor.

[55]John Hick, "Is Christianity the Only True Religion, or One Among Others?" 2001. Available at "John Hick: the official website," http://www.johnhick.org.uk/article2.html.

[56]Jesus Christ may hold such an ultimacy for Christians but certainly not for others—and in an absolute sense not even for Christians, either: "There is a valid sense in which, for those of us who are Christians, Christianity *is* the only true religion, the only one for us. For we have been formed by it. It has created us in its own image, so that it fits us and we fit it as no other religion can. And so for most of us who are Christians it is the right religion, and we should stick with it and live it out to the full. But we should also be aware that exactly the same is true for people formed by the

One of Hick's key assumptions concerns the gap between human beings' perceptions of deity and the ultimate reality of deity:

> Between ourselves and God as God is in God's ultimate transcendent being there is a screen of varied and changing human images of God—not graven images but mental images, or pictures, or concepts of God. And our awareness of God is always through and in terms of these human images. We worship God through our own images of God, to which our human ideas and cultural assumptions have inevitably contributed. These mental images not only differ considerably between religions, but also within a given religion.[57]

With respect to contextual influence on people's thinking, Hick's analysis sounds remarkably similar to what we have espoused here in our overall discussion. However, there are two absolutely crucial differences between Hick's framework and how we have reckoned with Christ's deity in relation to Christian missions and the plurality of religious traditions. First, Hick draws a clear "distinction between the divine reality as it is in itself and as variously imaged by us, [hence] our Christian doctrines are about the ultimate divine reality as conceived by us, in distinction from that reality as it is in itself."[58] Our discussion, by contrast, has maintained a true, corresponding knowledge between God and human beings; we truly hear God speaking intelligibly to us, his image-bearing creatures.

Second, Hick takes his pluralism a significant step further by claiming that "the different truth-claims of the different religions are claims about *different* manifestations of the Ultimate to different human mentalities formed within different human cultures and different streams of religious history. As such, they do not contradict one another."[59] Not only, then, is there a post-Enlightenment Kantian difference between human knowers and the perceived "Ultimate": somehow that Ultimate exudes different manifestations to various human communities. Hick's pluralism has taken distinctions and differences to the ultimate extreme of diversity, it seems. Here, however, we have kept sight of the universal side of Christianity's universal-particular faith. The Bible's and our commitment is to one creator-redeemer, the triune God who has communicated himself as the incarnate Son of God—"which [apostolic eyewitnesses] have heard, which we have seen with our eyes, which we looked upon and have touched with our

---

other world religions. They also should stick with the religion that has formed them and live it out, though in each case gradually filtering out its ingrained claim to unique superiority" (ibid.).
[57] Ibid.
[58] Ibid.
[59] Ibid.; emphasis original.

hands" (1 John 1:1)—and in vernacular languages throughout the tapestry of human communities scattered throughout the earth.

It is important to note as well that the concrete particularity of Jesus just mentioned is what "constitutes an offence to a pluralist society." With respect to "the controversy over Jesus [that] concerns *who he is*," our discussion's recognition of Jesus' deity stems from the fact "that no human category . . . can do justice to the evidence of his words and actions. No category short of deity itself is sufficient."[60] The universal-particular interplay of the Christian faith finds its ultimate example, and offense to a pluralist mind-set, in Jesus the incarnate God-man.

One more recent proponent of a pluralist understanding of religions— this one a more explicitly Christian approach—about whose views we need to comment (and about which, interestingly enough, John Hick comments[61]) is S. Mark Heim. One central component of Heim's views is the multiple types of truthful relations human beings have with God, namely, multiple truthful religions, that correlate with God's Trinitarian complexity:

> Christians believe in a complex God, three co-eternal persons living a single enduring communion. The divine life has varied dimensions and allows human interaction with the triune God to take different forms. God's channels are open on many frequencies. . . .
>
> There cannot, then, be only one simple way of relating to God. The Trinity is a map that finds room for, indeed requires, concrete truth in other religions, because it allows for a variety of ways of relating to God. It is impossible to believe in the Trinity instead of the distinctive religious claims of all other religions. If Trinity is real, then at least some of these specific religious claims and ends must be real also. If they were all false, then Christianity could not be true.[62]

Set in context of our discussion here, rather than seeing the fact of religious plurality based on varying contexts (superintended by the triune God, including of course God the Son), Heim roots his religious plural-

---

[60]Ramachandra, *The Recovery of Mission*, 181; emphasis original.

[61]Hick offers comments both positive ("This is probably the most philosophically accomplished of the current wave of Christian attempts to solve the problem of religious plurality by appeal to the doctrine of the Trinity") and negative ("His elegantly presented proposal is indeed richer and more interesting than traditional inclusivism, and deserves to be widely read. And yet, paradoxically, it is in the end less generous and less inclusive than the traditional version!"). John Hick, review of S. Mark Heim, *The Depth of the Riches: A Trinitarian Theology of Religious Ends* in *R&T* 8 (September 2001). Available at "John Hick: the official website," http://www.johnhick.org.uk/article6.html.

[62]S. Mark Heim, "A Trinitarian View of Religious Pluralism," *ChrCent* (January 24, 2001): 14. Available online at http://www.religion-online.org/showarticle.asp?title=2666.

ism in God's triune complexity, multidimensionality, and hence multiple "frequencies" for divine-human relations.

The second component of Heim's pluralism we need to consider is that of multiple "religious ends." Heim argues that Christians (as well as others) need to embrace the reality that "religious paths in fact lead persons to the distinctively varied states they advertise and on which they set such transcendent value."[63] Those advertised (and ultimately realized) states should not all be unfairly and inaccurately classified as "salvation," but instead need to be understood on their own terms, whether a Buddhist nirvana, a Hindu *moksha* or resolution of the individual atman into the ultimate Brahman, or any other "religious end."[64] One result is that "the religions play a truly providential role. They reflect the fact that every human response to any dimension of God's manifestation and revelation meets from God only affirmation, only God's 'yes' of grace."[65]

Clearly Heim is fixated here on the "searching" stool leg at the expense of the sin and satanic ones. But the crucial question for our discussion is this: Is Jesus Christ God for Heim? Christ is deity for Christians, since all adherents are to follow their own religions and receive that religion's promised goal. One could also surmise that, in light of Heim's Trinitarian understanding of God, Jesus Christ is God as a theological formulation. But in terms of being the actual Creator-Redeemer of the entire human race, who alone is the ultimate authority deserving every one of his creatures' ultimate allegiance, who orchestrates Christian missions to intrude into all contexts and to press his deity within all communities, who speaks in all peoples' languages and concepts to communicate to all of us the good news of his love, grace, and mercy—no.

We have had to be all too brief here in our considerations of two sophisticated, nuanced representatives of a many-sided understanding of the vast world of religious traditions. Nevertheless, it is clear enough that the ideology of religious pluralism cannot, does not, and will not accommodate Jesus the God-man.

Our Early Twenty-First-Century English-Language Confession
In his inexpressibly gracious treatment of the vast plurality of religious responses that people have been making to his inescapable presence, Jesus the God-man has been orchestrating the delivery throughout the world of

---

[63]S. Mark Heim, *The Depth of the Riches: A Trinitarian Theology of Religious Ends* (Grand Rapids, MI: Eerdmans, 2001).
[64]Heim, "A Trinitarian View," 15.
[65]Ibid., 18.

the good news of his reign and saving work on behalf of all those who will trust in him. Through his messengers Jesus has been speaking to human communities in their vernacular tongues, in our respective heart languages. The vast hosts of us who have come to believe in him have continuously been coming to grips with the reality that Jesus is our creator and the God of old-covenant Israel. He keeps pressing in on us, not allowing us to sink into complacency, self-preservation, and defense of the status quo but rather ever calling us to realize afresh his ultimate authority and our ultimate allegiance to him. Jesus the God-man boldly superintends and intrudes where he rightfully belongs anyway, namely, in the explosive, nuanced, and interrelated worlds of Christian missions, multiple religious traditions, and religious pluralism.

As early twenty-first-century English-language speakers, what is our faithful, appropriate, and relevant response to him within those interrelated worlds? "Jesus is God."

Selected Bibliography

Anselm. "The Incarnation of the Word." In *Anselm of Canterbury*. Vol. 3. Edited and translated by Jasper Hopkins and Herbert Richardson. Toronto and New York: Edwin Mellen, 1976.

Athanasius. "On the Incarnation of the Word." In *Nicene and Post-Nicene Fathers*. Second Series. Vol. 4, *Athanasius: Select Works and Letters*, 31–67. Grand Rapids, MI: Eerdmans, 1957.

Baillie, Donald. *God Was in Christ: An Essay on Incarnation and Atonement*. London: Faber & Faber, 1961.

Ball, David M. "'I Am' in John's Gospel: Literary Function, Background and Theological Implications." Journal for the Study of the New Testament: Supplement 124. Sheffield: Sheffield Academic Press, 1996.

Bauckham, Richard. *God Crucified: Monotheism and Christology in the New Testament*. Grand Rapids, MI: Eerdmans, 1998.

_____. *Jesus and the Eyewitnesses: The Gospels as Eyewitness Testimony*. Grand Rapids, MI: Eerdmans, 2006.

_____. *Jesus and the God of Israel: God Crucified and Other Studies on the New Testament's Christology of Divine Identity*. Grand Rapids, MI: Eerdmans, 2008.

_____. "Jesus, Worship of." In *Anchor Bible Dictionary*. Edited by David Noel Freedman. Garden City, NY: Doubleday, 1992.

_____. "Monotheism and Christology in the Gospel of John." In *Contours of Christology in the New Testament*. Edited by Richard N. Longenecker. Grand Rapids, MI: Eerdmans, 2005.

Bauer, Walter. *Orthodoxy and Heresy in Earliest Christianity*. London: SCM, 1972. Originally published in German, 1934.

Berkouwer, G. C. *The Person of Christ*. Studies in Dogmatics. Grand Rapids, MI: Eerdmans, 1954.

Bock, Darrell L. *Jesus according to Scripture: Restoring the Portrait from the Gospels.* Grand Rapids, MI: Baker Academic, 2002.

Bowman, Robert M., Jr., and J. Ed Komoszewski. *Putting Jesus in His Place: The Case for the Deity of Christ.* Grand Rapids, MI: Kregel, 2007.

Bray, Gerald. "Christology." In *New Dictionary of Theology.* Edited by Sinclair B. Ferguson, J. I. Packer, and David F. Wright. Downers Grove, IL: InterVarsity, 1988.

_____. *Creeds, Councils, and Christ.* Downers Grove, IL: InterVarsity, 1984.

Brown, Colin. *Jesus in European Protestant Thought: 1778–1860.* Grand Rapids, MI: Baker, 1988.

Brown, Harold O. J. *Heresies: The Image of Christ in the Mirror of Heresy and Orthodoxy from the Apostles to the Present.* Garden City, NY: Doubleday, 1984.

Bruce, F. F. *Jesus: Lord and Savior.* Downers Grove, IL: InterVarsity, 1986.

Burkett, Delbert. "The Son of Man in the Gospel of John." Journal for the Study of the New Testament: Supplement 56. Sheffield: Sheffield Academic Press, 1991.

Capes, David B. "Old Testament Yahweh Texts in Paul's Christology." Wissenschaftliche Untersuchungen zum Neuen Testament 2, no. 47. Tübingen: Mohr-Siebeck, 1992.

Capes, David B., April D. DeConick, Helen K. Bond, and Troy A. Miller, eds. *Israel's God and Rebecca's Children: Christology and Community in Early Judaism and Christianity: Essays in Honor of Larry W. Hurtado and Alan F. Segal.* Waco, TX: Baylor University Press, 2007.

Casey, Maurice. *From Jewish Prophet to Gentile God: The Origins and Development of New Testament Christology.* Louisville: Westminster, 1991.

Clark, Stephen. "Introduction." In *The Forgotten Christ.* Edited by S. Clark. Nottingham, UK: Inter-Varsity, 2007.

Cowan, Christopher. "The Father and Son in the Fourth Gospel: Johannine Subordination Revisited." *Journal of the Evangelical Theological Society* 49 (March 2006): 115–35.

Crisp, Oliver D. *Divinity and Humanity.* Cambridge: Cambridge University Press, 2007.

Cullmann, Oscar. *The Christology of the New Testament.* Translated by Shirley C. Guthrie and Charles A. M. Hall. London: SCM, 1959.

Dawe, Donald G. *The Form of a Servant: A Historical Analysis of the Kenotic Motif.* Philadelphia: Westminster, 1963.

Dumbrell, W. J. *Covenant and Creation.* Carlisle, UK: Paternoster, 1984.

Dunn, J. D. G. *Christology in the Making: A New Testament Inquiry into the Origins of the Doctrine of the Incarnation.* 2nd ed. Grand Rapids, MI: Eerdmans, 1996.

_____. "The Making of Christology—Evolution or Unfolding?" In *Jesus of Nazareth: Lord and Christ. Essays on the Historical Jesus and New Testament Christology.* Edited by Joel B. Green and Max Turner. Grand Rapids, MI: Eerdmans, 1994.

Erickson, Millard J. *The Word Became Flesh: A Contemporary Incarnational Christology.* Grand Rapids, MI: Baker, 1981.

Evans, Craig A. *Fabricating Jesus: How Modern Scholars Distort the Gospels.* Downers Grove, IL: InterVarsity, 2006.

Fee, Gordon D. *Pauline Christology: An Exegetical-Theological Study.* Peabody, MA: Hendrickson, 2007.

Fox, Richard Wightman. *Jesus in America: Personal Savior, Cultural Hero, National Obsession.* San Francisco: HarperSanFrancisco, 2004.

Gathercole, Simon J. *The Pre-existent Son: Recovering the Christologies of Matthew, Mark, and Luke.* Grand Rapids, MI: Eerdmans, 2006.

Giles, Kevin. *Jesus and the Father: Modern Evangelicals Reinvent the Doctrine of the Trinity.* Downers Grove, IL: InterVarsity, 2006.

Gomes, Alan W. "Faustus Socinus's *A Tract Concerning God, Christ, and the Holy Spirit." Journal of the International Society of Christian Apologetics* 1, no. 1 (2008): 37–57.

_____. *Unmasking the Cults.* The Zondervan Guide to Cults and Religious Movements. Edited by Alan W. Gomes. Grand Rapids, MI: Zondervan, 1995.

Green, Joel B., and Max Turner, eds. *Jesus of Nazareth: Lord and Christ: Essays on the Historical Jesus and New Testament Christology.* Grand Rapids, MI: Eerdmans, 1994.

Green, Michael, ed. *The Truth of God Incarnate.* Grand Rapids, MI: Eerdmans, 1977.

Grillmeier, Aloys. *Christ in Christian Tradition.* Vol. 1. 2nd ed. Translated by John Bowden. Atlanta, GA: John Knox Press, 1975.

Gruenler, Royce C. *The Trinity in the Gospel of John: A Thematic Commentary on the Fourth Gospel.* Grand Rapids, MI: Baker, 1986.

Hamerton-Kelly, Robert G. *Pre-Existence, Wisdom and the Son of Man.* Society for New Testament Studies Monograph Series 21. Cambridge: Cambridge University Press, 1973.

Hardy, Edward Rochie, ed. *Christology of the Later Fathers.* Vol. 3 of Library of Christian Classics. Philadelphia: Westminster, 1954.

Harner, Philip B. "Qualitative Anarthrous Predicate Nouns: Mark 15:39 and John 1:1." *Journal of Biblical Literature* 92 (1973): 75–87.

_____. *The "I Am" of the Fourth Gospel.* Facet Books. Philadelphia: Fortress, 1970.

Harris, Murray J. *Jesus as God: The New Testament Use of* Theos *in Reference to Jesus.* Grand Rapids, MI: Baker, 1992.

_____. *Three Crucial Questions about Jesus.* Grand Rapids, MI: Baker, 1994.

Hengel, Martin. *Studies in Early Christology.* Edinburgh: T&T Clark, 1995.

Hick, John. *The Metaphor of God Incarnate: Christology in a Pluralistic Age.* 2nd ed. Louisville: Westminster, 2006.

_____, ed. *The Myth of God Incarnate.* Philadelphia: Westminster, 1977.

Hurtado, Larry W. *How on Earth Did Jesus Become a God? Historical Questions about Earliest Devotion to Jesus.* Grand Rapids, MI: Eerdmans, 2005.

_____. *Lord Jesus Christ: Devotion to Jesus in Earliest Christianity.* Grand Rapids, MI: Eerdmans, 2003.

Jennings, J. Nelson. *God the Real Superpower: Rethinking Our Role in Missions.* Phillipsburg, NJ: P&R, 2007.

_____. "God's Zeal for His World." In *Faith Comes By Hearing: A Response to Inclusivism.* Edited by Christopher W. Morgan and Robert A. Peterson. Downers Grove, IL: IVP Academic, 2008.

Karkkainen, Veli-Matti. *Christology: A Global Introduction.* Grand Rapids, MI: Baker Academic, 2003.

Kelly, J. N. D. *Early Christian Doctrines.* 2nd ed. New York: Harper & Row, 1960.

Köstenberger, Andreas J. "The Glory of God in John's Gospel and the Apocalypse." In *The Glory of God.* Theology in Community. Edited by Christopher W. Morgan and Robert A. Peterson. Wheaton, IL: Crossway, 2010.

_____. "The Seventh Johannine Sign: A Study in John's Christology." *Bulletin for Biblical Research* 5 (1995): 87–103.

_____. *A Theology of John's Gospel and Letters.* Biblical Theology of the New Testament. Grand Rapids, MI: Zondervan, 2009.

Köstenberger, Andreas J., and Michael J. Kruger. *The Heresy of Orthodoxy: How Contemporary Culture's Fascination with Diversity Has Reshaped Our Understanding of Early Christianity.* Wheaton, IL: Crossway, 2010.

Köstenberger, Andreas J., and Scott R. Swain. *Father, Son and Spirit: The Trinity and John's Gospel.* New Studies in Biblical Theology. Downers Grove, IL: InterVarsity, 2008.

Ladd, George E. *New Testament Theology.* Grand Rapids, MI: Eerdmans, 1974.

Lee, Aquila H. I. *From Messiah to Preexistent Son: Jesus' Self-Consciousness and Early Christian Exegesis of Messianic Psalms.* Wissenschaftliche Untersuchungen zum Neuen Testament 2, no. 192. Tübingen: Mohr-Siebeck, 2005.

Lewis, C. S. *Mere Christianity.* New York, NY: Macmillan, 1952.

Liddon, H. P. *The Divinity of Our Lord and Saviour Jesus Christ.* London: Longman, Green, 1890.

Longenecker, Richard N. *Christology of Early Jewish Christianity.* London: SCM, 1970.

_____, ed. *Contours of Christology in the New Testament.* Grand Rapids, MI: Eerdmans, 2005.

Machen, J. Gresham. *Christianity and Liberalism*. New Edition. Grand Rapids, MI: Eerdmans, 2009.

Macleod, Donald. *Jesus Is Lord: Christology Yesterday and Today*. Geanies House, UK: Mentor, 2000.

_____. *The Person of Christ*. Contours of Christian Theology. Downers Grove, IL: InterVarsity, 1998.

Marshall, I. Howard. *New Testament Theology*. Downers Grove, IL: InterVarsity, 2004.

_____. *The Origins of New Testament Christology*. Downers Grove, IL: InterVarsity, 1976.

Martin, Ralph P. *Carmen Christi*. Cambridge: Cambridge University Press, 1967.

Martin, Walter R. *Kingdom of the Cults*. Minneapolis: Bethany Fellowship, 1965.

Mastin, B. A. "A Neglected Feature of the Christology of the Fourth Gospel." *New Testament Studies* 22 (1976): 32–52.

Matera, Frank. *New Testament Christology*. Louisville: Westminster, 1999.

McCready, Douglas. *He Came Down from Heaven: The Preexistence of Christ and the Christian Faith*. Downers Grove, IL: InterVarsity, 2005.

McGrath, Alister E. *The Making of Modern German Christology: 1750–1990*. 2nd ed. Grand Rapids, MI: Zondervan, 1994. Reprinted Eugene, OR: Wipf & Stock, 2005.

Moule, C. F. D. *The Origin of Christology*. Cambridge: Cambridge University Press, 1977.

Murray, John. *Collected Writings of John Murray*. 4 vols. Carlisle, PA: Banner of Truth, 1977.

Nichols, Stephen J. *For Us and for Our Salvation: The Doctrine of Christ in the Early Church*. Wheaton, IL: Crossway, 2007.

_____. *Jesus Made in America: A Cultural History from the Puritans to the Passion of the Christ*. Downers Grove, IL: IVP Academic, 2008.

Panikkar, Raimundo. *The Unknown Christ of Hinduism*. Revised edition. London: Darton, Longman & Todd, 1981.

Pelikan, Jaroslav. *Jesus through the Centuries: His Place in the History of Culture*. New Haven, CT: Yale University Press, 1999.

Prothero, Stephen. *American Jesus: How the Son of God Became a National Icon*. New York: Farrar, Straus & Giroux, 2003.

Ramm, Bernard L. *An Evangelical Christology: Ecumenic and Historic*. Nashville, TN: Thomas Nelson, 1985.

Reim, Günter. "Jesus as God in the Fourth Gospel: The Old Testament Background." *New Testament Studies* 30 (1984): 158–60.

Reymond, Robert L. *Jesus, Divine Messiah: The New and Old Testament Witness*. Ross-shire, Scotland: Mentor, 2003.

Ridderbos, Herman. *Paul: An Outline of His Theology.* Grand Rapids, MI: Eerdmans, 1975.

Rowdon, Harold H., ed. *Christ the Lord: Studies in Christology Presented to Donald Guthrie.* Downers Grove, IL: InterVarsity, 1982.

Runia, Klaas. *The Present-Day Christological Debate.* Downers Grove, IL: InterVarsity, 1984.

Schreiner, Thomas R. *New Testament Theology: Magnifying God in Christ.* Grand Rapids, MI: Baker, 2008.

Stott, John R. W. *The Authentic Jesus.* London: Marshall, Morgan & Scott, 1985.

Tertullian. "Against Praxeas." In *The Ante-Nicene Fathers.* Vol. 3, *Latin Christianity*, 597–628. Edited by A. Cleveland Coxe. Grand Rapids, MI: Eerdmans, 1957.

Turner, H. E. W. *The Pattern of Christian Truth: A Study in the Relations between Orthodoxy and Heresy in the Early Church.* London: Mowbray, 1954.

Vos, Geerhardus. *The Pauline Eschatology.* Grand Rapids, MI: Eerdmans, 1953.

Wallace, Daniel B. *Granville Sharp's Canon and Its Kin: Semantics and Significance.* Studies in Biblical Greek 14. New York: Lang, 2009.

Warfield, B. B. "The Divine Messiah in the Old Testament." In *Biblical and Theological Studies.* Philadelphia: Presbyterian and Reformed, 1968.

_____. *The Lord of Glory.* Reprint. Grand Rapids, MI: Baker, 1974.

Wells, David F. *The Person of Christ: A Biblical and Historical Analysis of the Incarnation.* Wheaton, IL: Crossway, 1984.

Williams, Catrin H. *I Am He: The Interpretation of 'ani hu' in Jewish and Early Christian Literature.* Tübingen: Mohr-Siebeck, 2000.

Witherington, Ben, III. *The Many Faces of the Christ: The Christologies of the New Testament and Beyond.* Companions to the New Testament. New York: Crossroad, 1998.

Wright, N. T. *The Challenge of Jesus: Rediscovering Who Jesus Was and Is.* Downers Grove, IL: InterVarsity, 1999.

_____. *The Climax of the Covenant: Christ and the Law in Pauline Theology.* Minneapolis: Fortress, 1992.

_____. "Jesus." In *New Dictionary of Theology.* Edited by Sinclair B. Ferguson, J. I. Packer, and David F. Wright. Downers Grove, IL: InterVarsity, 1988.

_____. *The Resurrection of the Son of God.* Vol. 3 of Christian Origins and the Question of God. Minneapolis: Fortress, 2003.

Author Index

Subject Index

Scripture Index

Also Available
in the
Theology in Community Series

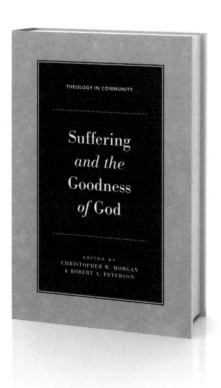

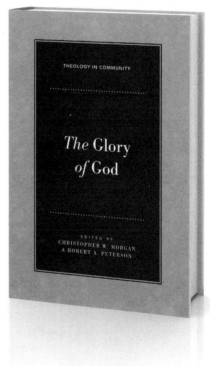